Exploring the 'Legal' in Socio-Legal Studies

Palgrave Macmillan Socio-Legal Studies

Series Editor

David Cowan, Professor of Law and Policy, University of Bristol, UK

Editorial Board

Dame Hazel Genn, Professor of Socio-Legal Studies, University College London, UK

Fiona Haines, Associate Professor, School of Social and Political Science, University of Melbourne, Australia

Herbert Kritzer, Professor of Law and Public Policy, University of Minnesota, USA

Linda Mulcahy, Professor of Law, London School of Economics and Political Science, UK

Carl Stychin, Dean and Professor, The City Law School, City University London, UK

Mariana Valverde, Professor of Criminology, University of Toronto, Canada

Sally Wheeler, Professor of Law, Queen's University Belfast, UK

Exploring the 'Legal' in Socio-Legal Studies

Edited by

David Cowan

University of Bristol Law School, UK

Daniel Wincott

Cardiff Law School, Cardiff University, UK

First published 2016 by
PALGRAVE

Palgrave in the UK is an imprint of Macmillan Publishers Limited,
registered in England, company number 785998, of 4 Crinan Street,
London, N1 9XW.

Palgrave Macmillan in the US is a division of St Martin's Press LLC,
175 Fifth Avenue, New York, NY 10010.

Palgrave is a global imprint of the above companies and is represented
throughout the world.

Palgrave® and Macmillan® are registered trademarks in the United States,
the United Kingdom, Europe and other countries.

ISBN 978–1–137–34436–6 hardback

This book is printed on paper suitable for recycling and made from fully
managed and sustained forest sources. Logging, pulping and manufacturing
processes are expected to conform to the environmental regulations of the
country of origin.

A catalogue record for this book is available from the British Library.

Library of Congress Cataloging-in-Publication Data
Names: Cowan, David (David S.), editor. | Wincott, Daniel, editor.
Title: Exploring the 'legal' in socio-legal studies / [edited by]
    David Cowan, University of Bristol Law School, UK, Daniel Wincott, Cardiff Law
    School, Cardiff University, UK.
Description: New York : Palgrave Macmillan, 2016. | Series: Palgrave
    Macmillan socio-legal studies | Includes index.
Identifiers: LCCN 2015038167 | ISBN 9781137344366 (hardback)
Subjects: LCSH: Sociological jurisprudence. | Sociological
    jurisprudence—Research. | BISAC: LAW / General. | LAW / Comparative. |
    LAW / Reference.
Classification: LCC K370 .E968 2016 | DDC 340/.115—dc23
LC record available at http://lccn.loc.gov/2015038167

Printed and bound by CPI Group (UK) Ltd, Croydon, CR0 4YY

Contents

Notes on Contributors

Paul James Cardwell is Reader in EU External Relations Law at the School of Law, University of Sheffield. He was also Deputy Head of School and Director of the Sheffield Centre for International and European Law (2012–2015). He is an Honorary Fellow of the Europa Institute, University of Edinburgh, and was an Invited Professor at Sciences Po Paris in 2015. He is also Treasurer of the University Association for Contemporary European Studies. His research has focused on the engagement of the EU with the outside world, particularly neighbouring countries, and his first monograph was published by Routledge in 2009. He has published widely on the development of EU foreign policy, democracy promotion and the relationship between EU and international law and he is currently exploring the use of new modes of governance in EU migration management.

Helen Carr is a Professor of Law at Kent Law School, University of Kent, Canterbury. She also sits as a part-time judge at the First Tier Tribunal (Property Chamber). Helen's research interests lie primarily in the fields of housing, homelessness and social care. She is particularly interested in the relationship between law and the politics of austerity and the problems facing advocates of social justice. She is currently working with Caroline Hunter on a book concerned with socio-legal approaches to homelessness. Recent publications include Socio-Legal Encounters with Homelessness: Regulating People at the Margins, 'The Right to Buy, the Leaseholder, and the Impoverishment of Ownership' [Online] 38(5) *Journal of Law and Society* 19–54 and, with Dave Cowan, 'The Social Tenant, the Law and the UK's Politics of Austerity' (2015) [Online] 5 Oñati Socio-legal Series 73–89. Exploring Experiences of Shared Ownership Housing: Reconciling Owning and Renting (Canterbury/Bristol: University of Kent/University of Bristol (with Dave Cowan and Alison Wallace).

Emilie Cloatre is a Senior Lecturer in Law at Kent Law School, University of Kent. Her research interests lie at the intersection between law and contemporary 'science and society' issues. Her publications include the books *Pills for the Poorest: An Exploration of TRIPS and Access to Medicines in Sub-Saharan Africa* (Basingstoke: Palgrave Macmillan 2013) and *Knowledge, Technology and Law* (London: Routledge, 2015, with Martyn Pickersgill).

David Cowan is editor of the Palgrave Macmillan Socio-Legal Series and a Professor at the University of Bristol Law School. He researches housing and land issues. He is the author of a number of books on those subjects, including *Great Debates in Property Law* (Basingstoke: Palgrave Macmillan 2013) and *Housing Law and Policy* (Cambridge: Cambridge University Press 2011). His current research is about shared ownership, a subject on which he has recently published a monograph, *Exploring Experiences of Shared Ownership Housing: Reconciling Owning and Renting* (Canterbury/Bristol: University of Kent/University of Bristol, with Helen Carr and Alison Wallace).

Sharon Cowan is a Senior Lecturer and the Director of Research at the University of Edinburgh School of Law. Her research interests include: gender, sexuality and the law; feminist legal theory; criminal law and criminal justice; and asylum studies. Recent projects include a national empirical project, along with Helen Baillot of the Scottish Refugee Council, and Vanessa Munro of the University of Nottingham, funded by the Nuffield Foundation (2009–2012), looking at the way in which women asylum claimants, whose applications are based on a claim of rape, are treated by the Asylum and Immigration Appeal Tribunal. Sharon is presently working on a comparative socio-legal project looking at the impact of law on transgender people.

Danielle Griffiths is a Research Fellow in Bioethics and Law within the institute for Science, Ethics and Innovation at the University of Manchester. Her research and teaching interests lie in medical and criminal law, particularly as these concern health and health policy. She is engaged in a wide range of teaching and research activities, including many interdisciplinary and international collaborations involving people from a variety of fields.

Tamara K Hervey, LLB, PhD, FAcSS, is Jean Monnet *ad personam* Professor of European Union Law at the University of Sheffield. She researches, teaches and writes on: EU social and constitutional law, in particular its application in health fields; equality law; interfaces between biosciences and (European) law; social rights; legal pedagogy; and global health law. She also pursues a long-standing interest in research methodologies, particularly in the context of EU law – see, for example, Tamara Hervey, Robert Cryer, Bal Sokhi-Bulley and Alexandra Bohm, *Research Methodologies in EU and International Law* (Oxford: Hart 2011).

Caroline Hunter is a Professor at York Law School, University of York. Her research interests lie at the intersection of housing law, policy and practice. She has conducted a number of empirical studies on evictions, the regulation of antisocial behaviour and homelessness. She has published extensively on these subjects and is a co-author of Arden and Partingon's *Housing Law*. She is currently jointly authoring with Helen Carr a book provisionally entitled

Socio-Legal Encounters with Homelessness: Regulating People at the Margins. She sits as a part-time judge of the First-Tier Tribunal (Property Chamber).

Natalie Ohana is a final-year PhD Student and Teaching Fellow in the Faculty of Laws, University College London. Prior to commencing her PhD, Natalie was the Head of the Legal Department in a refuge for women fleeing domestic violence in Jerusalem, representing women in civil and religious courts, and advocating for policy and legislation changes in legal responds to domestic violence. Natalie's dissertation reveals the manners by which discourse mechanisms in charge of producing legal knowledge operate to exclude realities and voices. Alongside her PhD, Natalie designed and conducted an academic public engagement project for which she was awarded UCL's Provost's Award for Public Engagement for 2015. The project was aimed at revealing perceptions of people subjected to legal processes towards the legal system, by integrating between mediums of art and dialogue. Natalie's current research interests are the intersection between art and law, especially the ability of art to bridge gaps posed by legal language, and the intersection between trauma studies and law, analysing the legal interpretation and meaning of the trauma.

Andreas Philippopoulos-Mihalopoulos is Professor of Law and Theory at the University of Westminster, and founder and Director of the Westminster Law and Theory Lab. He has been awarded the 2011 Oxford University Press National Award for the Law Teacher of the Year and has since been invited to join the judging committee. His research interests are radically interdisciplinary and include space, bodies, ontologies, post-humanist studies, critical autopoiesis, literature, psychoanalysis, continental philosophy, gender studies, art theory, and their connection to the law. His books include the monographs: *Absent Environments* (London: Routledge-Cavendish 2007); *Niklas Luhmann: Law, Justice, Society* (London: Routledge 2009); *Spatial Justice: Body Lawscape Atmosphere* (London: Routledge 2014) – and the edited volumes: *Law and the City* (London: Routledge-Cavendish 2007); *Law and Ecology* London: Routledge (2011); *Luhmann Observed: Radical Theoretical Encounters* (Basingstoke: Palgrave Macmillan 2013, co-edited with Anders La Cour); and *Knowledge-Creating Milieus in Europe: Firms, Cities, Territories* (London: Springer 2015, co-edited with Augusto Cusinato). Andreas is the editor (with Christian Borch) of the Routledge-Glasshouse series Space, Materiality and the Normative.

Jiří Přibáň is Professor of Law at Cardiff University in the UK. He graduated from Charles University in Prague in 1989 and became Professor of Legal Theory, Philosophy and Sociology in 2002. He was appointed Professor at Cardiff Law School in 2006 and has held visiting professorships and fellowships at a number of academic institutions such as University of California Berkeley, New York University, European University Institute, University of Pretoria and University of New South Wales in Sydney. He is author and editor of many books in Czech and English, such as *Sovereignty in Post-Sovereign Society* (Aldershot: Ashgate 2015), *Legal Symbolism* (Aldershot: Ashgate 2007), *Dissidents of Law* (Aldershot: Ashgate 2002), *Liquid Society and Its Law* (ed.) (Aldershot: Ashgate 2007), *Systems of Justice in Transition* (co-ed. with P Roberts and J Young) (Aldershot: Ashgate 2003), *Law's New Boundaries* (co-ed. with D Nelken) (Aldershot: Ashgate 2001) and *The Rule of Law in Central Europe* (co-ed. with J Young) (Aldershot: Ashgate 1999). He regularly contributes to the international and Czech media.

Annelise Riles is the Jack G Clarke Professor of Law in Far East Legal Studies and Professor of Anthropology at Cornell University and she serves as Director of the Clarke Program in East Asian Law and Culture. Her work focuses on the transnational dimensions of laws, markets and culture across the fields of comparative law, conflict of laws, the anthropology of law, public international law and international financial regulation. Her most recent book, *Collateral Knowledge: Legal Reasoning in the Global Financial Markets* (Chicago: University of Chicago Press 2011) is based on ten years of fieldwork among regulators and lawyers in the global derivatives markets. Her first book, *The Network Inside Out* (Ann Arbor: University of Michigan Press 2000) won the American Society of International Law's Certificate of Merit for 2000–2002. Her second book, *Rethinking the Masters of Comparative Law* (Oxford: Hart Publishing 2001), is a cultural history of comparative law presented through its canonical figures. Her third book, *Documents: Artifacts of Modern Knowledge* (Ann Arbor: University of Michigan Press 2006), brings together lawyers, anthropologists, sociologists and historians of science. She is the founder and Director of Meridian 180, a virtual think-tank on Pacific Rim issues. She also writes about law markets and culture on her blog, http://blogs.cornell.edu/collateralknowledge.

Andrew Sanders is Professor of Criminal Law and Criminology and Head of the School of Law, Politics and Sociology, University of Sussex (from 1 July 2015). He has held academic posts at the universities of Birmingham, Bristol, Manchester and Oxford, and at Manchester Metropolitan University. Andrew is a member of the Bar Standards Board and Chair of its Education and Training Committee, and an external member of the Criminal Cases Review Commission Research Committee. He has been a member of the Parole Board for England and Wales, the Parole Commission for Northern Ireland, the Criminal Justice Council, and the Attorney General's Advisory Board of the Crown Prosecution Service Inspectorate. He has also been an EU 'expert' on victim policy, and Chair of the Committee of Heads of University Law Schools in England and Wales.

Christopher Tomlins is Professor of Law (Jurisprudence and Social Policy), University of California Berkeley, and Affiliated Research Professor, American Bar Foundation, Chicago. His research concentrates on Anglo-American legal history from the sixteenth to the twentieth centuries. He is the author of *Freedom Bound: Law, Labor, and Civic Identity in Colonizing English America, 1580–1865* (Cambridge: Cambridge University Press 2010); *Law, Labor, and Ideology in the Early American Republic* (Cambridge: Cambridge University Press 1993); and *The State and the Unions: Labor Relations, Law, and the Organized Labor Movement in America, 1880–1960* (Cambridge: Cambridge University Press 1985, reprinted 2010). He has also been editor/co-editor of several other volumes and journals. His books have been awarded the Littleton-Griswold Prize of the American Historical Association, the Hurst Prize of the Law and Society Association (twice), the Reid Prize of the American Society for Legal History, and the Bancroft Prize of the Trustees of Columbia University. He is currently working on a history of the Turner Rebellion and slavery in antebellum Virginia.

Daniel Wincott is Blackwell Professor of Law and Society at Cardiff University and Head of Cardiff School of Law and Politics. Before moving to Cardiff he was Professor of European and Comparative Politics at the University of Birmingham and had also worked in politics departments and law schools at the universities of Leicester and Warwick. His substantive work is concerned with territoriality across multiple levels of governance and focuses on social policies. His most recent books are *Citizenship after the Nation-State* (co-ed. with Charlie Jeffery and Ailsa Henderson) (Basingstoke: Palgrave Macmillan 2013) and *The Political Economy of European Welfare Capitalism* (co-author with Colin Hay and winner of the 2013 Choice Outstanding Academic Title) (Basingstoke: Palgrave Macmillan 2012). He has a long-standing interest in theory and method in the social sciences.

1
Exploring the 'Legal'

David Cowan and Daniel Wincott

The animating questions

'Exploring the legal' could sound rather banal – after all, on one level, it is something that law students, lawyers and normal people do every day and have always done. However, in our seemingly eternal search for 'the social', we, in socio-legal studies, have rather forgotten that which is in front of us and appears authoritative: 'the legal'. This book (and the conference that underpinned many of the contributions) was designed not just to accompany Dermot Feenan's inspired collection, *Exploring the 'Socio'* (Feenan, 2012), but also to offer reflections on the socio-legal project from its most obvious starting point. Indeed, we go further and, as Christopher Tomlins (this volume, p. 35) puts it, we 'target[] the assumption ... that "the social" is the essential explanatory other of the legal'.

At the outset, our project drew inspiration from the work of Annelise Riles (2005; 2011) and Mariana Valverde (2009), both of whom encouraged socio-legal scholars to take back the legal technicalities and use them for our own ends. As Riles puts it, unless we 'take on the technicalities', we contribute to our own marginalization; moreover, as she argues with rhetorical flourish, 'the kind of politics that [we] purport to analyse is encapsulated there, along with the hopes, ambitions, fantasies and day-dreams of armies of legal engineers'. For Riles and Valverde technicalities do considerable work, and it is their analyses that provided us with our stepping-off point.

But we also recognize risks in using this conceptual language to address the work done by law, lawyers and jurists. The publisher's (anonymous) reviewer wondered whether the term 'legal technicalities' might reinforce the very disdain for the legal to which Riles also draws attention. This issue may be a question of semantics, but we are also hesitant about the language of legal technicalities for other reasons. It may convey a suggestion that there is non-technical legality or imply that legality is always

1

merely technical and mechanical. Many of our contributors engage with questions of technical legality – that range from counterfeit drugs to constitutions, care plans to leases, prosecutorial decisions to human rights in possession cases – without othering them as mere technicalities. Yet, other chapters in this book disrupt narratives of 'mere' technicality by suggesting alternative ways of thinking about legalities that go beyond, or do not reduce them to, the technical (for example, Cloatre, Cardwell and Hervey, Tomlins, and Přibáň). Across these chapters, the tools used are those of our trades. They cover a wide terrain, from techniques of legal history to ethnographic studies of life or death decisions, from reading law to the craft of judging.

So, while we began from Riles and Valverde, our project is theoretically pluralist and methodologically impure: we seek to draw on diverse ways of understanding (perhaps appreciating is a better word) the legal, through the various technicalities, doctrine and other practice with which we are individually engaged. Our perspective has also been influenced by other theories, traditions and approaches. We have, for example, been particularly affected by the work of Zenon Bankowski and Geoff Mungham (1976), Roger Cotterrell (1992) and Patricia Ewick and Susan Silbey (1998). In addition, Robert Gordon's (1984) critical legal history, and related conceptions of 'mandarin' doctrine and 'vernacular' deployment of legal concepts and categories (Gordon, 2012), also connect with our concerns.

In the rest of this chapter, we explore these animating questions and metatheoretical issues. In the next section, we describe and develop our primary aspiration for this collection. After that, we seek to clear through the disciplinary reeds, asking our questions by reference to the debates in other disciplines. As we are not alone in our angst, so to speak, this is essential ground-clearing work. We then go on to deal with our title, working through its constituent parts in turn: 'exploring', 'the legal' and 'legal technicalities'. Each of these sections shows that socio-legal studies engages with a variety of metatheoretical issues, including the relationships between time and space, structure and agency, and ideas and materiality. Next, we offer two brief case studies by way of illustration of our themes. Finally and briefly, we map out the chapters in the book and draw links between them.

A primary aspiration

Our primary aspiration, to contribute to methodology (rather than, say, to legal theory or the philosophy of law), involves provoking a discussion about how socio-legal research is undertaken. In so doing we can hardly avoid engaging with a variety of theories and particularly with what we will call 'metatheory'. Calling for attention to be focused on socio-legal metatheory – 'the way sociolegal method understands the world and itself' (Philippopoulos-Mihalopoulos this volume) – might appear to be an indulgent distraction, irrelevant to those involved in grounded socio-legal research. We agree that there is a risk of indulgence here. To avoid it, methodologically oriented reflection on the legal (including technicalities and doctrine) must remain connected to concrete or grounded socio-legal research. It also has the potential to enrich research of this kind. So the rest of this book is organized around our methodological and metatheoretical agenda. It is divided, admittedly fairly roughly, into two parts: the first addresses methodological issues, while the second is made up of individual case studies. The division is 'rough' because there are crossovers between the chapters and parts, which we will discuss in more detail below; we see a link between each 'methodological' chapter and at least two of the cases studies. We also recognize that some of the case study chapters range across alternative methodological perspectives. Finally, the roughness encourages us in the belief that the metatheoretical challenges taken up by these authors are real and productive.

By providing a level of analysis above the particular commitments of multiple theories and approaches, metatheory has other uses and virtues for our 'impure', methodologically focused project. It provides a level at which we can explicitly address higher order questions. For example, the question of whether, on the one hand, the legal is ubiquitous in, or basically constitutive of (cf. Gordon, 1984), 'society', or on the other is either an epiphenomenon of social or economic relations or perhaps vanishes in materiality, in the midst of 'things' (as Pottage, 2012, suggests) has a metathoretical quality. Rather than being an either–or choice, perhaps we are confronting a both–and paradox – if the legal is 'everywhere', then it may not be 'anywhere'. The 'ubiquity paradox', which we have found ourselves confronting repeatedly in this project, has variously puzzled and animated powerful influences on our conception of this project (including Ewick and Silbey, 1998; Mezey, 2001 – cf. Sharon Cowan's contribution to this volume).

Moreover, identifying a 'higher' level of metatheory can help us reflect on dilemmas, puzzles and relationships that emerge repeatedly across socio-legal theories and in grounded (or 'concrete') socio-legal research. Key conceptual distinctions underpin the kinds of 'metatheoretical issues' (cf. Marsh, 2010) to which we refer here; they include: those between law, space and place; that between continuity and change; structure and agency; the material and ideational; the socio-legal and soterial. Some of these issues have been explicitly and fruitfully discussed in (landmark) socio- and critical legal research. So, for example, the structure–agency issue animates

Ewick and Silbey's *Common Place of Law* (1998). The relationship between materialism and idealism is at stake in Gordon's (1984) influential account of critical legal history – as well as in the debates it continues to generate (Blumenthal, 2012; Edwards, 2012; Gordon, 2012; Tomlins, 2012) – and is also addressed in Ewick and Silbey (1998). A socio-legal research agenda on the 'materiality' of law has been inspired by science and technology studies (STS), especially in the form of actor–network theory (ANT). But, in contrast to some cognate disciplines in the humanities and social sciences (cf., in politics, Marsh, 2010), metatheoretical issues have not, as such, become an explicit focus in socio-legal studies.

As well as being present in a variety of theories and approaches to social and legal analysis, metatheoretical issues and the conceptual distinctions they reference also animate debates in other disciplines (economics, politics and sociology). In fact, these issues typically cut across disciplines. Given that the disciplinary location of law remains contested (Siems and MacSithigh, 2012, p. 660) discussion of metatheory may contribute to our understanding of the place of legal and socio-legal studies within the broader setting of the humanities, social sciences and, indeed, the natural sciences. So, for example, divisions and distinctions exist between what Peter Hall and Rosemary Taylor (1996) have called the logics of 'calculus' and 'culture' (see also Hay and Wincott, 1998). The difference between these logics also reflects the (sometimes aspirational) affinities of students of the social (broadly defined) with the wider disciplinary groupings of the humanities, the social 'sciences' and the 'natural' sciences.

Law, legality and other disciplines

In this section, we think about law in relation to other social science and humanity disciplines. By thinking about our disciplinary others, we are able to locate the key themes and understandings that underpin both this chapter and the rest of this book. Key questions for us are: what counts as legal research? What makes some research 'research on/in law' rather than something else? What of the distinctiveness of the methods – or perhaps more precisely the methodologies – of doctrinal legal analysis and 'legal technicalities'? At one level, legal methods appear as a form of textual analysis, recognizable to scholars in other disciplines. Equally, their inaccessibility to non-lawyers suggests that they may represent a distinctive method or method*ology*. Making the legal more accessible to, and useful for, social analysis more broadly might be a potential benefit of foregrounding the legal in socio-legal studies and of seeking to make its methodology more explicit. Answers to these questions are, of course, historical and ideological constructions. Thus, Tomlins reminds us that legal technicalities are as much technicalities of theology, particularly when, prior to the twentieth century, law and religion were effectively spliced; and, as Natalie Ohana argues, it is precisely the discontinuities in histories that are significant.

Without wishing to rely too heavily on the distinction between methods and methodology, we note, first, that, generally speaking disciplines in the social science and humanities share a set of methods. Quantitative methods are based on shared mathematical/statistical principles, while a range of qualitative methods – from interviews, by way of textual, content or discourse analysis, to ethnographies – are shared across a range of disciplines. Particular methods may have an association with specific disciplines – like that between anthropology and ethnography or rational choice theory and economics. Once established, these methods are applied to and taken up in other contexts and disciplines.

So, what elements identify and define academic disciplines? Aside from the institutional organization of the academy itself, there are at least two broad elements – related to subject matter and approach – that contribute to the definition of disciplines. The topic or subject matter studied by a discipline (the law, economy, government) can be defined institutionally and/or in terms of the 'field' or 'system' under investigation. Understood in these ways, the topics tend to be demarcated from one another and, by default, as exclusively and exhaustively defined within their disciplinary boundaries. By contrast, at least for some disciplines – including law, along with politics – we shall see that the subject matter may be understood less exclusively, as a particular moment of social relations, understood more broadly. Additionally – or perhaps alternatively – at least some disciplines can be understood as adopting a distinctive approach or approaches. This may be partly a matter of method and theory, but is probably most helpfully defined in terms of methodology.

We seek to situate legal and socio-legal studies in the context of cognate social science disciplines – including sociology, economics and geography – but our principal comparison is with the study of politics. Each discipline struggles with a ubiquity paradox – both the legal and the political are at once everywhere and nowhere. There are also clear areas of institutional and substantive overlap between the disciplines – most obviously in the area of public law and public administration, but on wider definition politics spills out to areas of private law as well – and we shall see that they share a preoccupation with power. Like socio-legal studies, politics is also, for the most part, a borrowing discipline in methodological terms. As an academic discipline, neither politics nor law has made strong claims to be the dominant discipline of the social sciences or humanities – indeed, law has remained rather aloof from the academy. Neither has it yet been a source of methodological innovations taken up by other disciplines (or applied to their main substantive concerns) – although socio-legal studies may learn lessons from the engagement of political analysts with metatheory over the past couple of decades. Partly pragmatic (reflecting the background of one editor), this disciplinary comparison is primarily motivated by these substantial similarities between the disciplines, but we will also identify a significant difference between political and socio-legal studies.

The study of politics and the study of law share a sense of having a core subject matter and set of institutions. It is easy to think of legal and political functions, while it is a commonplace to refer to the political system or the legal system (perhaps partly linked to the idea that some institutions are distinctively political or legal) (cf. Přibáň, this volume). While often presented as largely distinct from one another, functional and institutional definitions of politics and the law can have a circular quality – or are at least entwined with one another. We identify a function as legal because it is principally undertaken in legal institutions, and we know those institutions are legal because they fulfil legal functions (cf. Dunleavy and O'Leary, 1987, on definitions of the state). Equally, however, functional definitions raise the possibility that neither law nor politics can be confined to those institutions that are conventionally understood as legal or political.

A contrast with other disciplines may also help to clarify what law and politics share. Economics provides a classic example of a methodologically defined discipline – defined by its techniques, but also arguably by something of a shared wider mindset, which is widely applied beyond its historic subject matter of the economy. Economists became the most assertive social scientific imperialists, seeking to colonize other domains of social inquiry. By the 1970s, Gary Becker's influential monograph, *The Economic Approach to Human Behaviour* (1978), made the claim that the method(ology) (and perhaps the sensibility) of economists had a – probably *the* – key contribution to make to explaining social, political and legal as well as economic phenomena. More recently, of course, economics changed direction somewhat, having been strongly influenced by behaviouralism – which uses radically different methods and assumptions.

Sociology appears as the broadest of social science disciplines. Echoing Bruno Latour's insight (2006) that the social is glued together by many other types of connections, it makes little sense to argue that sociology is concerned with the social moment in social relations. Sociology aspired to – and to some extent achieved – the position of dominant social science during the 1950s and 1960s, at least in the Anglosphere. This position was based partly on the sweeping claims of Parsonian sociology to provide an encompassing framework within which other fields or (sub) systems of human existence were included (cf. C Wright Mill's influential critique of Parsonian sociology – in his celebrated work on *The Sociological*

Imagination (1959) – identifying sociology and social science in general as a craft, explicitly in place of an emphasis on method). A similar sense of the social system encompassing a range of sub-systems (the law, politics, the economy and so on) also pervades contemporary Luhmannian systems theory.

Geography also claims breadth but differs from sociology in the form it takes. The geographer's claim is based on the ubiquity – or at least potential ubiquity – of a particular 'moment' of social relations; the spatial moment or dimension. For law – and politics – it is worth reflecting on ways of thinking about a discipline. While broad in scope – human geography covering the breadth of (geographical) aspects of human existence and social relations – the discipline is not associated with strong claims to disciplinary dominance or methodological imperialism. A question for geography is whether space (broadly understood to include place, locality and territory) in its own right provides a distinctive subject matter for the discipline.

In one sense, then, both law and politics appear more modestly focused than economics, sociology or geography. Yet both disciplines overspill their traditional, institutional boundaries. So, to take politics first, traditionally the discipline and practice of politics was focused on the public sphere and defined in contrast to the private. But this definition of politics has been deeply challenged. Feminists, among others, uncover politics in private and intimate contexts and start to confront the ubiquity paradox: when we start to look for it, we can find politics 'everywhere'. But if the scope of politics is expanded in this way, it risks being rendered vapid through over-extension – if everything is political, the concept is emptied of content.

Hay argues that a wider definition of politics (or the political) can be developed around a core concept, power: *'power is to political analysis what the economy is to economics'* (2002, p. 168, emphasis in original). This move, he suggests, allows us to make sense of the (potential) ubiquity of 'politics' without overextending this concept and emptying it of content (2002, p. 74). So, rather than being defined by institutions or functions, politics is in play in any context in which power is exercised, a point on which Jiri Přibáň (this volume) expands. (Hay's definition appears to attach economics with a 'sector' of activity – in contrast to our methodological definition – while he identifies political analysis with a concept.) This conceptual move has two key implications. First, it makes politics *ubiquitous* (in the sense of being potentially present in all social relations). Second, it means that the political is *only one aspect* or moment of those social relations. So politics may be placed in the analytical foreground, so long as we recall that it also needs to be set among other moments of the social. In identifying a key disciplinary 'moment', this strategy might align political analysis more with geography than economics or sociology. In practice, of course, this conceptual definition of politics sits alongside – and in a creative tension with – other understandings and connotations of the word, including the more traditionally institutional.

While there are strong claims about its 'constitutive' character for wider social and economic relations (Gordon, 1984, is one example), as a discipline, law has generally been rather more modest than economics or sociology. Like politics, law could refer to the core domain – topics, institutions, functions and/or systems, while (socio-)legal studies places a particular aspect or aspects (dimensions or 'moments') of social relations in the foreground – whatever the topic or instance of social relations under investigation. That socio-legal scholars might want to share the power 'moment' Hay claims for politics (or to resist that claim) reinforces our suggestion of a significant overlap between the disciplines. Equally, it might be helpful to think of (socio-)legal scholars as addressing the legal aspect of social relations (say, in the form of 'legality'). (Socio)-legal studies might be thought of as researching the law as a topic and legality as a moment of social relations.

Taking this approach could provide a creative way of confronting the ubiquity paradox of legality. Echoing the political analysts' concerns, socio-legal theorists have been concerned that researchers have come to find legality and legal consciousness everywhere, and thus empty them of content (Silbey, 2005). To paraphrase Hay on the political (2002, p. 75), though legality may be everywhere, nothing is wholly or completely legal. So, rather than repudiating the concept of legal consciousness, legality could be understood as widespread to the point of ubiquity, without suggesting that anything is *exhaustively* legal. How then can we escape it? This is the point addressed by Sharon Cowan. If law is everywhere, of equal salience is that we seem to retain our faith in it. Drawing on Judith Butler's idea of the 'double gesture', Sharon Cowan argues that we can both work within and resist the law: 'Suspicion of law can be encouraged even while legal rights claims are pursued.' Her analysis is rather more nuanced than even this suggests in that she argues that, in this double gesture, we should also be 'resisting the temptation to rely on law to mould the social world around us' through engagement in diverse strategies.

So, as disciplines, law and politics share some clear similarities. Each has a core set of concerns and institutions that appear unimpeachable as 'law' or 'politics' respectively (some of which – the institutions of government – they share). Equally, both disciplines are impatient with the limits of these traditional cores and desire to branch out from the study of (legal or political) arenas to functions or to processes. But the two disciplines are also pockmarked by differences. For example, the study of politics, or political science, often seems to lack a distinctive approach or methodology.

Instead, it continues to draw heavily on economics and game theory (particularly in the form of rational choice approaches), statistics, behavioural science and systems theory, as well as history/historiography. While socio-legal scholars also draw methods from other disciplines, 'blackletter' and/or doctrinal analysis as well as a focus on legal technicalities can give law (and socio-legal studies) a distinctive approach – and perhaps even a particular methodology – which is not immediately accessible to the uninitiated.

Turning from disciplines to metatheory, the emerging socio-legal study of 'technicalities', we believe, raises metatheoretical questions in a particularly powerful way – an issue to which we will return at the end of this section. We aim to provoke a discussion of socio-legal metatheory and of an analytical 'level' and set of 'issues' as metatheoretical. Here, again, we think that socio-legal studies may have something to learn from the explicit debate in politics over the past 20 years about metatheory and methodology. Some socio-legal analysts have drawn explicitly on metatheoretical debates in politics (see Sarat and Scheingold, 2005) and the attention given to structure and agency as well as to materialism and idealism in Ewick and Silbey (1998) resonates with contemporary preoccupations in political analysis.

Socio-legal studies should not ape politics in engaging with metatheory – there are certainly differences of emphasis in the metatheoretical questions raised by socio-legal studies, including in the analysis of technicalities. Influenced by law and geography, much more attention has been given to ideas of space, place and territory in socio-legal studies than in politics. Our conception of metatheory has, we think, strong roots in influential, often empirically grounded, socio-legal (and critical) analyses over the past two or three decades – our corpus here includes Bankowski and Mungham (1976), Gordon (1984), Cotterrell (1992), Ewick and Silbey (1998), Riles (2005), Valverde (2009).

Politics has displayed an explicit engagement with various theoretical, epistemological and ontological questions – and political analysts have focused attention on a number of metatheoretical issues that are implicit in or explicitly raised by empirical research and can be identified across – and abstracted from – a number of theories. Three (interrelated) issues have garnered particular attention:

1 the concepts of structure and agency;
2 questions of time and temporality or continuity and change;
3 the relationship between idealism and materialism (or the ideational and the material).

In addition, a long-standing debate about power also has something of a metatheoretical quality (see Hay, 2002, pp. 168–93). Often, these issues have a dualistic quality – apparently forcing (or at least suggesting) a choice between structure or agency, continuity or change and ideas or material-ity (see Hay, 2002, p. 118; cf., in a socio-legal context, Ewick and Silbey 1998, pp. 38–9). These issues are all interlinked – both in the sense that one cannot simply 'pick and mix' elements into any combination and that beginning from any one of them is likely to implicate aspects of some others. And, at least within certain epistemological and ontological tradi-tions, there may be a sense in which some of these metatheoretical issues are deeper, more primitive or fundamental, than others. For example, Hay seems to treat the structure–agency issue – and more specifically what he calls the 'problem of agency' (2002, p. 50; also 1995) – as being primitive or having a more fundamental status than the issues of continuity and change, power or materialism and idealism (a status that owes something to the influence of critical realism).

Clearly, discussions of structure and agency, temporality and the ideational/material relationship are not exclusive to a particular disci-pline. In fact, many of the key contributors and sources of these debates lie in other traditions of social analysis. For example, drawing on the nineteenth-century classics, social theorists including Anthony Giddens (1984) Margaret Archer (1995), Roy Bhaskar (1979) and Pierre Bourdieu (1977; 1984) developed accounts of structure and agency as presupposing one another, or mutually constituting. Giddens' conception of structura-tion, Bhaskar's critical realism developed into a morphogenetic approach to structure and agency by Archer, and Bourdieu's concepts of fields and habitus, all seek to understand structure and agency relationally. That is, in Hay's words (2002, pp. 116–17), all these theorists accept:

> the view that agents are situated within a structured context which presents an uneven distribution of opportunities and constraints ... . Actors influence the development of that con-text over time through the consequences of their actions. Yet, at any given time, the ability of actors to realize their intentions is set by the context itself.

Engagement with the structure–agency debate by scholars of politics (and initially particularly of international relations) during the 1990s drew heavily on these arguments, sometimes explicitly offering social theories of political phenomena (Wendt, 1999, is emblematic here).

If socio-legal studies might learn from the move towards 'applied metatheory' in political analysis, it is also important to highlight dif-ferences between the disciplines. Among political analysts, interest in metatheory has been associated with an increasing interest in the idea-tional, in contrast to the privileging of 'material interests' (variously in

Marxist or economic liberal forms). The animating concerns of the traditional academic discipline of law are different: law has been preoccupied with rules and norms. Rather than ideas, recently 'applied metatheory' in socio-legal studies has retrieved the materiality of legality and legal processes. And some of the methodologies and metatheoretic positions that have been adopted by 'socio-legal' researchers suggest an evisceration – or even erasure – of law and the legal (Pottage, 2012).

Equally, though, and by contrast with the study and practice of politics, it certainly makes sense to speak of a legal method, albeit one perhaps more strongly associated with legal practice than legal scholarship. In as much as legal method is important for doctrinal scholarship, it has been treated as a matter of experience and craft at least as much as explicit knowledge and training. Again, our concern with legal technicalities' methods, methodologies and sensibilities in this volume – thinking about how they might be drawn to the surface as a matter for study and reflection – is partly to draw out the insights they offer in producing the social or some other; such as Tomlins' sustained analysis of the Nat Turner rebellion and its translations through Thomas Gray's contemporaneous pamphlet recalling Turner's confessions. Tomlins' analysis leads us to the conclusion that the search for the social from the legal blinkers us to other constructions – in this case, the soterial (the Christian salvation) by contrast with the social (which Tomlins describes as the profane, 'the world of fallen humanity', p. 35).

'Exploring'

When we explore something, it is often, perhaps usually, for the first time. We are like Alfred Schuetz's 'stranger', seeing things for the first time, reflexively developing our theory in order to get by. Exploration, in this sense, requires us to:

> orientate [ourselves] in [the legal] and to know it. Nothing is self-explanatory ... [We] may, of course, refer to a map of the town, but even successfully to use the map he must know the meaning of the signs on the map, the exact point within the town where [we] stand[] and its correlative on the map, and at least one more point in order correctly to relate the signs on the map to the real objects in the city. (Schuetz, 1943, p. 132)

The cartographer provides the map from a single disciplinary perspective, although one which bleeds governing power (see, for example, Rose, 1999, pp. 36–7).

Common to the chapters in this book is a version of the limited role of the state. Such a limit forms the starting point for Přibáň's reflections, which draw on different readings of legal pluralism, Eugen Ehrlich's 'living law', and Gunther Teubner's societal constitutionalism. Přibáň offers a trenchant critique of the latter, arguing that it suffers from the paradoxes, prescriptions and limitations of Ehrlich's sociology of law. In fact, for Přibáň, such approaches which deny the role of politics and the state and civil society in the formations of global legal pluralism are themselves in denial of the central role redefinition of the state as part of the 'global "meta-power game"' (p. 75) outside the structures of state sovereignty. There are affinities between Přibáň's methodological reflections and David Cowan's case study, although their social theoretical starting points are different. For David Cowan, whose key conceptual tools are territory and territoriality – not as fixed two-dimensional jurisdictional maps, but as things constantly being remade – the interaction of such global and local processes produces pragmatic compromises out of contestation. His case study concerns human rights and possession cases. His argument is that the territories of the home, the courts, the national and European, produce a narrow sense of the social obligation in housing. Rather than protecting 'rights', the legal protects both itself and its totalizing discourse of property as being defined by its exclusivity.

Drawing on Latour (1986), Nikolas Rose (1999, p. 37) makes the point that 'Inscription devices [such as maps] are "intellectual techniques": material techniques of thought that make possible the extension of authority over that which they seem to depict.' Plenty of examples of such devices, with their own *agencement* (Muniesa et al., 2008) adorn this book. The lease, the care plan, the 'human right', the legitimate medicine, the single legal order, the medical manslaughter prosecution (respectively, Hunter, Carr, David Cowan, Cloatre, Cardwell and Hervey, Sanders and Griffiths, all in this volume) are all examples of these things, techniques which are both made up and make us up (or, fabricated: Pottage, 2004). These are the things around which narratives of legal meaning are created, a creative process which may be collective or social, as Cover (1983, p. 11) suggests.

And explorations, just like maps, seek out and provide boundaries. The boundaries of this book are fixed by our use of legality as its central structuring concept. However, the boundaries of legality itself have proved a particularly fertile research resource for socio-legal studies (Cooper, 1998; Holder and Harrison, 2003; Sassen, 2006; Johns, 2013). Indeed, boundaries – both imagined and real – and silences are produced by our very subjects/objects of study, by our attempts at simplifying mess (Law, 2004; Latour, 2010), despite (or because of?) our effort to think more generally (Cooper, 1998; Sassen, 2014). As Johns (2013, p. 11) puts it, in her treatment of the boundaries of non-legality in international law, her:

forays into non-legality … are, then, hardly ventures into clearly bounded fields of negation of emptiness. On the contrary, attention to the ways in which *some* kinds of legal technique, institution or analysis are understood to be lacking or inoperative in particular areas of intentional legal work (in other words, the sense that non-legality prevails) may render *other* legal norms and practices more visible or significant. (emphasis in original)

In their case study of (non-)prosecutions of medical manslaughter, Andrew Sanders and Danielle Griffiths (this volume) provide yet further evidence of the silences engendered by legal decision-making silences. These silences produce non-legality. Why, they ask, are there so few medical manslaughter prosecutions (a finding in itself against the grain, as the usual argument is that there are more such prosecutions)? From a detailed ethnographic study they discover how prosecutors appear to prioritize a case of which they have barely heard, one ignored in the textbooks, and which appears also to have been misinterpreted. This classic socio-legal study offers a damning critique of prosecutors' 'frames' as 'traditional forms of deference disguised through the adoption of a legal test that is not required'.

Our explorations, techniques and boundaries are historically situated. This feels like a trite point – as Saskia Sassen (2006, p. 4) observes 'the "new" in history is rarely simply *ex nihilum*. It is deeply imbricated with the past, notably through path dependence, and … through a tipping dynamic that obscures such connections to the past.' As it contorts itself to spawn new exceptions and new principles, the common law has a habit of hoodwinking us into an assumption of legal progress and that we do not need legislators. Roger Cotterrell (2012, p. 2) makes this point nicely:

> Most of the important theoretical questions about law are not at all timeless but very timely – others are issues about the way law is shaped, works and develops in specific historical contexts. They are about what law means to those who are concerned with it or confronted by it, and this meaning cannot be abstracted as though it were unrelated to time and place.

Time often folds in on itself – the geographers' analogy is with the folding of a handkerchief – in the process of creating the common law. So, for example, in developing principles of property law, we might hark back to sixteenth-century principles, apparently fit for today's purpose (see, for example, *Berrisford v Mexfield Housing Co-operative Ltd* [2011] 2 WLR 423; [2011] UKSC 52; Cowan et al., 2012). However, the temporalities are often rather more complicated than the monochrome of the common law – Franz von Benda-Beckmann and Keebut von Benda-Beckmann (2014, p. 31) put this rather well when they argue that:

> legal spaces and places are perpetually perishing, as Harvey pointed out, but also that they 'come and go'; that is, they move and alternate with other spaces, but they do so at different paces, depending, among other things, on the kind of legal system that constitutes the space, for each legal (sub)system has characteristic ways in which spaces are being 'timed'. (see also Valverde's use of chronotopes (2014) in the same volume)

In their chapters, Tomlins and Ohana are both particularly concerned with histories. Their perspectives are different, to be sure: Ohana offers a Foucauldian method, while Tomlins is inspired more by seeing beyond the social. But, though different, each uses a case study to locate the legal. From another perspective, Caroline Hunter demonstrates how the techniques used to make the lease as historical artefact defined through precedent speak to modern technologies. That artefact can, of course, be our descriptive narrative of the development of law – law's onward march of progress through time, as portrayed in the various editions of our textbooks. This narrative of legal progress must be disrupted – a task Gordon (1984) took up, and which is engaged for EU law by Paul James Cardwell and Tamara Hervey here.

Finally, when we think about methodology we may be like Schuetz's stranger. In contrast to non-vocational social science disciplines, the legal academy has paid relatively little attention to (research) methodology, never mind to metatheory. In relation to:

> both methods and theory ... sociolegal scholarship has borrowed tools from various schools of critical social science, from Marxist structuralist theories of world capitalism to anthropological tools that shed light on the legal consciousness of ordinary people at more local and human scales. (Valverde, 2014, pp. 53–4)

Not least as a consequence of its disdain for the legal 'technicalities', in methodological and theoretical terms socio-legal studies has been a borrowing discipline. Socio-legal scholars have sought to awaken legal scholarship from the slumbers of doctrinalism by deploying the latest social theory (Valverde, 2009, p. 146). At best, legal thought and legal practice 'act merely as objects of study' (Valverde, 2014). In fact, as Riles (2005, p. 976) suggests 'humanistically oriented legal scholars are liable to find [legal technicalities] profoundly uninteresting at best, and offensive at worst'.

The legal

A key series of moves made in law and society scholarship in recent years has been away from thinking about 'law and' towards thinking about legalities in society. These moves are most clearly addressed in Ewick and Silbey's classic, *The Common Place of Law* (1998). They critique the 'law first' tradition of scholarship, arguing that it has drastically narrowed our vision; and that, despite the research which shows that law 'has no center and little uniformity, it is often implicitly assumed that the law is still recognizably, and usefully distinguishable from that which is not law' (p. 19). If we unhinge law from its institutional setting, and think about the cadences of legalities in everyday life, 'we must tolerate a kind of conceptual murkiness'. The key move for our purposes here is away from 'law' to legality, a term that Ewick and Silbey use 'to refer to the meanings, sources of authority, and cultural practices that are commonly recognized as legal, regardless of who employs them or for what ends'. They provide a material example of this shift – an old chair left on a public street, where snow has been cleared, to hold a parking spot might be seen in a Lockian sense as a marker of exclusivity, ownership/possession as a result of the labour. Silbey and Cavicchi (2005, p. 561) see this chair as 'a visual image of the law from the bottom up and from outside of legal institutions'. It signals a type of ownership and 'often elicits the same sorts of deference and respect accorded more conventional types of property: Other drivers park elsewhere.'

Uncoupling formal law from legality in this sense has risks (Engel, 1998), in particular, of the ubiquity paradox that, as we have already noted, when everything is potentially legal, legality itself becomes meaningless, a container term. As Naomi Mezey (2001, p. 153) suggests: 'the law is everywhere so much so that it is nowhere'. And, if that is the case, how do we speak to data which suggests that:

> more salient factors eclipse the force of law on [women in the street-level drug economy] conscious decision-making and on their understandings of their situation. Economic realities, gender hierarchies, peer pressure, fear, the need for personal safety – all of these considerations call for extralegal (or quasi-legal) measures to ensure survival on the street. (Levene and Mellema, 2001, p. 180; also Přibáň, this volume)

Sharon Cowan helpfully suggests that, if law is everywhere, it must come with a health warning about its inadequacies.

However, the retreat back (or return?) to legality may well prove particularly enticing for socio-legal scholarship that seeks to imbricate or fabricate persons with things. This is Ohana's point in this volume about the legal as a knowledge-power relation. While it may be a familiar trope for socio-legal studies, Ohana offers fresh insights through her consideration of the act of legal labelling, 'as a reflection of silenced and invisible social struggles within legal discourse' (p. 80). Her case study is the naming of 'domestic violence'. Her analytical tools – classification, continuity and translation – combined with concepts – statement, discourse, history and discontinuity – enable her to provide novel reflections on the legal as an arena of struggle. Emilie Cloatre takes a similar approach in her case study (this volume) of counterfeit medicines. Her research question is consequential on labelling. She asks how labels condition the possibility of materials circulating in a situation where the labels themselves do not provide clarity. The 'counterfeit' label is translated for different purposes in different ways.

These observations bring us back to socio-legal metatheory. Typically, a socio-legal scholar might have addressed a legal issue (or an issue with a legal dimension) by choosing (or borrowing) a particular approach (a theory and/or a methodology) and framing a research project within it. The borrowing often comes from other humanistic or social scientific disciplines and research traditions, rather than generating theories or approaches internal to the discipline itself. Where socio-legal scholars do take account of methodological and metatheoretical issues, the work is done typically from within a particular theoretical position, which aligns ontology, epistemology and methodology (although not necessarily in that 'order'). Self-consciously choosing to work within a particular theoretic tradition tends to bring with it a set of metatheoretical pre-commitments. Although often fruitful, the use of borrowed 'off-the-peg' theories and methods treats these 'legal technicalities' (the law or legal aspects) as, at best, little more than a subject matter. And, if we start (only) from a particular theory, we are generally likely to adopt the metatheoretical positions associated with it, but without necessarily reflecting as such on the issues these positions raise. In short, because metatheory often develops from, or involves, a second-order reflection on (or abstraction from) theory and method, the relative weakness of distinctively socio-legal theory and method production has contributed to the neglect of metatheory. Alternatively, a good deal of legal research – perhaps particularly scholarship that is focused on legal technicalities or doctrine – is sceptical of 'theory'. Reflection on methodology is only rarely a feature of this sort of work – and questions of epistemology and ontology appear still more arcane and abstruse.

Our approach here differs from the ways in which legal scholars carrying out empirical research might otherwise come across questions of methodology, ontology and epistemology. Rather than approaching metatheory primarily from a particular theoretical position, we seek to develop another way of thinking about these issues that might be more accessible and appealing to (mainstream) scholars of legal technicalities – and also, we hope, to socio-legal researchers. While it may not be possible to do full justice to the richness of the metatheoretical positions of each and every theory, it is (we think) possible to identify some broad themes, questions or dilemmas that are raised from a variety of these positions in and for research in law (and, indeed, in cognate humanities and social sciences). We hope that fruitful reflections on the legal will emerge from socio-legal engagement with metatheory.

Legal technicalities

The metatheoretical distinction between materialism and idealism – heavily implicated in political analysis as well as having a significant role in some socio-legal work (cf. Hay, 2002; Ewick and Silbey, 1998) – also underpins our concerns about legal technicalities. Full-blooded idealism remains rare in socio-legal scholarship – and is unusual even in other heterodox approaches to legal analysis. For example, while Gordon's (1984) classic critical analysis of legal histories seemed to accentuate the role of ideas, he has vigorously repudiated Tomlins' (2012) suggestion that it was an anti-materialist account – 'To the charge of idealism, I am quite sure I want to plead not guilty' (Gordon, 2012, p. 204). Increasingly, the distinction of ideas from materiality is recognized as no more than a preliminary step as analysts seek to move 'beyond' materialism and idealism. In so doing, political analysts and socio-legal scholars place emphasis on 'the *contingent* or *open-ended* nature of social and political processes and dynamics' (Hay, 2002, p. 201, emphasis in original, see, generally pp. 194–215).

As Riles (2005, p. 976) notes, the technical character of law 'encompasses diverse and at times even contradictory subjects, ideologies and practices', including 'ideologies, actors, the problem-solving paradigm and the *form* of technical legal doctrine and argumentation' (original emphasis). But, as she goes on to analogize using the example of a leaky faucet (pp. 979–80), this distinction between materialism and idealism breaks down. We set out this analogy in full because it provides the framework for our project:

> It is something like a very leaky faucet – a crucial but terribly dull piece of plumbing that becomes apparent only by virtue of the troublesome fact that it stubbornly refuses to work as it should. Now the faucet contains nothing that on its surface would render it of interest to those with a penchant for cultural questions: it is not adorned with interesting mouldings or set in unusual mosaic; it is just an old-fashioned, ordinary, leaky faucet.
>
> To the extent that humanistic legal scholars would find any reason to pay attention to the poor device at all, it might be to critique the distributive consequences of plumbing, or the

gendered division of labor it has produced, or to show the power of the plumber who comes each week to hoodwink the consumer into buying yet another new faucet-fixing gadget. Alternatively, a humanist with a great deal of creative energy might explore the persons and practices that produced the leaky faucet: he or she might describe the meetings of the leaky faucet fixers' association in all its exotic and ironic detail and show how the fantasies of repair and disrepair mirror wider forces at work in parallel fields of greater interest to humanists – perhaps he or she could find parallels to images of chaos and coherence in art or literature, for example.

Yet what of the faucet itself? In each of the projects it is somewhat beside the point – a mere pretext for telling the story of persons, practices, economic incentives or power politics. Would it be possible for the humanist truly to find something of interest in the mundane technologies of (faulty) plumbing – to take this crucial territory back from the plumbers of the legal discipline? Here, we would want to find a way to describe these techniques as something more than just the consequence of wider cultural trends, and as something more robust than putty in the hands of the technocrat. In other words, we would want to account for the agency of technocratic legal form.

In a rather nice way, Riles' analogy sets the parameters of our project, drawing out the relationship between the material and ideational. Hunter (this volume) engages in similar work when considering the humble technology of the lease, which is drawn on the basis of what went before it – indeed, as she puts it, a *reverence* for what has gone before. In this sense, precedent makes it both immutable and immobile, although paradoxically it must have a certain mobility to meet the exigencies of everyday life. Hunter's case study is of the lease, drawn in time-honoured fashion, and an apparent conflict with the use of solar panels; to put it crudely, the old, mundane technology and the technology-rich, modern solar panel. The tribunal had to use the abstraction of the 'reasonable person' to determine the outcome, and constructed this person as having no such sensibilities against modern technology (bearing in mind the already existing satellite dishes about which complaint had not been made).

An intellectual lineage can be traced to Riles' 'leaky faucet' from the stories told by William Twining (1967) in his inaugural lecture, 'Pericles and the plumber'. Socio-legal studies have often focused on the gap between law and everyday lives (see Sanders and Griffiths, this volume), and various forms of materialism – including Marxism – have had a significant impact on socio- and legal analysis. Nevertheless, in default mode, legal analysts appeal to ideas and norms rather than materialism. Academic legal analysts focus on the *text* from which they apparently abstract themselves, occasionally assuming the 'social context' as if it were an independent variable that can be superimposed on their text – and train students to operate in the same way.

In their chapter on EU law and scholarship, Cardwell and Hervey retell standard narratives that have taken on the status of truths. They do so through a study of legal technicalities in EU law and scholarship as metaphors of 'single legal order' or spaces/places (perhaps like the plumbers' convention in which different methods of dealing with the leaky faucet are discussed). Cardwell and Hervey also reflect on a paradox in their analysis. It 'embraces the very dichotomy it rejects' (p. 175) between the social and legal, because the narrative form forces it upon them: the narrative form traps them.

Although Riles and Valverde are theoretically peripatetic, both are influenced by STS. A comparatively recent accompaniment to the theoretical/empirical armoury of socio-legal studies, STS offers a way of intertwining the material and ideational. STS – and its close relation ANT – appeal particularly to scholars interested in bringing the materiality of law onto the foreground of socio-legal studies. This might be seen as part of a reaction against the background idealism of legal scholarship. Artefacts are typically described as passive 'things' in everyday language; by contrast ANT understands them distinctively as (something like) agents. Analysis in the ANT tradition typically proceeds through detailed and close ethnographies that 'begin in the midst of things' (Pottage, 2012, p. 168) and follow human and non-human 'actors' around. In its accounts of science and technology, ANT starts in specific settings and moves to assemble networks of actors. That is, like Foucault, ANT is sceptical of 'universals' – 'general categories or rational entities such as the state, sovereignty, law, or power' (Agamben, 2009, p. 23).

We should make it clear that in ANT the notion of material agency is not understood as 'an innate quality of' the 'artefacts' themselves. Agency is not 'inherently either human or non-human'. Instead, as Alain Pottage (2012) suggests, it is an 'emergent effect of the composition' and 'reciprocal engagement or co-variation' 'of humans and non-humans' or 'hybrid actants'. John Law's study (1986) of the Portuguese imperial expansion in the fifteenth and sixteenth centuries provides a neat example of this hybridity, as he shows how the technological, economic, political, social and natural became interrelated within different networks (the ship, the navigational system, and the imperial system as a whole, or, as he puts it, 'documents, devices, and people'). 'Materialities', as the points in which the transition of these processes become visible and traceable, become ciphers for 'materiality' as a kind of dynamic condition of existence. Hence the proposition that 'materiality is sociality ... ultimately materiality becomes a signifier of contingency' (Pottage, 2012, pp. 168–9; Carr, this volume).

Latour – the doyen of the ANT approach to STS – himself distinguishes law from science. As noted above, Latour describes law as a regime of enunciation distinct from the institution(s) in which it is articulated – assembling or binding statements and texts. Law is a textual or rhetorical world, not a material world like that of science and technology. That is, for Latour, law lacks the technologies and material artefacts that are so central to his account of science and technology. Not all socio-legal scholars would agree with this position: some apply Latour's STS approach more directly to law – drawn to do so for its potential to emphasize (law's) materiality (see, for example, Cowan and Carr, 2008; Cloatre and Wright, 2012; Rooke et al., 2012); or, as Cloatre and Pickersgill (2014, p. 1) put it, how legality 'is talked into existence'.

These questions are at the heart of Helen Carr's chapter, in which she interweaves technical law and considerations of the 'crisis' in social care. On one level, Carr is writing a critique of a UK Supreme Court decision (*Mcdonald v Kensington & Chelsea* RLBC), in which it was held that care could legitimately be provided to Ms McDonald by means of incontinence pads and absorbent sheeting rather than assistance with the use of a commode, which would have required a night-time carer. The question was one of resources. But, the analysis offers much more than that rather simple critique. One might observe that there can be little that is more material and symbolic (in this case of a lack of dignity) than incontinence pads and absorbent sheeting. Carr's argument – embedded in her project about the jurisdictional space of conscience – is about the way these things are translated into, or perhaps around, questions of dignity. Ultimately, these questions contrast with legal technicalities; that is, the very technicality obscures the issue. Rather than focusing on Ms McDonald's dignity, the judicial focus was on the documentation. The judiciary's sole role is to put right technical failures. Carr's biting critique of the judgment is a reflection on the welfare settlement. As she puts it, 'the jurisdictional project is no longer the vulnerable adult, but rather the documentation of that person's needs' (p. 214). It is not about civility and/or dignity, but about resources and the mundane proper completion of forms.

There is, however, something of a tension between the various ways in which socio-legal scholars have appropriated the concept of materiality from ANT. On the one hand, Riles (2005) and Valverde (2009) have used it to emphasize legal 'technicalities', promoting what is, in a sense, an 'internal' analysis of law and what 'detailed studies of legal governance' can teach 'social theory' (Valverde 2009:, p. 140; Carr, this volume). By contrast, Pottage rejects 'the lawyer's sense of law' 'and almost pre-theoretical commitment to law' that 'trumps profound differences in theoretical architecture or strategy'. Instead, he suggests (2012, pp. 182–3) that 'we should begin with materiality rather than "law"; and, in so doing, we should recognize that the vicissitudes of "materiality" dissolve the instances – in this case "law" – that they are supposed to constitute'. This would seem to suggest that there are no specifically 'legal' technicalities.

A different approach is offered by Cloatre and Martyn Pickersgill (2014, pp. 7–8), who argue that what is at stake in STS-inflected studies of law:

> are the meanings of things in the shaping of legal processes, and in turn the significance of the law in producing forms of materiality – and the inevitable interrelationships between these. Such explorations reveal how materials become sites that produce, stabilize and perpetuate particular kinds of power, and help render apparent (potential) displacements of 'traditional' forms of political action. Objects become socially charged both in regards to what they project of the law, and in what they enable (users of) the law to do. (see also Ohana, Carr, this volume)

They see 'social studies of law' falling out from this interweaving of STS and law. Building on this, and offering a complementary if disturbing question, Cloatre (this volume) asks what happens to law when it becomes '*un*-technical'. And, rather than offering a binary contrast between the two, she questions the inherent obscurity in legality, the blurred lines in apparently clear definitions. Her case study concerns 'counterfeit medicines', which is a term covering a broad range of types and she finds that human actors (medics and pharmacists) deploy this term in different ways. As she puts it, 'what counts as "law" for them underlies their engagement with legal technicalities' (p. 101). The product of these blurred untechnical lines of legality is an outcome in which copies and generics are treated as counterfeit, a conclusion which is (of course) reinforced by and for the pharmaceutical industry itself.

Two illustrations

Let us now proceed to illustrate through the use of two examples how a study of legal technicalities might enhance socio-legal studies. The first illustration – flowerpots – is about the humble technology of the lease and the relationships it creates or diverts (Cowan et al., 2015). The second illustration produces something very mundane and technical from the exciting – the data held by David Miranda, confiscated by the state, and the *Guardian's* application for an interim injunction.

What is it that the flowerpot might come to symbolize? On the shelf, it lacks meaning; it is passive. Yet, when placed in a garden or outside a front door or on a pavement, it may come to have rather more complicated meanings. In this illustration, it comes to have a double meaning – about ownership and its divisibility from the social. It becomes active, as a symbol of what the lease stands for (or is taken by the owners to stand for). The illustration is derived from Cowan, Carr and Alison Wallace's study of a phenomenon called 'shared ownership' (2014), under which a household buys a share of a property, with a social landlord retaining the rest of the share.

In their work, Cowan et al. (2014) encountered a shared owner household, Mark and his daughter, for whom flowerpots provided a powerful set of markers:

> *if you saw outside my flat and some of the others, people have got some potted plants and stuff?*
>
> I: OH, YES, I THOUGHT THAT WAS NICE.
>
> *Yes, I think it's nice, and it's one of the things – and also, the lower floors from here are tenants; the upper floors are shared owners. One of the differences between the floors is the shared owners have more of that kind of ... decoration and sort of personalisation, a sense of making it a nice environment. Because we've all got a stake in it and it's our flats, and maybe some of the social problems that exist in some of the other properties aren't – you don't get that with the shared owners. I'm talking, like, people out of prison, I'm talking about people with drug habits and so on and so forth. So looking after some nice flowers outside their front thing may not be their priority.*
>
> I: NO, FAIR ENOUGH.
>
> *But for the shared owners it's like, we don't have gardens here, and that is just one nice thing to do, to sort of take care of the thing and have a bit of pride in it, and try and make it a nice environment for everybody.*

The inherent fragility of their 'ownership', their difference from the social renters on the floor below, was brought home to this household because their social landlord asked for the flowerpots to be removed. The flowerpots were described as a health and safety hazard. The household felt their lack of control. Flowerpots and ownership of the common walkway became contentious but the lease was clear.

And because what they were saying was just ridiculous, and they were saying, 'Oh, well, there's been cases in other places where children have stepped up onto the plants and fallen' – you know, and toppled down and fallen three storeys. And I said, 'Well, I'm the only person on this floor with a child. I can live with the – you know, like, I'm prepared to be a grown-up and take the risk and live with the risk'. Because it's not a real issue. It's a non-issue. And the idea that it might somehow obstruct the emergency services if there was a problem: again, a completely, completely ridiculous objection. And so, yes, we ended up basically saying, … 'and if you want to escalate it, we will be kind of taking to, like, the local media, and actually saying, 'Look at this housing association with their ridiculous rules who don't want people to have a nice quality environment'; and at some point they sort of backed down and we heard nothing more. But we had to have a bit of a battle with them about that.

In this story, law (leases) and legalities (flowerpots as tenure comparators and health and safety issues), the material and the ideational, all become enmeshed. The householder speaks with pride about how they won the battle of 'common sense'.

The tale of David Miranda offers a rather different take on law, and here we are referring to formal law. On 18 August 2013, David Miranda was stopped by two counter-terrorist officers at Heathrow Airport en route from Germany to Rio. He was detained for eight hours. Miranda is the partner of Glenn Greenwald, the *Guardian* journalist who was involved in the revelations about the security services resulting from Edward Snowden's copying of US National Security Agency and UK Government Communications Headquarters files. Miranda's:

> hand luggage was examined, and items retained which … included encrypted storage devices. Mr Oliver Robbins, Deputy National Security Adviser for Intelligence, Security and Resilience in the Cabinet Office, indicates … that the encrypted data contained in the external hard drive taken from the claimant contains approximately 58,000 highly classified UK intelligence documents. Many are classified SECRET or TOP SECRET. Mr Robbins states that release or compromise of such data would be likely to cause very great damage to security interests and possible loss of life. (*Miranda v Secretary of State for Home Department* [2014] EWHC 255 (Admin), [13])

Various questions were raised by this stop-and-search procedure in which socio-legal scholars are likely to be interested. There is a key spatial question of jurisdiction over the transit lounge, which, in turn, relates to the ambit of the controversial counter-terrorist powers in Schedule 7 of the Terrorism Act 2000. There are procedural questions about the mechanisms used by the security services and police counter-terrorism service to communicate – the 'port circulation sheet' had to be completed three times before it was sufficient to enable the police to stop Miranda. There are detailed considerations about the interaction between Schedule 7 and the Human Rights Act 1998. We might be interested in the ways in which social media was deployed around the supposed security issues by all parties.

However, for our purposes here, there is a rather more mundane question raised at the interlocutory stage about whether Miranda was entitled to interim relief. Was he entitled to stop the security services from interfering with the data he was carrying prior to the hearing of the main claim in his case so as 'to protect the confidentiality of the journalistic material seized and the identity of journalistic sources'? (*Miranda v Secretary of State for Home Department* [2013] EWHC 2609 (Admin), [23]). As it happened, the issue for the court resolved to a three-day period between 27 and 30 August 2013, a period during which the court was being asked to grant an injunction preventing the Secretary of State from interfering with the material. After 30 August 2013, the issue would become substantive, in the sense that the Secretary of State undertook to provide the evidence on which she relied by that point. In the end, the court balanced the convenience by granting an injunction that was more limited pending the full hearing, entitling inspection and disclosure for those purposes.

How does a court make such a decision? The principles were laid down in *American Cyanamid Co v Ethicon Ltd* [1975] AC 396, a case which concerned a patent over absorbable sutures, and what most such cases turn on is the 'balance of convenience' test. Lord Diplock said:

> My Lords, when an application for an interlocutory injunction to restrain a defendant from doing acts alleged to be in violation of the plaintiff's legal right is made upon contested facts, the decision whether or not to grant an interlocutory injunction has to be taken at a time when *ex hypothesi* the existence of the right or the violation of it, or both, is uncertain and will remain uncertain until final judgment is given in the action. It was to mitigate the risk of injustice to the plaintiff during the period before that uncertainty could be resolved that the practice arose of granting him relief by way of interlocutory injunction; but since the middle of the nineteenth century this has been made subject to his undertaking to pay damages to the defendant for any loss sustained by reason of the injunction if it should be held at the trial that the plaintiff had not

been entitled to restrain the defendant from doing what he was threatening to do. The object of the interlocutory injunction is to protect the plaintiff against injury by violation of his right for which he could not be adequately compensated in damages recoverable in the action if the uncertainty were resolved in his favour at the trial; but the plaintiff's need for such protection must be weighed against the corresponding need of the defendant to be protected against injury resulting from his having been prevented from exercising his own legal rights for which he could not be adequately compensated under the plaintiff's undertaking in damages if the uncertainty were resolved in the defendant's favour at the trial. The Court must weigh one need against another and determine where 'the balance of convenience' lies.

The balance of convenience test was, in itself, a matter of convenience – the law had previously been that the claimant had to show a strong *prima facie* case, which caused the interim hearing in *American Cyanamid* itself to be lengthy (three days before a High Court judge and eight days in the Court of Appeal). As *The White Book* (the well-known book which expands on civil procedure in England and Wales) puts it (pp. 15–18):

[*American Cyanamid*] is also consistent with the view that, in the interest of husbanding scarce judicial resources, the court should not be expected to devote an inordinate amount of time to the hearing of applications for interlocutory injunctions. Further, the approach should have the effect of discouraging interlocutory appeals, because, as a practical matter, a respondent party is likely to find it more difficult to upset on appeal a judge's finding arrived at by applying a lower threshold test.

It is a matter of the success of legal engineering that such matters are now dealt with every day, often in county courts beyond view (in the sense that they are not reported) in short hearings. A test as banal and meaningless as the 'balance of convenience' has been one of simple application, transportation and translation from complex sutures to (for example) warring neighbours to high issues of state in *Miranda*. Its meaninglessness is, of course, betrayed by the incommensurables at stake in *Miranda* – the protection of national security against journalistic sources – and the complete lack of evidence beyond the written words in the port circulation sheet. It was argued that 'what the court does have are serious assertions by responsible persons' ([30]). These were that national security, including putting people's lives at risk, was threatened but that is, or should be, no basis for decision-making on high constitutional matters. And just what is 'convenience', let alone how is this supposed convenience to be balanced? The diversity of circumstances to which this test is to be applied means that there is no coherent body of law beyond the principle – there is no systematic body of empirical knowledge (cf. Cotterrell, 1998) – precisely because of that diversity (which also impacts on the possibility of appeal).

We might use sociological ideas to think about the balance of convenience test, as Cotterrell (1998) encourages us to do, perhaps drawing on the sociology of ideas itself. In the same vein as Thomas Osborne (2004), we might think of the balance of convenience test as a vehicular idea. A vehicular idea moves things on; it brings in critique and such ideas:

> have something of the principled theory or committed ideology to them, but in many ways are resistant to theorization in any rigorous sense. And this is not exactly their point. Rather, they serve as inclusive umbrellas under which quite a range of advocates can shelter, trade and shift their alignments and allegiances. (McLellan, 2004, p. 485)

Yet, there is also something rather more interesting in the concept of the balance of convenience test, for in its shallowness it has drawn in all sides; it has become second nature for lawyers; in a sense, it has become a metaphor for a legal political rationality, one in which the material and the ideational intertwine just as in our flowerpot example above.

The framework of this book

The chapters that make up this book are divided, perhaps a little artificially, into two major sections. The first is more theoretically and, particularly, methodologically focused; the second is made up of case studies. But the chapters in the first section ground their methodological reflections in concrete examples, while each of the case studies also engages with methodological issues. The chapters in the first section range across approaches to legal histories (Tomlins), social theoretical perspectives on legal pluralism (Přibáň) and labelling (Ohana), as well as sex/gender perspectives on legalities (Sharon Cowan). Tomlins distinguishes the 'social' from 'soterial' and reminds us of the call to justice (which, in the material he analyses is grounded in the sacral). His close focus on the Nat Turner Rebellion shows the reader how methodological insight is most persuasive when illustrated through concrete context and narrative. Tomlins asks the reader to grapple with what is for us a key question: '[W]here is legality/law?' (p. 52) And in doing so, he models a fresh and profoundly effective methodological approach.

Přibáň reminds us how state law is decentred when viewed through a legal pluralism lens – but no complex global legal system takes its place. Further, his insistence that pluralist theory should take power into account in a serious way is important in sensitizing the abstract to the concrete. He asks how a global legal pluralist methodology might shape an exploration of the 'legal' in a way that enriches and complements the 'social' or 'sociological' in socio-legal scholarship.

Ohana demonstrates how that which is not always easy to 'classify', 'name', 'translate' can provide important ways to examine the legal. She demonstrates the use of these tools in action (using the example of domestic violence) and shows the significance of labelling to the interdisciplinary process that is part of legality's essence. She reminds us again of the significance of the relationship between knowledge and power, which underpins the techniques she discusses.

Carol Smart (1989) warned against turning to the 'power' of law in order to 'fix' the very problems identified in law in the first place. Beginning from this insight, Sharon Cowan shows us that the need to address deeper questions and to find law's 'place' have perhaps always been part of the most convincing narratives in feminist legal theory and socio-legal scholarship, rather than necessarily being produced (or characterized by) the 'bees to honey' phenomenon of focusing on law reform. Again, her analysis is rooted in and derived from empirical illustrations (sexual violence and same-sex marriage) of these themes.

Each of these chapters offers a different way into our subject and they range across wide theoretical terrain. In each case, however, their considerable theoretical purchase is rooted in concrete illustration. We hope that their methodological pluralism provides a welcome and an orientation for readers, various kinds of 'anchor' that may appeal to socio-legal scholars who start from differing theoretical points.

The second major section contains a series of case studies. They range from pharmaceuticals (Cloatre) to medical manslaughter (Sanders and Griffiths); leases (Hunter) to mandatory possession (David Cowan); the story of EU law (Cardwell and Hervey) to the dignity of vulnerable adults needing care (Carr). The sources and sites are mostly British and European, but they travel as well – we hope that jurists in any tradition, system or jurisdiction would understand the issues in real property, intellectual property, criminal proceedings and administrative decision-making.

Indeed, at their essence, the questions asked in these chapters are about the nature, form and function of legalities and, in this way, they all link back to the methodological issues discussed in the first section. Each of the four chapters in the first section has, we think, particularly clear links with two of the case studies. So Ohana's concern with legal labelling connects with Cloatre's discussion of counterfeit pharmaceuticals, as well as with Hunter's discussion of clauses in the leases. Hunter's understandings of the leases as being steeped and rooted in historical interpretations can be read alongside Tomlins' soterial histories, as might Sanders and Griffiths' understandings of prosecutorial decision-making. Sharon Cowan's understandings of law's 'place' links with Carr's detailed examination of the background and foreground to law's place in adult social care narratives. Similarly, Cardwell and Hervey's dissection of the temporalities of EU law scholarship suggest that different visions of law's place underpin the different phases of European integration. As well as connecting with Sharon Cowan's analysis, the diverse images of EU law painted by Cardwell and Hervey link with Přibáň's global legal pluralism analysis, which also finds its imperfect shape in David Cowan's local story about the different influences and structures in apparently mundane mandatory possession proceedings where external legal influences have become significant.

Cases

American Cyanamid Co v Ethicon Ltd [1975] AC 396
Berrisford v Mexfield Housing Co-operative Ltd [2011] 2 WLR 423; [2011] UKSC 52
Miranda v Secretary of State for Home Department [2013] EWHC 2609 (Admin); [2014] EWHC 255 (Admin)
R (on the Application of McDonald) v Royal Borough of Kensington and Chelsea [2011] UKSC 33; [2011] 4 All ER 881

References

Agamben, G (2009) *What Is an Apparatus?* (Stanford: Stanford University Press)
Archer, M (1995) *Realist Social Theory: The Morphogenetic Approach* (Cambridge: Cambridge University Press)
Bankowski, Z and G Mungham (1976) *Images of Law* (London: Routledge & Kegan Paul)
Becker, G S (1978) *The Economic Approach to Human Behaviour* (Chicago: University of Chicago Press)
Benda-Beckmann, F von and K von Benda-Beckmann (2014) 'Places that Come and Go: A Legal Anthropological Perspective on the Temporalities of Space in Plural Legal Orders' in I Braverman, N Blomley, D Delaney and A Kedar (eds), *The Expanding Spaces of Law: A Timely Legal Geography* (Stanford: Stanford University Press)
Bhaskar, R (1979) *The Limits of Naturalism* (Brighton: Harvester Wheatsheaf)
Blumenthal, S (2012) 'Of Mandarins, Legal Consciousness, and the Cultural Turn in US Legal History' 37(1) *Law and Social Inquiry* 167–86
Bourdieu, P (1977) *Outline of a Theory of Practice* (Cambridge: Cambridge University Press)

Bourdieu, P (1984) *Distinction: A Social Critique of the Judgement of Taste* (Cambridge, MA: Harvard University Press)

Braverman, I, Blomley, N, Delaney, D. and Kedar, A. (eds) (2014), *The Expanding Spaces of Law: A Timely Legal Geography* (Stanford: Stanford University Press)

Cloatre, E and M Pickersgill (2014), 'Introduction' in E Cloatre and M Pickersgill (eds), *Knowledge, Technology and Law* (London: Glasshouse)

Cloatre, E and N Wright (2012) 'A Socio-legal Analysis of an Actor-world: The Case of Carbon Trading and the Clean Development Mechanism' 39(1) *Journal of Law and Society* 76

Cooper, D (1998) *Governing out of Order: Space, Law and the Politics of Belonging* (London: Rivers Oram Press)

Cotterrell, R (1992) *The Sociology of Law: An Introduction* (Oxford: Oxford University Press)

Cotterrell, R (1998) 'Why Must Legal Ideas Be Interpreted Sociologically' 25(2) *Journal of Law and Society* 171

Cotterrell, R (2012) 'Socio-legal Studies, Law Schools, and Legal and Social Theory' Legal Studies Research Paper No 126/2012 (London: Queen Mary University of London School of Law)

Cover, R (1983) 'The Supreme Court, 1982 Term – Foreword: Nomos and Narrative' 97(1) *Harvard Law Review* 4

Cowan, D and H Carr (2008) 'Actor–Network Theory, Implementation and the Private Landlord' 35 *Journal of Law and Society*, Special Research Issue 149

Cowan, D, H Carr and A Wallace (2015), *Reconciling Owning and Renting in Shared Ownership Housing: Moving Forward* (Bristol: University of Bristol/York: University of York)

Cowan, D, L Fox O'Mahoney and N Cobb (2012), *Great Debates in Property Law* (Basingstoke: Palgrave Macmillan)

Dunleavy, P and O'Leary, B (1987) *Theories of the State: The Politics of Liberal Democracy* (Basingstoke: Macmillan)

Edwards, L (2012) 'The History in "Critical Legal Histories"' 37(1) *Law and Social Inquiry* 187–99

Engel, D (1998), 'How Does Law Matter in the Constitution of Legal Consciousness?' in B Garth and A Sarat (eds), *How Does Law Matter?*, Fundamental Issues in Law and Society Research, Volume 5 (Evanston: Northwestern University Press)

Ewick, P and S Silbey (1998) *The Common Place of Law: Stories from Everyday Life* (Chicago: University of Chicago Press)

Feenan, D (2012) *Exploring the 'Socio' in Socio-legal Studies* (Basingstoke: Palgrave Macmillan)

Giddens, A (1984) *The Constitution of Society* (Cambridge: Polity)

Gordon, R (1984) 'Critical Legal Histories' 36(1) *Stanford Law Review* 57–125

Gordon, R (2012) '"Critical Legal Histories Revisited": A Response' 37(1) *Law and Social Inquiry* 200–15

Hall, P and Taylor, R (1996) 'Political Science and the Three Institutionalisms' 44(4) *Political Studies* 935–57

Hay, C (1995) 'Structure and Agency' in D Marsh and G Stoker (eds), *Theory and Method in Political Science* (London: Macmillan)

Hay, C (2002) *Political Analysis* (Basingstoke: Palgrave Macmillan)

Hay, C and Wincott, D (1998) 'Structure, Agency and Historical Institutionalism' 46(5) *Political Studies* 951–7

Holder, J and C Harrison (2003) *Law and Geography* (Oxford: Oxford University Press)

Johns, F (2013) *Non-Legality in International Law: Unruly Law* (Cambridge: Cambridge University Press)

Latour, B (1986) 'Visualisation and Cognition: Thinking with Eyes and Hands' 6(1) *Knowledge and Society* 1

Latour, B (2006) *Reassembling the Social: An Introduction to Actor–Network Theory* (Oxford: Oxford University Press)

Latour, B (2010) *The Making of Law: An Ethnography of the Conseil d'Etat* (Cambridge: Polity)

Law, J (1986) 'On the Methods of Long Distance Control: Vessels, Navigation, and the Portuguese Route to India' in J Law (ed.), *Action and Belief: A New Sociology of Knowledge?* Sociological Review Monograph 32 (London: Routledge)

Law, J (2004), *After Method: Mess in Social Science Research* (London: Routledge)

Levine, K and V Mellema (2001) 'Strategizing the Street: How Law Matters in the Lives of Women in the Street-level Drug Economy' 26(1) *Law and Social* Inquiry 169

McLellan, G (2004) 'Travelling with Vehicular Ideas: The Case of the Third Way' 33(4) *Economy and Society* 484–99

Marsh, D (2010) 'Meta-theoretical Issues' in D Marsh and G Stoker (eds), *Theory and Method in Political Science* 3rd edn (Basingstoke: Palgrave Macmillan)

Marsh, D and G Stoker (1995) *Theory and Method in Political Science* (Basingstoke: Palgrave Macmillan)

Marsh, D and G Stoker (eds) (2010) *Theory and Method in Political Science* 3rd edn (Basingstoke: Palgrave Macmillan)

Mezey, N (2001), 'Out of the Ordinary: Law, Power, Culture, and the Commonplace' 26(1) *Law and Social Inquiry* 145

Muniesa, F, Y Millo and M Callon (2008) 'An Introduction to Market Devices' in M Callon, Y Millo and F Muniesa (eds), *Market Devices* (Oxford: Blackwell)

Osborne, T (2004) 'On Mediators: Ideas and the Ideas Trade in the Knowledge Society' 33(4) *Economy and Society* 430–47

Pottage, A (2004) 'Introduction: The Fabrication of Persons and Things' in A Pottage and M Munday (eds), *Law, Anthropology and the Constitution of the Social: Making Persons and Things* (Cambridge: Cambridge University Press)

Pottage, A (2012) 'The Materiality of What?' 39(1) *Journal of Law and Society* 167

Riles, A (2005) 'A New Agenda for the Cultural Study of Law: Taking on the Technicalities' 63(4) *Buffalo Law Review* 973

Riles, A (2011) *Collateral Knowledge: Legal Reasoning in the Global Financial Markets* (Chicago IL: University of Chicago Press)

Rooke, C, E Cloatre and R Dingwall (2012), 'The Regulation of Nicotine in the United Kingdom: How Nicotine Gum Came to Be a Medicine, But not a Drug' 39(1) *Journal of Law and Society* 39

Rose, N (1999) *Powers of Freedom: Reframing Political Thought* (Cambridge: Cambridge University Press)

Sarat, A and Scheingold, S (eds) (2005) *The Worlds Cause Lawyers Make: Structure and Agency in Legal Practice* (Stanford: Stanford University Press)

Sassen, S (2006) *Territory, Authority, Rights: From Medieval to Global Assemblages* (Princeton: Princeton University Press)

Sassen, S (2014) *Expulsions: Brutality and Complexity in the Global Economy* (Cambridge, MA: Harvard University Press)

Schuetz, A (1943) 'The Problem of Rationality in the Social World' 10(38) *Economica, New Series* 130–49

Siems, M and MacSithigh, D (2012) 'Mapping Legal Research' 71(3) *Cambridge Law Journal* 651–76

Silbey, S (2005) 'After Legal Consciousness' 1 *Annual Review of Law and Social Science* 323–68

Silbey, S and A Cavicchi (2005), 'The Common Place of Law: Transforming Matters of Concern into the Objects of Everyday Life' in B Latour and P Weibel (eds), *Making Things Public: Atmospheres of Democracy* (Cambridge, MA: MIT Press)

Smart, C (1989) *Feminism and the Power of Law* (London: Routledge)

Tomlins, C (2012) 'What is Left of the Law and Society Paradigm after Critique? Revisiting Gordon's "Critical Legal Histories"' 37(1) *Law and Social Inquiry* 155–66

Twining, W (1967) 'Pericles and the Plumber' 83(3) *Law Quarterly Review* 396

Valverde, M (2009) 'Jurisdiction and Scale: Legal "technicalities" as Resources for Theory' 18(2) *Social and Legal Studies* 139

Valverde, M (2014) '"Time Thickens, Takes on Flesh": Spatiotemporal Dynamics in Law' in I Braverman, N Blomley, D Delaney and A Kedar (eds), *The Expanding Spaces of Law: A Timely Legal Geography* (Stanford: Stanford University Press)

Wright Mills, C (1959) *The Sociological Imagination* (Oxford: Oxford University Press)

Part I
Methodological Issues

2
Debt, Death and Redemption: Towards a Soterial–Legal History of the Turner Rebellion

Christopher Tomlins

In law and society scholarship, 'socio-legal' means pertaining to the relationship between law and society, and to the representation of law as a social phenomenon. Socio-legal research rejects the techniques of doctrinal exegesis commonly associated with legal scholarship in favour of social science disciplines and their quantitative empirical (or qualitative social–theoretical) methodologies. A recent introductory text states that: '"Real law" is law as it is lived in society,' and is to be explained by what lies outside its formal representation, that is by 'forces *outside* the box' (Calavita, 2010, pp. 3, 4, emphasis in original). According to this approach, 'the legal' on its own tells us relatively little. Explanation of it lies in what accompanies it.

This chapter does not dissent from the base proposition that explanation of the legal is materially enhanced by summoning perspectives that do not themselves originate within the legal. Nevertheless, it targets the assumption, current since the time of Oliver Wendell Holmes Jr, Frederick William Maitland, and Roscoe Pound, that 'the social' is the essential explanatory other of 'the legal' (Tomlins, 2007, pp. 59–61). In particular it recommends that we reopen the door that Holmes et al. slammed shut at the end of the nineteenth century, the door labelled metaphysics (Tomlins and Comaroff, 2011, pp. 1039–41). Hence the chapter's subtitular reference to 'soterial–legal' history. Soterial means salvific, pertaining to salvation, to the eschatology of redemption. If social connotes the profane, the world of the creature, the world of fallen humanity, where law reigns and justice is an afterthought, soterial connotes the sacral, beyond law, where justice is eternal (Jacobson, 2003, pp. 157–232). When in Book 12 of *Paradise Lost* Milton's Adam asks the archangel Michael 'Why to those /Among whom God will deigne to dwell on Earth /So many and so various Laws are giv'n?' Michael replies 'Doubt not but that sin /Will reign among them, as of thee begot /And therefore was Law giv'n them to evince /Their natural pravity'. But, Michael promises, 'blood more precious' will be 'paid for Man, /Just for unjust' by him 'whom the Gentiles "Jesus" call ... who shall quell /The Adversary Serpent, and bring back /Through the world's wilderness long wandered man /Safe to Eternal Paradise of rest' (Milton, 2005, pp. 292–3). The soterial stands at about as stark a polar opposite to the social as it is possible to imagine. Here lies our point of purchase.

I

The turn to the social as law's companion in the unceasing play of explanans and explanandum was intended to be, and ever since has been, resolutely antimetaphysical (Parker, 2011, pp. 6–11, 16–22, 279–92). As Marianne Constable (2005, p. 9) has written:

> [m]ost texts of and about law today take law to be a social phenomenon. All manner of scholars take even religious law and customary law to be products of the societies of their times. Even scholars interested in what they would call the 'normative' aspect of law situate law in an empirical social world. That 'society' is real, that 'reality' is social and empirical, holds such sway that one wonders what else law could possibly be.

The result is the dominance of what Constable terms 'sociolegal positivism', an account of law in which the premises of legal positivism and the expertise of sociology have combined in the presumption that all law is 'humanly articulable power' either in 'the declarations of officials or in scholars' descriptions ... of the order and dynamics of human social systems', and which 'relegates connections between law and justice, if any, to empirically contingent social realities' (2005, p. 10). One could not ask for a better example of socio-legal positivism at work than Holmes' pithy observation (1897, p. 457) that to study law is not to study 'a mystery' but to engage in 'the prediction of the incidence of the public force through the instrumentality of the courts'. Current accounts of law, Constable remarks (2005, p. 11), stress its function 'as instrument or strategy within a field of social power'.

In the relentless twentieth-century campaign to empiricize the world, to render it, as Weber classically put it, calculable, social history has been sociology's faithful companion. Calculability did not mean, Weber (1958, p. 139) stressed, 'an increased and general knowledge of the conditions under which one lives' as such. It meant rather that if one wished to acquire such knowledge one could, that 'no mysterious incalculable forces' stood in the way. In his own genteel fashion, Maitland (1965–1995) had made the same point in a letter to A V Dicey in 1896 (that is, at more or less the same moment as Holmes was busily hacking out his 'Path of the Law'). To study legal history was to learn 'that each generation has an enormous power of shaping its own law', to be freed from 'superstitions'. Robert Gordon (2012, pp. 200, 212–13) has drawn Maitland's words to our attention in his most recent exposition and defence of 'critical legal history'. Maitland's position, he says, was that of a historicist; that is, one who holds that any social practice or document, such as law, is 'a product of the preoccupations of the people of its own time and place'. By locating law in a social context, the legal historian makes it an empirical phenomenon explicable not by the weight of tradition, or fate, or other such ineffable forces beyond human capacity to influence, but by its context. By stripping humanity of the magical thinking that hindered its capacity to engage in self-realizing activity, Gordon argues (alongside Maitland) that a social history of law tells us pragmatically 'that opportunities for remaking law always exist'.

I propose to test this historicist conception of the utility of legal history by examining which – the social or the soterial, empiricism or metaphysics – helps us better understand an incident in antebellum US history. The incident is the Turner Rebellion, a slave revolt that occurred in Southampton County, Virginia, in August 1831. Which of them unleashes from that incident the energy that might alter the way we understand American history and, not incidentally, the way we understand law?

The Turner Rebellion began in the early hours of 22 August, just west of the hamlet of Cross Keys, when the slave known as Nat Turner entered the house of his master, Joseph Travis, and with six confederates killed all five occupants: Travis, his wife and three children. During the next 12 hours, members of the group attacked a further 15 farmsteads, killing most of their white occupants – 50 people in all, largely women and children – and recruiting many of their slaves. By the afternoon of 22 August, the rebels, now approximately 60 in number, mounted and armed, were within about 3 miles of the Southampton county seat, the town of Jerusalem, when they were confronted by a party of white militia who had ridden out from the town to investigate news of the uprising. There occurred the first in a series of skirmishes that over the next 24 hours would completely disperse Turner's group, killing or capturing virtually all participants except Turner himself (Greenberg, 1996).

Beginning on 31 August 1831, some 40 summary trials of slaves accused of participating in the 'insurrection', as it was called, took place in the Southampton County courthouse in Jerusalem. Of the 43 defendants, 30 were sentenced to death, eleven with recommendations of commutation (Tragle, 1971, pp. 177–245). Turner himself remained at large in the locality until the end of October when he was captured. He was tried on 5 November and hanged on 11 November.

It is not difficult to determine what Southampton County was like at the time of the Turner Rebellion. No Deep South plantation district, it was a region of predominantly small farms producing mixed crops of corn, hogs and cotton, and tending apple orchards for apple brandy (Crofts, 1992, pp. 75–104). In a population of just over 16,000, whites at 6600 were slightly outnumbered by the enslaved black population of 7700. The remaining 1700 were free people of colour (Howe, 2007, p. 323). When it comes to the rebellion itself, historians have resorted to the usual array of archival sources employed to write the histories of notorious events – court records, newspaper accounts, state government documents, militia records, the odd cache of personal papers (Tragle, 1971). The pickings are relatively slim. But one document distinguishes the Turner Rebellion – a 24-page pamphlet entitled *The Confessions of Nat Turner, the Leader of the Late Insurrection in Southampton, Va. As fully and voluntarily made to Thomas R Gray, In the prison where he was confined* (Gray, 1967).

Gray's pamphlet 'immediately became the standard account' of the Turner Rebellion (Allmendinger, 2003, p. 40). It continues to be central to all examinations of the affair. But like all documents generated by white investigators of slave revolts, alleged or actual, *The Confessions of Nat Turner* presents problems. In 2001, the historian Michael Johnson launched a detailed critical assault on three new histories of the 1822 Denmark Vesey conspiracy in Charleston, South Carolina, because their authors had relied upon the *Official Report* of the inquiry into the alleged plot undertaken by the Charleston Court of Magistrates and Freeholders. According to Johnson (2001, pp. 915–16), the court had:

> colluded with a handful of intimidated witnesses to collect testimony about an insurrection that … was not about to happen; that Denmark Vesey and the other men sentenced to hang or to be sold into exile were not guilty of organizing an insurrection; [and] that, rather than revealing a portrait of thwarted insurrection, witnesses' testimony discloses glimpses of ways that reading and rumors transmuted white orthodoxies into black heresies.

Scholarly histories that depended on the very sources used to convict those accused for information about who they were, what they did, and what they hoped to do, inevitably became 'unwitting co-conspirators with the court in the making of the Vesey conspiracy'.

Obviously, in Turner's case, as in Vesey's, one must be careful in relying upon white-created documents (see e.g. Sundquist, 1993, p. 80). There are, of course, differences. Most obviously, there really was a Turner Rebellion. We are dealing with an actual event rather than a plot, alleged or authentic. Second, Gray's account of the Turner affair was not an official report of the activities of a public body, but a document produced to cash in on the notoriety of the Southampton County 'insurrection' (Parramore, 1978, pp. 105–7, 119–20). Acknowledging a need for care, how should one read Gray's pamphlet?

The Confessions is a document of two halves and two personalities (Santoro, 2008, p. 116). By the time he met with Turner, Gray had accumulated considerable independent knowledge of the rebellion, and the second half of the *Confessions*, literally a blow-by-blow narrative of the rebellion, bears all the signs of methodical preparation. There is not much in this half of the confession that Gray did not already know (Allmendinger, 2003, p. 37). The first half of the confession is quite different. This half dwells on Turner's life from his birth until the rebellion, matters of which Gray could have had little detailed knowledge. Its central concern is the ascent of a severely ascetic personality to a state of grace and the consequences attending that outcome. This half is written in a discontinuous, staccato, non-linear form. One can readily imagine the first half of the confession as a hastily written draft based on notes taken during Gray's extended jail cell conversation with Turner.

If *The Confessions of Nat Turner* is indeed a document inhabited by two personalities, what distinguishes them? How do their accounts of the Turner Rebellion differ? Essentially, they offer two completely distinct epistemologies, the one social, the other soterial. The social presents empirical data in a purposeful manner that produces a narrative of relevant circumstance. Gray takes 24 hours of *confusion* and methodically *organizes* it. Here temporality is linear and causality is secular. The account of the progress of the rebellion presented in the second half of the confession is an *accounting*, complete with careful lists of deceased whites and captured blacks. Gray seeks to make the rebellion knowable by making it calculable. In turning the chaos of action into knowledge he establishes the terms on which it shall be known.

What were those terms? They were terms of contradiction and conflict between reality and irrationality. What was reality? '[E]very thing upon the surface of society wore a calm and peaceful aspect' (Gray, 1967, p. 4). What was irrationality? '[A] gloomy fanatic was revolving in the recesses of his own dark, bewildered, and overwrought mind, schemes of indiscriminate massacre to the whites' (p. 4). The rebellion was irrational not because it occurred, but because 'it was *not* instigated by motives of revenge or sudden anger', which though doubtless unjustifiable would be at least comprehensible (p. 5). It was irrational because it was 'the offspring of gloomy fanaticism' (p. 5). The result is a sequestration of ideation (mentalité), its confinement to a specific *taxis* explaining the relationship between belief and action. The social renders rationality a consequence or function of one's social–cultural locale, one's context. The disjunction between Turner's imputed worldly situation – a calm and peaceful environment, a kindly master, no provocation given, no vengeance sought – and his thought process proves him an irrational fanatic, 'excited by enthusiasm'.

Gray was actually quite right. There is little direct evidence, in Turner's case, of correlation between worldly situation and mentalité, between context and ideational outcome. Turner's mentalité was one of faith, which engaged him in an entirely different situation, possessed of a distinct temporality and a distinct causality, than the profane, creaturely world of the gaol and the courthouse. At least as conceived by Nat Turner, the Turner Rebellion was an act of and for God. Its temporality and causality were eschatological.

Such claims are usually met with scepticism, and not only from secular humanist scholars made uneasy by religiosity. One of the principal channels through which the modern American mainstream made its acquaintance with the Turner Rebellion was William Styron's fictionalized autobiography, *The Confessions of Nat Turner*, first published in 1967. In appraisals of his own work years after the book first appeared, Styron (1993b, p. 52) advertised the repulsion he felt for Turner's 'religious mania'. Styron didn't want to write about a 'dangerous religious lunatic' but to explore, as he put it, 'subtler motives, springing from social and behavioral roots' that would allow the man to be 'better understood' (1993b, pp. 441, 442). The result? Styron's Turner is a sexually frustrated, homoeroticized celibate, who learns 'an exquisitely sharpened hatred for the white man' from the quotidian behavioural intimacies and humiliations of his enslavement (Styron, 1993a, pp. 258–9). Though religious, his religiosity is not 'mania' but rational response – in Styron's eyes it assumes the comprehensible form of 'Old Testament vengeance' (1993b, p. 442; see also Sundquist, 1993, p. 258). Styron's assumptions, in short, reproduce Gray's. The social *explains* the ideational. Ideation that the social is unable to explain is insanity.

Suppose instead we start with belief. And instead of trying to construct belief as a consequence of context, let us allow belief its own primal force. To return to the only available source, Gray's *Confessions*, what does it tell us about Nat Turner's mentalité?

The first half of the confession grants us access to Turner's life history as a narrative of three braided threads. The first is a story of self-isolation, of withdrawal from others, of 'austerity of … life and manners', of 'fasting', continual prayer, developing spirituality and, at last, assurance of election (Gray, 1967, pp. 8–9, 10). The second thread, a crucial component of an ascetic Protestant life, asks that life's central question: what is my calling? This is a question, for obvious reasons, acutely problematic for a slave to answer. It was doubly problematic for Turner, of whom it had been remarked in his childhood – as he reported – 'that I had too much sense to be raised, and if I was, I would never be of any use to any one as a slave' (p. 8). Finding that he had become an adult and nonetheless *was* a slave, 'I began to direct my attention to ... the purpose for which, by this time, I felt assured I was intended' (p. 9). The third thread comes from Turner's eventual formulation of an answer to his question of purpose. A maturing consciousness of messianic mission finds fulfilment in the life story from its inception.

Turner's search for his life's spiritual meaning begins in early adulthood, signified by his preoccupation with Christ's Sermon on the Mount, and in particular with Luke 12:31, 'seek ye the kingdom of God; and all these things shall be added unto you'. Intense prayer brings an initial revelation – 'the spirit spoke to me' – that affirms the admonition to seek God's kingdom.[1] Continual prayer brings, two years later, the same revelation, 'which fully confirmed me in the impression that I was ordained for some great purpose in the hands of the Almighty'. But *what* purpose remains unknown. At this point Turner first directly confronts the apparent contradiction between his quest for his calling and his slavery. He has become confident of his eventual ordination 'for some great purpose'. Yet he carries with him that childhood prediction that he 'would never be of any use to any one as a slave'. The second proposition blocks the first. Turner's solution is to abscond. By running away he would cease to be a slave and hence remove the obstacle to the realization of his great purpose. He is so confident in the correctness of his solution that he boasts to his 'fellow servants' that 'something was about to happen that would terminate in fulfilling the great promise that had been made to me' (Gray, 1967, p. 9).

Belatedly, however, Turner realizes he has misunderstood God. And so, '[a]fter remaining in the woods thirty days I returned'. God had made no promise; rather he had instructed Turner that his purpose lay in seeking God's kingdom. Turner had failed to obey. '[T]he Spirit appeared to me and said I had my wishes directed to the things of this world, not to the kingdom of Heaven, and that I should return to the service of my earthly master'. For a third time, in other words, Turner was admonished to seek God's kingdom, and this time with the unmistakable injunction to do God's will rather than interpret that will to suit himself, as a 'promise' with earthly consequence. Turner observes in self-reproach, once more referencing Luke's rendition of the Sermon on the Mount, 'he who knoweth his

---

1 Turner identifies 'the spirit' as 'The Spirit that spoke to the prophets in former days' (Gray, 1967, p. 9) or, in other words, as a direct manifestation of the God of the Old Testament.

Master's will, and doeth it not, shall be beaten with many stripes', adding the words that the spirit had spoken to him, 'and thus have I chastened you' (Gray, 1967, pp. 9, 9–10).

This passage of the confession is often interpreted as a form of *tu quoque*: Turner the rebel in chains reminds his white interlocutor of the fate of those who would defy God's will by keeping others in bondage. Turner had indeed beaten Southampton's white slaveholders with many stripes. But although available, this reading is implausible. Turner here is speaking of his own abject failure to understand God's will, his shallow interpretation of his revelations as 'promises' rather than injunctions pointing him towards grace. His reappearance at his master's plantation after a month's absence is an act of penitence. No doubt it earned him punishment, as well as the incredulity of his fellow slaves, who, he says, 'murmured' against him (Gray, 1967, p. 10). Turner is at this point profoundly isolated, humiliated and quite conceivably – given God's reproof – unable to comprehend the meaning of his revelations. He has been chastened spiritually while in the wilderness and, likely, physically on his return. Yet we should note that, at the same time, God has quite pointedly dissolved the blockage that led Turner to abscond in the first place. By requiring that he return to his master, God has underlined the irrelevance of Turner's earthly condition to the achievement of his purpose. He has indicated that it is *as a slave* that – if at all – Turner will realize his calling.

This acute moment of psychological crisis and self-examination produces Turner's most intense vision to this point:

> I saw white spirits and black spirits engaged in battle, and the sun was darkened – the thunder rolled in the Heavens, and blood flowed in streams – and I heard a voice saying, 'Such is your luck, such you are called to see, and let it come rough or smooth, you must surely bare it'. (Gray, 1967, p. 10)

The vision has two clear textual points of reference, Revelation and once again Luke. Revelation's apocalyptic conflict and blood imagery supplies Turner's vision with most of its visual cues. From Luke 3: 4–5, meanwhile, comes the vision's voice, specifically the voice of John the Baptist, preaching repentance and the coming of the Messiah, 'Prepare ye the way of the Lord ... the crooked shall be made straight, and the rough ways shall be made smooth'.

Onto these twinned moments of intense eschatological anticipation, Turner imposes a specific coding – 'white spirits and black spirits engaged in battle'. Almost invariably this is read as an intimation of racial violence some eight years before the event. To be so, however, it must be turned around – the white spirits of Revelation, after all, have been made white 'in the blood of the Lamb'. They are the souls of those saved from tribulation, who serve God 'day and night'. Neither Testament of the Bible, meanwhile, furnishes a single positive connotation for blackness of any kind, or darkness of spirit. In any case, Turner has been specifically warned *against* preoccupation with the creaturely world. His purpose is to learn God's will and obey it. Hence, he resumes, as far as possible for one in his situation, his ascetic withdrawal from the world. His objective is to 'serv[e] the Spirit more fully' (Gray, 1967, p. 10). They commune once again, and Turner at last begins to understand the meaning of God's creation. He becomes more confident of his own spiritual maturity, his capacity to obtain 'true holiness', his ability to receive 'true knowledge of the faith'. He finally experiences grace. 'And from the first steps of righteousness until the last was I made perfect; and the Holy Ghost was with me' (p. 10). It is difficult to read these words as anything other than the description of an experience, and a temporality, at once sacral and ecstatic. Turner is at last at one with the – necessarily eternal – will of God.

Turner's experience of grace is accompanied by further visions once again informed by Revelation. 'Behold me as I stand in the Heavens' the Holy Ghost commands him. 'Behold' says Revelation of Christ, in an absolutely key passage, 'he cometh with clouds; and every eye shall see him, and they also which pierced him'. Turner sees the 'lights of the Saviour's hands' stretched across the sky 'even as they were extended on the cross on Calvary for the redemption of sinners' (Gray, 1967, p. 10). Revelation says 'he had in his right hand seven stars'. It explains that the seven stars are 'the angels of the seven churches' to which Christ instructs the author of Revelation, John of Patmos, to write. Turner says that the 'children of darkness' name the lights wrongly. Throughout Revelation 2 and 3 Christ, through John, warns the seven churches to repent 'from whence thou art fallen'. Only those who 'have not defiled their garments ... shall walk with me in white'.

The meaning Turner ascribes to his vision is understandably apocalyptic, anticipating the imminent return of Christ – 'the Saviour was about to lay down the yoke he had borne for the sins of men, and the great day of judgment was at hand' (Gray, 1967, pp. 10–11). He shares his knowledge of what is to come with a white overseer named Etheldred Brantley (it seems frankly improbable that if Turner was planning race war the first person to be let in on the secret would be a white overseer.) Both are baptized by the Spirit. As the coincidence of second coming and last judgment indicate, Turner's eschatology has taken on a distinctly postmillennialist slant. The apocalyptic tension is tightened even further in the wake of Turner's baptism, when:

> on the 12th of May, 1828, I heard a loud noise in the heavens, and the Spirit instantly appeared to me and said the Serpent was loosened, and Christ had laid down the yoke he had born for

> the sins of men, *and that I should take it on* and fight against the
> Serpent, for the time was fast approaching when the first should
> be last and the last should be first. (Gray, 1967, p. 11, emphasis
> added)

The serpent is, of course, the serpent of Genesis, Satan, the cause of the fall
of man. In Revelation the final loosening of the serpent comes after Christ's
thousand-year reign on earth and presages the Last Judgment. From this
point onward Turner is living entirely in sacred space and time, beyond
Armageddon, his calling – finally clarified – to fight the final battle against
Satan so that the Last Judgment could take place, completing humanity's
redemption, and the new Jerusalem appear.

Turner must now wait, in silence, for the sign to commence the battle
with Satan – 'to arise and prepare myself, and slay my enemies with their
own weapons'. When the sign appears – an eclipse of the sun that occurred
in February 1831 – a 'seal' is removed from his lips, and he at once commu-
nicates his purpose to four others. The enormity of the task defies imagination – 'Many were the plans formed and rejected by us'. Turner nearly
buckles under the burden; he becomes sick with tension. A plan is con-
cocted, hurriedly and haphazardly, only after a second unambiguous sign
(Gray, 1967, p. 11). The events that we know as the Turner Rebellion begin
immediately.

Asked by Gray whether, chained in his cell, his fate does not prove him
mistaken in his convictions, Turner replies curtly, 'was not Christ crucified'
(Gray, 1967, p. 11), confirming the third and final thread of his narrative.
The account of his life that Turner has offered as he awaits trial is of a
life, as was Christ's, of preparation: a precocious infant gifted with uncanny
knowledge; an adult tested in the wilderness, come to grace and baptism,
confronted in his maturity by an immense task that nearly breaks him,
on the outcome of which rides the salvation of all. Indeed, his reply to
Gray may signify more, that Turner's account is one of his own transfigu-
ration *as* Christ, or – in a sense the same thing – as Christ's antitype. To
understand what this means requires that we delve a little into Protestant
hermeneutics.

II

The roots of evangelical Protestantism in antebellum Virginia lay in the
revivals of the 1750s and particularly of the 1760s, when Virginia's dominant Anglican church was challenged first by the influence of Baptist dis-
senters spreading northward across the border from North Carolina, and
then by an internal rupture as Methodism split off to create a separate
denomination (Heyrman, 1997, pp. 9–27; Scully, 2008, pp. 19–92). Nat

Turner's original master, Benjamin Turner, was an Anglican-turned-Methodist; Turner himself has been linked to Barnes Methodist Church, located on the southern border of Southampton County. Though described at the time of the rebellion as a Baptist preacher (see e.g. Tragle, 1971, p. 54) Turner's own account of his experience of grace, and particularly his realization of perfection, is classically Methodist (Weber, 2002, p. 96). Methodists were generally not, unlike the Baptists, Calvinist – that is, disposed to believe in predestination.[2] The two denominations also differed in principles of church organization. Ideationally, however, they were not dissimilar. Both were intensely ascetic and pietistic. Both – but particularly the Baptists – were millenarian in eschatology. Baptists were largely premillennialist; Methodists inclined to millenarianism were postmillennialist or amillennialist in sensibility (see generally Bloch, 1985; Howe, 2007).

Millenarian hermeneutics were of considerable importance to the religious revivals of the eighteenth and early nineteenth centuries wherever they occurred across Europe and America. Among their American exponents, none was more formidable than the Northampton Massachusetts Congregationalist cleric Jonathan Edwards (1703–1758). A figure of major importance in Northampton's own revival of 1733–1735, Edwards was one of the most important religious intellects anywhere in the Atlantic world. He enjoyed lasting influence on American evangelicalism far beyond Massachusetts, through writings published during his life and after his death. Of these, the most comprehensive eschatological statement was his *History of the Work of Redemption*, which originated as a series of 30 sermons preached in Northampton in 1739 but was not published in book form until 1774. The *History* was republished frequently in the later eighteenth and early nineteenth centuries, both in its original edition and in augmented editions. It has been credited with 'enormous influence' on American popular culture between the Revolution and the Civil War, both as 'a manual of Calvinistic theology suited for lay readers and popular preachers' and as an explanation of evangelical thought that helped to diffuse a millenarian sensibility throughout American Protestantism. The *History* 'set up exceptionally long-lived and significant resonances within the popular culture'. It 'securely anchored American experience in a cosmic setting, locating it by means of reference to sacred Scripture, and investing it with preeminent significance for concluding the drama of Christian redemption' (Wilson, 1989, pp. 56, 82).

The hermeneutics of Edwards' *History* are essentially as follows: first, throughout the entire span of scriptural time, from the fall to the Last

---

2 However, those strands of Methodism associated with the itinerant revivalist George Whitefield (1714–1770) rather than John Wesley (1703–1791) were Calvinist in orientation, notably the Countess of Huntingdon's Connexion, which had a number of African-American adherents, among them Olaudah Equiano and Phillis Wheatley.

Judgment and end of the world, God's principal relationship to the world is expressed in his work of redemption (salvation) of humanity, of which the most visible expression is 'remarkable pourings out of the Spirit at special seasons of mercy' (Edwards, 1989, pp. 120–5, 143). Redemption is the greatest of God's works because its culmination is a renewal of creation that extends for all eternity. Second, all God's work of redemption belongs to an eternal covenant entered into between Father and Son, God and Christ, before the beginning of the world, which elected Christ as mediator between God and humanity (Edwards, 1989, p. 130; Milton, 2005, 55–67). Third, the entire span of scriptural and human history is manifested in three phases: the first phase from the fall until Christ's incarnation in human form is one of preparation for the purchase of redemption. The second phase, which is that of Christ's first coming, lasting from his incarnation until his resurrection, is the phase in which the purchase of redemption is actually accomplished through the perfection of Christ's obedience, his humiliation and his resurrection. At this point, for the first time, Christ's kingdom of heaven becomes a reality upon earth. The third phase, which lasts from Christ's resurrection until the end of the world, is one of constant struggle to complete the work of redemption by extending Christ's kingdom upon earth until it encompasses all humanity, a struggle necessarily undertaken in constant confrontation with Satan (Wilson, 1989, pp. 25, 38–40, 52–6).

To create a detailed historical account of the work of redemption, Edwards relied on scriptural evidence, notably the currents of prophecy (revelation of what would come to pass) that recur throughout Old and New Testaments, and on what he terms 'profane' history, that is, non-scriptural chronicles of events (Wilson, 1989, pp. 48–9). To establish the meanings and connections that rendered scriptural time holistic, he employed several distinct hermeneutical strategies: first, the interpretation of certain Old Testament events as betokening the presence of Christ in scriptural narrative prior to his New Testament incarnation (Edwards, 1989, pp. 176, 184, 196–8); second, prophecy (Wilson, 1989, p. 32); and third, a neo-allegorical theory of 'shadows' or 'images' in which one scriptural or historical reality discloses or represents another more fundamental reality (e.g. Edwards, 1989, p. 218). The strongest and most detailed form that this neo-allegorical hermeneutics takes is typology, which expressed a broad Protestant literalist and historical rejection of Catholic scriptural exegesis. Essentially, typology was a figuralist hermeneutics that unified the Bible by identifying Old Testament events and individuals as prefigurations of Christ (Wilson, 1989, pp. 45–8). Protestant typology literalized figuralism – a common example is that the Old Testament figure of David is read as the type fulfilled by Christ as antitype. Edwards greatly expanded the range of typological interpretation by treating the New Testament – notably the Book of Revelation – and the recorded history of the Christian church as sources for types that would be fulfilled by future antitypes, and hence as means to predict the course of the work of redemption during that part of his third period, from the resurrection until the end of the world, yet to occur.

What has this to do with Nat Turner? Consider two interrelated propositions. First, as I have already argued, Turner understood himself to be the fulfilment of Christ at the moment of his second coming. Turner's account of himself in the first half of the confession is not simply an account of a figure that is Christ-like. Considered typologically, Turner creates himself as the antitype of the Christ of the New Testament, the re-materialization in human form of the Christ whose return in a postmillennial eschatology coincides with the Last Judgment.[3] This proposition can best be substantiated if one is prepared to accept the second and more controversial proposition, which is that Turner actually had read Edwards' *History of the Work of Redemption*, or at least was acquainted with it well enough to have been greatly influenced by it. Though the claim cannot be substantiated, the *History*'s wide circulation and immense influence among 'lay readers and popular preachers' – or in other words people like Nat Turner – lends it plausibility. Turner was a lay preacher. He was highly intelligent (this is generally accepted) and he was highly literate. Gray's *Confessions* attests to his possession of the kind of knowledge that a familiarity with widely circulating texts such as almanacs would impart (Gray, 1967, p. 8). A circumstantial case for his knowledge of Edwards' *History* can be made.

Consider, initially, Edwards' representations of Christ in his human form and compare Turner's self-description. First Edwards: Christ was born into 'uncommon humiliation and sufferings ... as though he had [been] meaner and viler than a man, and not possessed of the dignity of the human nature, but ... of the rank of the brute creatures'. He was 'persecuted in his infancy. They began to seek his life as soon as he was born'. He was subjected to 'great humiliation' by his 'servile, obscure life in a mean, laborious occupation'. He spent 'the first thirty years of his life ... among mean, ordinary men, as it were, in silence'. He lived a life of 'spotless purity and eminent holiness ... in great measure hid in obscurity ... he was little taken notice till after his baptism' (Edwards, 1989, pp. 324, 325). Now Turner: He was born 'the property of Benj. Turner, of this county'. He was early in life told by a white onlooker that 'I had too much sense to be raised, and *if* I was, I would never be of any service to any one as a slave'. (Does this

---

3 In hermeneutic usage 'antitype' does not mean 'opposite' but rather that which is 'shadowed forth' or represented by the 'type' or 'figure'.

not read as the recollection of a threat?) He was a slave, whose time was 'devoted to my master's service'. He emphasized both the 'austerity of my life and manners' and that his had been a life hidden in obscurity – avoidance of 'mixing in society', devotion to 'fasting and prayer'. Turner's claim to a precise knowledge of his date of birth – 2 October 1800 – is particularly noteworthy, both because such knowledge was impossibly rare among slaves, and because the date he claimed meant that, like Christ, he too was 30 years old when the time came to 'arise and prepare myself' (Gray, 1967, pp. 7, 8, 9, 11).

Consider, second, certain turns of phrase or images that Turner uses in the confession. One, obviously, is his frequent invocation of 'the Spirit', which parallels Edwards' repeated reference to 'the remarkable pouring out of the Spirit' – of God, of Christ, or just 'of the Spirit' – throughout the *History* (Wilson, 1989, pp. 50, 60). A second example is found in Turner's references to blood. Like Turner, Edwards drew widely on Revelation for his *History*, but, as we have seen, he also treated Old Testament events as typological figurations ('types') for Christ, notably (in this case) the waters of the Flood for Christ's saving blood. His description of a sinful world drowned in a tempest of blood resonates with Turner's first major vision, which he likens to a storm – darkened sun, thunder in the heavens and blood flowing in streams (Edwards, 1989, pp. 151–2). Likewise, we find elsewhere in the *History* blood images that closely match those used by Turner to describe Christ's blood 'shed on this earth ... ascended to heaven for the salvation of sinners ... now returning to earth again in the form of dew'. As Moses redeemed his people 'from hard service and cruel bondage' when others were destroyed by 'the sprinkling of the blood of the paschal lamb', says Edwards, so Christ saves his people and his church 'from the cruel slavery of sin and Satan' by 'the sprinkling of the blood of Christ when the rest of the world is destroyed' (Gray, 1967, pp. 10; Edwards, 1989, pp. 175–6).

A more particular example arises from the turn of phrase that Turner uses to specify 'the great work laid out for me to do' (itself of course redolent of Edwards' multiple references to God's 'great work' of redemption). It is to 'slay my enemies with their own weapons' (Gray 1967, p. 10). This seems innocuous for the expression is now familiar. But its familiarity is deceptive. Despite its biblical ring it is not a biblical phrase. And, in fact, etymological evidence suggests the phrase had no extended currency before the mid-nineteenth century.[4] Jonathan Edwards, however, employs virtually the same phrase as Turner and uses it to convey precisely the same auspicious redemptive meaning: 'God preserved him [David] from him

---

4 *Oxford English Dictionary*, weapon, n. 2b, available at www.oed.com/view/Entry/226597?rskey=birpKp&result=1#eid.

[Goliath], and gave him the victory over him, so that he cut off his head with his own sword and made him therein the deliverer of his people, as Christ slew the spiritual Goliath with his own weapon, the cross, and so delivered his people' (Edwards, 1989, p. 206; see also Edwards, 2001, p. 580). In Edwards' *History* this sentence appears in the paragraph immediately following a disquisition upon David as type to Christ's antitype that describes David as 'low of stature and ... of despicable appearance' whereby God showed how Christ, who was 'despised and rejected [of men]', would 'take the kingdom from the great ones of the earth ... thus was the frequent saying of Christ fulfilled, "The last shall be first and [the first last]"' (Edwards, 1989, pp. 205–6). In the confession, the same three ideas are intimately associated – that Turner was reviled of men, that 'the time was fast approaching when the first should be last and the last should be first' and that 'I should arise and prepare myself, and slay my enemies with their own weapons'. They occur in the same order as in the *History*, on the same page of Gray's pamphlet, and within a very few lines of each other. If the first half of Gray's *Confessions* is indeed a reasonably accurate transcription of what Turner said, in the order he said it, the conjunction is noteworthy.

Consider finally the tenor of Turner's postmillennialism. Where does it come from? That he should have embraced a millenarian world-view is not itself remarkable – millenarianism was a central element of early nineteenth-century American popular culture, and of a religious culture dominated by the morphology of revival-driven conversion. Nor was postmillennialism a rare eschatology in the early republic. 'A minority position in earlier generations' writes Daniel Walker Howe (2007, p. 289) 'postmillennialism became the most widely held viewpoint ... among Protestants in antebellum America'. But Howe is writing here of the period's 'middle-class mainstream', the urbane white citizenry that embraced progress and uplift, whose celebration of 'reformers, inventors, and Christian missionaries' folded evangelical religion seamlessly together with lyceums and mechanics' institutes, with utopian communities and collegiate education, to compose an antebellum civic identity of respectable expectation. Was this a mentalité one should expect to find amid the fetid squalor of small-scale rural slavery in Southside Virginia?

Turner's was not the complaisant postmillennialism of Howe's emergent bourgeoisie, but the altogether more urgent, revolutionary eschatology of Edwards' *History*, in which Christ's kingdom does not await his second coming but is a reality upon earth from the moment of his resurrection, and in which human history from that moment onward becomes a history of the struggles of Christ's suffering, visible church to advance his kingdom against the earthly powers of Satan, struggles attended by extraordinary danger, by miraculous successes against impossible odds brought about by

the glorious 'pouring out of the spirit of God', and accompanied throughout by Revelation's chorus of martyred souls slain for their faith: 'How
long, O Lord, holy and true, dost thou not judge and avenge our blood on
them that dwell on the earth?' (Edwards, 1989, pp. 352–3, 372–4, 381–4,
387–98). This is the revolutionary postmillennial sensibility that Turner
brings to the extraordinary moment of supreme danger to the whole work
of redemption that precedes finality, the moment when Satan is 'loosed
a little season', when 'the church of Christ ... shall be reduced to narrow
limits again' and 'shall seem to be imminently threatened with a sudden
and entire overthrow' by a human wickedness and apostasy incompara-
bly greater than ever before seen (Edwards, 1989, pp. 488–90). This is the
moment, Edwards insists, of Christ's second coming, once again 'in his
human nature', when 'the wickedness of the world will remarkably call
for Christ's immediate appearing in flaming fire to take vengeance' (pp.
490, 495). This is the moment Turner describes, but winds to an even more
exquisite level of eschatological tension: 'I heard a loud noise in the heavens, and the Spirit instantly appeared to me and said the Serpent was loos-
ened, and Christ had laid down the yoke he had borne for the sins of men,
and that I should take it on and fight against the Serpent' (Gray, 1967,
p. 11). Suddenly the entire burden of the purchase, the fate of the entire
work of redemption, the salvation of humanity, had been laid on the thin
shoulders of a 30-year-old Southside slave.

In light of all this, what then was 'the great work laid out for me to do'
that Turner and his four confidants discussed repeatedly during the first
eight months of 1830? It was, he says, 'the work of death' (Gray, 1967,
p. 11). We must ask, who were to be the slain? As it turned out, a dozen
wretched Southside farmers and their families. But in Turner's intent, at
least, were the slain not to be the 'blasphemous, murtherous enemies'
pressing in on Christ's church, 'wicked persons ... not fit to live' whose
threat to the final realization of the work of redemption Turner had been
charged to end, against utterly impossible odds, in what one might therefore represent as the most wonderful 'pouring out of the spirit of God'
of all? (Edwards, 1989, pp. 491, 503). Just as Christ crucified had been
brought 'under the power of death' to complete the purchase of human
redemption, as Edwards repeatedly noted, so Christ's enemies had themselves finally to be brought under the power of death to complete the work
of redemption.

III

We have canvassed death and redemption, but not yet, directly, debt. Debt
is central to Protestant theology, as the conceptual structure of Edwards'

History makes clear. The hinge upon which God's work of redemption turns is Christ's purchase of salvation for sinners. 'Then' says Edwards was '[the] whole debt paid. Then finished the whole of the purchase of eternal life' (Edwards, 1989, p. 331). All prior history leads to that payment; all subsequent history is the struggle to complete the purchase, to realize the meaning of Christ's self-sacrifice. It is a moment that has attracted innumerable commentators, among them, perhaps most famously, Friedrich Nietzsche, who described it as Christianity's stroke of genius, the 'horrific and paradoxical expedient' that ensured that obligation was forever moralized as guilt and that simultaneously gave humanity an exit from moral torture: 'God sacrificing himself for the guilt of man ... the creditor sacrificing himself for his debtor, out of *love* (are we supposed to believe this?), out of love for his debtor!' (Nietzsche, 2008, p. 72). In his acclaimed *Debt: The First 5000 Years*, David Graeber thinks Nietzsche's commentary was a knowing attempt to tease out a bourgeois discourse of identity borne in commerce to its ultimate shocking consequences as a theory of unpayable primordial debt cancelled by God (2011, pp. 78–9). Surprisingly, however, Graeber's tour de force does not otherwise have much to tell us about the place of debt in Protestant theology.

Jonathan Edwards' sharp answer to Nietzsche would have been that he had completely misunderstood the work of redemption. God did not sacrifice himself out of love for his debtor. Humanity is actually quite incidental to the work of redemption, merely the occasion for it rather than its centrepiece. The true purpose of the work of redemption is God's self-glorification (Wilson, 1989, pp. 40–1). Recent work by Giorgio Agamben (2011, p. 216), formulated – appropriately – as a triune paradox, suggests agreement:

> The paradox of glory has the following form: glory is the exclusive property of God for eternity, and it will remain eternally identical in him, such that nothing and no one can increase or diminish it; and yet, glory is glorification, which is to say, something that all creatures always incessantly owe to God and that he demands of them. From this paradox follows another one, which theology pretends to present as the resolution of the former: glory, the hymn of praise that creatures owe to God, in reality derives from the very glory of God; it is nothing but the necessary response, almost the echo that the glory of God awakens in them. That is (and this is the third formulation of the paradox): everything that God accomplishes, the works of creation and the economy of redemption, he accomplishes only for his glory. However, for this, creatures owe him gratitude and glory.

A profane antitype of the salvific debt–economy of glory exists in the creaturely debt-economy of slavery. Conceptually, as indeed Graeber (2011, pp. 167–71) recognizes, enslavement is built on debt – the existential debt owed by the captive to the captor in the Christian law of nature and nations for death withheld, to be paid for ever more by the body's service (Tomlins, 2010, pp. 420–3). Perhaps not surprisingly, as Americans turned scientifically racist in the early republic, one of the popular justifications peddled for the enslavement of Africans was a tale of primordial indebtedness: Africans were the seed of Ham, cursed by their ancestor's guilt in looking upon the nakedness of his father, Noah, to live for ever in servitude (Braude, 1997, pp. 103–4). American law, too, treated slaves as debtors. As Stephen Best (2004, pp. 80–1, 171) has argued, both in 1793 and 1850, federal laws governing the return of fugitive slaves conceptualized labour as a service owed, that is as a debt due the claimant, as indeed, arguably, does the enabling clause of the US Constitution. (Best also argues that this has the effect of remaking the *fugitive* slave as a debtor, but in this I think he is incorrect. Labour is owed whether or not the slave has absconded. Fugacity adds nothing, other than the imperative that the fugitive be returned to resume the interrupted, endless payment of what is owed.)

One issue still remains. In all of this soteriality, where is legality? How is law implicated here? Why does the title for this chapter invoke soterial–*legal* history?

The first and simplest answer is that it was a trial that provided the occasion for Nat Turner's soterial monologue. Had Turner not been captured and held for trial, we would not have his confession to ponder. His drama encompasses the trial itself, where he continued to present himself as the antitype of Christ – who, Edwards says, complied with his abasement and 'endured when he was dumb and opened not his mouth' (Edwards, 1989, p. 322). Turner, according to Gray's pamphlet, tells the court that he has spoken through his confession and has 'nothing more to say' (1967, pp. 4–5). And so he is duly found guilty and sentenced to die – an outcome that Gray could only have approved, for Gray in his empirical rationality is also very much a positivist. Turner's fate 'is calculated also to demonstrate the policy of our laws in restraint of this class of our population, and to induce all those entrusted with their execution, as well as our citizens generally, to see that they are strictly and rigidly enforced. Each particular community should look to its own safety, whilst the general guardians of the laws, keep a watchful eye over all' (pp. 4–5). In Thomas Ruffin Gray's mentalité the restoration of positivist normalcy was the goal – the crushing of 'gloomy fanaticism' beneath the ordered rationality of empirical explanation and panoptic law.

But if we can trust Gray's pamphlet, in one short sentence uttered in court Nat Turner spoke volumes that answered both Gray's positivism and the court's creaturely jurisdiction. 'The court ... having met for the trial of Nat Turner, the prisoner was brought in and arraigned, and upon his arraignment pleaded *Not guilty;* saying to his counsel, that he did not feel so' (1967, p. 20, original emphasis). The plea is unremarkable, the accompaniment is not. Turner did not say that he *was* not guilty, he said that he did not *feel* guilty. In refusing the guilt that the court insists he bear, he frees himself of the yoke of sin that he was enjoined to assume. 'To those that look for him he shall appear the second time without sin to salvation', writes Edwards of the 'success of Christ's purchase' bestowed at the day of judgment. 'So it is called redemption' (Edwards, 1989, p. 493).

A second and more general answer to the question of how law is implicated is, of course, that at least prior to the twentieth-century's assault on metaphysics it is actually rather difficult to effect a meaningful distinction between law and religion. Law necessarily plays an utterly central role in Edwards' *History*, though not the laws of humanity, or even the Mosaic law of the Old Testament, but the law of God breached at the fall, the law that sinful humanity is incapable of fulfilling and that can be fulfilled perfectly only by Christ in his human aspect (Edwards, 1989, p. 312). It is the perfection of Christ's obedience to *God*'s law that completes the purchase of redemption.

Finally, lest we think that theology lies only on Turner's side of the bar, let's note that nestling amid the aggressive secularities of Gray's pamphlet we find the following attestation of its authenticities (1967, pp. 5–6), given on behalf of the Southampton County Court:

> I, James Rochelle, Clerk of the County Court of Southampton in the State of Virginia, do hereby certify, that Jeremiah Cobb [and five others] ... were members of the Court which convened at Jerusalem, on Saturday the 5th day of November, 1831, for the trial of Nat *alias* Nat Turner, a negro slave ... and that *full faith and credit* are due, and ought to be given to their acts as Justices of the peace aforesaid.

The meaning at common law of 'full faith and credit' is evidentiary – it attests to the truth of a record, or the confidence one may have in an agent's representation of a principal. What is at issue here is not the use of the formula, but the words *in* the formula. 'Full faith and credit' displays the 'double form' of law to which Peter Goodrich (2011) has drawn our attention: at once an agency of economy, which is to say of governance; and of glory, which is to say of the transcendent sovereignty that Christianity locates in God.

To explore that double form is to undertake an exercise that Annelise Riles (2005) has described as 'taking on the technicalities'. Riles has in mind the technicalities of law, but in this instance the technicalities are those of theology, the technicalities of the evangelical Protestant eschatology that so deeply implicate *both* the events *and* the legalities of the Turner Rebellion.

Nat Turner was not a theologian, but he was a devout Christian and a deeply intelligent man. I hope it is now clear why I describe his rebellion as an act of God. But to conclude on that note does not completely satisfy the scholarly project attempted here, which was to counterpose the soterial to the social as an exercise that could yield scholarly returns. So let me end differently. We can think of the Turner Rebellion as a fracture in the social–historical and socio-legal normalization of the world, the normalization that Thomas Ruffin Gray laboured so hard to re-establish in the wake of its interruption. Such fractures are useful: by peering through them we can discover other orderings, other *taxes*, of the phenomena with which as scholars we concern ourselves, realms of human motivation and action that are otherwise literally incomprehensible to us because unimaginable by us. By peering through this particular fracture in the continuum of normalcy, one can catch a glimpse of a profoundly theological metaphysics at work in an American history and law that we have been taught to think of in determinedly atheological terms.

References

Agamben, Giorgio (2011) *The Power and the Glory: For a Theological Genealogy of Economy and Government* (Stanford: Stanford University Press)

Allmendinger, David F, Jr (2003) 'The Construction of *The Confessions of Nat Turner*' in Kenneth S. Greenberg (ed.), *Nat Turner: A Slave Rebellion in History and Memory*, pp. 24–42 (New York: Oxford University Press)

Best, Stephen M (2004) *The Fugitive's Properties: Law and the Poetics of Possession* (Chicago: University of Chicago Press)

Bloch, Ruth (1985) *Visionary Republic: Millennial Themes in American Thought, 1756–1800* (Cambridge and New York: Cambridge University Press)

Braude, Benjamin (1997) 'The Sons of Noah and the Construction of Ethnic and Geographical Identities in the Medieval and Early Modern Periods' 54 *William and Mary Quarterly* 103–42

Calavita, Kitty (2010) *Invitation to Law and Society: An Introduction to the Study of Real Law* (Chicago: University of Chicago Press)

Constable, Marianne (2005) *Just Silences: The Limits and Possibilities of Modern Law* (Princeton: Princeton University Press)

Crofts, Daniel W (1992) *Old Southampton: Politics and Society in a Virginia County, 1834–1869* (Charlottesville: University of Virginia Press)

Edwards, Jonathan (2001) 'The Excellency of Christ: Doctrine' in M X Lasser (ed.) *The Works of Jonathan Edwards: Sermons and Discourses, 1734–1738* vol. 19 (New Haven: Yale University Press, 2001), pp. 560–95

Edwards, Jonathan (1989) *A History of the Work of Redemption: The Works of Jonathan Edwards* vol. 9, John F Wilson (transcr. and ed.) (New Haven: Yale University Press)

Goodrich, Peter (2011) 'Specters of Law: Why the History of the Legal Spectacle Has Not Been Written' 1 *University of California Irvine Law Review* 773–812

Gordon, Robert W (2012) '"Critical Legal Histories Revisited": A Response' 37 *Law and Social Inquiry* 200–15

Graeber, David (2011) *Debt: The First 5000 Years* (Brooklyn: Melville House Publishing)

Gray, Thomas Ruffin (1967) *The Original Confessions of Nat Turner: A Facsimile of the 1831 Edition* (Ann Arbor: Uniprint)

Greenberg, Kenneth S (1996) 'The Confessions of Nat Turner: Text and Context' in Kenneth S Greenberg (ed.), *The Confessions of Nat Turner and Related Documents* (Boston and New York: Bedford St Martin's), pp. 1–35

Heyrman, Christine Leigh (1997) *Southern Cross: The Beginnings of the Bible Belt* (Chapel Hill: University of North Carolina Press)

Holmes, Oliver Wendell, Jr (1897) 'The Path of the Law' 10 *Harvard Law Review* 457–78

Howe, Daniel Walker (2007) *What Hath God Wrought: The Transformation of America* (New York: Oxford University Press)

Jacobson, Eric (2003) *Metaphysics of the Profane: The Political Theology of Walter Benjamin and Gershom Scholem* (New York: Columbia University Press)

Johnson, Michael (2001) 'Denmark Vesey and his Co-Conspirators' 58 *William and Mary Quarterly* 915–76

Maitland, Frederick William (1965–1995) in C H S Fifoot and P N R Zutschi (eds), *Letters of Frederic William Maitland* (London: Selden Society)

Milton, John (2005) *Paradise Lost*, Gordon Teskey (ed.) (New York: Norton)

Nietzsche, Friedrich (2008) *The Genealogy of Morals*, Douglas Smith (trans.) (Oxford and New York: Oxford University Press)

Parker, Kunal M (2011) *Common Law, History, and Democracy in America, 1790–1900: Legal Thought before Modernism* (Cambridge and New York: Cambridge University Press)

Parramore, Thomas C (1978) *Southampton County, Virginia* (Charlottesville: University of Virginia Press)

Riles, Annelise (2005) 'A New Agenda for the Cultural Study of Law: Taking on the Technicalities' 53 *Buffalo Law Review* 973–1033

Santoro, Anthony (2008) 'The Prophet in his Own Words: Nat Turner's Biblical Construction' 116 *Virginia Magazine of History and Biography* 114–49

Scully, Randolph Ferguson (2008) *Religion and the Making of Nat Turner's Virginia: Baptist Community and Conflict, 1740–1840* (Charlottesville, University of Virginia Press)

Styron, William (1993a) *The Confessions of Nat Turner* (New York: Random House)

Styron, William (1993b) 'Nat Turner Revisited' in William Styron, *The Confessions of Nat Turner* (New York: Random House), pp. 433–55

Sundquist, Eric J (1993) *To Wake the Nations: Race in the Making of American Literature* (Cambridge, MA: Harvard University Press)

Tomlins, Christopher (2007) 'How Autonomous is Law?' 3 *Annual Review of Law and Social Science* 45–68

Tomlins, Christopher (2010) *Freedom Bound: Law, Labor, and Civic Identity in Colonizing English America, 1580–1865* (Cambridge and New York: Cambridge University Press)

Tomlins, Christopher and John Comaroff (2011) '"Law As …": Theory and Practice in Legal History' 1 *University of California Irvine Law Review* 1039–79

Tragle, Henry Irving (1971) *The Southampton Slave Revolt of 1831: A Compilation of Source Material* (Amherst: University of Massachusetts Press)

Weber, Max (1958) 'Science as a Vocation' in H H Gerth and C Wright Mills (eds), *From Max Weber: Essays in Sociology* (New York: Oxford University Press), pp. 129–56

Weber, Max (2002) 'The Protestant Ethic and the "Spirit" of Capitalism' in Peter Baehr and Gordon C Wells (eds), *The Protestant Ethic and the "Spirit" of Capitalism and Other Writings*, (New York: Penguin), pp. 1–202

Wilson, John F (1989) 'Editor's Introduction' in Jonathan Edwards, *A History of the Work of Redemption: The Works of Jonathan Edwards*, vol. 9, John F Wilson (transcr. and ed.) (New Haven: Yale University Press), pp. 1–109

3

The Concept of Law in Global Societal Constitutionalism

Jiří Přibáň*

The recent popularity, great variety and conceptual innovations of global legal and constitutional pluralism theories often lead to the academic ritualization and banalization of the very concepts of pluralism, constitutionalism and global society. Nevertheless, the pluralistic conceptualizations of law beyond the basic norm and the rule of recognition also lead to the most original and innovative adoptions of sociological and socio-legal methods by legal theory and jurisprudence.

Exploring 'the legal' in global society is impossible without the sociology of law and social theory. The system of globally evolving positive law and its operations require the sociological concept of law. Apart from radically questioning legal theories and doctrines, it offers what social systems theories call a second-order observation focusing on law's general function and specific operations beyond the legalist framework of national and international institutions, political bodies, territories, metaphors and normative hierarchies.

Global law evolves beyond the state and is functionally differentiated from similarly globalized systems of politics and economics. Instead of the law's imperial constitution of global society, it is the social coding of legality and varieties of constitutionalizations that need to be studied by the sociological theory of global law. In this chapter, I therefore pursue the goal of critically examining and reconceptualizing theories of global legal pluralism and societal constitutionalism. In the first part, I establish the connection between legal globalization and theories of legal pluralism. In the second part, I focus on more radical theories of legal pluralism and

---

* Some sections of this chapter draw on earlier research outcomes published in the article 'Asking the Sovereignty Question in Global Legal Pluralism' (2015) 28(1) *Ratio Juris* 31–51.

globalization, criticizing the very concept of official state law and drawing on Ehrlich's sociological notion of living law and spontaneously evolving normative orders and regulatory regimes. Critically assessing Teubner's most original and inspiring sociological theory of societal constitutionalism, civil constitutions and global legal pluralism, I finally discuss the concepts of law and power and their reconfigurations within the global legal and political framework.

In my theoretical analysis, I focus on different forms of adopting the concept of legal pluralism, including the social theoretical conceptualization of systemic pluralism and functional differentiation by recent legal and socio-legal theories. I emphasize originality of Teubner's eclectic theoretical perspective taking the concept of constitutionalism beyond the restrictive framework of legal science and applying it to the most general societal processes and developments. Teubner's social theoretical perspective thus breathes a new life into the conceptual framework of modern jurisprudence and legal theory. However, I criticize this and other theories of global legal pluralism and societal constitutionalism inspired by the autopoietic social systems theory for their normative hopes and visions of global civil society and law. I conclude by arguing that the functionally differentiated systems of globalized law and politics continue to be structurally coupled and power as a medium of the political system cannot be removed from global politics by civil constitutions like caffeine from coffee beans by decaffeination.

Globalization and theories of legal pluralism

It is now a generally accepted legal and social theoretical view that structures of globalized law and politics do not replicate the hierarchies and symbolic centrality of the nation state, its sovereignty and constitutional normative basis. The state has become a less important organization in contemporary globalized politics, law and economy (Strange, 1996). The affiliation between the modern state and law is radically challenged by global legal and political developments (Sassen, 1998). Nevertheless, although economic globalization has led to the decline of national economic sovereignty and weakened the regulatory economic instruments of national governments, political and legal globalization has not resulted in the same level and forms of institution-building, governance and self-regulation as economic globalization has.

Though it may seem logical that the evolution of the global economic system should coincide with the evolution of similarly complex global political and legal systems, a global democratic polity of cosmopolitan values (Held, 1995, pp. 267–83) continues to be just a utopian project while voters and citizens persistently associate political responsibility with their national politicians and identify with them. International human rights treaties may be considered a force for the globalization of law, unifying state constitutions and subjecting them to a supreme legally binding interpretation (Habermas, 2008, pp. 448–9), but cosmopolitan democracy, human rights and a global political constitution continue to look more like a legalistic utopia and less like a viable project for a politically pluralistic and socially fragmented global society.

Despite many differences, some themes have been common to many theories of legal globalization, especially their focus on legal pluralism evolving in a global society. While the concept of legal pluralism may have different theoretical meaning and contextualization, the remark that '[L]egal pluralism concerns the idea that more than one legal system operate in a single political unit' (Sousa Santos, 2002, p. 89) can be taken as the minimum common understanding of legal pluralism.

In the context of legal theory, legal pluralism means the absence of a basic norm or rule of recognition, or any other jurisprudential fiction of unity and authority operating within the system of positive law (Cotterrell, 2008, p. 9). The problem of several basic norms or rules of recognition has to be addressed as the primary condition of contemporary supranational and transnational legal systems.

Furthermore, theories of legal pluralism often criticize the concept of law as a normative order sanctioned by the state's monopoly on political violence. While monistic views look for a clear specification of legal authority and rules of legal validity, pluralistic views claim that these specifications are impossible in the presence of more legal systems operating in the same social environment. They criticize methodological individualism, instrumentalism and the assumption of the state's normative monopoly as typical failures of theories of state legal centralism (Griffith, 1998, p. 206).

Recent theories of legal and constitutional pluralism involve a great variety of conventional jurisprudential conceptualizations of the basic fact of the plurality of legal and political orders (Tsagourias, 2007). These jurisprudential theories of legal pluralism acknowledge the existence of different legal orders and ultimate rules of recognition that do not communicate with each other in terms of hierarchy and supremacy established by a superior rule-based process (Kumm, 1999). Instead of the ideal rule of law limiting politics and containing power, the legal pluralist condition typifies the absence of a juridical hierarchy and the presence of permanent contestations and confrontations between political forces promoting the currently most persuasive juridical arguments and interpretations (Mellisaris, 2009, pp. 27–43).

For legal pluralists, drawing on a much more radical and sociologically inspired concept of pluralism, jurisprudential theories of the pluralism of basic norms, their interpretations and enactments, however, represent a 'weak' pluralism considered theoretically unremarkable because of its reliance on the concept of official state law and conventional models of adjudicative cooperation (Griffith, 1986, pp. 5–8). The difference between 'weak' and 'strong' or 'radical' pluralism established by John Griffith and other sociologists and anthropologists of law certainly contributed to high-lighting methodological differences between the sociology and jurispru-dence of legal pluralism. It strictly separated legal pluralism studies from analytical jurisprudence and sociological positivism, exploring unofficial and/or living law from legal positivism and the legalism of officially sanc-tioned rules (Griffith, 2002).

The plurality of laws represents a highly contested reality in global soci-ety, unlimited by the constitutional structures of the modern state (Nelken, 2007) and often driven by the specific regulatory demands of non-state legal sectors (Delmas-Marty, 2009). For some scholars, the challenges of legal plurality in global society subsequently call for the radical rethink-ing of the systems of national and international modern politics and law. Instead of taking the modern state as the natural political and legal unit, the uncoupling of the modern state and law in global society allegedly calls for a new paradigm and theory of social and political transformation – 'a new legal common sense' (Sousa Santos, 2002).

With the modern state's loss of its monopoly over law, it allegedly is possible to recouple the concept of law with multiple non-state and state-organized polities which exist in global society (Sousa Santos, 2002, pp. 85–98). The state is supposed to adapt to the social movement, accommo-dating the oppositional legality of different polities challenging new global hegemonies 'from below' (Sousa Santos and Rodriguez-Garavito, 2005). The paradigm of global legal pluralism is considered part of this complete semantic overhaul of legal and political theory and its apparent opposi-tional potential in global society.

'Strong' sociological theories of legal pluralism thus go far beyond the 'weak' notion of a plurality of official legal orders enforced by different social agencies and institutions. They favour a radical version of the plu-ralism of unofficial legal orders spontaneously recognized by communities and operating despite a state legal order rather than as its parallel supple-ment. These theories commonly emphasize the basic fact of the plurality of social reality and its relevance for the legal system, especially the limits of the system's self-regulation and its external dependence on spontaneously recognized non-state and non-legal normative orders of society. According to these views, formal rules of official law and their sanctioning by the sov-ereign state are just one of many different normative structures and orders of society (Teubner and Fischer-Lescano, 2004).

These radical theories are often driven by a critique of official state law and present themselves as critical theories of state power and authority enforced on the state's territory and its populations (Galanter, 1981). They also commonly perceive the state and its law as a form of hegemony that needs to be challenged by alternative politics emerging at subnational, national and transnational levels of global society (Rajagopal, 2005). Finally, and most importantly, radical theories of legal pluralism often contrast the concept of constitutional authority and political sovereignty with spontaneously evolving sectors of society which, instead of being constituted by political force, engage in the parallel processes of self-constitutionalization and constitutional fragmentation (Krisch, 2011; Teubner, 2012).

The concept of global living law: on the importance of Ehrlich's sociology of law for the global legal system

Though Eugen Ehrlich never established a theory of legal pluralism and did not even use the concept at all, his sociology of law continues to be perceived as a profound source of inspiration for legal pluralism studies (Griffith, 1986, pp. 23–9). For instance, Klaus Ziegert critically stated that reinventing Ehrlich as the founding father of legal pluralism studies is misguided because Erhlich's sociology of law primarily focused on core elements of the operation of legal systems, especially the reflexivity of normative expectations and legal communication (Ziegert, 2002, pp. xli, xlv). Ehrlich's goal was nothing less than to establish a general theory of law. Nevertheless, the sociological concept of legal pluralism continues to be closely associated with Ehrlich's concept of living law because theories of legal pluralism, like the sociology of law, focus on the internal operations and different regulations of society as a whole (Merry, 1998, p. 873).

Furthermore, by extending the concept of law to the realm of social customs and reformulating it as a blurred domain of genuinely binding and socially heterogeneous rules, Ehrlich certainly overcame the modern identification of law and sovereign political power and the methodological limits of normativist legal logic. Following the then popular distinction between society and community and adopting it in the context of legal theory, Ehrlich actually redirected academic attention from the official rule of society by state law to the spontaneously enforced rules of communal life beyond statehood. His concept of living law was a non-state concept of law recognized by a particular community. The unity of society was to be secured by the variety of spontaneously ordered associations of which people are members mutually coordinating their actions and reactions (Ehrlich, 2002, p. 27).

Against the mainstream legal theoretical canon of official law sanctioned by the state, Ehrlich argued that the effectiveness of legal norms depends on the inner order of associations and its internal forms of enforcement rather than the power and organization of the modern state. According to this view, threats of force and official sanctions have very little effect and may indeed be counterproductive (Ehrlich, 2002, p. 402), and the normative order of society evolves without the state's sanctioning power.

No wonder this theoretical ambition was criticized not only by theorists of law for its methodological contradictions and holistic notion of society but also, directly and indirectly, by sociologists of law for using too broad a concept of law and neglecting specific self-regulatory aspects of legal reality as an intrinsic part of social reality.

For instance, Hans Kelsen (1961) dismissed Ehrlich's theoretical views giving precedence to society and its general rules of existence and evolution over the system of positive law as a methodologically regressive return to the concept of natural law. Kelsen severely criticized Ehrlich's sociology of law for confusing facts and norms and turning autonomous legal normativity into a mere function of the forces and ultimate laws operating in society. The identification of law and society in Ehrlich's concept of 'living law' allegedly leads to the loss of methodological clarity and the reintroduction of the old-style metaphysical difference between positive and supra-positive law. According to Kelsen, this kind of sociology of law treating social facts indiscriminately as 'living law' faces the impossible task of establishing itself as a separate discipline independent from both general sociology, which focuses on the social facts of human behaviour, and legal science, which studies the normative character of a legal order (Kelsen, 2003).

Similarly, Ehrlich's peculiar form of the philosophy of life, translating into the concept of living law as law prevailing in the social struggle for recognition, was completely foreign to Carl Schmitt's notion of political struggle and the enemy/friend distinction (Schmitt, 1985). Ehrlich's concept of society drawing on general forces constantly recreating the unity of pluralistic social life and spontaneously recognized as law was the opposite of Schmitt's world full of frictions, differences and conflicts. Indeed, Schmitt's vigorous criticisms of theories of political and legal pluralism because of their identification of legal and political reality with social totality applied to Ehrlich's sociological theory of law.

Ehrlich was criticized by sociologists as much as by legal theorists and political philosophers. For instance, Max Rheinstein criticized Ehrlich's confusion of law with custom and his reduction of legal science to sociology, and prudence to popular sentiment (1938, pp. 232–9). More significantly, Ehrlich's sociological method as a basis of a general theory of law was ignored by Max Weber who established his sociology of law by using common jurisprudential concepts of law, legal norms and sanctions or the relationship of law, the modern state and legal legitimacy (Weber, 1978).

The concept of living law was considered obscure and problematic by sociologists and social theorists because of its emphasis on social recognition, spontaneity and the evolution of normative orders rather than their political enforcement, rational organization and guidance by expert knowledge. Nevertheless, it almost looks as if Eugen Ehrlich, so severely criticized by Kelsen, dismissed by Schmitt, and ignored by Weber and other scholars of his time, is having the last laugh in the current condition of global society. His sociological method and emphasis on law as an order of rules spontaneously recognized by social associations appears appropriate for understanding the complexities of globalized law. It even led Gunther Teubner, a leading theorist of global societal constitutionalism (2004, p. 3) whose work is discussed in the following sections of this chapter, to remark that Eugen Ehrlich's sociology of law was perhaps wrong at the time of its writing at the beginning of the twentieth century, but turned out to be the most comprehensive and realistic response to our current globalized society, nicknamed 'global Bukowina' (Teubner, 1997).

Global society and its plurality of subnational, supranational and transnational legal orders support anything but Kelsen's monistic belief in one ultimate basic norm overcoming the duality of national legal systems and international law. Current legal structures and networks are characterized by contestations, fragmentations and differences. In this society, different legal systems coexist and make independent claims of legal validity and authority (Merry, 1998). The ultimate validity of the basic norm is replaced by a multiplicity of simultaneously valid basic norms of different and mutually independent legal orders – something considered logically impossible by Kelsen (1961, p. 363).

Pluralism and the functional differentiation of global society – the autopoietic social systems theory perspective

Current legal pluralism and societal constitutionalism debates actually replicate a number of fundamental arguments and polemics related to the problems of legal theoretical methodology discussed in the first half of the twentieth century by Ehrlich, Kelsen, Schmitt, Heller, Smend and other legal scholars. They, therefore, often continue to be illuminated by the triadic conceptual structure of 'will' (*Wollen*), 'norm' (*Sollen*), and 'fact' (*Sein*) which has always informed modern legal and social theory.

Some classical jurisprudential differences are being reinvented and reconceptualized in the context of contemporary global society, its politics and law. As Kaarlo Tuori observed, legal and political theories and philosophies draw on the tension between power and norm, respectively will and reason, from ancient times to the postmodern globalized systems of transnational politics and law. The law's normative coherence depends on its capacity to manage the intrinsic tension between law's *voluntas* and *ratio* and it remains unimportant whether the legal system couples with political institutions of the nation state or supranational and transnational organizations (Tuori, 2010, p. 287).

Similarly, the typically modern sociological differentiations, such as state/ civil society, society/community and living law/lawyers' law, find their specific uses in theories of global legal pluralism, non-state law and societal constitutionalism. Transnational and supranational legal orders persuasively demonstrate the impossibility of identifying the notion of society with the concept of national society and the notion of a legal system with the legal system of the nation state. Nevertheless, theories reflecting on these legal and social changes often continue to use modern conceptual distinctions and contrast state law and its political authority with the spontaneously evolving laws of civil associations and networks.

However, legal and political globalization and the emergence of different sectors of transnational law cannot be simply considered as either democratically illegitimate structures resembling pre-modern autocratic political settlements, or the most recent example of what Jeremy Bentham described as 'anarchical fallacies' (1843, p. 491) of law that are not commanded by the political sovereign and draw on hasty generalizations and abstract propositions susceptible to moral and political abuse. Instead, global legal pluralism involves concurrent processes of fragmentation and constitutionalization that are part of the autopoiesis of globalized law.

The concepts of global legal pluralism and societal constitutionalism can actually signify the complexity, self-constitution and plurality of different social systems in current global society. According to this social systems theoretical view, global society consists of a plurality of specific societies and communities which are connected by the rationality of structurally pluralistic but globally functioning social systems of economy, law, politics, education, science, etc. This plurality of functionally differentiated global social systems is a lot more important and reflective of recent social developments than simple cultural plurality that has always been experienced and existed even in the pre-modern world (Luhmann, 1997). Global social and technological changes have led to the emergence of new forms of social communication, networks and structures beyond the typically modern hierarchies and establishments of the nation state, popular sovereignty, constitutional power and democratic self-government.

According to the autopoietic systems theory (see especially Luhmann, 1995; 2004; for the legal context, see Teubner, 1993; Přibáň and Nelken, 2001; King and Thornhill, 2006), society is a functionally differentiated and globally operating system consisting of different sub-systems, such as politics, law and economy, which are cognitively open but normatively closed (Luhmann, 1995, p. 102). It means that an autopoietic social system uses information from its environment but this external reference between the system and its environment does not affect the system's operations. Systems are autopoietic in the sense that they self-create their operations and their functioning is guaranteed by self-referential communication (Luhmann, 1995, pp. 437–77) using the system's binary coding, such as 'legal/illegal' in the legal system and 'government/opposition' in the democratic political system (Rasch, 2000, p. 151).

The functional differentiation of society into autopoietic social systems operating concurrently without any hierarchical ordering replaces the Parsonsian image of specific social systems supporting the functioning and cultural integration of overall society. Systemic differences are more significant than societal unity and the concepts of self-reference, self-production and self-organization are introduced to concurrently describe the internal normative closure and external cognitive interference and interdependence between different autopoietic social systems (Luhmann, 1990, p. 93).

The living law of global civil society?

According to many theoretical conceptualizations of transnational law and global legal pluralism, the constitutional state as a typically modern form of political and legal organization cannot withstand the social pressure of globalization, and modern structural co-evolution of the state and law is replaced by new forms of societal self-constitutionalization as part of 'global law without a state' (Teubner (ed.), 1997). The spontaneity of social and legal evolution is preferred to the iron cage of the state's official legality and bureaucratic organization.

Montesquieu and Savigny's silently operating social forces appear to be much more significant than legislated laws. These elements of the classical difference between politically organized *society* and spontaneously evolving *community* are detectable even in highly sophisticated theories of global governance and social steering (Teubner, 1993, p. 64). In this context, Ehrlich's concept of living law is also reformulated as signifying the process of spontaneous juridification and even the constitutionalization of different sectors of global society without polity, such as commerce, intellectual property, the internet, sport, the environment etc. The well-established theoretical semantics differentiating between living and legislated law, respectively law in action and law in books, is supplemented by new distinctions, such as hard law/soft law, national government/transnational governance and state/societal constitutionalism.

Ziegert, for instance, reinterprets Ehrlich's sociology of law and the concept of living law as the most persuasive critique of statist legal theory which corresponds to our current state of self-ordering and self-regulating global society and its legal system operating without the state (2009, p. 223). He understands Ehrlich's analysis of the ethnic and legal diversity of communal life as part of a functional–structural concept of society based on the differentiation of the reciprocal actions and reactions of individuals in their associations. Ziegert even considers Ehrlich's theory a general theory of society rather than just another theory of law. According to this reading of Ehrlich's living law, social order:

> emerges as a relational and structural result of generalised, practised observation of others, that is, having respect for the actions and reactions of the other members of the association. This order cannot be singularly 'hijacked' or commandeered by any one individual. It develops over time, and becomes entrenched so deeply that the original, practical reasons for those 'actions and reactions' get lost in the cultural, intergenerational transmission. What there is to be 'vigorously' kept and preserved by the associations are the forms of relational conduct, that is, social norms. (Ziegert, 2009, pp. 227–8)

Ziegert argues that these norms stabilize the inner order of association through social evolution and communicative experience. Social stability is conditioned by this self-regulatory primary order whose functionality – rather than a special apparatus of political enforcement – guarantees the effectiveness of valid norms. It is the factuality of social life rather than the normativity and/or rationality of a political order that facilitates the legitimacy of law. The living law dominates social life, and legal propositions and documents need to be recognized by these dynamic inner orders of human associations.

Ziegert reinterprets Ehrlich's conceptual separation of living law and lawyers' law as an example of the functional differentiation of society and a challenge for modern society that needs reflexively to reconstruct expert legal knowledge and legal propositions formulated by lawyers as part of living law (2009, p. 230). He even treats Ehrlich's view of living law as:

> a prophetic glimpse at the emerging world law of human rights … reminiscent of Kant's design of a cosmopolitan civil society of non-governmental 'associations' supported by law (international legal decision-making), together with the power play of states held in check by treaties. This civil society does not have nor needs to have a corresponding 'world government', but is anchored in and promoted by non-aggressive and humanitarian states … (Ziegert, 2009, pp. 235–6)

This optimistic assessment and surprisingly prescriptive 'civil' interpretation of Ehrlich's sociology of living law builds on the contrast between artificially integrated political order and spontaneously evolving global civil society (Nelken, 2009, pp. 262–3).

However, Ehrlich's distinction between lawyers' law and living law can scarcely be reinterpreted as an example of functional differentiation because the living law, according to Ehrlich, dominates life, including the life of legal propositions, decisions and expert knowledge. The theory falls short of the heterarchies of a functionally differentiated society and its self-regulatory legal system because Ehrlich expands the meaning of law by finding it everywhere in society and thus blurs its social boundaries and differentiation from other social normative orders (Hertogh, 2009, pp. 2–8).

If living law depends on the life of associations and the recognition of their members, the meaning of law becomes semantically expanded beyond the point of obscurity. If every normative order is to be called law, what about the relationship between the legal order and other social normative orders? Is law really any order that people use and call 'law' (Tamanaha, 2001, p. 167)? And does not the whole distinction of lawyers' law and living law, respectively state law and non-state law, rather confirm the importance of the state as a law-making institution (Roberts, 1998, p. 105)?

The problem with Ziegert's interpretation is that Ehrlich's concept of living law has an integrating rather than a differentiating effect in the study of legal reality. Ehrlich's difference between living law and lawyers' law was segmental and not functional and signified the contrast between modern rationality and historical tradition, society and community, organization and spontaneity, human alienation and organic bonds.

This segmentation could be discovered in a number of theories and philosophies of society and politics of Ehrlich's time, for instance, in the Marxist critique of modern industrial capitalism and utopian hopes of a post-revolutionary classless society and socialist beliefs in economic and political self-organization. It also was typical of various forms of modern nationalism and ethno-politics drawing on 'the decline of civilization' and the need to protect communal bonds and national traditions against the destructive forces of modern industry and bureaucratic political organizations. It permeated modern nationalism and political struggles for national self-determination as well as the socialist belief in converting the state from an organ superimposed upon society into one subordinate to it.

Beyond the legal concept of constitution: on Teubner's societal constitutionalism

Unlike the image of the living law's commonality of global civil society, supranational and transnational legal and political developments are characterized by fragmentation, asymmetries, structural irritations

and collisions. These cannot be contained by some form of civil unifica-
tion or cooperation between states and non-state agents at global level.
Rapidly evolving sub-systems of global society pursue their specific self-
constitutionalization. Instead of the constitutionalization of a global
political society, different sectors of global society establish their constitutions through functional differentiation and not by means of political
integration facilitated by the deliberative political efforts and cooperation of state governments (Teubner and Fischer-Lescano, 2004, p. 1014).
The legal system of global society is typified by a multiplicity of what
Sciulli describes as societal constitutions (1992) in which sovereign states
may continue to have some operative capacity but characteristically lose
their constitutive power within the system of international law and state
constitutionalism.

Gunther Teubner adopted Sciulli's theory of societal constitutionalism and reinterpreted it in the same original manner which informed his
unorthodox reading of Luhmann's autopoietic social systems theory and
Ehrlich's sociology of law. He argues that the functional dynamics of the
global legal system are part of global societal constitutionalism (Teubner,
2011, p. 220). He thus challenges the old semantics of international law,
the hierarchies of the nation state, and its sovereign constitution of both
the political system and the whole nation. The domain of international law
is considered just a sectorally differentiated part of the global legal system
in which political and legal sovereignty, both internal and external, ceases
to play the role of the essential precondition of legal communication.

Teubner's eclectic theoretical approach represents a fascinating and original attempt at taking the concept of constitutionalism beyond the restrictive framework of legal science and applying it to the most general societal
processes and developments. Social theory thus breathes a new life into
one of the most important concepts of modern jurisprudence and legal
theory.

According to Teubner, the state and its hierarchies are equally inadequate
when dealing with non-state global social actors and the horizontal effects
of fundamental rights guaranteed at supranational level and pursued
through multiple transnational networks and institutions. He subsequently
reformulates the process of global constitutionalization as a process in
which:

> [t]he constitution of world society does not come about exclu-
> sively in the representative institutions of international poli-
> tics, nor can it take place in a unitary global constitution which
> overlies all areas of society, but, instead, emerges incrementally
> in the constitutionalisation of a multiplicity of autonomous
> sub-systems of world society. (2004, p. 8)

This concept of societal constitutionalism has to be taken as a system of constitutions *in* society rather than the constitution *of* society. According to this perspective, different social systems, such as global law, politics or economy, often collide with each other and do not lead to some form of ultimate constitutional settlement of global society that would be able to replicate the national constitutionalization paradox by representing a politically sovereign global authority and symbolically expressing the totality of global society. Instead, this perspective represents a view of global law functionally differentiated from global politics and internally differentiated into a multiplicity of self-constituted and self-constituting sub-systems.

The intrinsic tension between the political dimension of constitutions and their expressive symbolism covering the totality of society is reconceptualized as a non-representational politics of constitutionalization of autonomous sectors of global society pursued by both state and non-state agencies (Teubner and Fischer-Lescano, 2004). The global context of functional differentiation makes nation-state constitutionalism just one of many processes of constituting political organizations which are impossible to replicate in global law and politics. Constitutional theories centred on the dynamics of politics need to be replaced by an analysis of global social polycontexturality and its constitutionalizations beyond the state and politics (Teubner, 2011).

The radicalism of this view arises from the fact that constitutionalizations of global law evolve not only without the state or any other global political authority but also as multiple processes of the differentiated social sectors of global economy, technology, science and so on (Teubner, 2011). According to Teubner, the political constitutionalization of global society is just a constitutional illusion driven by fantasies of cosmopolitan politics and global statehood. Nation-state constitutions cannot be replicated at the level of global society: 'the constitutional totality breaks apart and is dissolved by a type of *constitutional fragmentation*' (2011, p. 220; 2012). A global political community has no constitution, and nation-state constitutions and supranational or transnational political attempts at constitutionalizing the global political system are just fragments of global societal constitutionalism.

The nation-state constitution is challenged by global self-constitutionalizations without a state and beyond the realm of constitutional law (Callies and Zumbansen, 2010). Instead of normative projects and politics, a genuinely radical theory of legal pluralism emerges as a theory of a global legal system which is functionally differentiated from global politics, economy or science. It is a system of internal paradoxes, deparadoxifying operations and fragmentations rather than a system of rules and doctrinal contestations. It effectively dismantles the boundaries and regulatory structures of national legal systems and makes legality a global function-specific communication.

Drawing on these notions of spontaneously evolving legal orders beyond political organizations and constitutionalism without the state, constituent power and polity, some scholars even reject the very idea of pluralistic transnational or postnational constitutionalism and contrast it to a pluralist vision of global societal governance (Krisch, 2010). According to these radical voices, the coherence and unity associated with any constitutional system and global governance needs to be treated as its pluralistic and fractured structural alternative. As Nico Krisch comments:

> [I]n pluralism, there is no common legal point of reference to appeal to for resolving disagreement; conflicts are solved through convergence, mutual accommodation – or not at all. It is a vision that takes societal fragmentation to the institutional level. (2010, p. 69)

Nevertheless, the concepts of law and constitutionalism can scarcely be so easily contrasted with the concepts of postnational governance and pluralism, if only because of the strong semantic tradition and common theoretical uses of the concept of legal and constitutional pluralism. Unlike Krisch and other scholars who completely renounce the concept of constitutionalism, Teubner suggests that the process of functional differentiation in global society guarantees that the concurrent constitutionalizations of specific sub-systems institutionalize their internal mechanisms of self-restraint. They thus effectively avoid the risk of society-wide expansion and constitutional interventions into other sectors of global society.

Teubner is convinced that the autonomy and civil self-constitutionalization of these sectors counter the risk of de-differentiation and the expansion of political instrumentalization and remarks:

> Strengthening the autonomy of spheres of action as a counter-movement to trends of de-differentiation seems to be the general response at work both in the traditional political constitutions and in the emerging civil constitutions. If it was the central task of political constitutions to uphold the autonomy of other spheres of action against the expansion of the polity, specifically in relation to political instrumentalisation, then, in today's civil constitutions, it is presumable to guarantee the chances of articulating so-called non-rational logics of action against the dominant social rationalisation trend, by conquering areas of autonomy for social reflection in long-lasting conflicts, and institutionalising them. (Teubner, 2004, pp. 12–13)

Societal constitutionalism as the depoliticization of global society

Removing the process of constitutionalization from the fiction of the ultimate normative foundations of law, Teubner questions major orthodoxies of legal and political theory and asks constitutional and international law theorists to embrace not just the form of constitutionalism without the state but even more distant forms of the self-constitutionalization of sectors of private law and governance regimes (2012, pp. 1–2). He states that the radical concept of global societal constitutionalism without the state, polity and the symbolic image of ultimate social unity is difficult for constitutional and political theorists to digest. It would require 'breaking a taboo' (2004, p. 8).

However, there is another taboo even Teubner does not break, that of 'civility'. Teubner's theory of global legal pluralism surprisingly draws on the typically modern social science orthodoxy, namely the duality of hierarchically organized *political* constitutions and spontaneously evolving *civil* constitutions (Teubner, 2004, pp. 27–8). His distinction between political and civil constitutions is not just a reflection of transnational globalized society and the international politics of sovereign states. In a vein not too distant from Ziegert's view of global civil society, Teubner reformulates the classical difference between society and the state in the context of the autopoietic systems theory of global legal pluralism by contrasting the instrumental rationality of legality and the bureaucratic administration of the state to the multiplicity of social sub-systems and their specific modes of rationality.

Teubner prefers the concept of a 'regime constitution' of different sectors of global society as more inclusive than the state organization-driven concept of a political constitution. He even reintroduces the regime's centre/periphery differentiation, which was refuted by Luhmann as a distinction signifying segmental rather than functional differentiation, to encompass informal institutions, organizations and actors operating beyond the central formal organization of a regime constitution (Teubner, 2011, pp. 222–3). However, this strange retro-semantics of state/society and centre/periphery distinctions would effectively mean that the dynamics of the functional differentiation of global legal and global societal constitutionalism continues to be exposed to the persisting segmental differentiation of formally organized centres and informally evolving and interacting social peripheries.

These theoretical problems are further exposed by Teubner's call for a 'hybrid regulation', combining the internal regulation of function systems with external pressure from other social spheres, in particular, public discussions, protests, movements, non-governmental organizations and trade unions, to guarantee the effective self-limitation of the function systems. According to him:

> [p]olitical-legal regulation and external social influences can only succeed if they are transformed into the self-regulation of systemic dynamic. This requires massive interventions from politics, law and civil society: interventions, however, which, as a matter of fact, are translated into self-limiting impulses and transformed into a regime constitution. (2011, p. 225)

However, this conclusion effectively means that the self-regulation of global societal constitutionalism is safeguarded by global societal interventions in legal rationality rather than by legal autopoiesis.

The concepts of civil constitutions and societal constitutionalism are profoundly influenced by the idea of the self-constitution and self-regulation of civil society spontaneously evolving and gradually reducing the power and instrumental rationality of the state. However, the concept of civility is extremely rich and diverse in meaning. It represents a specific normative project rather than merely blind social processes of functional differentiation. Moving beyond the limits of state politics-centred constitutionalism does not change the political character of collectively binding decisions and decision-making processes associated with any kind of constitutionalism.

As Hans Lindahl notes, societal constitutionalism cannot dispose of its politics (2011, p. 234). Furthermore, one can ask what is meant by the 'civility' of functional differentiation and constitutionalization in, for instance, global science, technology and sport. Is the evolution of the global *lex mercatoria* (Teubner, 2002) and *ius humanitatis* (Sousa Santos, 2002, pp. 301–11) just a more sophisticated version of the early modern process of the evolution of civil society analysed at the dawn of political modernity by, for instance, Adam Fergusson? Will it lead to the global political establishment of a self-organized and spontaneously evolving civil society unconstrained in its forms by the state's organization and its limiting hierarchies? Do globally communicating media and technologies involve some form of civility?

The operative closure of constitutions by the external semantics of civility

Teubner's concept of fragmented global societal constitutionalization beyond the state suffers from the same opaque and insufficiently differentiated conceptualization typical of Sciulli's theory of societal constitutionalism, which can be attributed to a great variety of social developments and different forms of social communication that have nothing in common with legal or political operations. While Luhmann considers a constitution as the social organization of a structural coupling between law and politics (2004, p. 410), Teubner treats many different depoliticized and non-legal forms of spontaneously evolving social organizations as constitutions. However, this perspective necessarily leads to profound conceptual confusion as regards the basic difference between constitution as political organization and constitution as the social semantics of the self-organization, self-regulation and self-reference of specific sectors and systems of global society.

Teubner's use of the concept of civility is not linked to some prescriptive notion of a global civil society based on the notion of an ethical human life. Nevertheless, it indicates the possibility of some form of overarching commonality in the sectorally and functionally differentiated global society. The 'civil' operates as a precondition of the self-constitutionalizations of different sectors of global society and thus resembles the tradition of civil society as a basis of the differentiation of economy, politics, family and other sectors of modern social life (Teubner, 2012, p. 16).

Teubner's theory of the civil self-constitutionalizations of different sectors of global society is a peculiar mixture of self-referencing legal autopoiesis and the constitutive civility of non-state actors as its external reference. The concept of post-sovereign civil constitutions without the constitutional state relies on external reference to the notion of civility rather than the self-reference of globally pursued legality. Global civility is expected to operate in the same manner as a 'civil religion', limiting constitutional power by external reference to a set of political and social values. Tocqueville's famous claim that the effectiveness and persistence of political institutions depend on their entrenchment in everyday social life and society's moral fabric (Tocqueville, 2000, chs 2–3) thus finds yet another of its original theoretical conceptualizations, this time within the context of autopoietic social systems theory.

The external reference to the civility of self-constitutionalization effectively means that the global legal system can never fully achieve its systemic differentiation and operative closure. Legality is not the only medium of the global legal system and the whole concept of societal constitutionalism is unthinkable without the external semantics of civility which is particularly burdened by the difference between the organized state and spontaneously evolving society. Civility becomes a stabilizer of the most general process of societal constitutionalization.

Teubner's theory of self-constitutionalized sectors of global law is thus both uniquely inspired and haunted by the spectre of Ehrlich's sociology of law and its paradoxes, prescriptions and limitations. Teubner establishes a

sticated theory of autopoietic sub-systems of functionally differenti-
global law but also pursues the goal of eliminating political power and
on from the definition of law. Structural pressures of legal and politi-
obalization allegedly lead to the abandonment of Schmitt's concept of
cal sovereignty and Kelsen's concept of the basic norm but also need
ep using the typically modern concept of civility. This is the only way
terarchical, polycentric and spontaneously evolving global civil soci-
imagined by Teubner can structurally prevail over political hierarchies
d bureaucratic organizations emerging at national, subnational, supra-
ational and transnational levels of global society.

Conclusion: on the concepts of law and power in global society

Theories of global societal constitutionalism and legal pluralism transcend the limitations of institutions and values associated with the modern rule of law and the constitutional democratic state. However, they can
also fail to attribute any sociological importance to power as the medium
of modern politics coupled with the rule of law. In this respect, Sousa
Santos, therefore, correctly observes that the state 'is a central player even
in producing its own downsizing' (2002, p. 94) in the process of globalization. Global legal plurality subsequently cannot be interpreted merely
as non-state spontaneous and heterarchical social evolution and constitutionalization, because the state, its official laws and power continue to
be part of the process of globalization. However, the state's decentraliza-
tion in global society (Jacobsen and Lawson, 1999, p. 205) leads to the
reconfiguration of structural coupling between globalized law and politics which actually replicates state power practices (Sousa Santos, 2002,
p. 489).

As regards functional differentiation and asymmetries in legal and political globalization, Luhmann, for instance, treated the legal system of global
society as 'a special case' (2004, p. 481) and warned against overlooking
huge legal differences in different parts of the globe. In the absence of
globally centralized legislation and decision-making, a global legal order,
according to Luhmann, evolves through the generalized semantics of
human rights and their violations. Legal globalization is facilitated by the
general expectation that states, these differentiated 'segments' of the global
political system (Luhmann, 2004, p. 487), are responsible for their compliance with human rights and make them an intrinsic part of legislation
and law enforcement (Luhmann, 2004, pp. 482–7). The divergence in legal
developments at the level of global society, nevertheless, is so significant
that it raises the very question of the functionality of a global legal order
(Luhmann, 2004, p. 488).

Unlike Luhmann, Teubner never doubts global legal autopoiesis. Nevertheless, his concept of societal constitutionalism cannot be simply dismissed as just another normative project of global civil society and a theory of depoliticization by societal constitutionalism and global governance. Teubner contrasts spontaneously evolving global civil constitutions to politically deliberated constitutions, but this spontaneity, rather than politically designed and regulated, is socially conditioned. Chris Thornhill then rightly notes that the weakness of societal constitutionalism is that 'it is not yet sociological enough' (2011b, p. 245) because it does not take into consideration transformation of political power as an autonomous medium of global social communication and subsequent changes and fragmentations in the constitutional relation between power and law (2011a, p. 7).

Power has not disappeared as the political medium in globalized society (Keohane and Nye, 1977). It cannot be removed from global politics by depoliticized governance like caffeine from coffee beans by decaffeination. Constitutional power practices and strategies can lead to both the renationalization and transnationalization of politics and law in global society. States thus redefine themselves as part of the global 'meta-power game' (Beck, 2005, p. 168) beyond the limitations of state sovereignty.

State and politics are two distinct categories and the modern sovereign state is just one of many semantic forms of modern contingent power structures (Thornhill, 2011b, p. 246). Instead of the pronounced end of the state and its law in global society, sovereign states continue to operate as political and legal organizations in global society. The international legal order, depending on sovereign states, coexists with transnational orders in globalized politics and law (Hurrell, 2007). The nation state is still the most common form of political organization, not just in the supranational system of European society but even in global society characterized by a great variety of international, supranational and transnational institutionalizations and organizations (Holton, 1998).

Modern society does not have one 'super-medium' which could unify all social communication in all of its sub-systems and both legality and power as fully developed symbolically generalized media of the systems of law and politics can perform only specific operations without any possibility of fully integrating and founding a global polity and/or a basic norm of global society (Luhmann, 2012, p. 214). Nevertheless, this *societal neutralization of moralism* looking for normative foundations of the global systems of law and politics can hardly lead to the opposite conceptual and theoretical extreme which considers any form of secondary coding and structural coupling between different social systems a form of societal constitutionalism and civil constitutions beyond politics and its medium of power.

In global society, the sovereign state's power becomes part of much more complex and contingent supranational and transnational power structures and asymmetries. The existence of global social plurality in itself, therefore, cannot justify normative expectations of the horizontal effect of transnational human rights, heterarchical structures of global governance and soft laws of self-regulated segments of global economy, politics, administration and/or technology.

Power as the medium of political communication is subject to a secondary coding by the medium of legality and thus makes political power itself subject to the law or amends the existing laws only through the legal process. This self-referential juridification of power is described as the rule of law, which is purely defined by the secondary coding of power and its structural coupling with legality and thus may be distinguished from moral and ideological concepts of the rule of law of liberal and constitutional statehood (Luhmann, 2012, p. 213). This secondary coding even makes the rule of law independent of organizational constraints of the modern state and stretches the self-constitution and self-inclusion of mutual coupling between the media of power and legality to the level of global society and its multi-layered organizations, networks and regimes. The self-inclusion of power in the medium of legality makes it more efficient at the level of global society because it is not referred to merely in terms of the success/failure distinction but also the compliance/non-compliance distinction.

Power subsequently cannot be treated as a universal medium of controlling global society, but requires further juridical specification of its universal competence. The secondary coding of power by the medium of legality rather contributes to the functional differentiation of global society and both power and legality serve as catalysts for the differentiation of the functional systems of politics and law of global society and its segments, such as European society evolving through the structures and semantics of the EU.

Theories of global societal constitutionalism need to profoundly reflect on this structural coupling between politics and law and explore power structures evolving at global level and their various forms of constitutionalization. The modern state's paradox of constitutionalism as the permanent communication of political power through the medium of legality cannot be resolved by the claim that constitutionalism is just another name for the juridification of functionally differentiated sectors of global society completely dissociated from the power operations and asymmetries of constitutional politics. The constitutionalization of different sectors of global society is a process of increasing rather than limiting power operations and their globalized legal forms regulating these sectors.

The global systemic plurality of functionally differentiated society thus calls for theoretical reconsideration and reconceptualization of legality and power as communication codes of the globalized and structurally coupling systems of positive law and politics concurrently using and stretching beyond organization of the constitutional sovereign state. This reconceptualization could be a truly radical contribution by the theory of societal constitutionalism to contemporary social theory of law and politics.

References

Beck, U (2005) *Power in the Global Age: A New Global Political Economy* (Cambridge: Polity Press)

Bentham, J (1843) 'Anarchical Fallacies' in J Bowring (ed.), *The Works of Jeremy Bentham*, vol. II (Edinburgh: Tait), pp. 491–524

Callies, G P and P Zumbansen (2010) *Rough Consensus and Running Code: A Theory of Transnational Private Law* (Oxford: Hart Publishing)

Cotterrell, R (2008) 'Transnational Communities and the Concept of Law' 21(1) *Ratio Juris* 1–18

Delmas-Marty, M (2009) *Ordering Pluralism: A Conceptual Framework for Understanding the Transnational Legal World* (Oxford: Hart Publishing)

Ehrlich, E (2002/originally published in 1936) *Fundamental Principles of the Sociology of Law* (New Brunswick: Transaction)

Galanter, M (1981) 'Justice in Many Rooms: Courts, Private Ordering and Indigenous Law' 19(1) *Journal of Legal Pluralism and Unofficial Law* 1–47

Griffith, A (2002) 'Legal Pluralism' in R Banakar and M Travers (eds), *An Introduction to Law and Social Theory* (Oxford: Hart Publishing), pp. 289–310

Griffith, J (1986) 'What Is Legal Pluralism?' 24(1) *Journal of Legal Pluralism and Unofficial Law* 1–55

Griffith, J (1998) 'Legal Pluralism and the Theory of Legislation: With Special Reference to the Regulation of Euthanasia' in H Petersen and H Zahle (eds), *Legal Polycentricity: Consequences of Pluralism in Law* (Aldershot: Dartmouth), pp. 201–34

Habermas, J (2008) 'The Constitutionalization of International Law and the Legitimation Problems of a Constitution for World Society' 15(4) *Constellations* 444–55

Held, D (1995) *Democracy and the Global Order: From the Modern State to Cosmopolitan Governance* (Stanford: Stanford University Press)

Hertogh, M (2009) 'From "Men of Files" to "Men of the Senses": A Brief Characterisation of Eugen Ehrlich's Sociology of Law' in M Hertogh (ed.), *Living Law: Reconsidering Eugen Ehrlich* (Oxford: Hart Publishing), pp. 1–17

Holton, R J (1998) *Globalization and the Nation State* (Basingstoke: Palgrave Macmillan)

Hurrell, A (2007) *On Global Order: Power, Values, and the Constitution of International Society* (Oxford: Oxford University Press)

Jacobsen, M and S Lawson (1999) 'Between Globalization and Localization: A Case Study of Human Rights versus State Sovereignty' 5 *Global Governance* 203–19

Kelsen, H (1961) *General Theory of Law and State* (New York: Russell & Russell)

Kelsen, H (2003) 'Eine Grundlegung der Rechssoziologie' in H Kelsen and E Ehrlich, *Rechtssoziologie und Rechtswissenschaft: Eine Kontroverse (1915/1917)* 'Baden-Baden: Nomos Verlagsgesellschaft)

Keohane, R O and J Nye (1977) *Power and Interdependence: World Politics in Transition.* Boston, MA: Little, Brown.

King, M and C Thornhill (eds) (2006) *Niklas Luhmann's Theory of Politics and Law* (Basingstoke: Palgrave Macmillan)

Krisch, N (2010) *Beyond Constitutionalism: The Pluralist Structure of Postnational Law* (Oxford: Oxford University Press)

Krisch, N (2011) 'Who Is Afraid of Radical Pluralism? Legal Order and Political Stability in the Postnational Space' 24(4) *Ratio Juris* 386–412

Kumm, M (1999) 'Who is the Final Arbiter of Constitutionality in Europe?: Three Conceptions of the Relationship between the German Federal Constitutional Court and the European Court of Justice' 36(2) *Common Market Law Review* 351–86

Lindahl, H (2011) 'Societal Constitutionalism as Political Constitutionalism: Reconsidering the Relation between Politics and Global Legal Orders' 20(2) *Social and Legal Studies* 230–7

Luhmann, N (1990) *Essays on Self-Reference* (New York: Columbia University Press)

Luhmann. N (1995) *Social Systems* (Stanford: Stanford University Press)

Luhmann, N (1997) 'Globalization or World Society: How to Conceive of Modern Society?' 7(1) *International Review of Sociology* 67–79

Luhmann, N (2004) *Law as a Social System* (Oxford: Oxford University Press)

Luhmann, N (2012) *Theory of Society,* vol. 1 (Stanford: Stanford University Press)

Mellisaris, E (2009) *Ubiquitous Law: Legal Theory and the Space for Legal Pluralism* (Aldershot: Ashgate)

Merry, S E (1998) 'Legal Pluralism' 22(5) *Law and Society Review* 869–96

Nelken, D (2007) 'An Email from Global Bukowina' 3(3) *International Journal of Law in Context* 189–202

Nelken, D (2009) 'Ehrlich's Legacies: Back to the Future in the Sociology of Law?' in M Hertogh (ed.), *Living Law: Reconsidering Eugen Ehrlich* (Oxford: Hart Publishing), pp. 237–72

Přibáň, J and N Nelken (eds) (2001) *Law's New Boundaries: The Consequences of Legal Autopoiesis* (Aldershot: Ashgate)

Rajagopal, B (2005) 'The Role of Law in Counter-Hegemonic Globalization and Global Legal Pluralism: Lessons from the Narmada Valley Struggle in India' 18 *Leiden Journal of International Law* 345–87

Rasch, W (2000) *Niklas Luhmann's Modernity: The Paradoxes of Differentiation* (Stanford: Stanford University Press)

Rheinstein, M (1938) 'Sociology of Law, Apropos Moll's Translation of Eugen Ehrlich's Grundlegung der soziologie des Rechts' 48 *Journal of Ethics* 232–9

Roberts, S (1998) 'Against Legal Pluralism' 42 *Journal of Legal Pluralism and Unofficial Law* 95–106

Sassen, S (1998) *Globalization and Its Discontents: Essays on the New Mobility of People and Money* (New York: The New Press)

Schmitt, C (1985) *Political Theology: Four Chapters on the Concept of Sovereignty* (Chicago: University of Chicago Press)

Sciulli, D (1992) *Theory of Societal Constitutionalism: Foundations of a Non-Marxist Critical Sociology* (Cambridge: Cambridge University Press)

Sousa Santos, B de (2002) *Towards a New Legal Common Sense* (London: Butterworths) (2nd edn)

Sousa Santos, B de and C A Rodriguez-Garavito (eds) (2005) *Law and Globalization from Below: Towards a Cosmopolitan Legality* (Cambridge: Cambridge University Press)

Strange, S (1996) *The Retreat of the State: The Diffusion of Power in the World Economy* (Cambridge: Cambridge University Press)

Tamanaha, B (2001) *A General Jurisprudence of Law and Society* (Oxford: Oxford University Press)

Teubner, G (1993) *Law as an Autopoietic System* (Oxford: Blackwell)

Teubner, G (1997) '"Global Bukowina": Legal Pluralism in the World Society' in G Teubner (ed.), *Global Law without a State* (Aldershot: Dartmouth), pp. 3–28

Teubner, G (ed.) (1997) *Global Law without a State* (Aldershot: Dartmouth)

Teubner, G (2002) 'Breaking Frames: Economic Globalisation and the Emergence of Lex Mercatoria' 5 *European Journal of Social Theory* 199–217

Teubner, G (2004) 'Societal Constitutionalism: Alternatives to State-Centred Constitutional Theory?' in C Joerges, I J Sand and G Teubner (eds), *Transnational Governance and Constitutionalism* (Oxford: Hart Publishing), pp. 3–28

Teubner, G (2011) 'Constitutionalizing Polycontexturality' 20(2) *Social and Legal Studies* 210–29

Teubner, G (2012) *Constitutional Fragments: Societal Constitutionalism and Globalization* (Oxford: Oxford University Press)

Teubner, G and A Fischer-Lescano (2004) 'Regime Collisions: The Vain Search for Legal Unity in the Fragmentation of Global Law' 25(4) *Michigan Journal of International Law* 999–1046

Thornhill, C (2011a) *A Sociology of Constitutions: Constitutions and State Legitimacy in Historical-Sociological Perspective* (Cambridge: Cambridge University Press)

Thornhill, C (2011b) 'Constitutional Law from the Perspective of Power: A Response to Gunther Teubner' 20(2) *Social and Legal Studies* 244–7

Tocqueville, A de (2000) *Democracy in America* (Chicago: University of Chicago Press)

Tsagourias, N K (ed.) (2007) *Transnational Constitutionalism: International and European Perspectives* (Cambridge: Cambridge University Press)

Tuori, K (2010) *Ratio and Voluntas: The Tension between Reason and Will in Law* (Aldershot: Ashgate)

Weber, M (1978) *Economy and Society* 2 vols (Berkeley: University of California Press)

Ziegert, K (2002) 'Introduction to the Transaction Edition' in E Ehrlich, *Fundamental Principles of the Sociology of Law* (New Brunswick: Transaction Publishers)

Ziegert, K (2009) 'World Society, Nation State and Living Law in the Twenty-first Century' in M Hertogh (ed.), *Living Law: Reconsidering Eugen Ehrlich* (Oxford: Hart Publishing), pp. 223–36

4
Portraying the Legal in Socio-Legal Studies through Legal-Naming Events

Natalie Ohana[1]

Introduction

In this chapter I wish to explore 'the legal' in socio-legal studies. I see it as a relationship between knowledge and power. The legal is a relational phenomenon that can be uncovered by identifying the mechanisms of legal-knowledge production, including the social meanings that those mechanisms either accept or exclude from legal discourse. I illustrate this crucial power relation between the techniques of knowledge production and knowledges themselves by analysing acts of legal naming: acts of granting a legal name to a social phenomenon or constructing the legal meaning of a name already given.

The nature and characteristics of the act of legal naming are the twin focus of the first part of the chapter. Based on Foucault's knowledge/power theory, the essence of the act of naming is revealed as a site of social struggle. These sites are zones of battle between social actors who strive to render their own meaning the accepted one by society. Their nature as struggle enables us to see the legal as a reflection of silenced and invisible social struggles within legal discourse.

In the second part, I present a research method, tailored to reflect the legal among these terms, through analysing acts of legal naming. The method consists of four basic concepts – statement, discourse, history and discontinuity – and analyses three discourse techniques – classification, continuity and translation. Their actual effects and operations in monitoring meanings accepted by or excluded from legal discourse are the defining bricks of the legal. To illustrate my method I take examples from my

1 I wish to thank Professor Alison Diduck for her invaluable support and direction throughout the writing process.

current research on the legal naming of domestic violence against women by courts in England.

The act of naming as a social battle zone

The act of naming is an act of power. To name is to create, recognize, to give a life to the named element, to make it real. On the other hand, to name a phenomenon is also to conceal, erase and render other elements forgotten or invisible. A name is able to define, transform, legitimize and delegitimize the named element – whether an object, a subject or a social phenomenon. Naming is never a singular or final act. Through numerous moments in time and space and as long as the existence of the element is acknowledged, its name can always be reshaped, disappeared, recreated and scattered. Socially accepted names are foundational bricks in the creation of accepted knowledge, around which disciplines, institutions, professions and policies are formed.

Naming events, the occasions in which acts of naming take place, are political in their nature. They are encounters between different social actors, who may or may not be aware of the power struggle in which they are engaged to render their preferred name the popular or accepted one by society. As the balance of power between actors shifts from time to time, different names may be produced and accepted.

To try to reveal social power dynamics through naming events is to conduct genealogical research. Genealogical research looks at the named element as the result of social struggle and seeks to examine the dynamics of that struggle (Foucault, 2003). By asking questions such as who can speak and who is silenced, what can be said and which speech is forbidden or disregarded, we develop a genealogy that reveals the 'winners' and 'losers' in the struggle, the knowledge that was accepted and acceptable and the possibilities of knowledge that was not. Crucially, however, genealogy also *recreates* the battle while changing it entirely: in genealogical research we see actors who did not participate previously or were silenced become part of the struggle, and their voices, previously silenced or buried, become heard and highlighted.

Subjugated knowledge is the term Foucault used to name buried, marginalized and silenced knowledge (Foucault, 2003). He typologized two categories of subjugated knowledge: historical and disqualified. Historical knowledge is content that was present at the time of struggle but was systematically concealed. Disqualified knowledge is content that is referred to as naïve, 'primitive', popular, beneath the required level of scientificity and, therefore, inadequate. Both types of knowledge, once revealed, bear the potential of revealing struggles over discursive meaning.

> It is surely the following kinds of questions that would need to
> be posed: what types of knowledge do you want to disqualify in

the very instant of your demand: 'Is it a science'? Which speaking, discoursing subjects ... do you then want to diminish when
you say: 'I who conduct this discourse am conducting a scientific discourse and I am a scientist'? (Foucault, 1980)

Legal names are a form of social names. They are distinctive names when
compared to names given by other disciplines and actors in society. The
legal system is vested with a unique power to produce socially authoritative
names, which also become the foundation of legislation and policy. Legal
names are thus able to transcend the borders of the legal system itself and
construct the meanings accepted by society as a whole:

> Law is the quintessential form of the symbolic power of naming
> that creates the things named. (Bourdieu, 1986–1987, p. 838)

Legal naming is an act of knowledge-production by which a social phenomenon is granted a name accepted by legal discourse. It is also the act
of reinforcing, constructing or changing the meaning of a name already
accepted by legal discourse. For the purpose of outlining a legal that is
based not only on 'acceptable' knowledge but also excluded knowledge,
the legal-naming act is one through which we can see a struggle between
different possible meanings and which therefore provides a different perspective on the meaning of the legal. It does not simply accept the names
of legal phenomena as given.

Research method

In this part, I present a method with which to analyse legal-naming events
in order to reveal through the events themselves a new meaning for the
legal in socio-legal studies.

As well as presenting its components, I demonstrate how the method
can be applied by using examples from my current research on the
legal naming of domestic violence against women in England. I start
by briefly introducing this case study, which I use as an exemplar, and
explain what renders it apt for addressing the question of outlining
the legal according to exclusionary operations. In order to be able to
examine the struggles that take place in legal-naming events regarding domestic violence against women, I have to first observe the different meanings attributed to this social phenomenon by non-legal
disciplines.

A case study exemplar

Domestic violence erupted into social discourses in the UK during the
late 1960s and 1970s, after decades of vigorous feminist activism during
Labour as well as Conservative periods of government. Domestic violence

was located on the agenda at the time as one of the most urgent and central issues to address.[2] Law, sociology, psychiatry, psychology and later medicine responded to this eruption (Freeman, 1979; Dobash and Dobash; 1980, Williamson, 2000; Humphreys, 2003). Domestic violence became a locus around which knowledge was (and remains) concerted in the form of new expertise, new professions and special institutions.

The name 'domestic violence' was and is still used by many different actors in various social locations. In a multidisciplinary reading on the meanings of domestic violence, which included sociology, psychology and psychiatry, I traced a struggle between two main streams of knowledge trying to render their own meaning the dominant one. These streams do not conform to the borders of the three disciplines, but exist in all of them.

According to the first stream, the dominant one, domestic violence is understood as an *episodic* phenomenon. It is defined through the various violent episodes inflicted by the perpetrator against his victim in the context of an intimate relationship. The episodes are described in a decontextualized way; seen in isolation from each other. This stream understands 'violence' as mainly physical violence and perceives physical injury as its main harm. Gradually, other forms of violence were recognized, mainly sexual and psychological violence, but the understanding of such extra types remained episodic in nature. Domestic violence was understood as one or a series of separated and isolated events, defined by beginning and end points, whether physical, sexual or psychological (Gelles, 1972; Straus, 1979; Dobash and Dobash, 1980; Gelles, 1985; Walker, 1989; Dutton, 1992; Walker, 1999; Dekeseredy, 2000).

The second stream started to emerge at the beginning of the 1980s. It developed at a much slower pace than the first one. Women who experienced domestic violence were given time to explain these experiences; and scholars and practitioners cast this experience-based knowledge in disciplinary terms, which have become the foundation of what is today a body of knowledge spanning over 30 years (Herman, 1992; Johnson, 1995; Johnson and Ferraro, 2000; Smith et al., 2002; Stark, 2007). According to this stream, domestic violence is *coercive control,* achieved by a *pattern* of behaviours used by the perpetrator against his partner. Behaviours against women in a coercive control relationship are directed at three aims: *isolation* from social and economic support – family, friends, professional support and economic means; *control* over bodily autonomy, for example, over number of sleeping hours, what to wear and what to eat; and *intimidation* – putting a person in fear of violence. Through achieving these three aims the perpetrator subjects his partner to a state of

---

2   For example, the first government Select Committee on Violence in Marriage sat in 1974 (Select Committee on Violence in Marriage, 1975).

psychological captivity. Women's accounts of coercive control share core commonalities with accounts by people who were captives in political forms of captivity (Herman, 1992). Only by looking at the *entirety* of the relationship can the harm of coercive control be identified. That harm will remain invisible when one observes the violent relationship through its violent episodes since behaviours that constitute a pattern of coercive control are not necessarily episodic in their nature. The indicator of a violent relationship, its severity and dangerousness, is this *pattern itself* and not the distinct violent episodes. According to this stream, the fundamental and most *lethal* harm caused to women in a violent relationship is the harm of coercive control, or of being subjected to behaviours aimed to reach this state. The other harms caused by violent episodes such as physical or sexual attacks are not overlooked but are recognized as additional to the core harm.

In my analysis of *legal*-naming events of domestic violence against women, I search for both meanings of domestic violence. I examine whether a struggle exists between them, and if so, what is the nature of its dynamic. I focus on operations in legal discourse that both exclude or include meanings.

The legal-naming events I analyse in my case study are the ones revealed in judgments given by English courts between 1972 and 2012.[3] In these judgments the name and meanings of domestic violence against women were produced, constructed and reinforced. I am interested in revealing whether both meanings of domestic violence were able to be present and to compete equally in these struggles throughout those 40 years.

The subject of my case study is specific. It examines the naming of one particular social phenomenon by analysing discourse written by courts, a component of, though not independent of the legal system: on the one hand, bound by legislation and, on the other, able to shape legal meanings through its power to exercise discretion, determine relevance and admissibility of evidence and shape and identify the legal issues before it.

I now turn to present the concepts and tools of analysis which form the research method.

---

3 At the beginning of 2015 s. 76 was added to the Serious Crimes Act 2015 entitled 'Controlling or coercive behaviour in an intimate or family relationship'. A critical reading of this new offence – which *named* coercive control legally for the first time – exceeds the space of this chapter. I will add one remark though that the offence presents a risk that coercive control will be understood as an *additional* form of harm inflicted in a violent relationship rather than as the underlying element through which conduct, harm and risk must be assessed. In my view, the difference between the two is crucial.

Concepts

Statement, discourse

A statement is the atom of the method; the smallest part within a text that is core to the research. A statement can be a word, a sentence or a few sentences together. However, in order for something to be considered a statement, it should be able to reveal something relevant in the struggle over naming (Foucault, 1972). The following types of questions are therefore asked regarding statements. Which statements vanished immediately after their appearance and which kept being repeated? Which statements became the dominant ones and which were dismissed as irrelevant or disqualified? Examples of statements from the case study are:

> The term 'domestic violence' rose to prominence in the 1970s in connection with 'battered wives' – women who, whether married or not, suffered violence at the hands of their husband or partner. (*Yemshaw v Hounslow LBC* [2011] UKSC 3; [2011] 1 WLR 433, [39])

> Of course, it was known that physical violence was not the only form of abuse which women suffered … But, understandably, the predicament of women who were the victims of physical violence was at the forefront of demands for the law to be reformed. (Ibid. [40])

> The judge also noted that there were no lasting physical injuries to the appellant's wife. (*Regina v Ali Abbass Khan* [2011] EWCA Crim 2782, [12])

These three extracts are examples of statements in which courts actively constructed or reinforced the meaning of domestic violence as predominantly the use of physical violence in a context of an intimate relationship.

Importantly, at the start of analysis, statements should be analysed separately, free from any assumptions about their connections with other statements. Only after statements are analysed separately can the researcher examine the relations between them. She can then observe whether they are in fact isolated statements, or if they form a group or several groups. If they are connected, she can then identify the rules of grouping that connect them. A group identified in this way is a *discourse*. It is contrasted with a group of statements that is assumed to be such before studying the statements separately. When analysing statements taken from English judgments, one should not assume at the outset that they are part of a unified 'legal discourse', but study the statements separately to see which types of unities they form between them. The researcher can then examine whether they form a group which is unique to the legal system and can therefore be titled a legal discourse – or whether they connect with other groups that transcend the legal system's borders (Foucault, 1972).

The statements quoted above are examples of statements that were repeated many times in judgments. After looking at them first as isolated statements, the rule of grouping that formed a unity between them, a discourse, emerged. They are connected to each other in their content, in perceiving domestic violence as predominantly the use of physical violence. But the analysis of statements searches not only for their unities but also asks whether those unities are part of a larger discourse. As I will demonstrate below under tools of analysis, statements naming domestic violence against women revealed two unities of statements: one that is based on the perception that domestic violence is an episodic phenomenon in its nature and the other on the perception that physical violence is its main harm. Examining the relations between those unities revealed that they are actually attached to each other and are part of one larger discourse.

History, discontinuity

The method applies to research that is historical in its nature. Legal-naming events occur at different points in time and, therefore, their study generates a historical observation of legal practice. *History* is not perceived as a gradual, linear and monotonous curve, in which one event leads harmoniously to the next. In this method, we are freed from the urge to portray the legal as a 'process', or to divide it into organized periods or tenets. We do not accept the division between 'major' and 'minor' events as reflecting a division between the meaningful and the insignificant; nor do we try to present such events as if they are somehow in accord with each other (Foucault, 1980, 1991). Rather, *discontinuities* – which are instances of breaks, transformations or interruptions that disturb the harmonious path of statements – are perceived as significant in the analysis.

> How is it that at certain moments and in certain orders of knowledge, there are these sudden take-offs, these hastenings of evolution, these transformations which fail to correspond to the calm, continuist image that is normally accredited. (Foucault, 1980, p. 112)

The concepts that form the foundation of my genealogical method, therefore, are statement/discourse and history/discontinuity. With this conceptual foundation laid, let me turn to my tools of analysis.

Three discourse techniques

The method consists of three analytical tools. Each tool is essentially a technique operated within legal discourse(s) that determines the names and meanings that can be accepted into them. The tools are classification, continuity and translation. By revealing their operation, I suggest we can demonstrate as much about the naming process as we can about its outcomes, and how this process, as much as the outcomes, constitutes the legal.

Classification

In naming events, a named element goes through classification acts as part of the naming process. Acts of classification define the limits of the named element and divide it to sub-categories. Classification acts, as naming itself, continue as long as the named element – whether object, subject or social phenomenon – is acknowledged (Foucault, 1972).

Classification is a technique of knowledge production, prevalent in most disciplines, but fundamental within legal discourse. The reliance of legislation and case law on word and text makes the classification technique a foundational one with which to produce clearly defined legal concepts. Although some legal concepts are intentionally left ambiguous, others go through processes of classification aimed at rendering them more clear and accurate. They are classified and reclassified, divided continuously into sub-categories.

The technique of classification is a mechanism that monitors the dynamics between different meanings that compete with each other in legal-naming events. The act of classification constructs the meaning of a named element by defining the limits within which it can be understood and thereby separating it from other possible meanings. Classification thus prevents new, challenging and different meanings from entering the discourse that do not correlate with that defined space. First acts of classification divide the element off and set the paths through which it can be further understood. Additional classification acts continue through the directions set by those first acts and so strengthen and solidify them. The more classification acts that pile on top of that initial definition and are guided by it, the harder it becomes for new and different possibilities of meaning to uproot the existing realms of understanding in order to be heard and accepted.

The first acts of classification, revealed in statements within judgments, construct and reinforce the legal meaning of domestic violence in a fundamental way. Through acts of classification the entirety of a violent relationship becomes nothing more than discrete and isolated timed *incidents*. Statements reveal that courts see violent episodes as the relevant factors with which to assess the severity of conduct and harm inflicted by the perpetrator and as the indicators of his dangerousness.

The following judicial statement is representative of those that reflect the mechanism of classification:

> Mr B gave evidence admitting certainly some of the incidents
> of violence of which Mrs B had made complaint but seeking, if

> not to excuse, at all events to explain the circumstances in which
> those incidents had occurred, so as to minimize their significance.
> (*B v B (Domestic Violence: Jurisdiction)* [1978] Fam 26 CA, [32])

According to this statement, taken from a civil case, domestic violence is understood through the violent episodes it entails. The repetition of statements that share the same content indicates they are part of a unit – discourse.

The effect of this act of classification is the erasure of the harm of coercive control, the most lethal harm of domestic violence, which can only be recognized when the violent relationship is looked at as an entirety and not through its episodes.

Statements also revealed a second, fundamental act of classification, built on the first act presented above, that monitors the meaning accepted into discourse. Through the first act of classification the path was laid for further classifications. The violent episodes, perceived as the relationship itself, are divided into categories of violence according to their *form*: physical violence, sexual violence and emotional/psychological violence.

The following statement, taken from a family case, represents how this act of classification actually operates:

> I accept her account that she has been subjected by her husband
> to sustained emotional, physical, and sexual abuse stretching
> back to the early days of their relationship and continuing until
> its conclusion ... The emotional abuse consisted of: ... Examples
> of the wider course of physical abuse are: ... Examples of the
> wider course of sexual abuse are: ... (*DT v LBT (Abduction: Domes-
> tic Abuse)* [2010] EWHC 3177 (Fam); [2011] 1 FLR 1215, [10])

This statement is representative of a discourse emerging in judgments. The discourse is responsible for fragmenting a relationship, experienced by victims as one reality, into separate sub-categories that are divided to the extent that they are perceived as separate social phenomena. This act of classification adds another layer that prevents the harm of coercive control from being understood and accepted. When domestic violence is understood as coercive control it becomes apparent that the different forms of violence that achieve this state are secondary in their importance, in comparison to the harm of coercive control itself. Coercive control is the root, ground, cause and harm achieved by different behaviours organized in a pattern. Focusing on forms of violence, and perceiving them as separate social phenomena, conceals their common root, which is also a lethal harm.

These acts of classification in the legal naming of domestic violence exclude women's experience of coercive control. Women do not experience coercive control as fragmented into different phenomena but as one experience. Each separate phenomenon constructed by the discourse can be mistakenly perceived as requiring a different legal remedy. The oneness of all forms of violence within one relationship is left unseen. The consequence is that coercive control, the lethal harm described above, is concealed in this process, since it can only be seen when the one source that generates all violent forms is acknowledged.

Moreover, these acts of classification reveal a strategy of naming: the meaning of domestic violence is constructed not by engaging directly with the question *'What is* domestic violence?' but by establishing channels through which it can be judged. In order to be assessed legally, the discourse requires that domestic violence be adapted in its form to the episodic, categorical understanding.

Continuity

Continuity is the act of affiliating a newly acknowledged phenomenon to existing phenomena that were previously recognized and named (Bourdieu, 1986–1987; Foucault, 1972). Attaching a newly recognized phenomenon to previously accepted and named phenomena is a particularly prevalent technique of knowledge production used by the legal system. New judgments, legislation and policies are based on, enabled and conditioned by existing ones. The common law system and the primacy of the precedent are designed to provide these with established grounds on which new legal phenomena can be acknowledged.

Continuity operates to monitor the meanings acceptable to legal discourse. Like classification, it sets out the path along which the new phenomenon can be understood and defines its limits. It is therefore exclusionary in its nature and effect.

To analyse the effects of the continuity mechanism on legal-naming events, we must ask whether the researched phenomenon was named or its meaning constructed by affiliating it or attaching it to a different, previously named phenomenon (Foucault, 1972).

I uncovered a fundamental form of continuity in legal-naming events regarding domestic violence. Judicial statements tended to subject the phenomenon of domestic violence to the traditional meaning of the concept 'violence', as inflicting bodily harm through the use of physical force. These are two representative statements that reflect the dominant view shaped by this form of continuity:

> 'Battered wives' is a telling phrase. It was invented to call the
> attention of the public to an evil. Few were aware of it. It arose
> when a woman suffered serious or repeated physical injury from

the man with whom she lived. (*Davis v Johnson* [1978] 2 WLR 182 CA Civ, [187])

In my view, there is no doubt that violence means the same, whether it comes from a person associated with the victim or from a third party. (*Yemshaw v Hounslow*, [44])

This form of continuity establishes a 'real' or 'actual' violence, as opposed to other forms of behaviour that are not considered as harmful. By extricating the physical harm from other harms inflicted in the same relationship it constructs a misleading understanding that the harms *are* actually separate from each other, a separation that is not experienced by women in a violent relationship. Moreover, by perceiving physical violence as the most serious harm, a hierarchy between harms is created: physical violence positioned at the top of the hierarchy and other harms positioned lower down.

A connection exists between the two techniques: the classification technique fragments the relationship into separate phenomena – physical, sexual and psychological violence; the continuity technique hierarchizes them, rendering them phenomena that represent different degrees of harm and risk. The two unities of statements uncovered when analysing the statements according to classification and continuity – one unity being the episodic understanding of domestic violence and the other being the perception that physical violence is its main harm – were revealed as attached to each other, as being part of the same discourse.

The effect of the revealed discourse is that domestic violence is misunderstood, the harm of coercive control is concealed and the discourse becomes more and more shielded, not allowing a gap for coercive control to enter and become visible and accepted.

In *Yemshaw v Hounslow*, the Supreme Court was concerned with interpreting the concept 'violence' in the context of domestic violence in the Housing Act 1996. In Lady Hale's judgment, we see several statements that reveal exclusion and inclusion.

The following statement written by Lady Hale might seem to be a sign of discontinuity, a sign that courts begin to alter their perception of domestic violence as physical violence:

'Violence' is a word very similar to the word 'family'. It is not a term of art. It is capable of bearing several meanings and applying to many different types of behaviour. These can change and develop over time. (*Yemshaw v Hounslow*, [27])

However, by stating that violence can mean other forms of behaviour, the court still perceives domestic violence along the lines established by forms of classification and continuity. Even as the nature and harms of new types of violent events are affiliated with the accepted meaning of violence, the phenomenon is still perceived as episodic in nature and 'actual' physical violence is still seen as the severest harm of the relationship. The statement renders the concept 'violence' as open, broad, fluid and discretion-based, but one that does not challenge those embedded ways of understanding. The lethal harm of coercive control is not rendered visible by perceiving the concept 'violence' as a broad concept. Rather, it is left to the discretion of each judge to decide whether circumstances that constitute coercive control fall into the concept. But again, forms of classification and continuity make that task difficult. The following statement from Lady Hale's judgment reveals that even though violence is acknowledged as a broad concept, domestic violence remains beholden to the existing legal understanding:

> There may also be a concern that an expanded definition is setting the threshold too low. The advantage of the definition adopted by the President of the Family Division is that it deals *separately* with *actual* physical violence, *putting a person in fear of such violence* and *other types of harmful behaviour*. (*Yemshaw v Hounslow*, [34]) (emphasis added)

In the example of domestic violence, courts' naming operations ground the episodic and hierarchical channels of understanding and these are more powerful than the occasional acts in which courts directly alter or rename the definition of violence.

There is, however, one statement in Lady Hale's judgment that we can view as a crucial sign of discontinuity. Here, she is directing the housing authority on the test it needs to apply when deciding whether a woman is a victim of domestic violence:

> Was this, in reality, simply a case of marriage breakdown in which the appellant was not genuinely in fear of her husband; or was it a classic case of domestic abuse, in which one spouse puts the other in fear through the constant denial of freedom and of money for essentials, through the denigration of her personality, such that she genuinely fears that he may take her children away from her however unrealistic this may appear to an objective outsider? (*Yemshaw v Hounslow*, [36])

Here, Lady Hale clearly describes the harm of coercive control. She calls this harm the 'classic case' of domestic abuse. Yet, she chose not to include it as part of her *ratio decidendi* in a case that was concerned solely with the meaning of domestic violence.

I see this statement as an important judicial-naming strategy revealed. On the one hand, Lady Hale *named* (*acknowledged*) the phenomenon: she described the harm and titled it the 'classic case' of domestic abuse. Titling coercive control as a classic case of domestic abuse renders it a central phenomenon and not merely an example of a possible form of domestic violence. On the other hand, by adding it only as an end remark, part of general guidance to the housing authority, and by using the word 'abuse' and not 'violence', she presented it in a way that concealed its revolutionary meaning, as if she was describing a harm that had long been acknowledged and not a harm that was still mostly invisible to courts. This statement reflects a judicial strategy of shifting accepted legal meanings by means that seem entirely marginal to the judgment itself.

Translation

Upon entry to the legal system, an acknowledged social phenomenon will go through a process in which it needs to put on new 'clothes' tailored to suit the legal space into which it enters (Bourdieu, 1986–1987). Its admission requires more than it merely becoming measurable and provable. Social phenomena must go through transformations that enable them to join the legal system harmoniously and become an integrated part of it.

> Entry into the juridical implies the tacit acceptance of the field's fundamental law, an essential tautology which requires that, within the field, conflicts can only be resolved *juridically* – that is, according to the rules and conventions of the field itself. (Bourdieu, 1986–1987, p. 832)

This is essentially a process of translation: processing a social phenomenon in order to render it legal in its form and nature, an integral part of the legal discourse. This process is a crucial part of the legal-naming act. In a similar way to the operations of classification and continuity, when the courts reject, receive or alter meanings presented to them by external actors they monitor the struggle between accepted and excluded legal meanings.

Acts of translation are clearest when courts are presented with new meanings – not yet acknowledged legally – brought to them by non-legal actors. In these meeting points, different possibilities exist: the court might ignore the new meaning altogether, preventing it from entering the discourse; it might change its form or essence in the process of allowing its entry; or it might accept it as it is.

In the context of domestic violence, acts of translation can be identified whenever actors from different disciplines present the court with the understanding that domestic violence is something other than an episodic phenomenon defined by the seriousness of physical violence.

I identified these meeting points in criminal appeals regarding sentencing of domestic-violence offenders, in which non-legal actors – probation officers, who are usually trained as social workers, psychologists or psychiatrists – presented courts with their evaluation regarding the future risk of offenders towards victims or the general public. I found acts of translation in courts' reactions to these evaluations. I wanted to examine the courts' reactions to evaluations of risk based on coercive control, rather than on traditional acts of physical violence.

The following statement by the court comes from the probation officer's pre-sentence report. The probation officer evaluated the offender as presenting a high risk towards the victim:

> It is my assessment that Mr Zelder's behaviour bears the hallmarks of a violently controlling man who has lost the power over his victim. The loss of his relationship appears to have enraged him to the point of almost killing Ms Johnson ... Again, the threats against her initially gave him his desired outcome of Ms Johnson dropping the charges against him, keeping her within his control by placing her in fear of her life. ...
>
> Of particular concern are his aggressive, controlling behaviour and his power over Ms Johnson, resulting in her becoming unconscious. (*R v Zelder (Mitchell)* [2009] EWCA Crim 2958, [11])

This is the only place the court mentioned facts of coercive control. Although it accepted the final conclusion that the offender is dangerous, it refrained from repeating the controlling behaviour as a ground for that conclusion. Instead, it accepted the aggravating features listed by the Crown Court to ground the offender's sentence:

> In our view, the judge was entitled to take the view that it was. He spelled out in his sentencing remarks the aggravating factors. They included the fact that the victim came closer to death than any other case seen by the pathologist, the cunning way in which the appellant sought to lay a false trail immediately after the attempted murder so as to prevent any assistance coming to the victim that evening, the fact that he himself made no attempt to summon medical assistance, despite knowing or believing that his victim was still alive when he left the premises on that night, and the fact that he left the victim's four-year-old son alone in the flat with the victim overnight, as well as the subsequent attempts to

intimidate the victim so as to avoid the consequences of his actions. (*R v Zelder*, [16]).

By quoting the part from the pre-sentence report that is based on coercive control but not repeating it in the judgment itself, thus acknowledging it as a legal concept, the court delivers the message that this factor is significant only from a probation officer's point of view. The court refrained from granting coercive control a *legal* significance. In this example, the court held back from integrating the new meaning into legal discourse by ensuring its place as external; referring to it as a non-legal factor and shying away from granting it legal importance.

Conclusion

In this chapter, I have argued that a crucial portrait of the legal in socio-legal studies sees it as space, an arena of struggle. In a sense the legal is the space in which the power/knowledge nexus operates, as much as it is the result of that struggle. The actual way in which social meanings are accepted into or excluded from legal discourse is one approach to understanding the legal in socio-legal studies. I have presented a research method with which to analyse these processes, which I have termed legal-naming events. My method relies upon a set of concepts and tools to make visible the power dynamics in legal naming. Together they form a complex structure of exclusionary mechanisms, including exclusion in techniques of knowledge-production – classification and continuity – and exclusion in meeting points between the legal and other disciplines – translation. Importantly, I do not argue that these mechanisms present a full picture of the exercise of power in legal naming, rather that the method allows us to see the legal in socio-legal studies *as* the operations and effects of these mechanisms.

The method is focused on local, specific, routine, everyday practice. It sees the dynamics within local incidents as the defining elements of the legal itself. Accordingly, I used the legal naming of domestic violence against women by courts in England as an example of a case study on which to apply the method. The examples emphasize the effects of discourse techniques in naming instances and offer a glimpse of the portrait of the legal according to this case study. These effects presented a legal that cannot be outlined in a coherent line. Most statements supported an image of an excluding legal, one that is too ordered and controlled and is mainly occupied with validating its own accepted meanings: the effect of classification acts having shattered domestic violence into separated fragments to the extent that the most crucial conduct and harm in the relationship was concealed. Through acts of continuity, the phenomenon was subjected to the previously defined notion of 'violence' which caused a distortion in its understanding. Lastly, new understandings brought to courts by professionals were met with relative reluctance to adopt and change the conventional understandings. This part of the analysis revealed the dominant role and violent operations of discourse techniques in the production of accepted legal knowledge. The judgments correlated with the techniques, not with women's actual (fatal) harm. Carr's perception (this volume) reflects the exact same operation that has been revealed here: the very technicalities obscured crucial human realities. This is a violent operation in its essence since its consequence is to render relevant fatal realities absent. Cloatre (this volume) shows how a blurry definition constructs instability in the defined object. In my analysis, the same type of relationship is revealed but the definition I examined is the opposite of blurry. It is too clear and too stable, and was able to generate a corresponding controlled and ordered discourse (that continued to reinforce the meaning of the definition itself) that leaves very little room for mobilization.

However, few statements managed to provide a glimpse of preliminary signs of discontinuities in this largely stable image. A particular statement reflecting a discontinuity was identified which provides evidence of the struggle taking place within these incidents of naming and the existence of a certain shaky dimension that they entail.

Defining the legal as constant struggles over accepted knowledge, through analysing the role of discourse techniques in monitoring the dynamics in these struggles, allows us to question existing legal knowledges while acknowledging new ones and rendering them real, legitimate and important as we continue to study the legal.

Cases

B v B (Domestic Violence: Jurisdiction) [1978] Fam 26 CA
Davis v Johnson [1978] 2 WLR 182 CA Civ
DT v LBT (Abduction: Domestic Abuse) [2010] EWHC 3177 (Fam); [2011] 1 FLR 1215
R v Zelder (Mitchell) [2009] EWCA Crim 2958
Regina v Ali Abbass Khan [2011] EWCA Crim 2782
Yemshaw v Hounslow LBC [2011] UKSC 3; [2011] 1 WLR 433

References

Bourdieu, P (1986–1987) 'The Force of Law: Toward a Sociology of the Juridical Field' 38 *Hastings Law Journal* 814
Dekeseredy, W S (2000) 'Current Controversies on Defining Nonlethal Violence against Women in Intimate Heterosexual Relationships: Empirical Implications' 6 *Violence Against Women* 728

Dobash, R E and R P Dobash (1980) *Violence against Wives: A Case against Patriarchy* (London: Open Books)

Dutton, M A (1992) 'Understanding Women's Responses to Domestic Violence: A Redefinition of Battered Woman Syndrome Symposium on Domestic Violence' 21 *Hofstra Law Review* 1191–242

Foucault, M (1972) *The Archaeology of Knowledge* (London: Tavistock)

Foucault, M (1980) *Power/Knowledge Selected Interviews and Other Writings in 1972–1977* (New York: Knopf Doubleday Publishing Group)

Foucault, M (1991) 'Nietzsche, Genealogy, History' in P Rabinow (ed.), *The Foucault Reader* (London: Penguin Books)

Foucault, M (2003) *Society Must Be Defended: Lectures at the College de France 1975–1976* (London: Penguin Books)

Freeman, M D (1979) *Violence in the Home* (Farnborough: Saxon House)

Gelles, R J (1972) The Violent Home. A Study of Physical Aggression between Husbands and Wives (London: Sage Publications)

Gelles, R J (1985) 'Family Violence' 11 *Annual Review of Sociology* 347–467

Herman, J L (1992) *Trauma and Recovery* (New York: Basic Books)

Humphreys, C (2003) 'Mental Health and Domestic Violence: "I call it symptoms of abuse"' 33 *British Journal of Social Work* 209–26

Johnson, M P (1995) 'Patriarchal Terrorism and Common Couple Violence: Two Forms of Violence against Women' 57 *Journal of Marriage and the Family* 283–94

Johnson, M P and K J Ferraro (2000) 'Research on Domestic Violence in the 1990s: Making Distinctions' 62 *Journal of Marriage and the Family* 948–63

Select Committee on Violence in Marriage (1975) *Report together with the Proceedings of the Committee* vol. 1 (London: HMSO)

Smith, P H, G E Thornton, R Devellis, J Earp and A L Coker (2002) 'A Population-Based Study of the Prevalence and Distinctiveness of Battering, Physical Assault, and Sexual Assault in Intimate Relationships' 8 *Violence Against Women* 1208–32

Stark, E (2007) *Coercive Control: The Entrapment of Women in Personal Life* (New York/Oxford: Oxford University Press)

Straus, M A (1979) 'Measuring Intrafamily Conflict and Violence: The Conflict Tactics (CT) Scales' 41 *Journal of Marriage and Family* 75–88

Walker, L E (1989) *Terrifying Love: Why Battered Women Kill and How Society Responds* (New York: Harper & Row)

Walker, L E (1999) *The Battered Woman Syndrome* (New York: Springer)

Williamson, E (2000) *Domestic Violence and Health: The Response of the Medical Profession* (Bristol: Policy Press)

5
Fluid Legal Labels and the Circulation of Socio-Technical Objects: The Multiple Lives of 'Fake' Medicines

Emilie Cloatre

Introduction

In this chapter, I explore what the politics of 'fake' medicines in Ghana have to contribute to understandings of the law and of legal (un)technicalities. Socio-legal scholarship has developed multiple strategies to explore the meanings and multiple existences of law, within and outside the formally defined 'legal space'. The ways in which law is defined, perceived, experienced and understood by those sitting at its edge, encountering the legal system occasionally or 'sideways' have, for example, been explored by some strands of legal consciousness scholarship (e.g. Silbey and Ewick, 1998).

At the same time, calls have been made for a more careful attention to the ways in which legal technicalities and the 'law within' matter to the constitution of the social (it being understood here as inherently constitutive of and constituted by legal interactions, rather than as a distinct space). This attention to the day-to-day and the technical of law finds its roots both in legal anthropology and in science and technology studies (STS), both of which have opened avenues for questioning the boundaries of law, as well as the ways in which its routinized deployment comes to shape its identity and meaning. Alongside these developments, STS has also opened up significant sets of questions about how we can conceive of social interactions, relationships and constitution of norms, but also about how social processes can be exemplified or enriched by a close look at material connections and the gathering of relationships within localized materials.

Thus, in this chapter I bring together several of these strands of interests and disciplinary traditions by exploring what happens to law when it becomes un-technical; and also how those who sit on the edge of law come to constitute the boundaries between legitimate and illegitimate, 'real' and 'fake', in fields that are defined, unusually for law, by blurring, rather than clear determination, of legal categories. In doing so, I also question how legal uncertainty impacts on the constitution of unsettled material existences, or in other words, how a blurry legal definition of a thing constructs instability in this same object.

In particular, this chapter uses the example of counterfeit medicines, and the fight against counterfeits, to discuss how legal (un)certainty and (un)technicalities translate into ontological and material uncertainties for particular medicines. It focuses on the complex relationships between the politics of counterfeits and the politics of access to medicines, using examples of their entanglement at several sites, from spaces of transnational decision-making to local practices in Ghana. It links the difficulties faced by the circulation of generic medicines in Ghana to the entangled discourses that link legitimate generics to discourses on 'fakes' and 'counterfeits' in other instances. In this manner I seek to unpack the social and political implications of the shifting definition of what counts as a 'legitimate' device for pharmaceutical treatment. Methodological tools are drawn from actor–network theory's (ANT) attention to materiality and day-to-day practice in the constitution of social processes (Latour, 1993; Mol, 2003; Latour, 2005; Law, 2008), as well as more broadly from STS scholarship that has unpacked the way drugs emerge and stabilize in social networks and practices in particular ways (Lakoff, 2005; Hayden, 2007; Pollock, 2008; Hayden, 2011; Pollock, 2011).

This exploration begins from an apparent paradox in the practice of access to medicines in Ghana – though this is not unique to Ghana. Like others in sub-Saharan Africa, the government of Ghana has developed extensive strategies to attempt to broaden the use of generic medicines in the country. Nonetheless, these medicines are repeatedly excluded from the prescription and usage practices of many health professionals and patients, rendering the country far less reliant on generic medicines than it would hope. At the same time, the health system of Ghana has struggled for many years with the issue of fake or substandard medicines being sold illegally on the local market. These two problems are closely related, and here I argue that the difficulty in generalizing the use of generic medicines, while finding its roots in a long history of contestation surrounding these drugs (Greene, 2011), is also deeply grounded in a broader set of relationships, shifts and blurriness that emerge at the global level in the definition of legitimate/illegitimate, legal/illegal, real/fake drugs. The story of counterfeit medicines in Ghana provides an interesting platform upon which to explore the effacement of legal technicalities and how this effacement translates when moving across networks that are mostly animated by actors sitting on the edge of the legal system, interacting with law only in particular and occasional ways. Specifically, it provides a useful instance in which to question how the blurring and shifts that are at play in this situation impact on the constitution of a particular set of socio-technical entities: medicines.

The chapter draws on qualitative fieldwork, organized primarily around in-depth, loosely structured interviews with 20 policy-makers and health professionals involved in the regulation, procurement, use and distribution of medicines in Ghana. It emerges from a larger empirical study concerned with the interaction between regulation and the shaping of pharmaceutical markets in sub-Saharan Africa that was therefore not exclusively focused on counterfeit medicines, but from which counterfeit medicines emerged as one determinant of the complex movements that directed patients, health professional and policy-makers towards certain drugs and away from others (Cloatre, 2013). Interviews were carried out with those involved in the importation of medicines, their prescription and distribution, and checks and controls over the market – this included wholesalers, pharmacists (private and hospital), doctors, members of the Food and Drugs Board and the Pharmacy Council, members of non-governmental organizations (NGOs) and academics who were or had been involved in relevant policy committees, as well as those involved in intellectual property policy. Where available, policy documents were analysed and followed up in interviews as appropriate. This chapter brings together this empirical data with an analysis of global discourses on counterfeit drugs to conceptualize the blurring of boundaries between the technical and un-technical, legal and non-legal, intentional and unintentional which emerged from paying attention to day-to-day medicinal use and distribution.

In the first half of the chapter, I locate the questions that need to be addressed by revisiting the relevant strands of available scholarship. I then turn to elaborate on the notion of counterfeit, and why it offers a useful site to explore un-technical law. In the second half of the chapter, I explore the shifting understandings of counterfeits in the public health practices of Ghana and reflect on what this means for conceptions of law and its understanding in socio-legal scholarship.

Labels, myths and un-technical names

My analysis borrows from several strands of scholarship. First, it relates to questions surrounding the link between imagined social conditions and social realities which has a long history in sociology. Following the ideas of symbolic interactionism, engagement with social labelling opened questions that can be summed up by this early statement: 'If men define situations as real, they are real in their consequences' (Thomas and Thomas, 1927, p. 572). Labelling theories have grown to explain how processes of identification, classification and attribution of social labels impact on social constitution and behaviour. Underlying this is the assumption that beliefs are as determinant (if not more) as objective or material reality in shaping social action (e.g. Lemert, 1967; Lindesmith et al., 1999). In other words, what we believe to be factual comes to shape actions, regardless of the possible misconceptions that affect these beliefs.

My understanding links into some of the questions that this literature has raised, in so far as this literature interrogates the power of legal categorization and processes of branding of social activities and movement. However, a particular concern in this chapter is to question the links between names and the allocation of labels to materials and objects, rather than only or primarily to human actors. By teasing out the links between beliefs and practice, my concerns also echo, in turn, those of scholarship on 'legal myths' that have explored specifically how beliefs held about what the law states, or about the formation of legal facts or phenomena, impact on social behaviour in ways that the letter of the law, or actual legal events, do not necessarily warrant or explain alone (Daniels and Martin, 1991; Almond, 2009). Again, when investigating the effects of the label 'counterfeit' on the use and distribution of different kinds of medicines, beliefs become merged with (uncertain) legal definitions in shaping attitudes and behaviours. However, in this example, the myth also finds its roots in the complex uncertainty of the processes of legal labelling at play and comes to challenge further the boundaries between definitions, actions and intentions.

Although sharing some of these classic concerns, the approach in this chapter differs from both these sets of literature in at least two ways. First, the central focus of the chapter is on the relationship between labels and the constitution and movements of socio-technical objects and it explores how labels that become, intentionally or accidentally, attached to things, condition the possibility of their mobilization and circulation. Second, it interrogates a type of label that is, at several levels of its making and deployment, largely un-technical, and does not sit neatly in either the 'legal' or 'non-legal' categories, therefore bringing into question the meaningfulness of this categorization itself. The ambivalence of the notion of counterfeit is played out at different levels: first, as a term that appeals to a sense of law yet is most often used in a non-technical way, by actors to which legal technicalities are not of central concern; second, by its use to refer to medicines that can either be dangerous chemical products or only breach intellectual property rules; and third, consequently, by affecting the processes deployed in facilitating access to good quality generic medicines, as well as those that surround the fight against low-standard drugs – I return to this in the next section (Holstein and Miller, 1993).

Therefore, the chapter interrogates how the constitution of the notion of counterfeit, arguably both legal and non-legal in its making and deployment, conditions the ways in which medicines come to be used or distributed in Ghana. This uncertain, shifting and largely un-technical label is transposed from medicines that are caught by at least some of its uncertain definition to others whose legality is not in question. In doing so, the case study places questions about the role of legal technicalities (Riles, 2010; 2011) at the core of its analysis, and interrogates specifically the effacement of legal technicalities, both in its making and deployment. Finally, it should be noted that most of the actors that are relevant to this case study are not lawyers, but medical practitioners or health policy-makers. Their definition of 'law' might not fit the understanding of lawyers, yet what counts as 'law' for them underlies their engagement with legal technicalities.

Generics, copies, fakes and counterfeits

In recent years, the international community has been increasingly concerned with the risks posed by fake medicines (Outterson and Smith, 2006; Bunker, 2007; Yar, 2008). Reports of the seizing of 'counterfeits' are regularly issued, as are health warnings to the general public; and these concerns have become more acute as medicines have started being sold in a wider range of spaces, notably on the internet, often with limited levels of regulation (Oliver, 2007). In particular, the risk of encountering dangerous fake medicines has been heavily associated with the markets of so-called developing states, and with much of sub-Saharan Africa in particular, and reminders that counterfeits are also found 'in the West' are often issued with the implicit understanding that counterfeits were originally a problem of the 'South'.

The processes at play are deeply rooted in, and inevitably entangled with, broader politics of access to medicines – the crude, nitty-gritty questions of who gets what, where, when and under which conditions. Access to medicines has been a concern for the international community for many years and has been articulated as such at least since the 1970s, when the World Health Organization (WHO) issued its first Essential Medicines List (T'Hoen, 2010). Since the end of the 1990s, however, it has also become a problem heavily associated with intellectual property rights and the global politics of ownership.

Since the adoption of the Trade Related Aspects of Intellectual Property (TRIPS) has opened debates on intellectual property and access to medicines, the importance of generic medicines – cheaper replicates of innovator brands – to improve healthcare for the poor has become increasingly acknowledged. Nonetheless, generic medicines have continued to meet significant sets of practical barriers and resistance; constituted largely from a mixture of pressure from pharmaceutical companies, a persistent effect of patents (exceeding at times the role that law had attached to them by providing market exclusivity in practice beyond the terms of the law), but also more subtle sets of habits, routines and practices from which the key players of prescription and distribution in parts of sub-Saharan Africa have still not successfully extracted themselves (Cloatre, 2013; Cloatre and Dingwall, 2013). These networks have come to shape branded medication as what Michel Callon has named, in a different set of contexts, obligatory passage points – a point through and towards which all other networks and actors repeatedly, and almost inevitably, travel (Callon, 1986), leaving generic medicines in the position of an uncertain Other, repeatedly faced with exclusion. This uncertain position of generic drugs is aggravated and conditioned by a broader instability of the real/fake, good/bad medicine distinctions, that find some of its roots in the use of legal discourse through non-technical means and, in particular, by the ill-defined category of counterfeit drugs.

Defining the 'real' drug

'The problem with drugs is quality. If you lower quality, they are not drugs'

In this section, I start interrogating the meaning of a 'real drug', by looking at how 'fake drugs' are defined. The subtitle of this section, a quote from the statement of a Ghanaian informant, offers one particular entry point into questioning what differentiates the 'medicine' from the 'non-medicine'; and one that is certainly highly defendable – focusing on the material itself, its content and assuming that the ontology of a medicine is defined primarily by its potential effects on a patient's body. We know, however, that drugs are defined and produced as much by their regulatory framing as they are by their substance (Jackson, 2012). Medicines come to be 'things patients can use' once they have been authorized through particular practices and institutions, and products that have not done so retain a much more unstable and contested position. They are, in this way, socio-legal hybrids, of the type that Caroline Hunter also explores in her contribution to this volume.

In this context, the fluidity of the concept of counterfeit medicines, the term that has come to designate the fake drugs that patients and policy-makers are warned against, is particularly interesting (Outterson and Smith,

2006; Bunker, 2007). At one level, 'counterfeit' drugs are precisely what the above quote suggests – they are substandard medicines that can either contain dangerous or harmful substances or, instead, contain no active products, or low levels of an active product. The danger presented by those drugs (or 'non-drugs', as the quote suggests) has generated widespread and legitimate concern among policy-makers, health professionals and patients around the world.[1] Innovative technological solutions are frequently proposed to try to facilitate patients' awareness and risk reduction. Quantifying the size of the market in these dangerous fake (non)medicines is problematic, but most commentators and policy-makers agree that the problem is significant and increasingly fuelled by poorly regulated sales and underlying poverty issues (Obi-Eyisi and Wetheimer, 2012). Undoubtedly, this is also the category of counterfeit medicines that has most strongly captured public attention. They have become influential in shaping practices of buying and using medicines, a point to which I return later in this chapter.

Yet the fake or counterfeit drug can also be defined more centrally by its relationship to the law – as opposed to its chemical make-up. For example, drugs can be caught within the definition of counterfeit by being in breach of regulations on sales and distribution. This may be because the outlets in which they are sold should not be allowed to sell them; or they are sold without medical prescription when the law requires them to be prescribed; or they may be labelled in ways that are incomplete, in a language other than the official languages of the country, packaged poorly, or stored in inadequate conditions. More problematically, and importantly for my purpose, a drug can be defined as 'counterfeit' because it breaches intellectual property rights (Intellectual Property Watch, 2012). The very reality of drugs in those discourses comes to be defined in relation to a set of rights that, as well as being politically contested by many, are not directly related to their physical constitution, or their relationship with patients' bodies.[2] This is problematic as the use of the law, including the deployment of ill-defined legal terminology in public discourses, is significant in determining the social reality of drugs. Here, the seizing of the notion of fake drugs by those seeking to protect intellectual property rights has come to blur and therefore destabilize the medical, and common-sense, definition

---

1 For example, both the US Food and Drug Administration and the Medicine and Healthcare Products Regulatory Agency have detailed information and updates on fake and dangerous medicines known to be in circulation. See: www.fda.gov/Drugs/ ResourcesForYou/Consumers/BuyingUsingMedicineSafely/CounterfeitMedicine/ default.htm and www.mhra.gov.uk/Safetyinformation/Generalsafetyinformationan dadvice/Adviceandinformationforconsumers/counterfeitmedicinesanddevices/Falsi fiedmedicines/index.htm.

2 For a problematization of 'generics', 'copies' and the licit/illicit divide in a different context, see Hayden (2011).

of a 'fake' drug. This phenomenon is reminiscent of the seizing of the notion of 'piracy', in the years preceding TRIPS, to capture the activities of the legal and legitimate generic industry in countries like India that did not protect pharmaceutical product patents – entirely legally at the time.

In addition to these broadly defined current meanings of the word, counterfeiting has encompassed further practices and products over the years: in the early days of the generic industry, substitution by pharmacists of a generic when a brand name had been prescribed was, for example, considered as 'counterfeiting' (Greene, 2011). The uncertainty and political loading of the term is therefore not peculiar to contemporary discourses. It is interesting that a term that is so strongly connected to, and generated in or by, legal documents has come to be defined in such an uncertain, though not unique, way. One problematic consequence of this is that the notion of counterfeit medicines has come to be entangled in at least two very different types of actions (that could arguably be defined, in the sub-Saharan context at least, as having diametrically opposite interests at heart) – actions to protect patients' health and bodies, on the one hand, and, on the other, campaigns to protect intellectual property rights and a section of the pharmaceutical industry. In response to this, new categorizations and labels have progressively been developed, such as the terms 'falsified medicines' or 'low-quality drugs' to focus specifically on the public health issues at play, but they have not yet dented the generalized use of the term counterfeit in most public discourses to refer to medicines that do not comply with intellectual property rights.[3]

The significance of the term counterfeit and its relationship to law are complex. Although the word immediately appeals to a certain sense of the law, through its engagement of the 'illegal', the concept of counterfeit medicines is a strangely ill-defined category and, even in formal settings, the term is used in shifting ways. Here, the collusion of different socio-technical realities under a loosely used label has some problematic consequences for the management of public health – a problem that several NGOs have started to voice (e.g. Oxfam, 2011). For many, the problem is one of the pharmaceutical industry, and those seeking to protect its intellectual property rights, using this uncertainty to mobilize further control of the pharmaceutical trade and exploiting the well-founded fear of substandard medicines to mobilize further resources in the fight for intellectual property rights (Anderson, 2009; Médecins Sans Frontières, 2009; Oxfam, 2011; Health Poverty Action, 2012). Specific initiatives, such as the Anti-Counterfeiting Trade Agreement (ACTA) have been attacked for contributing to this problem (McManis and Pelletier, 2011; Rens, 2011; Liberman, 2012).

---

3 See Pfizer in the *New York Times*: www.nytimes.com/2012/11/29/opinion/counterfeit-medicines.html?_r=0.

However, it is useful to look beyond, and unpack, this proactive role, and observe in more detail how the effacement of technicalities in the context of counterfeit medicines translates in the day-to-day lives of those who experience law from its edge and, in turn, how it impacts on the position occupied by legitimate, generic medicines. In these movements, unsettled realities of what are the real/fake, good/bad medicines are performed, blurring the boundaries between public and private interests. I now turn to reflecting further on how deep-running this issue of uncertainty and instability is, by looking at how uncertain legal labelling translates into an uncertain ontology of the 'real' or 'good' drug in the context of Ghana and in turn comes to confuse and destabilize the social existence and deployment of medicines, especially medicines that are produced outside of a particular Western context.

Translating 'fake' drugs in Ghana

In this section, I turn to how the ambivalent legal definition of the 'fake' medicine translates into an uncertain definition of the 'fake' drug in the practice of public health actors in Ghana. I explore how, in turn, this uncertainty surrounding the fake medicine comes to challenge the stability of generic medicines whose legality is not at issue, by associating brands, and certain localities, with a sense of safety. Throughout, the lack of a clear, technical legal definition of the real/fake divide comes to blur categories of medicines and challenge the social positioning of legal replicates, creating policy difficulties as well as theoretical questions.

For health professionals, fake medicines are first and foremost low-quality drugs, described by policy-makers mostly in terms of their chemical make-up:

> a lot of these cheap medicines have no active ingredients … In terms of medicines, some don't have any active ingredients. But also some have lower levels of active ingredients. (public health policy-maker)

Health professionals, in turn, tended to define these drugs in relation to their impact (or lack of impact) on patients' bodies:

> Sometimes they are really really sick and you are giving them a drug that may be really half strength of what it's supposed to be. Basically, you are under-dosing them. They aren't getting enough of the drug. They aren't getting enough of the treatment and also you are building up resistance to these sicknesses. (medical doctor)

The causes and dynamics behind the proliferation of low-quality medicines in Ghana – arising from a mix of underlying poverty, difficulty in overseeing trade for an under-resourced government, and porous borders, among other factors – are multiple and highly complex and the purpose of this chapter is not to provide a detailed review of these (Cloatre, 2013). Instead, it interrogates more specifically the impact of this trade, and of the blurry discourses that surround definitions of counterfeit, on the constitution of the real/fake medicines divide, through law and in spite of law.

The divide between real and fake drugs is partly constituted, and made visible, through the practices of avoidance that surround particular drugs, and through the processes of selection. Those deemed to be fake drugs are avoided, eliminated, or targeted through two predominant techniques. First, the government of Ghana deploys, to the best of its material capabilities, systems of checks and surveillance to identify, test and seize low-standard medicines. Campaigns of information for patients and health professionals have also been deployed to try to encourage them to avoid counterfeits. Some of these actions are interlinked with global actions, and Interpol is also instrumental in some of the activities of the Ghanaian government in this field. The aim is to identify drugs that are not of the nature or quality that they claim to be. However, once again, the shifts in the notion of what constitutes this nature itself, and in turn what is a fake medicine, are visible in some of these global campaigns. So, for example, the Interpol website shifts between notions of risk, fake medicines and counterfeits, without clearly locating how breaches of intellectual property fit with its broader activities.[4] Second, alongside these governmental actions, patients and health professionals deploy their own strategies to avoid fake medicines. Through their practices, the co-constitution of real and fake, good and bad medicines illustrates how uncertain legalities translate into uncertain sociality of certain types of medicines. In other words, the constant shifts in defining the label of counterfeit/fake in legal documents, and in discourses that surround them, impact on how particular medicines – licit or illicit – are constructed.

At the core of these shifts is the constant blurring of boundaries between issues of brand and intellectual property, on the one hand, and of safety and medicinal standard, on the other. As the label of counterfeit has come to encompass both low-quality medicines and medicines that are in breach of regulatory regimes (such as intellectual property) that do not directly reflect on their safety, practitioners of medicine have come to associate safety with visible signs that are reflective of and, arguably, exclusively of intellectual property. In turn, this results in the frequent exclusion of good

---

4 www.interpol.int/Crime-areas/Pharmaceutical-crime/Pharmaceutical-crime

quality generic medicines from the day-to-day lives of patients. In other words, uncertainty in legal technicalities has resulted in a fragility of use of a wide range of medicines, some of which do not formally fall under any of the shifting legal definitions. At the same time, as the boundaries between fake and real, and between licit and illicit, have been rendered unclear, the boundary between 'unsafe copy' and 'valid generic' has become uncertain in the beliefs and the practices of those involved in their use. This effect goes against much of the efforts that access to medicines campaigns have been deploying over the years. At the same time, it raises questions in relation to the way in which legal instability participates in the fragility of particular medicinal devices. In the absence of legal 'technicalities', other factors, such as names, aspects and place, come to condition what is constituted as a real or fake medicine.

Patients' mistrust of generic medicines has been documented in a vast range of contexts, and earlier studies have demonstrated how establishing the bioequivalence of branded and generic medicines was itself become entangled in complex socio-political issues, themselves significantly shaped by the strategies of brand-name manufacturers (Carpenter and Tobbell, 2011). In Ghana, where substandard medicines are a serious everyday concern for policy-makers, health professionals and patients alike, explicit links between fake medicines and generic medicines were commonly drawn:

> Generics, I think it started in 97 and then it gained ground in 2000 … I think it was then that counterfeit started coming up more. People felt the counterfeits more with generics. (private pharmacist)

The ambiguity expressed by this participant potentially alludes to two related issues: the easier spread of counterfeit medicines in more diversified markets; and an increased feeling of exposure to the fake in the face of the emergence of new, less well-known medicines. Both elements are relevant where the government has deployed vast efforts to increase the distribution of generic medicines in its healthcare system, but yet failed to see their use become generalized, both in public hospitals and the private sector (Ghana Ministry of Health, 2007).

The shifts between notions of fakes and the concept of generics are also central to the question of the reality of the copy – copies being 'real' and occupying an ambiguous place in the history of intellectual property (Pottage, 2014). Notably, these shifts are widespread in the discourses of health professionals, as this conversation with a doctor illustrates. I was trying to find out how doctors identified low-quality or fake medicines. Soon enough, the discussion became one in which the notion of 'low quality' was assimilated into that of 'generics':

Respondent: ... Sometimes you get very good results with a particular antibiotic, brand of antibiotics in a way that you don't get normally if you just ask them to get a generic.

Interviewer: That's interesting. They are supposed to be the same ... if they are good quality generics, they are supposed to be the same, aren't they?

Respondent: They are supposed to be the same, but sometimes you don't. Maybe also it's erm, maybe it's out of habit. Maybe it makes doctors feel comfortable with a particular drug ... maybe there is a bias in that ... But it's not only about having a bias. I think some of these biases are based on real experience that happen on the ground ... It's the same base drug but just by a different company, different brand and you get good results.

The suggestion that responses to particular drugs can vary, even when they are meant to be faithful replicates, is not exceptional, and indeed this is entangled in a long history of contestation dating back to the emergence of the first non-proprietary drug names (Carpenter and Tobbell, 2011). What is visible, however, in this excerpt of conversation is the uncertainty with which a particular doctor seemed to engage the links between brand and reliability – reflecting back on what may make them trust one drug rather than another.

There are several reasons for the difficulties that generic medicines have in becoming 'normalized', in Ghana and elsewhere. Blurry discourses on fake medicines and fears of counterfeits are by no means the only reasons for their difficulties. Rather, they play a part in othering (or 'excluding') generic drugs. Because of the legitimate anxieties that have developed around low-quality medicines in Ghana, patients and health professionals have developed extensive strategies to try to avoid fake medicines. Often, however, the 'other' of fake medicines seems to have become the branded medicine. Here, the visible signs of intellectual property have come to constitute what is perceived as a reliable drug – even though the faking of these very signs is at the core of what is denounced elsewhere in the fight against counterfeit (that is, fake branded medicines are known to be produced and sold, and brands are therefore not an absolute guarantee of safe origin). Greene (2011) has explored the importance of the brand in generating trust in medicines, and how generics have progressively become recognized as valuable since the 1970s, as the meaning of brand progressively shifted away from being a unique guarantee of safety. In Ghana, it is fair to say that brands continued to form a primordial part of what constitutes a real drug, in the face of the ill-defined counterfeit.

In attempting to break down further some of the ways into which brands become associated with safety, and different regimes come to collide in building trust, a myriad of issues emerge, including those related to space, history and localities in the constitution of valid medicines. The following comment by a doctor illustrates well some of these issues:

> In some cases, you just don't want to take any chances with any-thing generic, especially in the very young kids. I don't want to take any chances with something I'm not familiar with ... One was made by this five star company ... I have seen it work ... I have seen the research and it's been proven. I want to use some-thing good, proven to be good. No offence to those who haven't proven their products. I just don't want to take any chances. With the more expensive popular brand names, you know that there has been some research done. They are more convincing. The generic things kind of come out of nowhere, no offence. I don't really know too much about them. Probably haven't seen a presentation or read a paper about some research that was done on them. They have put out this legal document that says, my drug contains this and this and this. If it's made in some village in Kumasi it is still the drug. If that's what the patient go for then, cool. You pray that it's not chocolate inside the medication ...

The history of generic medicines demonstrates how brands gained their significance through the meaning associated with a particular form of industry. Indeed, the research-based pharmaceutical industry has long defended the importance of brand in guaranteeing that a drug is made to certain standards – something to which many have objected over the years (Greene, 2011). In Ghana, in response to significant fears of low-quality drugs, the importance of spaces of production re-emerged. This plays at two levels. First, 'real' drugs are produced by a certain type of industry – research-based industries have developed strategies to provide expertise; they build trust in particular products and processes, including regulatory processes: 'companies are producers not only of pills but also knowledge about their safety and efficacy, and their gifts to doctors of travel to confer-ences and workshops provide access to the latest expertise' (Lakoff, 2005, p. 140). As explained by one of my informants:

> [Most of my seniors] are familiar with the pharmaceutical reps and have even been on some seminars and stuff, organised by these pharmaceutical companies. Even if I don't have first hand experience with that drug I can always ask them, what do you recommend?
>
> (medical doctor)

Second, this industry has a geographical base that is judged trustworthy. This is heavily entangled in historical and postcolonial relationships which impact on the positioning of different places and firms. In Ghana, where generics are sold and used, distinct markets exist for 'UK generics', and for cheaper and less trusted 'Indian generics'. Patients who can afford them will tend to choose generic medicines produced in the UK, and pharmacists have in turn adapted their own sources of imports to the demands of their particular clientele, and to their own perceptions of what are the 'better', 'safer' or more 'trustworthy' medicines. Generics produced in India, while remaining more affordable than their UK competitors, have, in turn, seen their share of the market diminish as they became increasingly perceived as less reliable than pricier alternatives. An ill-defined notion of realness and fakeness plays a key role in shaping perceptions of places of production.

Overall, the enrolment of cheaper generic medicines in Ghana is threatened by the joint workings of innovator brands on the one hand and low-quality counterfeits on the other, together with the various practices, routines and habits that are associated with each. The need to turn to, and rely on, links with the pharmaceutical industry is increased and aggravated by the growing fear of fake and dangerous medicines that are, in legal discourses, conflated under the same label as ill-branded medication. As low-quality drugs are an undeniable reality on the Ghanaian markets, one of the key priorities is to learn how to identify the differences between different types of fakes and the different networks to which they relate. It is also crucial to ensure that good quality generic medicines remain clearly distinct in public understandings from drugs that patients and health professionals are encouraged to avoid. Any confusion and overlap in this area aggravates both problems of access and the problem of low-quality medicines itself, since the latter is fuelled by the former.

Those with a deeper understanding of the different functions of intellectual property and other forms of pharmaceutical regulations in Ghana were aware of some of the difficulties that occur as a result of this repeated lack of clarity and the assimilations it produces. They were, in turn, critical of the stance taken by the international community in acknowledging and responding to this problem and of the lack of attention to the power of definitions:

> The WHO is trying to harmonise the rules for pharmaceuticals and counterfeiting. But I tell them, it is not all about counterfeits. And some people also refer to generics as counterfeits, and this is wrong. I tell them that is about definition. (intellectual property policy-maker)

Two concerns emerge from this. One is an issue of how various sets of pressures come to produce particular sets of 'powerful' and 'disempowered' objects. The second is the fear that new regulations result in stabilizing further the extension of ideas of fakeness that receive support because of public health concerns to products that only breach intellectual property rules. This latter concern was illustrated by the examples of Uganda and Kenya, two countries that have recently adopted laws relevant to counterfeit medicines, in further conversations with local experts (Anderson, 2009). In both cases, the law, although responding primarily to public health concerns from local actors, has become drafted with the effect of reinforcing the fight against products that breach intellectual property rules. Policy experts in Ghana have been very resistant to this model, emphasizing instead the problems with a system in which the object of the law itself remains so indeterminate, or contested. Indeed, the practice of counterfeits, from global politics to local practices and to its re-enactment in new laws, is unclear about either the nature of the problem, the definition of counterfeits as objects, or the nature of the boundary between real and fake, illegitimate and legitimate, medicines.

Conclusion

The definition of a counterfeit medicine is uncertain and blurry and has, over the years, come to encompass different categories of products in different sets of laws and different discourses. The uncertainty of this label is both generated by its conflicting legal definitions and by the seizing of this term (with legal origins and connotations) in discourses for which the letter of the law does not really matter – extending, hence, further the fluidity of this term. In this chapter, I chose to discuss this as an issue of (un)technicality, in response to the recent contributions of the work of Annelise Riles and other scholars interested in technicalities. The research example in this chapter sought to follow how law matters when it occupies a less certain space than may be expected. Generic medicines are essential tools of public health policies. They have also, historically, been fragile and uncertain objects, contested in particular by research-based industries which denied their reliability, stability and effects. As their position has progressively become strengthened in many national contexts, they remain fragile in those where they are possibly most needed – including sub-Saharan Africa. I have argued that this fragile position is aggravated by fears of fake medicines, and by the lack of effort of policy-makers to relocate the role of brands clearly, and the limits of its relevance, to defining the real/fake boundary for medicines. Uncertainties and shifts in the legal domains that notions of counterfeiting appeal to have come to blur distinctions between policy programmes and interests, merging concerns over intellectual property and concerns over risks in ways that in turn complicate, and become entangled with, the everyday practice of medicine and the constitution of real/fake medicines.

'Big pharma' has played a determinant role in those movements and, indeed, its involvement in the campaigns against counterfeit medicines often does little to clarify how important it is not to assimilate different types of counterfeits, or to assimilate legitimate generics with fake medicines. However, the processes at play are also more complex than this. They are deeply rooted in the ambivalence of law-makers at various policy levels on the nature of the drugs that are being targeted and of the types of networks to which they belong. As a result, well-intentioned campaigns aimed at targeting dangerous products may simply not yet have done enough to engage with the impact that these campaigns have on the trade in valid generics. In addition to this, some of the most deep-rooted relationships between doctors and patients and branded medicines are rooted in subtle sets of habits and routine that are not only or directly the result of intense lobbying by the industry. The definition of 'good' and 'bad' drugs is therefore the result of a tight set of movements, beliefs, relationships and language. The law and the ways in which legal language is being deployed have a significant impact on those movements while, when unacknowledged or unaddressed, legal language becomes a powerful tool in maintaining positions of power, as held in this case by branded products and, in turn, by a particular type of industry. The example utilized in this chapter is not unique in relation to what it suggests about the social effects of legal misconceptions. Instead, it invites further reflection on how misconceptions and blurriness are messy both in their making and in their practical effects. One of the effects of an (un)technical legal label becomes its ability to destabilize particular objects and policies, while opening possibilities to maintain the dominance of others that are associated with particular sites of knowledge, and particular localities.

References

Almond, P (2009) 'The Dangers of Hanging Baskets: "Regulatory myths" and Media Representations of Health and Safety Regulation' 36(3) *Journal of Law and Society* 352–75

Anderson, T (2009) 'Confusion over Counterfeit Drugs in Uganda' 373 *The Lancet* 9681, pp. 2097–8

Bunker, A (2007) 'Counterfeit Pharmaceuticals, Intellectual Property and Human Health' 89 *Journal of the Patent and Trademark Office* 493

Callon, M (1986) 'Some Elements of a Sociology of Translation: Domestication of the Scallops and the Fishermen of Saint Brieuc Bay' in J Law (ed.), *Power, Action and Belief: A New Sociology of Knowledge?* Sociological Review Monograph 32 (London: Routledge & Kegan Paul), pp. 196–233

Carpenter, D and D A Tobbell (2011) 'Bioequivalence: The Regulatory Career of a Pharmaceutical Concept' 85 *Bulletin of the History of Medicine* 93–131

Cloatre, E (2013) *Pills for the Poorest: An Exploration of TRIPS and Medicines in Sub-Saharan Africa* (London: Palgrave Macmillan)

Cloatre, E and R Dingwall (2013) '"Embedded Regulation": The Migration of Objects, Scripts and Governance' 7(1) *Regulation and Governance* 365–86

Daniels, S and J Martin (1991) 'Myth and Reality in Punitive Damages' 75(1) *Minnesota Law Review* 1–65

Ghana Ministry of Health (2007) *Study on Low Generic Prescribing in Ghana* http://ghndp.org/images/downloads/Ghana_KABP_on_Generics.pdf

Greene, J A (2011) 'What's in a Name? Generics and the Persistence of the Pharmaceutical Brand in American Medicine' 66(4) *Journal of the History of Medicine and Allied Sciences* 468–506

Hayden, C (2007) 'A Generic Solution? Pharmaceuticals and the Politics of the Similar in Mexico' 48(4) *Current Anthropology* 475–95

Hayden, C (2011) 'No Patent, No Generic: Pharmaceutical Access and the Politics of the Copy', in M Biagioli, J P Aszi and M Woodmansee (eds), *Making and Unmaking Intellectual Property: Creative Production in Legal and Cultural Perspective* (Chicago: University of Chicago Press), pp. 285–304

Health Poverty Action (2012) 'Counterfeit Medicines Briefing' www.healthpovertyaction.org/wp-content/uploads/downloads/2012/07/counterfeitBriefingfinal1.pdf

Holstein, J A and G Miller (eds) (1993) *Reconsidering Social Constructionism: Debates in Social Problems Theory* (New York, Aldine de Gruyter)

Intellectual Property Watch (2012) 'G8 Countries Take Hard Line on Counterfeit Medicines' www.ip-watch.org/2012/05/31/g8-takes-hard-line-on-counterfeit-medicines

Jackson, E (2012) *Law and the Regulation of Medicines* (London: Hart Publishing)

Lakoff, A (2005) *Pharmaceutical Reason: Knowledge and Value in Global Psychiatry* (Cambridge: Cambridge University Press)

Latour, B (1993) *We Have Never Been Modern* (Brighton: Harvester Wheatsheaf)

Latour, B (2005) *Reassembling the Social: An Introduction to Actor-network Theory* (Oxford: Oxford University Press)

Law, J (2008) 'Actor-network Theory and Material Semiotics' in Bryan S Turner (ed.), *The New Blackwell Companion to Social Theory* (Oxford: Blackwell) (3rd edn), pp. 141–58

Lemert, E (1967) *Human Deviance, Social Problems and Social Control* (Englewood Cliffs: Prentice Hall)

Liberman, J (2012) 'Combating Counterfeit Medicines and Illicit Trade in Tobacco Products: Minefields in Global Health Governance' 40(2) *Journal of Law and Medical Ethics* 326–47

Lindesmith, A, A Strauss and N Denzin (1999) *Social Psychology* (Sage: Thousand Oaks)

McManis, C and J Pelletier (2012) 'Two Tales of a Treaty Revisited: The Proposed Anti-Counterfeiting Trade Agreement (ACTA)', Washington University in St Louis Legal Studies Research Paper No 12–04–10

Médecins Sans Frontières (2009) 'Counterfeits, Substandard and Generic Drugs' www.msfaccess.org/content/counterfeit-substandard-and-generic-drugs

Mol, A-M (2003) *The Body Multiple: Ontology in Medical Practice* (Durham: Duke University Press)

Obi-Eyisi, O and A Wertheimer (2012) 'The Background and History of Counterfeit Medicines' in A Werteimer and P Vang (eds), *Counterfeit Medicines: Policy, Economics and Countermeasure* (Lichfield: ILM Publications)

Oliver, A (2007) 'Internet Pharmacies: Regulation of a Growing Industry' 28(1) *Journal of Law, Medicine and Ethics* 98–101

Outterson, K and R Smith (2006) 'The Good, the Bad and the Ugly' 16 *Albany Law Journal of Science and Technology* 525–43

Oxfam (2011) 'Crisis of Poor Quality Medicines Being Used as an Excuse to Push up Prices for Poor' www.oxfam.org/en/pressroom/pressrelease/2011–02–02/crisis-poor-quality-medicines-being-used-excuse-push-prices-poor

Pollock, A (2008) 'Pharmaceutical Meaning-making beyond Marketing: Racialized Subjects of Generic Thiazide' 36(3) *Journal of Law, Medicine and Ethics* 530–6

Pollock, A (2011) 'Transforming the Critique of Big Pharma' 6(1) *BioSocieties* 106–18

Pottage, A (2014) 'Paper Prototypes' in E Cloatre and M Pickersgill (eds), *Knowledge, Technology and Law* (London: Routledge)

Riles, A. (2010) 'Collateral Expertise: Legal Knowledge in the Global Financial Markets' 51(6) *Current Anthropology* 795–818

Riles, A (2011) *Collateral Knowledge: Legal Reasoning in the Global Financial Markets* (Chicago: University of Chicago Press)

Rens, A (2011) 'Collateral Damage: The Impact of ACTA and the Enforcement Agenda on the World's Poorest People' 26(3) *American University International Law Review* 783–809

Silbey, S and P Ewick (1998) *The Common Place of Law: Stories from Everyday Life* (Chicago: University of Chicago Press)

T'Hoen, E (2010) 'The Revised Drug Strategy: Access to Essential Medicines, Intellectual Property and the World Health Organization' in G Krikorian and A Kapczynski (eds), *Access to Knowledge in the Age of Intellectual Property* (New York: Zone Books), pp. 127–41

Thomas, W and D Thomas (1927) *The Child in America: Behaviour Problems and Programs* (New York: Alfred Knopf)

Yar, M (2008) 'The Other Global Drugs Crisis: Assessing the Scope, Impacts and Drivers of the Trade in Dangerous Counterfeit Pharmaceuticals' 1(1) *International Journal of Social Inquiry* 151–66

Other web resources

Medicine and Health Products Regulatory Agency, counterfeit medicines www.mhra.gov.uk/Safetyinformation/Generalsafetyinformationandadvice/Adviceandinformationforconsumers/counterfeitmedicinesanddevices/Falsifiedmedicines/index.htm

US Food and Drug Administration, information for consumers on counterfeit medicines www.fda.gov/Drugs/ResourcesForYou/Consumers/BuyingUsingMedicineSafely/CounterfeitMedicine/default.htm

6

Sex/Gender Equality: Taking a Break from the Legal to Transform the Social

Sharon Cowan

Introduction

This chapter considers the place of law in current political debates about how best to address problems of social justice, with particular reference to sex/gender and sexuality. In examining recent 'moments' of successful law reform around issues of sex/gender and sexuality, I will argue that the contemporary thirst for law as a route to equality does not address deeper, more structural questions of inequality. Accommodation and assimilation of 'others' within the existing legal system will always leave open the question of what social justice could look like were it not understood autopoietically – solely and self-referentially within the confines of existing frameworks of legal rights and responsibilities. What is more, recent moments of sex/gender and sexuality law reform tell us something not only about the gap between law and 'the social' but also about the power of law and legal techniques. In this chapter I will explore what happens when, first, legal tools are used to adapt existing doctrinal approaches to include – co-opt – those who previously have fallen outwith the protection of the law; and second, how such techniques fail to deliver justice, despite the good intentions of those who aim for equality (albeit without the kind of radical rethinking that activists and critical scholars might desire).

In both cases, legal techniques leave intact underlying problematic and embedded binary gendered and heteronormative foundations. While law can permit certain kinds of agency, and produce certain kinds of agents – and for some, in this age of human rights, law may even be the condition for agency and autonomy – the focus on law-as-solution can lead to a kind of methodological blindness that instinctively accepts the centrality of legal techniques in our lives, to the detriment of other strategies. Other ways of knowing and seeing, that resist the lens of law, are possible and necessary for living. It is perhaps trite to say that some resort to law is still required, and that we cannot completely extricate ourselves from 'the legal', but at the very least law must come emblazoned with a health warning if we are to avoid the most common pitfalls associated with legal reform. I am suggesting an epistemological challenge to liberal conceptualizations of the importance of law, but also to those scholars who, in engaging with law, neglect the non-legal and therefore help to scaffold law into the fabric of the social. In this sense I am echoing Paddy Hillyard's plea (2014) that we stop using the law-and-order language of crime and criminality and, instead, think more broadly about social harm; that is, let's stop talking so much about law and legal categories and definitions, and focus more on whether legal concepts and techniques, such as problem-solving, comparison, analogy, drafting and interpretation, produce the kinds transformative effects that critical scholars and activists imagine (for a critique of legal techniques of interpretation, see Ohana, this volume). As Cardwell and Hervey (this volume) have observed, critical analysis of the use of these kinds of legal techniques can flag up 'the ways in which law sustains certain assumptions that support structures of power as "background rules of the game", essentially by hiding them from scrutiny'.

This chapter is divided into two parts: the first dealing with sexual violence; and the second with the issue of same-sex marriage. Given the apparent ubiquity of law in contemporary conversations about sex/gender and sexuality equality, in each section I will examine the contradictions, constraints and chances offered by law's desire to co-opt (but its failure to capture); and argue that the law is inadequate, and arguably powerless, to address deeply engrained social perceptions, stereotypes and injustices.

Harnessing the power of law – part I: legal techniques for addressing sexual violence

In the late 1980s, Mary Jane Mossman (1987) and Ann Scales (1986) provided early warnings against using legal standards, concepts and techniques (such as objectivity, neutrality and relevance) as ends in themselves rather than the means to the end of substantive equality; and the ways in which such standards, concepts and techniques resist structural challenge and are impervious to feminist critique.

In 1989, Carol Smart went further and published a book entitled *Feminism and the Power of Law*. I was a law undergraduate at the time, and hating every minute of it. When I finally reached third year in 1990 and realized that I could study subjects that were of actual interest to me, and of relevance to the world that I saw around me through 20-year-old idealistic eyes, I began to read books, whole books, about law, and found that I actually enjoyed some of them. *Feminism and the Power of Law* was one of the first of those books. It was a refreshing and provocative analysis of the disciplinary effects of law, and powerful in its exhortation that feminists should resist the 'siren call of law' – urging us to draw back from the ever-present dangers of relying on law as our sole or main vehicle to sex/gender equality. At the same time, though, Smart reminded us that law is not all-powerful, and is not the master narrative that determines the fate of its subjects in a universal or totalizing fashion. The significance and impact of this book has reverberated through time, culminating in a 2012 special edition of *Feminist Legal Studies*, devoted to articles that revisit the central claims of the book and their relevance both to contemporary feminist scholarship and to the operation of law in the real world.

As others have made clear, Smart did not argue that social justice can never be achieved through law (Barker, 2013, p. 172), only that caution should be exercised; law is 'a site of conflict and dispute and not a place of refuge or resolution' (Smart, 2012, p. 164). As such, we should never turn to law as our first resort, and feminists engaging with law must be prepared for as many gains as losses when turning to law as a tool for social change. Moreover, feminists should decentre law and look more optimistically to other sources of political sustenance and tools for change, including community-based grass-roots political work and academic scholarship.

Reflecting on the book more than 20 years later, Carol Smart has recently written of the chapter on rape in *Feminism and the Power of Law*:

> Although I would undoubtedly write that chapter differently now I certainly stand by its main argument that 'normal' rape cannot be comprehended by the criminal justice system and by juries. Every time I take note of the abysmally low conviction rates for crimes of rape in the UK I feel sorry that I was roughly right in my analysis about law's inability (unwillingness even) to understand the issues. Douglas is, of course, right to point out that in going to law women who experience domestic violence may also find real help from trained advocates and feminist support groups, but the legal process itself remains damaging and largely futile. Given this unchanging situation I still feel that it is worth considering cutting out the legal 'middle man' and just going straight to the feminist support networks. (2012, p. 162)

And yet many feminists, among others, still seem to be stuck in a way of thinking about the possibility of realizing equality (indeed, of conceptualizing equality) which relies centrally on legal techniques such as reinterpreting precedent,[1] applying existing rights and legal protections against discrimination and violence, and using tools of comparison and analogy to extend those protections to otherwise excluded individuals and groups (for the problems of reasoning by analogy, see also Carr, this volume). Turning to law as a first resort may for some be inevitable, at least to some degree; as Mary Eaton argued many years ago, law has been an effective tool for many of those who have been historically marginalized and subjected to violence, harassment and discrimination. For some then, the question is not *whether* we should engage with law, but rather, *how* (Eaton, 1994, p. 172).

The area of sexual violence is one place where law has been trusted to make changes that will improve the lives of those subjected to such violence. Many gains, both symbolic and practical, have been made in this area. In England and Wales, for example, wife rape is now a criminal offence, and by way of the 2003 Sexual Offences Act, the definition of the act of rape has been expanded to recognize the harm of non-consensual penile penetration not only of the vagina but also the mouth and anus. New and specific criminal offences have also been introduced to sanction non-penile penetration of the anus and vagina, as well as offences of trafficking for sexual purposes, offences of 'sex tourism' and offences involving an abuse of a position of trust, among others. The legislation has been subject to criticism for many reasons, not least the convoluted provisions on consent and the way in which it treats young people who have consensual sexual interaction (see, for example, Spencer, 2004; Cowan, 2007; McGlynn, 2010). These arguments aside, we might ask: is it the case that these legislative reforms have made a significant impact on the incidence of sexual violence, the willingness of women to report rape, the conviction rate,[2] or the way in which victims of sexual violence are treated by the criminal justice system? For McGlynn and Munro, the answer is no:

> Reforming rape law feels like a Sisyphean task with constant pressure leading to reforms only to have such 'successes' neutralized in practice; the boulder falling back down the mountain. (2010, p. 150)

There is no doubt that many hundreds of hours of hard graft went into the process of consultation leading up to the 2003 Act in England and Wales,

---

1 See, for example, the burgeoning 'Feminist Judgements' projects in Canada, the UK, Australia and Ireland, to name a few.

2 Wendy Larcombe (2011) has argued that aiming to increase the conviction rate for rape is not in itself a valid feminist law reform goal and that, rather, the goal should be to have rape complaints dealt with as 'occasions of respect'.

the precision with which the lawyers and drafters attempted to draw up the new provisions, and the final articulation of a commitment to principles of gender equality and sexual autonomy. But the intrinsic unevenness and unpredictability of law means, for critics like McGlynn and Munro, that any legislative gains are tainted with the constant risk of being undermined or thwarted in practice. And in the last three decades we have seen countless recursive attempts to further refine central concepts of rape law, such as consent and capacity, and many internationally comparative conversations about what is the best approach to defining rape (see, for example, McGlynn and Munro, 2010; Westmarland and Gangoli, 2011). Should we keep the offence of rape or move to sexual assault as the Canadians have done? Should the *actus reus* of rape include oral penetration as it does in England and Wales? Should women be included as potential perpetrators of rape, as they are in Finland? (And this is not even to approach the question of the evidential processes that accompany the substantive law.)

Answering these questions usually follows a pattern of campaigning (usually by feminists), followed by a Law Commission or government consultation exercise (but usually no empirical research), followed by a 'Report', followed by a draft Bill, followed by a shiny new piece of legislation. My representation of this process smooths over many bumps on the way to a final Act. But the point is that these techniques of fine-tuning and perfecting legal provisions – the drafting and redrafting – to ensure the correct language seem to imply that there is magic formula which, if only we can find it, will solve the 'rape problem'. These Herculean efforts do not, however, appear to have made much impact with respect to the incidence, prosecution and conviction of rape, calling into question both the appropriateness of this kind of process for reviewing important issues of social policy and social justice, and the notion that law can be successful as purely instrumental, as a means to an end, and part of a 'modern mass of interrelated parts that is the tool of social and economic engineering' (Riles, 2005, p. 1002).

While Annalise Riles argues that what makes the law 'hopeful' and full of potential is its 'as-if' quality, sheer optimism about the possibility of a positive outcome from legal reform is not a good enough end in itself when measured against low prosecution and conviction rates and the perpetuation of gendered stereotypes about responsibility and blame in rape cases (Ellison and Munro, 2009a; 2009b). Likewise, Gotell (2007) has highlighted the erosion of feminist-inspired law reforms, which were underpinned by a recognition of gender violence as a product of systemic relations of race, class and gender, and the 'disappearance' of sexual violence in Canada, due to a form of neoliberal governance that over-individualizes responsibility for sexual assault.

One critique then of the feminist engagement with law is that feminists risk disappointment, frustration and exhaustion by over-investing in law reform that promises much but delivers little, with considerable pomp and symbolic ceremony. Helen Reece has recently suggested that this is in part due to law's (unsuccessful) attempt to circumvent the impact of the vagaries of public opinion on the law, and that, recalling the work of Sutherland and Cressey, 'the law is only necessary because of the attitudes but because of the attitudes the law will not work' (Reece, 2013, p. 452). Law's techniques are themselves insufficient to take on the power of dominant, social sex/gender discourses and scripts. What is more, addressing the problem of rape via the criminal justice system is overly 'reactive' and only allows for engagement at a responsive, rather than at a pre-emptive, preventative level (Gotell, 2007, p. 221).

Another similarly robust critique is that in wholly engaging with the law in this way, feminists also risk their campaigns being co-opted by the state in a law-and-order approach that too easily over-criminalizes (Snider, 1990; Daly, 2002). Think of the debates over the appropriate type of criminal intervention in domestic violence. Some propose a mandatory arrest policy, so that criminal justice agencies are encouraged to take the offence seriously, and victims are protected from the perpetrator inflicting further violence as punishment for having chosen to press charges. On the other hand, others have argued that inflexible arrest policies are often over-inclusive in their application and can disproportionately target racialized poor women (and men) (Snider, 1998). The point here is that, when feminists harness themselves to the unruly strategy of law reform, they may – advertently or inadvertently – find themselves signing up to a punitive, over-expansive criminal justice system (Brown, 1995).

Lise Gotell has recently argued that it is over-simplistic to cast feminism as entirely and unquestioningly invested in law as a response to social harms such as sexual violence (2013). Canadian feminists in the 1990s, for example, did not solely resort to the criminal law; rather, they used the opportunity of consultation to call also for education and financial support for frontline activism. In other words, feminists seeking change with respect to rape did not *only* turn to law, at least in part because they recognize the ways in which rape law constructs and constrains female sexuality. Taking on the claims of Janet Halley and others, that 'governance' feminism has aligned itself with the aims of a carceral state such as to produce a kind of 'carceral feminism', Gotell suggests that we have forgotten Smart's important reminder that the power of law is uneven, and therefore any feminist influence on law reform does not necessarily equate with untrammelled punitiveness or criminalization, since the effect of law is always patchy. Halley and others (such as Reece) are too totalizing, she argues, in their discussion of the retributive drive of feminism and in portraying feminism as unified in its response to violence against women.

This is undoubtedly true – feminisms and feminists suggest many and various ways of dealing with problems of social harm. Gotell herself acknowledges, however, that many feminists have been too quick to dismiss less mainstream criminal justice responses to sexual violence, such as restorative justice, and that more care should be taken to ensure that a wide range of possible responses is kept in mind, even for the most difficult kinds of cases of social harm such as rape.[3] We have to think in a more open and complicated way, Gotell says, about how and whether a punitive response is appropriate. And while there are community justice projects that eschew the use of the criminal justice system entirely, Gotell reminds us that we cannot avoid law completely or the consequence will be a reprivatization and silencing of violence. And, as Hudson reminded us many years ago, while certain crimes such as property offences have been over-penalized and over-criminalized, sexual violence has been over-tolerated (Hudson, 1998, p. 245). Perhaps the trick, then, is to be alive to the possibility of *co-option* while resisting *capture*: that we must be tentative in accessing the power and authority of law and not lose sight of feminist values, such as empathy, compassion, respect and the relational, and feminist aims, such as promoting human flourishing, ending cycles of violence, and critiquing the unequal impact of state power upon already marginalized individuals. This broader focus is arguably equally as important as catching and convicting sex offenders.

And while feminists wishing to change what has been called a 'rape culture' have long recognized the need for social interventions other than law reform, such as education, the social world has a lot of catching up to do, particularly with respect to how rape and sexual violence are *seen*. Munro and Ellison's research with mock juries shows that presumptions and stereotypes about women's personal and sexual responsibility still drive their intuitions, and their verdicts, about whether or not sexual violence has taken place; they cannot *see* rape, regardless of how it is technically defined, unless it contradicts their socio-sexual expectations about what constitutes 'normal' heterosexual sex. It is not new to say that law alone cannot shift social preconceptions and attitudes; Temkin and Krahé's research with members of the legal profession, as well as the general public, found that people tend to rely on their preconceived stereotypical intuitions about gender-appropriate behaviour which lowers their propensity to

---

3 On the possibility of using restorative justice in sexual violence cases, see Daly (2002); for domestic violence, post-conviction, see Miller and Iovanni (2013).

blame and convict defendants and increases their inclination to blame the complainant (2008). These prevailing attitudes make it extremely difficult for a defendant to be brought to, and convicted at, trial, regardless of how well crafted the substantive law is.

Riles has suggested, referring to Latour, that 'when controversies flare up the literature becomes technical' (2005, p. 1008, fn. 109). Law-makers and lawyers – technocrats and engineers – are driven to define and refine, to precisely draft the wrong of sexual violence; in spite of this, great difficulty persists in achieving clarity in legal rules, with respect to language and scope, such that victims' grounded experiences of the harm of sexual violence might be acknowledged (Du Toit, 2007). Legal techniques are also ill-equipped to combat perceptions about sexual violence or to impact upon the rate of sexual violence occurring in the 'real world'. Nonetheless, many feminists continue to place too much faith in law reform as their champion in the fight against sexual violence.

Harnessing the power of law – part II: reforming sex/gender equality rights and equal marriage

The reliance on rights claims arguably had its fullest and most recent sex/gender manifestation in campaigns in the UK and USA (among other jurisdictions) for same-sex[4] marriage. Feminists and LGBT activists have long challenged the state's power to exclude certain individuals from marriage, particularly on the basis of sex/gender or sexuality. In the USA, these battles were fought most publicly in a series of cases in California, leading to the Supreme Court decision of *Hollingsworth v Perry* (570 US ____ (2013)), which in effect allowed same-sex marriage in California (but not elsewhere in the USA).

Not only did these cases illustrate the power of the court, rooted in its interpretation of the US Constitution, to confer rights, but also the power of law, or more precisely legal reform, to capture the public imagination and energy in powerful and productive ways. As a visitor to the University of California at Berkeley when the decisions came down, I had the opportunity to witness a community-wide sense of joy and celebration that was pervasive and deeply felt. Followed by the San Francisco Pride march but a week later, the decision led to a sense that the whole of California was revelling in the right to marry. The UK's Westminster Parliament has also now passed a law allowing same-sex marriage in England and Wales (though the

---

4 The terms same-sex and opposite-sex marriage imply there are only two sexes/genders. My work is committed to challenging this heteronormative binary framework, but the terms same-sex and opposite-sex are used in this chapter since this is the terminology used in political and legal debates on marriage equality.

extent of the celebrations does not bear comparison).[5] In both jurisdictions this has been cast as a victory for activists and advocates of equal rights, at least in terms of a formal equality approach. Perhaps it is a victory of sorts, and perhaps it is the sort of victory that could only have been achieved through legal reforms. So what could Carol Smart possibly object to in this tale of progressive law-making? As far back as 1984, Smart challenged marriage as legally and ideologically problematic because it is enshrined within gendered structural inequalities. Would advances in the social and legal treatment of marriage since 1984, most recently the embracing of same-sex couples within its fold, assuage her concerns?

Perhaps unsurprisingly, feminists have continued to be critical of marriage, even in its same-sex form. Boyd and Young (2006, p. 219) have argued, with respect to same-sex marriage in Canada (legal since 2005), that:

> [S]truggles to achieve legal recognition of same-sex relationships may require a normalisation of lesbian and gay intimate relationships to appear as marriage-like as possible, in turn leaving intact the hierarchies that are ideologically embedded within marriage ... the invocation of the equality rights section of the Canadian Charter has exacerbated this trend, requiring that litigants demonstrate that they have been discriminated against on the basis of sexual orientation. As a result, litigants must compare themselves to others in a relevant category, in a way that tends to suppress differences and emphasise similarities.

Other exclusions also operate in the debate over same-sex marriage. Legal 'engineers' and other proponents of same-sex marriage used techniques of comparison between same-sex marriage and anti-miscegenation laws; as Lenon (2005) has argued, in doing so, such analogies disaggregate race and sexuality in a way that implies they are mutually exclusive, assumes the 'whiteness' of the same-sex couple, and is thus othering of the non-white LGBT person. Again we see that legal techniques such as comparison, analogy and interpretation may be used to argue for the extension of legal protections, but in a way that often excludes already marginalized individuals and communities and obscures the fundamental issues at play (see also Carr, this volume). Marriage becomes a metaphorical and material

---

5 Scotland followed suit in 2014, though its Marriage and Civil Partnerships (Scotland) Act 2014 is more progressive in that it does not allow a spousal veto for transgender people wishing to apply for a GRC (see www.gaystarnews .com/article/why-trans-people-have-won-major-victory-scotland-gay-marriage-fight191213). Of course, other jurisdictions have allowed same-sex marriage well in advance of these 'ground-breaking' cases: Canada in 2005, Belgium in 2003 and the Netherlands in 2001.

container for potentially risky, deviant or 'other' sexualities – but only those that can be said to most closely resemble, and be recognized as, the (unraced, able-bodied) heteronormative ideal.

Across the pond, in England and Wales, it might be said that the new law is a mess, and that it fails even on its own terms to remedy the problem it explicitly sets out to address – that of equality for same-sex couples who want to get married. The law does not promote equality even on the formal basis that it promises because of four main subsisting problems. First, same-sex couples cannot get married in a place of religious worship unless the 'relevant governing body' of that religious organization consents to same-sex marriages taking place there. Given that the Church of England is still divided on this point, and that under s. 2(2) of the new Act no person working for that religious organization can be forced to conduct a marriage ceremony (in contrast to civil registrars who cannot opt out of conducting same-sex marriages), this does not put same-sex couples on an even footing with heterosexual couples. Second, there are some differences with respect to pension rights, in that companies can opt out of granting benefits accrued before 2005 to a surviving same-sex spouse, but not to a surviving heterosexual spouse – apparently on the grounds of cost to private-sector companies.

Thirdly, there is tension between the new marriage provisions and the provisions of the Gender Recognition Act (2004) (GRA). Before the new Act, because same-sex marriage was not possible, a trans person who had been legally married to someone of the sex 'opposite' to their own 'birth' sex (or more accurately, sex attributed to them at birth) would only be granted a gender recognition certificate (GRC), acknowledging their 'acquired' gender,[6] if they annulled their existing marriage – even where both people wanted the marriage to continue. In other words, either their gender identity or their marriage could be recognized by the state, but not both. Critics have pointed out the injustice of this (see, for example, Cowan et al., 2009). Since same-sex couples can now get married, one might be forgiven for thinking that an existing marriage would prove no impediment to state recognition of an 'acquired' gender identity. However, the GRC can only be granted if the trans person's spouse agrees, in writing, that they are happy to remain in the marriage. If they do not, only an interim certificate can be granted (for six months) until the marriage is dissolved. In other words, the spouse has the power to veto (at least temporarily) the granting of a GRC. As Barlow and Mason point out, while this preserves the autonomy of the cisgender spouse to decide whom they want to be married to, cisgender people make all sorts of major changes to their lives without having to

---

6 For a critique of the language used in the GRC, see Cowan et al. (2009).

gain the consent of the person they are married to: 'No consent is required to move abroad or financially destabilize the family or apply for medical treatment' (2013, p. 16).

Now it might be argued that the gender of one's partner is so profoundly important that individuals are perfectly entitled to end a relationship if their partner undertakes gender transition, and as such the new law does not result in injustice for trans people. It seems from the criminal justice context that the gender of a sexual partner has been taken to be so fundamental that lying about it before engaging in sex can lead to a sexual assault charge on the basis of fraud (see Sharpe, 2013). But this is an extremely complex issue. If someone is in an otherwise functional and satisfying relationship or marriage, why should a 'mistake' about their partner's gender identity undermine either consent to sex, or the ongoing status of the relationship itself? It is because gender – and thereby sexuality – is considered by many to be at the core of who we are and whom we are attracted to, to the extent that it is difficult to put it aside and focus on the other aspects of a person, perhaps particularly when a transition in gender identity or expression takes place. This calls to mind Friedson's (2013) argument that we are conditioned to filter out sex samenesses and concentrate only on sex differences; in the present context, sex difference becomes primary as the essence of attraction, identity and orientation. These heteronormative sex/gender assumptions, expectations and norms that underpin the new legislation are much more difficult to challenge than the terms of the Act itself.

Not only is this provision discriminatory against trans people (undermining the stated aim of marriage equality), as Adams (2013) says, the spousal veto of the GRC is unnecessary since any spouse who does not want to remain in a marriage can seek a divorce. It seems then that giving someone the power to block state recognition of a gender transition, even temporarily, merely allows them to act in anger or retribution and further 'punish' their spouse. Given that trans people often suffer harassment and abuse, or at the very least uncertainty and anxiety that harassment will occur when their identity documents do not match their gender presentation, delaying the GRC even by six months may cause unintended harm in the name of protecting the 'autonomy' of the cisgender spouse – an autonomy that can be just as convincingly expressed through an application for separation or divorce. This is not to mention the emotional impact of having a spouse intervene to delay transition in this way.

Fourthly and finally, if, as many heterosexual couples do, a same-sex couple in England or Wales seeks to the end marriage, the grounds on which they can do so differ from those that apply to heterosexual marriages. For example, straight couples can apply for an annulment of the marriage on the grounds of lack of consummation – same-sex couples cannot. There is also no ground of adultery for divorce in same-sex marriage. This seems to be a hangover from the Civil Partnerships Act 2004, which also neglected to include non-consummation as a ground for dissolution of the marriage. One reason for this might be because, as Barlow and Mason (2013, p. 16) suggest, the Westminster government seems squeamish about having to define what consummation in a same-sex intimate relationship might look like (see also Barker, 2013).

To be clear, I am not suggesting that the absence of same-sex sex in the new Act is unequivocally a bad thing. As Barker has argued, leaving (hetero)sexual scripts out of same-sex marriage may open up unintended spaces for non-heteronormative and queer practices such as non-monogamy and polyamory, as well as for non-conjugal relationships to take the form of and be valued as marriages (2013, p. 85). But the fact remains that the law here has failed to meet even its own formal equality goals. What is more, in applying legal techniques such as comparison and analogy, law (re)produces a certain kind of sexual citizen; and in casting the law as a triumph of equality, law-makers perpetuate the notion that law reform is the preferred solution to problems of social justice – as long as we don't peek behind the curtain and point out the real practical consequences of those reforms. The danger is, as feminists have pointed out with respect to rape law, that legislation that has been fought for long and hard, and seems to promise equality, operates in only the most superficial and minimalistic fashion and becomes a proxy for a properly grounded attempt to achieve social justice.

Writing in the radical anarchist magazine *Slingshot*, published in Berkeley, California, Joey (2013) suggests that one of the problems of legal debates that fetishize marriage is that they miss the point, or indeed the opportunity, to emphasize that, if marriage is for everyone, then it is not only for gays and lesbians that are 'just like us' (whoever that 'us' may be). For Joey, sanitized same-sex marriage debates that void the conversation of any possible threatening sexualized 'gay agenda', by casting it as a simple matter of formal equality, and of human rights, take the notion of sexuality as a site of exploration and adventure off the table, which is particularly problematic for young queers (see also Barker, 2013, p. 86, arguing that leaving sex out of same-sex partnership laws desexualizes gay and lesbian lives). In other words, it precludes any discussion of what it means to be young, queer, non-monogamous, and choosing intimacy beyond one's genetic family, and focuses instead on homonormatively, monogamously and neatly reproducing the established family structure. This is *not* to say that queers should not have families or celebrate their intimate partnerships. This is to say that there is more than one way – marriage – of experiencing and expressing the sexual self in relation to one's community, and that there might be a way of doing so without forcing queers to align themselves with the legitimate 'straight agenda' (marriage, monogamy, coupledom, vanilla sex, etc.).[7] Whether or not those 'other' experiences and expressions of the sexual self can be recognized by law, however, is another question. However, in learning what it is about law reform that keeps us coming back like bees to honey, it *is* also worth studying the 'failures' as well as the 'successes' of legal intervention, particularly as resistance and critique through failure – for example, failure to be granted equal status rather than success through assimilation and thus co-option by law – are part of the queer (legal) theory toolset (Halberstam, 2011; Leckey, 2014).

So, what happens now? The post same-sex marriage social and political terrain will most likely look pretty similar to the one previously inhabited – marriage stays, and lesbians and gay men will be ushered into its warm embrace. But will there really be a trickle-through of good will, a spread of happiness, joy and acceptance of the 'normalcy' of same-sex families, not to mention same-sex *sex*?[8] It seems that inclusion within law only applies to those who are most analogous to heterosexual couples and families – those who, as Dean Spade would say, but for the unfortunate characteristic of being gay are just like everyone else (and for everyone else read: tax-paying, law-abiding, monogamous, white, heterosexual citizens). It is not clear how reformed laws change any of the established socio-political terrain, either for queers and non-queers who don't fit the heteronormative model, or for marriage itself. As Spade has argued in another context: 'The resultant law reforms are so narrow in their understanding of the issues that they only provide access to the sought after right for those who do not have other intervening vectors of marginality' (2011, p. 160; see also Boyd and Young, 2006). And yet we are encouraged to celebrate the fact that the 'ancient' institution of marriage which has, through the ages, been a tool to oppress, contain and control women and children, the poor, and racialized and immigrant populations, is now open to gays and lesbians too. This seems somewhat anomalous when we consider Rosemary Auchmuty's point (2012) that marriage is dying out anyway; the marriage rate in 1987 was half what it was in 1970, and by 2007 it had halved again. What is more, the shifts in thinking in the UK that have led to the new law do not seem to have affected the incidence and fear of homophobia.[9]

---

7 www.theguardian.com/film/2014/apr/10/stacie-passon-concussion-lesbian-hooker. See also Boyd and Young (2006).

8 For a critique of the binary of hyper-sexualized urban bathhouse versus domesticated suburban wedlock that dominates cultural representations of queer lives, see Charles (2012).

9 see www.theguardian.com/world/2013/aug/25/homophobia-uk-survey

Of course, there are many countries in the world where identifying as lesbian or gay can lead to criminalization, or even execution. The timing of writing this chapter has brought some of the arguments about the positive role of law reform into focus for me. Currently, the Russian government is treating those who identify as homosexual as criminals, deviants and troublemakers.[10] To even discuss homosexuality is cast as its promotion, which has recently been said to be illegal. This has prompted campaigns and petitions across the world that aim to show support for LGB communities in Russia and, in so doing, put pressure on the Russian government to change its laws and policies. It is all very well, then, for me to call for an end to the focus on law reform from the safety of my sofa in a country where gay pride marches, gay parenting, gay adoption and now gay marriage are becoming, for want of a better word, the 'norm'. The juxtaposition of UK and Russia only serves to illustrate the privilege that allows me to critique the law as a site of symbolic and practical achievement for those of us who do not identify as heterosexual.

In any case, this 'victory' for equality in same-sex coupledom is not an indication that all is well in the garden of Eden for people with same-sex desire. In contrast to these moments of progressive social change for same-sex couples, despite extensive critical discussion (see Craig, 2013; Newman, 2013; Pothier, 2014), Trinity Western University in Canada has recently succeeded in introducing a new law degree programme into its curriculum. However, prospective students must sign a covenant that says that they will not, during their time at the university, engage in 'sexual intimacy that violates the sacredness of marriage between a man and a woman'.[11] What this means is that while students will be able to gain an LLB, the first step to practising law, and will have been made aware of materials relating to the equality provisions of the Canadian Constitution and the Charter of Human Rights and Protections, exclusion from the programme of students in same-sex marriages is somehow justified (i.e. non-discriminatory) on the basis of religious freedom (sexual activity between opposite-sex couples is also prohibited by the covenant *unless* the couple is married). Similarly, as suggested above, there are 'religious freedom' protections for those in the UK who do not wish to sanction marriage in their place of worship. Religion, it seems, is a particular sticking point when it comes to 'full equality' for same-sex couples, in the UK, North America and elsewhere. Balancing rights, or deciding 'hard cases' is the kind of exercise that has always taxed lawyers and judges,

---

10 www.theguardian.com/world/2013/jun/11/russia-law-banning-gay-propaganda

11 See http://twu.ca/studenthandbook/university-policies/community-covenant-agreement.html.

not least because the application of legal tools such as rights often leads to comparisons and analogies that can be manipulated and moulded to suit the purposes of those demanding or opposing the rights in question. When Elizabeth Kingdom asked in 1991, 'What's wrong with rights?' she was not posing a rhetorical question. Like Kingdom, and Smart before her, I would point to the persistent suggestibility and unevenness of the impact of rights, the fetishization of legal concepts such as objectivity and equality, and the overuse and over-technocrization of legal tools such as comparison and analogy, as well as the ways in which the aspirations of marginalized groups are fundamentally misplaced when the focus remains solely or mainly on legal protections. Some practices cannot, in reality, be prevented or regulated by law; law is often not the answer to socio-political disagreement (Cowan, 2008). This may be especially true when the freedom of religion appears to be at odds with other human or civil rights.

Concluding thoughts

What it is that makes law so irresistible to those that have historically been excluded from its protective shield? Why do people have faith in law? Sometimes, law seems like the most obvious way of protecting one-self, especially in extreme and immediate cases such as the infliction of violence. But oftentimes the system that ostensibly protects us in fact exacerbates structural inequalities, particularly since technical questions about the form, structure and content of law cannot be separated from the issue of who implements those laws on the ground.[12]

Riles (2005, p. 997) has suggested that technical legal tools help us to focus on what 'would best promote uniformity of decision and foresee-ability of outcomes', but arguably they do not adequately promote social justice. As Vivien Namaste (2000) reminds us, focusing only on legal iden-tity claims and rights can obscure the deeply felt ways in which other social and political institutions impact upon our lives. This, however, does not necessitate a wholesale rejection of law as a resource or tool, or a prohibition upon legal analyses of inequalities. Suspicion of law can be encouraged even while legal rights claims are pursued. Paisley Currah (2002–2003) argues, for example, that like critical race theorists who main-tain that it is possible to use the law to combat racial inequalities, even as

---

12 See, recently, in the USA: the shooting of Trayvon Martin http://edition.cnn.com/2013/06/05/us/trayvon-martin-shooting-fast-facts; the shooting of Michael Brown www.bbc.co.uk/news/world-us-canada-30193354; and the death of Eric Garner www.bbc.co.uk/news/world-us-canada-30323750. See also www.theguardian.com/us-news/2014/dec/13/civil-rights-marchers-in-washington-dc-set-protest-against-police-killings.

work is done to demonstrate the legal and social construction of racializa-
tion itself, working to dismantle gender as a normative system, and the
use of litigation strategies to end sex/gender discrimination, are not and
should not be mutually exclusive. Rather, the question is how to negotiate
the tensions. This is what Judith Butler (1993) would call the 'double gesture', interpreted here to mean that we can engage in legal tactics but
simultaneously challenge the authority and the power of law to shape the
world, and use sex/gender categories as the basis of rights claims, even as
we aim to undermine those same categories by demonstrating their failure to reflect the variety and depth of human experience. As Lenon (2005,
p. 406) has put it, the fact that heterosexuality tends towards perpetuating
itself does not mean that it 'can never be invaded, interfered with, and
critically impaired'. Building on Halberstam's (2011) work, then, attempting – and failing – to revolutionize and radicalize law is just as, if not more
important for critical scholars and activists, as meeting and beating it on
its own terms.

So, it might be possible, as Butler and others have suggested, to engage in
some sort of double gesture – using and undermining law's categories and
power at the same time. But perhaps what will make more impact is what
Dean Spade has called 'participatory resistance led from the bottom up'
(2011, p. 224) and 'community solutions to violence that do not rely on
the police' (2011, p. 210). In his book *Normal Life*, writing in the context
of a critical trans politics, and drawing on Foucault, women of colour
feminism, critical race theory and postcolonialism (to name but a few),
Spade argues that it is the administrative norms that structure everyday
life, and thus produce more lasting and endemic harms, that we should
focus on, rather than simply those moments of legal inequality, targeted
through legal reform efforts, such as employment discrimination: '(Hetero)
norms such as those relating to sex, gender, race, physical ability, education, nationality, and health, that seem to operate as neutral, often operate in the background of our systems of criminal punishment, nationality
and reproduction in a way that ensures more "security" for some and more
"vulnerability" for others' (2011, p. 24).

Focusing only on law as a 'top-down' form of power neglects the myriad
of ways in which diverse and decentralized forms of power permeate and
construct our lives: 'race and gender operate as vectors of the distribution
of life chances that cannot simply be solved by passing laws declaring that
various groups are now "equal"' (Spade, 2011, p. 119). Although Spade
does not eschew law reform efforts altogether, like Carol Smart he sees a
minimal role for law in addressing problems of social justice, in order to
shift the focus 'beyond the politics of recognition and inclusion' (2011,
p. 28) and towards both dismantling systemic injustice and supporting
those who are most vulnerable and disadvantaged (2011, p. 41). Thinking

about justice in this more localized and participatory way 'can also help us spot traps of co-optation and incorporation that our resistance projects face [and] how legal reform itself operates as one such trap' (2011, p. 26). The main vehicle to achieve this, he says, is 'a shared imagination of what ultimate transformative change we are pursuing, and what we think it will take to get there' (2011, pp. 156–7).

Changes in the law, such as rape reform, or same-sex marriage, can tell us that there has been some kind of 'tipping point' where the arguments in favour of equality have 'found the crack' and have levered their way sufficiently into the mainstream as to make some kind of difference, at least as far as the 'laws on the books'. But what they also tell us, even in the way they are written, such as the same-sex marriage law in England and Wales, is that equality, even in its formal sense, is often elusive. Conservative, neoliberal and hegemonic tendencies often find a way to creep back in. This new same-sex marriage law serves to illustrate that it is difficult to balance strong views in a community that disagrees about what counts as marriage, what marriage is for and what it means, and whether marriage is important, not to mention any of the similar yet more fundamental questions that arise about equality – what it is, what it means and how best to accomplish it.

In the context of sex/gender equality, as discussed above, the achievement of same-sex marriage in England and Wales comes with (the usual) inbuilt cautionary fail-safes that promote heterosexual, cisgendered monogamy, as well as the economy (in time-limiting pension benefits for same-sex surviving spouses) and the freedom of religion, at the expense of even the most basic, formal 'we are just like you' kind of equality. Although Janet Halley might argue that one reason to use the law is to get a better outcome for the pervert (2003, p. 636), Spade would caution us to be mindful of legal reforms that in fact protect the interests of the status quo, and perpetuate neoliberal logics of privacy, and of the law-abiding 'us' versus the deviant 'them' (2011, p. 158).

In the context of rape reform, social justice seems to be negated by resort to technical definitions and interpretations of language; prospects for real engagement with the harm of sexual violence are impeded by the legal tools and technologies that seem to be indifferent to those they are applied to. As Riles has argued:

> this love of and commitment to the tools also helps explain why it is that legal knowledge seems cut off from the 'social ends' it purports to instrumentalize, to exist in what the legal theorist Gunther Teubner terms an 'autopoietic' sphere of the technical, even as the stated goal of means–ends reasoning is precisely to make law relevant to real people, or real corporations, and

their problems. Once reframed as a problem-solving device, the means–ends relationship serves to limit the scope of law, to draw the device back in. (2005, p. 1028)

Engaging with sex/gender equality therefore means engaging in public debate about the social regulatory norms underpinning law, and the representations of sexuality and sexual behaviour they spawn, as well as bringing 'the technical into view' (Riles, 2005, p. 985), in order to question whether the traditional techniques of law are fit and able to foster social justice. But aiming for change also means grass-roots organizing across communities around local issues, creating and disseminating art projects, finding other ways of solving conflicts than calling for state criminal justice intervention, and harnessing the power of mainstream and independent news and social media, among other things – in other words, resisting both the temptation to rely on law and legal techniques to mould the social world around us, and the false goal of 'uniformity of decision and foreseeability of outcome's (Riles, 2005, p. 997).

Cases

Hollingsworth v Perry 570 US ____ (2013)

References

Adams, R (2013) 'Unequal Marriage? How the "Spousal Veto" Harms Transgender People' *Huffington Post* 9 July 2013 www.huffingtonpost.co.uk/richard-adams/unequal-marriage-and-transgenders_b_3560849.html

Auchmuty, R (2012) 'Law and the Power of Feminism: How Marriage Lost Its Power to Oppress Women' 20(2) *Feminist Legal Studies* 71–87

Barker, N (2013) *Not the Marrying Kind: A Feminist Critique of Same-Sex Marriage* (Basingstoke: Palgrave Macmillan)

Barlow, J and M Mason (2013) 'All Marriages Are Equal ... But Some Are More Equal Than Others' *New Law Journal*, 26 July 2013

Boyd, S and C Young (2006) 'Losing the Feminist Voice? Debates on the Legal Recognition of Same Sex Partnerships in Canada' 14 *Feminist Legal Studies* 213–40

Brown, W (1995) *States of Injury: Power and Freedom in Late Modernity* (Princeton: Princeton University Press)

Butler, J (1993) *Bodies that Matter: On the Discursive Limits of 'Sex'* (New York: Routledge)

Charles, C (2012) *Critical Queer Studies: Law, Film, and Fiction in Contemporary American Culture* (Farnham: Ashgate)

Cowan, S (2007) 'Freedom and Capacity to Make a Choice: A feminist Analysis Of consent in the Criminal Law of Rape' in V Munro and C Stychin (eds), *Sexuality and the Law: Feminist Engagements*, (London: Glasshouse Press/ Routledge-Cavendish), pp. 51–71

Cowan, S (2008) 'The Headscarf Controversy: A Response to Jill Marshall' 14(3) *Res Publica* 193–201

Cowan, S, R Sandland and A Sharpe (2009) 'Debate and Dialogue: The Gender Recognition Act' 18(2) *Social and Legal Studies* 241–63

Craig, E (2013) 'The Case for the Federation of Law Societies Rejecting Trinity Western University's Proposed Law Degree Program' 25(1) *Canadian Journal of Women and the Law* 148–170

Currah, P (2002–2003) 'The Transgender Rights Imaginary' 4 *Georgetown Journal of Gender and the Law* 705

Daly, K (2002) 'Sexual Assault and Restorative Justice' in H Strang and J Braithwaite (eds), *Restorative Justice and Family Violence* (Cambridge: Cambridge University Press)

Du Toit, L (2007) 'The Conditions of Consent' in R Hunter and S Cowan (eds), *Choice and Consent: Feminist Engagements with Law and Subjectivity* (London: Taylor & Francis)

Eaton, M (1994) 'Lesbians, Gays and the Struggle for Equality Rights: Reversing the Progressive Hypothesis' 17 *Dalhousie Law Journal* 130

Ellison, L and V Munro (2009a) 'Reacting to Rape: Exploring Mock Jurors' Assessments of Complainant Credibility' 49 (2) *British Journal of Criminology* 202–19

Ellison, L and V Munro (2009b) 'Of "Normal Sex" and "Real Rape": Exploring The Use of Socio-Sexual Scripts in (Mock) Jury Deliberation' 18(3) *Social Legal Studies* 291–312

Friedson, A (2013) *Blind to Sameness: Sexpectations and the Social Construction of Male and Female Bodies* (Chicago: University of Chicago Press)

Gotell, L (2007) 'The Discursive Disappearance of Sexualized Violence: Feminist Law Reform, Judicial Resistance, and Neo-Liberal Sexual Citizenship' in D E Chunn, S B Boyd and H Lessard (eds), *Reaction and Resistance: Feminism, Law and Social Change* (Vancouver: University of British Columbia Press)

Gotell, L (2010) 'Canadian Sexual Assault Law: Neoliberalism and the Erosion of Feminist-inspired Law Reforms' in C McGlynn and V Munro (eds), *Rethinking Rape Law: International and Comparative Perspectives* (London: Routledge), pp. 209–23

Gotell, L (2013) 'Carceral Feminisms' paper presented at the Canadian Law and Society Association Conference, Vancouver, 2–3 July 2013

Halberstam, J (2011) *The Queer Art of Failure* (Durham: Duke University Press)

Halley, J (2003) 'Gender, Sexuality and Power: Is Feminist Theory Enough?' (Parts III and VII) 12 *Columbia Journal of Gender and Law* 610–37

Hillyard, P (2014) 'Critique and Reaction: Zemiology's challenge to Criminology' paper presented to the Legal Theory Spring Workshop, University of Edinburgh, 29 May 2014

Hudson, B (1998) 'Restorative Justice: The Challenge of Sexual and Racial Violence' 25(2) *Journal of Law and Society* 237–56

Joey (2013) 'The Gay Agenda: How the Corporate Media Fails Queers' 112 *Slingshot* 8

Kingdom, E (1991) *What's Wrong with Rights?* (Edinburgh: Edinburgh University Press)

Larcombe, W (2011) 'Falling Rape Conviction Rates: (Some) Feminist Aims and Measures for Rape Law' 19(1) *Feminist Legal Studies* 27–45

Leckey, R (2014) 'States of Identity' paper presented at Who Are We?: The Quest for Identity in Law Conference, University of Dalhousie, Canada, 20–1 October 2014

Lenon, S (2005) 'Marrying Citizens! Raced Subjects? Rethinking the Terrain of Equal Marriage Discourse' 17 *Canadian Journal of Women and the Law* 405–21

McGlynn, C (2010) 'Feminist Activism and Rape Law Reform in England and Wales: A Sisyphean Struggle?' in C McGlynn and V Munro (eds), *Rethinking Rape Law: International and Comparative Perspectives* (London: Routledge-Cavendish)

McGlynn, C and V Munro (eds) (2010) *Rethinking Rape Law: International and Comparative Perspectives* (London: Routledge-Cavendish)

Miller, S and L Iovanni (2013) 'Using Restorative Justice for Gendered Violence: Success with a Postconviction Model' 8(4) *Feminist Criminology* 247–68

Mossman, M J (1987) 'Feminism and Legal Method: The Difference It Makes' 3 *Wisconsin Women's Law Journal* 147–68

Namaste, V (2000) *Invisible Lives: The Erasure of Transsexual and Transgendered People* (Chicago: University of Chicago Press)

Newman, D (2013) 'On The Trinity Western University Controversy: An Argument for a Christian Law School in Canada' (2013) 22(3) *Constitutional Forum/Forum constitutionnel* 1–14

Pothier, D (2013) 'An Argument against Accreditation of Trinity Western University's Proposed Law School' (2014) 23(1) *Constitutional Forum/Forum constitutionnel* 1–7

Reece, H (2013) 'Rape Myths: Is Elite Opinion Right and Popular Opinion Wrong?' *Oxford Journal of Legal Studies* 1–29

Riles, A (2005) 'A New Agenda for the Cultural Study of Law: Taking on the Technicalities' 53 *Buffalo Law Review* 973–1033

Scales, A (1986) 'The Emergence of Feminist Jurisprudence: An Essay' 95 *Yale Law Journal* 1373–403

Sharpe, A (2013) 'We Must Not Uphold Gender Norms at the Expense of Human Dignity: Sexual Intimacy, Gender Variance and Criminal Law' *New Statesman*, May 2013

Smart, C (1984) *The Ties that Bind* (London: Routledge & Kegan Paul)

Smart, C (1989) *Feminism and the Power of Law* (London: Routledge)

Smart, C (2012) 'Reflection' 20(2) *Feminist Legal Studies* 161–5

Snider, L (1990) 'The Potential of the Criminal Justice System to Promote Feminist Concerns' 10 *Studies in Law Politics and Society: A Research Annual* 143–73

Snider, L (1998) 'Towards Safer Societies: Punishment, Masculinities and Violence against Women' 38(1) *British Journal of Criminology* 1–39

Spade, D (2011) *Normal Life: Administrative Violence, Critical Trans Politics and the Limits of Law* (Brooklyn: South End Press)

Spencer, J (2004) 'The Sexual Offences Act 2003: Child and Family Offences' *Criminal Law Review* 328–60

Temkin, J and B Krahé (2008) *Sexual Assault and the Justice Gap: A Question of Attitude* (Oxford: Hart Publishing)

Westmarland, N and G Gangoli (2011) *International Approaches to Rape* (Bristol: Policy Press)

Part II
Case Studies

7

Solar Panels, Homeowners and Leases: The Lease as a Socio-Legal Object

Caroline Hunter

Introduction

> It has been said that the development of the lease as predominantly a contractual device gave it 'a plasticity which could conform to the finest shade of commercial requirements'. (Davey, 2006, p. 149, quoting Grove and Garner, 1963, p. 174)

> A lease is a sophisticated but somewhat inflexible institution, not easily adjustable to meet changing social and commercial expectations and this can limit its usefulness. (Clarke and Kohler, 2005, p. 609)

This chapter[1] is concerned with a rather dull and formal piece of paper: the lease. As a legal technical document it is (or was – the past looms large given the length of leases) created by conveyancers in a law office. We know little of its creation – something I shall return to later. But, as the quotes above show, the lease appears to be something of a contradiction – a flexible contract and an inflexible institution. Leases are usually studied as part of property law. It is generally accepted that '[p]roperty law tends to the regarded by students as both dull and difficult' (Clarke and Kohler, 2005, p. xvii). Within this, leases may be seen as particularly so, to such an extent that many English law schools simply do not bother to teach anything but the most basic principles of the distinction between leases and licences and certainly would not stray into the statutory regulation of the relationships

1 The author would like to thank the participants of the Challenging Ownership stream at the Socio-Legal Studies Association (SLSA) Annual Conference 2012 and the SLSA one-day conference Exploring the Legal in Socio-legal Studies – in particular Sarah Blandy and Nick Blomley for their helpful comments and suggestions. Thanks also need to go to the staff at York Law School for their comments following an internal staff presentation and to the editors of this book for their helpful comments. The usual caveats apply.

between leaseholders and freeholders, nor ask their students to read and interpret leases. If '[t]he machinery of law is often dismissed by critical legal scholars as "technical", with the contents of the "technical" black box being left to black-letter law professors' (Valverde, 2005, p. 427), here is a technical aspect that not even the black-letter law professors are very interested in.

But perhaps there is another way to think about the lease which takes it out of this dull and difficult world and starts to prise open some of the contradictions alluded to above. The story I wish to tell is partly one of implementation of government policy – a government policy that requires the use of new (scientific) technologies (in this case solar panels) and what happens when these new technologies come into conflict with the technology of the lease. There is a growing literature on the interaction of law and science, in particular how law regulates science. There is also a literature on how technology (broadly conceived) shapes law (see Faulkner et al., 2012). In addition there is a literature which seeks to show how law is a technology in its own right that is worthy of study as a cultural practice (Riles, 2005).

Technology has been conceived of in a variety of ways. Guggenheim (2010a, p. 443), following Luhmann (2000) and Latour (1991), defines it as 'an assemblage of things and practices that produces with the same input and the same output and thus makes processes predictable'. Thus technologies have stabilizing effects. They can become 'immutable mobiles' – 'hardened technologies, objects that are stable in varying circumstances and always perform the task assigned to them' (Guggenheim, 2010a, p. 444). It is in this sense that Riles (2005) also conceives of law as a technology. The content of technologies can become a 'black box'. The term comes from Latour's study of scientists. A black box is a complex machinery or set of commands about which scientists need to know nothing: 'no matter how controversial their history, how complex their inner workings, how large the commercial or academic networks that hold them in place, only their input and output count' (Latour, 1987, quoted in Riles, 2005, p. 999).

Latour is inextricably linked to the ideas of actor–network theory (ANT). While there may be disagreement about the nature of ANT, as Farias (2010, p. 2) notes:

> ANT is less a matter of precise definitions than one of an (allegedly) shared sense regarding the objects researchers investigate and are curious about ... It involves rather a certain sensibility towards the active role of non-human actors in the assemblage of the world, towards the relational constitution of objects, and the sense that all this calls for symmetrical explanations.

Lovell (2005, p. 816) underlines this approach to the inseparability of social and technical systems:

> politics, economics and culture are critical to the development (or not) of certain technologies, and likewise, technologies are important in shaping culture and society.

There has been an increasing interest in the role that ANT can play in explaining the role of law in the socio-material world (Valverde, 2005; Cowan and Carr, 2008; Faulkner et al., 2012; Cloatre, this volume). Latour (2010, p. viii) himself, writing about the study of the French Conseil D'Etat, has said that he found 'law much more technical and difficult to follow than science or technology'. His focus, however, was the nature of disputes once they enter the Conseil. Law and legal disputes, however, move from the work of lawyers (whether in a court setting or their offices) out into the lives of non-lawyers. As Valverde (2005, p. 422) notes: 'Latour is concerned only with the Conseil's own internal productive consumption of knowledge.'

Riles suggests that the technical aspect of law can seem mundane and an inherently uninteresting dimension of the law – the realm of practice rather than theory (2005, p. 974). It also has a self-conscious image of being 'neutral and agnostic'. Thus it is removed from the 'rough and tumble of fights over how to allocate scarce resources in society' (Riles, 2011, p. 67). This may be why leases are so overlooked in legal academia; a very dull but complex technology. As the quotes at the outset of this chapter indicate, there are different views from those interested in the lease as to whether it is useful.

But I would like to take up Riles' challenge to the culturalist and ask some different questions about the lease. As she suggests, we need to understand that legal technicalities are not the neutral and agnostic tools they appear but in fact have power to shape society with potentially profound distributive consequences (Riles, 2011, p. 67). I am seeking to examine whether the lease is a socio-legal object which Cloatre (2008, p. 264) has defined as an object 'with a legal origin/dimension studied in [its] social action through networks and connections'. Is it in fact a technology as defined by Guggenheim? In doing so, I want to ask some questions about the role that the lease plays in creating the social–material world and when and whether it is an active actor in social networks. Further, I want to consider how there might be an interplay between different technologies, of how the lease might facilitate and be part of a network that also includes another more conventionally scientific technology – the solar panel.

I am concerned here with leases of land. More often than not such a lease also includes a building on that land. Guggenheim (2010a, 2010b) considers whether buildings are themselves immutable mobiles. He concludes that they are not. Rather they are quasi-technologies:

> objects that are sometimes real technologies, functioning as black boxes, but at other times they lose this quality. They are turned from technologies, in the sense of black-boxed procedures, into 'mere' masses of materials. They become *materialized* ... To materialize in this sense means that an object is freed from its actor-network and reduced to its material qualities. (Guggenheim, 2010b, p. 165, original emphasis)

Guggenheim argues that buildings are mutable immobiles – the opposite of immutable mobiles. They are on a fixed location – hence immobile. They are also singular, unstandardized, with their own form and openness to users which make them changeable – hence mutable. This may be less true in the UK where Lovell (2005) suggests that new houses, speculatively built, are subject to a socio-technical system that has conservative tendencies and makes it difficult for technical innovation to take place: 'Technical knowledge, regulations and production methods are all aligned towards building dwellings in a particular way' (2005, p. 824).

Guggenheim is concerned with what happens when these mutable immobiles come into view within the law and, indeed, create a problem for the law. He does this in the context of zoning law and he addresses how the law 'fixes' the buildings with the power of the law (2010b, p. 174). In doing so, however, the law and its own technologies are not considered. What this chapter starts to explore is whether the technology of law can 'fix' the building more completely and to make the case for unpacking that black box of the lease.

The limitations of this chapter should be acknowledged from the outset. It is limited in its ambitions – necessarily so coming out of a single case (*Re 11 and 27 Parklands View*)[2] heard before a very minor tribunal. It is intended to explore a way forward that takes some of the literature referred to above away from its regular focus on the regulatory sphere of supranational organizations and governments, implemented through statute and statutory instrument, international treaty and other forms of soft law, and turns the gaze towards the technologies of private law arrangements – the contract, the lease, the legal precedent. Further, as Cowan and Carr (2008, p. 154) observe, referring to actor–network approaches, 'ethnographic

---

2 Case references MAN/00CF/LBC/2011/0002 and 0003. A transcript of the decision can be found at: www.residential-property.judiciary.gov.uk/search/decision_search.jsp.

methods are best suited to this type of approach. Observation studies are likely to be the most suitable methods by which actor-networks can be followed.' This chapter is not based on an ethnographic study. No interviews were conducted nor interactions observed. Indeed, at this stage I must confess to it being based on a single case in which I was an actant – the lawyer chair of the case.[3] Accordingly, in seeking a slightly broader frame to answer my questions, I have also drawn extensively on the work of Sarah Blandy – who has taken the study of the legal frameworks under which people live together beyond its dry and dusty technicalities into an understanding about how 'social life and (property) law are mutually constitutive' (Blandy, 2013).

Before describing the case, I will reflect on the role of the lease within a model of homeownership. I then examine the arguments that leases are constitutive of both physical space and social relations. I will then move on to some reflections on how we see this play out in relation to the particular instance of solar panels on roofs, before concluding with some thoughts about the way forward for the study of the lease as a potential socio-legal object and technology.

Role of the leasehold

The role of the 'home' in creating the social world is one that has been widely acknowledged. Debates have raged as to whether the form of legal rights to the home impact on our relationship with that space (cf. e.g. Gurney, 1990; Saunders, 1990; and the discussion in Fox, 2007, ch. 5), but it is clear that the last 40 years of government policy is a period that has seen the promotion of homeownership over other forms of occupation. Homeownership, however, is not an acknowledged legal classification. Where housing policy refers to owner-occupiers and tenants, the law draws a distinction between freeholders and leaseholders (Blandy and Goodchild, 1999). Sitting in an uncomfortable place between these classifications are long-leaseholders (i.e. those owners with a long – 21 years and usually a great deal longer – lease of a property purchased for a capital sum) – owner-occupiers in housing policy terms but leaseholders in legal terms.

We find long leaseholds most often used in relation to flats of houses, where they are used to provide for the maintenance of common parts (see Blandy, 2010, for a discussion of the different form of legal arrangements in cases of residential properties with common parts). However, houses have also historically been developed and sold on long leases (Davey, 2006)

---

3 I am, of course, writing in a purely personal capacity in this chapter. In referring to myself as an actant, I am adopting the 'ugly word' (Cowan and Carr, 2008, p. 152) used to indicate an active mediator in a network.

and, indeed, as the facts of the case discussed in this chapter indicate, they are still being developed and sold on long leases.

This hybrid position of long-leaseholders has led to a great deal of government intervention in the relationship between the leaseholder and the freeholder – a long campaign (Davey, 2006) gave long-leaseholders of houses a right to enfranchise. A set of, often difficult and complex, statutes has given long-leaseholders of flats a set of rights which permit them to extend their leases, change managers of the property, challenge service charges and collectively acquire the freehold (Davey, 2006; Carr, 2011). Most disputes arising in relation to the rights in these statutes are adjudicated before the Leasehold Valuation Tribunal (LVT) or, as it has been rather cumbersomely renamed since July 2013, the First Tier Tribunal of the Property Chamber. One further right which the most recent legislation (the Commonhold and Leasehold Reform Act 2002) has limited is the right of freeholders to forfeit a long residential lease (whether of a house or a flat). Before proceedings for forfeiture of such a lease can be brought, the freeholder must first obtain a ruling from the LVT that there has been a breach of the lease.

The hybrid position also means that long-leaseholders may feel differently about their homes than freeholders. As Carr (2011, p. 540) points out:

> [L]easeholders are permanently disappointed that their status fails to deliver the ownership and control that they expect. ... That disappointment reflects the economic vulnerability of this form of tenure.

A similar point is made by Bright and Hopkins (2011) in relation to the even more complex shared-ownership lease (see also Cowan and Wincott, this volume).

Having sketched this brief background to the place of the long lease in current housing policy, I want to explore two key questions. The first is whether there is any evidence that the legal form has a role in constituting the physical form. The second is the evidence as to how the legal frame constitutes social relations. Leading from this second question is the role of the legal form where disputes arise between parties, i.e. at a 'legal moment of social relations' (Cowan and Wincott, this volume, p. 8).

The lease and physical form

The last 30 years or so have seen a growth in city centre residential development (Bromley et al., 2007). In other jurisdictions, the condominium or strata title, rather than the lease, has become the form of ownership used for this high-density ownership requiring some shared ownership of common spaces. Harris (2011) has argued that the adoption of the legal form of condominium[4] in Vancouver in the late 1960s in fact help define the physical form that the city has now taken on.

> Vancouver without condominium would be very different from the city that has emerged. The legal form, introduced in the 1960s, enabled fuller rights of ownership to attach to a single unit in a multi-unit building than possible at common law or through cooperatives or residential tenancies. It is, at least in part, the opportunity to hold this fuller bundle of property rights that has brought people into the city as residents or as investors. (Harris, 2011, p. 721)

Thus, we have here an argument that the legal form is constitutive of the socio-material reality of the city. It is also notable that this form of legal innovation was not necessary for parallel developments in UK cities. Similar changes have taken place in many UK cities using the existing legal form – the lease and indeed the provision of a new legal form (the commonhold) in 2002 has not proved to be a success (Smith, 2009). In England therefore the lease continues to be used.

It is in some ways an empirical question as to whether the role of the legal form is an essential element of the development of cities. Harris is able to demonstrate the success of the condominium and its spread through Vancouver. He suggests that this success is due to the way in which the bundle of property rights is configured. But the question which remains is whether this particular configuration was necessary, or could a different one have produced the same or similar results? He points to an important distinction between UK and Canadian law in relation to whether ownership of land could be divided horizontally as well as vertically. He also points to the problem of the long lease as a wasting asset – which has led to the some of the complex legislation discussed briefly above, in order to facilitate the equivalent developments in England.

While Harris's study focuses on the condominium as shaping a particular physical form to the city, I would suggest that we might be able to take this insight in relation to other physical forms. This will be explored further below in relation to the use of solar panels.

The lease and social life

Blandy (2013) has explored how far the lease itself is constitutive of the social life of residents. This would seem to depend on the nature

---

4 Condominium (in some jurisdictions referred to as strata-title) is a statutory legal form of landholding which enables, through a particular bundling of property rights, private ownership in a single unit of a multi-unit building and common ownership of shared facilities among the owners of the units.

of the development in question. In a study of a co-housing development in the UK, she demonstrates how it developed its own rules but was also penetrated by the external legal system (Blandy, 2013, citing Moore, 1973). Blandy notes: 'It was striking how frequently formal law was invoked as a way of justifying the rules by which [the residents] live.' It was invoked to justify rules the lease did not contain and was frequently referred to in residents' meetings. In this instance the lease loomed large in constituting the material realities of the lives of the residents. However, in doing so, the lease had broken away from its legal moorings and moved beyond its technical limitations and become something which can be invoked as governing the relationships between the lives of the residents. This perhaps contradicts the image of the lease as immutable. While it is producing the associations, it is also being changed at least in its invocation, if not in its physical form, as an object.

In an account of a very different community, the lease takes on a very different level of agency, however. Blandy and Lister (2005) discuss the leases used in the development of a gated community in the UK. The covenants entered into 'aim to control the occupiers' behaviour and use of their property, in a way which seems at odds with our expectations of the freedoms enjoyed by owner occupiers' (Blandy and Lister, 2005, p. 296). Their study suggested that most residents were unaware of the covenants – thus backing up a study in the USA which found that less than 10 per cent of gated community residents had read the covenants prior to purchase (Alexander, 1994). When asked to consider the importance of the covenants most residents did not accord any importance to the fact that the covenants restricted their own behaviour, but felt it was very important that the restriction would ensure that all other residents kept to the terms of the lease (Blandy and Lister, 2005, p. 297).

Both these studies in different ways show that the lease may or may not be constitutive of the social life of residents. Cloatre (2008, p. 279) has suggested that the elusive nature of socio-legal objects might 'require that additional thought be given to how the modes of action of ... immaterial tools can be observed and analysed in practice'. In a homogeneous network, such as the residents of co-housing, Blandy has provided such an analysis of the immaterial tool of the lease in practice. As the network becomes less homogeneous in the gated community, we see less evidence of the action of the lease. My own experience of sitting on property disputes between leaseholders and freeholders is that the parties, even where the dispute reaches the tribunal, have rarely read and understood the lease (it might be added that legal representatives have not always done so either!). The actual technical content of the lease is therefore less important in terms of the day-to-day constitution of social relations than as a symbol of the relations.

However, I would not want to argue that the technical terms of the lease are not important – they have an important instrumental function. Although the freeholder enters into a separate lease with each leaseholder, those leases will also relate to each other. Thus, the lessor may well covenant to enforce the obligations imposed on other leaseholders within a particular development. The lease undoubtedly constitutes a network between all those who are signed up to such a term. But there is also a larger network here through which the lease resonates particularly where disputes arise. The lease will have had an originator – probably a conveyancer in a legal firm. The terms that have been specified will play a role in framing any dispute and in the outcome. But we know very little about how leases are created and why particular terms are included. Examining the lease at Parklands View illustrates some of the questions which might arise.

The development at Parklands View was very different from both of the communities studied by Blandy. It was on its face simply a new estate of 'executive-style' houses on the edge of a large city. It was neither a development of co-housing nor a gated community – there was no need for the creation of 'privately bounded spaces' (Harris, 2011) which we see in dense inner-city developments. It was therefore difficult to understand why houses were being sold on 200-year leases, with covenants that restricted the use of the property which would not occur in a freehold house.

Given the legal rights of leaseholders (particularly of houses) to enfranchise, there is an interesting question to be asked about why a developer would use a lease for this type of development. Undoubtedly, there is a role for lawyers here and something to be studied in relation to what Riles (2005) might call the aesthetics of property law – which lead to lawyers advising their clients to use this form of property arrangement. It may be linked to financial issues, but I would speculate there is something else going on about both the symbolism and the reality of the lease in terms of control. The reality arises, as in this case, where a developer is slowly building out an estate and will be selling houses prior to completion of the development. In such a case it may be felt to be important to keep control over how the homeowners behave and treat the houses because of the effect this might have on future purchasers (as discussed below this appeared to be some of the justification for taking action in the case). This, however, is speculative and requires further study.

Although parties may not be familiar with the terms of the lease, as we shall see, the terms may become important where disputes arise. Here we can consider another aspect of the lease and how its generation may become important to understanding the effect that it has. For a new development, the leases will be produced by the developer's lawyers. It is likely that they will be generated from some form of precedent. Here, I would argue, we see the implications of a form of legal technicalism (Riles, 2005, p. 976) coming into play. Lawyers are attracted to certainty of form – where precedents are used it is because they have been used before and shown to work, they have been interpreted by the courts, so that advice can be given on what they mean and how any disputes will turn out. There is, I would argue, an aesthetic to the lease, one that encompasses a reverence for what has gone before.

How else can one otherwise explain the fact that a lease entered into in 2003 provided this as one of its terms?

> Not to use the Demised Premises for any illegal or immoral pur-
> pose nor for any trade or business purpose whatsoever and not
> to keep pigs pigeons or poultry or any animal or animals other
> than the usual domestic pets and in any event not more than
> three for breeding purposes.

The thought of the purchasers of these executive homes keeping pigs or poultry (and, even in South Yorkshire, pigeons) seems unlikely – but this no doubt is the precedent that the lawyers had and knew and therefore used.

Butt (1993) suggests three reasons why lawyers write in traditional law-yers' language. The first is inertia (it is the way lawyers have always writ-ten), the second is necessity driven by the adversarial ethos – linked to the idea of certainty of form. The third provides an explanation of the use of exact precedents: 'the pace of modern legal practice reduces the time avail-able to research new ways of expressing old ideas; and when time is short it seems safer to stick to the old than risk adopting the new'. A similar point is made by Hyatt (1998) in relation to the terms of covenants in common interest communities in the USA. This last reason may also explain why not only is old-fashioned legal language maintained, but why terms which seem irrelevant are included.[5]

So, arguably, what we see here is a legal aesthetic generating a par-ticular legal form, which becomes a hardened technology, to be used in a variety of circumstances with no thought for its content. That form, while it may not impact on the daily social relations between the resi-dents on the estate and freeholder, becomes important when disputes arise. As Cowan et al. (2009) describe, some formal legal agreements may in fact fail to produce social relations or may only do so in certain lim-ited situations. In terms of the relationship between the freeholder and

---

5 My own experience in the LVT certainly indicates that precedent leases can be used and agreed to by all parties with little thought. In one case the lease of a Grade 2 listed house which had been converted into flats included provisions relating to the maintenance of the lift – there was no lift and clearly never would be given the Grade 2 listing.

leaseholder, the lease may not be mobile in the sense of creating and transforming the relationship on a daily basis, but once a dispute occurs it translates the parties into these respective roles. It is what Latour (2005, p. 207) refers to as a 'plug-in' – something which 'can simply *make* someone *do* something' (2005, p. 214, original emphasis). Despite its seeming lack of size, it exercises power (Cowan et al., 2009, p. 284). Here the relatively homogeneous social network is governed by the socio-legal object – the lease – created by actors who may know little or nothing of the physical reality of the spaces. Those actors tend to be backward-looking in relation to a socio-legal object which must govern relations over a long period of time.[6]

While the lease may not always be constitutive of day-to-day social relations, it sits in the background of the lives of lessors ready to be pulled out and relied on at particular points. The travel from the lawyer's offices to the lives of people in their homes indicates its mobility. It particularly travels over time – taking phrases from earlier leases into new leases which will potentially bind the owners of the particular land for several hundred years. Less clear is its immutability. It may well be that the lease becomes 'blackbox' like in the sense that there is little concern for its content, and only for the input and output. But Blandy's work might suggest that, although the lease may be constitutive of social life, the outputs (the nature of that constitution) vary and are not identical.

Solar panels on roofs

Having identified these two potential ways in which the lease is constitutive – of physical forms and social relations – this section of the chapter examines in more detail the context of and dispute in relation to solar panels and seeks to apply the insights above to the particular case.

The physical form

Government responses to climate change have been many and varied, but the Climate Change Act 2008 imposed legally binding targets on the government to reduce greenhouse gases. Domestic properties produce 25 per cent of CO_2 emissions (Department for Energy and Climate Change, 2014), so an improvement in the energy efficiency of homes and encouraging the use of alternative technologies to generate electricity for domestic use is a key component of climate change policy. According to some estimates,

---

6 Clarke (2006, p. 176) notes his experience as a chair of an LVT of cases coming before him of a lease of 500 years originally granted in 1563. The property had been subdivided to build individual houses – each by way of an assignment of part of the lease.

around 80 per cent of properties in the domestic sector that will be occupied in 2050 are already built (Boardman, 2007), so, in order to achieve change, it will be necessary to retro-fit many existing properties. One relatively simple technological step is to fit solar panels on the roofs of homes. Hence government policy has been to encourage the fitting of solar panels through the use of subsidized feed-in tariffs.

The problem for homeowners (whether freeholders or long-leaseholders) is that fitting solar panels requires a large capital outlay, which many homeowners cannot afford. In response to this, a number of firms have emerged seeking to take advantage of the feed-in tariffs. In order to do this and recoup a return, the firms required a return over a long period of time. The question was how this could be achieved in legal terms. Here was a (relatively) new technology which policy-makers wished to come into widespread use. Although financial incentives were on offer, this was not sufficient to make it happen. Those with the capital needed to interact with those with the physical space. The legal form which enabled these two to come together was the lease.

In some ways, this is simply a technical solution to the problem. A lease is used, rather than a contract, because of its technical possibilities. The lease can be registered, under the Land Registration Act 2002, as a proprietary right that binds future owners. Thus, if the property is sold, the lease will continue as against future owners. It also works because English law allows leases of airspace.

What we see here are two different technologies – the solar panel and the lease – being harnessed together to take advantage of government policies. At this moment we know very little of how this came about – the process which brings together the technologies and produces this network of associations between homeowners and solar panel firms. We do not know whether the firms offering a 'rent-a-roof' scheme were set up before the legal technology emerged or whether the legal technology was necessary in order for them to emerge. Are the leases used across the industry standard leases – have they in effect become black boxes?

Following this network and the role of the legal technology within it might enable us to understand better the problems of implementation of government policy. As Cowan and Carr (2008) and Rooke et al. (2012) have pointed out, there is a link between implementation studies and ANT. This is not an ANT study of the policy to put solar panels on roofs and the development of the rent-a-roof as one way of enabling it to happen. Could studying the lease (following its development and travel through the actors who developed the policy) as a socio-legal object give us an insight into the success of this policy?

Without being able to trace the reasons for the success of the policy empirically, one might argue that it was the legal form that was in part responsible for it. Thus, as with the condominium in Vancouver, it has come to shape our physical world in a particular way and further constitute our social relations as the solar panel becomes part of our normalized physical surroundings. Whether indeed such panels were normalized was part of the dispute which I turn to next.

The dispute and its resolution

The success of the scheme has led to a number of companies springing up which offer 'free' solar panels. One of these is A Shade Greener – 'the UK Market leader with over 11,000 free installs under our belt'. In the case of 11 and 27 Parklands View, the owners of the leaseholds on each of these properties had solar panels installed by this company. The installation, however, provoked a conflict with their freeholder who sought to invoke the power of the lease to prevent the use of solar panels.

In January 2011 the freeholder (Redmile) made an application to the LVT for a determination under s. 168(4) of the Commonhold and Leasehold Reform Act 2002 that the erection of the solar panels was a breach of the leases. Here I would argue that the network that had developed to enable the implementation of the government's solar panel policy has become disrupted by another network – that between the landlord and the tenant. It is one that was unexpected in this context – certainly for the leaseholders who, during the hearing, expressed their surprise and concern that as property 'owners' they could be treated in this way. The extent to which it was seen as disruptive to the network that the solar panel company had developed in its business was also indicated by the fact that it was the solar panel company which had apparently instructed (and presumably paid for) the barrister who represented the leaseholders at the hearing.

It was not at all clear why the freeholder had such strong objections to the panels that it was willing to incur the expenditure on litigation. The factual basis for the claim seemed to rest on some negative comments by potential purchasers and potential damage to the property from the loading on the roof, which in turn might invalidate guarantees. The former was not evidenced in any way at all and it was hard to discern the extent that it raised real commercial concerns for the freeholder in its role as developer.

The freeholder sought to invoke three clauses in the lease which it was alleged had been breached. One was based on the clause set out above, alleging use of the premises for a business. The second related to causing a 'nuisance or annoyance' and the third alleged a breach of the covenant not to make an alteration or addition without consent. I have already commented on the language used in the first of these. The reliance on older precedents was also obvious in the second which was in the following terms:

> Not to use the Demised Premises other than as a single private dwelling in the occupation of one family only with suitable outbuildings thereto and not to do or suffer thereon anything which may be noxious noisy or offensive or which may be or grow to be a nuisance or annoyance or cause damage or disturbance to the Lessor or any adjoining or neighbouring property or the owners or occupiers thereof.

As I have already suggested, this reliance on precedents may be motivated by a need for certainty. It may of course have do with more prosaic constraints of time and money which may encourage the use of existing precedents with little thought as to updating them to language and meaning that would be easily understood by the parties and would be relevant to problems that might arise in the future.

However it has been arrived at into its hardened technology, once invoked in a dispute the meaning of the lease becomes core to the outcome of the case. The certainty of the precedent comes into play at this stage as cases using the same or similar terms are invoked to indicate whether the behaviour complained of does in fact breach the term. Terms such as 'nuisance and annoyance' are commonplace and familiar. We have precedents where the courts have considered their meaning. In this case it was the word 'annoyance' that was particularly relevant. It had been considered in the case of *Tod-Heatley v Benham* (1889) 40 Ch D 80 at pp. 97–8:

> 'Annoyance' is a wider term than nuisance, and if you find a thing which reasonably troubles the mind and pleasure, not of a fanciful person or of a skilled person who knows the truth, but of the ordinary sensible English inhabitant of a house – if you find there is anything which disturbs his reasonable peace of mind, that seems to me to be an annoyance, although it may not appear to amount to physical detriment to comfort.

However, precedent only goes so far – the factual circumstances are never identical. In *Tod-Heatley* the court was dealing with a very different problem which would now be dealt with by regulatory mechanisms – i.e. someone setting up a hospital in a house they had leased. The premises were opened by the good Dr Benham as 'the *Queen's Jubilee Hospital* and Surgical Appliance Department for the treatment of diseases of the throat, nose, ear, skin, eye, fistula, and other diseases of the rectum, and various deformities of the human frame', which was intended for poor out-patients and supported by voluntary contributions. The key question was whether the attendance of the poor with these diseases constituted an annoyance.

But as is illustrated in the *Tod-Heatley* case, the term 'annoyance' has always been interpreted as an objective test of the reasonable person. So what would a reasonable person think of solar panels? This was something on which there were no reported decisions. Thus, in some senses the lease is both mutable and immutable. Its frame of interpretation 'the reasonable person' is immutable and fixed. However, the context for that interpretation becomes much more singular as Guggenheim (2010a; 2010b) suggests is also the case for the physical form (the building) to which it relates.

What the LVT found telling in the case was that many houses on the estate already had satellite dishes mounted on them. This is another form of technology that has (relatively) recently emerged and which it was a moot point whether the general provisions of the lease against nuisance and annoyance and against alterations prevented. The freeholder had to admit that it had taken no steps to prevent leaseholders putting these up. The tribunal members concluded:

> In our view a 'reasonable person' would no more find the panels annoying than they would the satellite dishes on the houses.
> (*Re 11 and 27 Parklands View*, [23])

In deciding this, the lease provides the conduit by which such a decision on the acceptability of solar panels can be made and through which the solar panel becomes part of the accepted physical fabric of our lives.

All the grounds for breach were dismissed by the tribunal.[7] In this instance, the freeholders were not able to use the lease to curtail the freedoms of the leaseholders as 'home owners'. The leaseholders had been surprised and upset by the assertion of control by the freeholders which had disrupted the way that they exercised ownership over what they considered 'their properties'. While they had been happy to cede legal rights through the lease of the air space, they had not been happy when the lease of the property had been used to limit their control. While the lease clearly created a relationship between the lessees and the freeholder, the relationship was not one of any depth and did not seem to play a significant role in the day-to-day lives of the leaseholders. The example of the satellite dishes indicated that it was only in certain circumstances (and it was not clear

---

7 The business use argument was a complete non-starter. The solar panels were, however, found to be an 'addition' which required consent, but the tribunal concluded that consent had been unreasonably withheld and that in one of the cases the breach had been waived by acceptance of ground rent.

what these were) that the lease would be invoked to constitute a relationship where the freeholder sought to control the property use. Thus, the lease was not constitutive of the daily material realities of the leaseholders and their relations with others.

Rather, the lease came into play when, for whatever reason, the freeholder decided that the particular behaviour came into conflict with its own interests. At that point, we see the particular form of the lease, using precedents which provide a very general but familiar (for lawyers) language, being invoked. Where, as here, the parties cannot resolve their differences, the matter is decided by the tribunal which becomes the arbiter of the application of these terms to the new technology. While the 'physical and textural integrity' (Valverde, 2005, p. 422) of the lease is retained, it is applied to a novel situation.

Conclusion

The intention of the chapter is to illustrate that the lease can be studied afresh through new eyes. It is not just a dry and dusty document full of clauses that only (or not even) lawyers understand. It operates, I would argue, as a socio-legal object. It potentially does this at different scales of network – in enabling and constituting the physical form of the world around us as part of the network which changes that form. Arguably, the lease here became an immutable mobile – a technology. Its form became static and, indeed, potentially black-boxed, but travelled from the lawyer's offices to the firms doing deals with homeowners.

Here, there is the close link with policy implementation. In the particular case of solar panels, the policy was seeking to introduce a new technology into a mass use. As the literature illustrates, the adoption of new technologies is not without problems (Lovell, 2005). In this case one of the problems was enabling recovery of the capital cost over a long period of time. This could not be achieved without the legal technicality of the lease, although the role of the particular legal form is one that has not been examined. But, it is hoped that, drawing on the work of Harris and through this example of solar panels, provides an illustration of how the particularity of legal documents and forms may be relevant to studies of policy implementation, and also to the particular built form in which we live. It indicates how it is necessary to consider how law may translate other technological change in the housing form.

But on a very different scale – of the day-to-day relations between neighbours and between those with different interests in the same property – the lease is also important. The story here is one of social relations without any particular policy implementation context, as are many of the relations between different occupiers and owners of houses. Thus, we may be interested in the very small and immediate relationship between a freeholder and a leaseholder. We may be interested in the relationships between a group of leaseholders in the same building, or a larger community on a development. In each case, these may be said to be connected together through the legal instrument of the lease. As Blandy has illustrated, the lease may be constitutive of those social relations. The effect of the lease may go beyond its actual working to be invoked to produce further rules and standards of behaviour. In this sense, it is a form of Foucauldian self-regulation. In order to understand how it acts a socio-legal object requires, as Cloatre (2008) suggests, further empirical study. In this situation it is certainly also mobile, but is it immutable? In physical terms it is certainly immutable – unlike the house which can be changed physically (and thereby have its use changed), the lease cannot be rendered different physically. In legal terms it is almost immutable because amending it without the consent of all the parties is very difficult.[8] But those who are associated through it may imagine, assume and act as if it has different contents from those contained within it. Is it therefore black-boxed or, rather, is it an empty box into which different understandings can be put? Does it at times lose its 'legal' nature?

It may also only come in to play at moments of falling-out and dispute. Such a dispute may occur where new technologies not envisaged by the creators of the lease are brought into play. Here, the type of wording that is used in the lease, while based on precedents which seem to give a form of certainty, often also leave room for an interpretative moment. Where the parties cannot agree, that interpretative task falls to the appropriate court or tribunal. Here a standard of the 'reasonable person' when interpreting terms permits the decision to move beyond the particular dispute between the parties and lay down a marker for other relationships governed by similar terms.

We know very little about how leases are created – which terms are included and why. What we do know is that those terms govern not only the relationship between the original parties to the lease, but also, potentially over hundreds of years, future owners of the property and of adjacent properties. Because the terms are then replicated in other leases, the process of interpretation by the courts and tribunals then means that those meanings speak to different leases at different times.

ANT makes us focus on how the social is created. It has been described as a sociology of associations (Callon, 1986). Within this, it treats the human

---

8 See the provisions of the Landlord and Tenant Act 1987, ss 35–7 which provide for application to vary a lease to the tribunal in certain limited circumstances.

and non-human equally and indifferently. This approach is not without its critics, particularly that the post-human focus leads to a lack of focus on human injustice and suffering (see Gabriel and Jacobs, 2008, for an overview in the context of housing research). Nonetheless, for legal scholars I would suggest that there is some merit in the approach. It allows us to think differently about the objects (leases, contracts, statutes) that lawyers create, to follow them through both time and space to view how they create socio-material realities.

Cases

Re 11 and 27 Parklands View case references MAN/00CF/LBC/2011/0002 and 0003
Tod-Heatley v Benham (1889) 40 Ch D 80

References

Alexander, G S (1994) 'Conditions of "Voice": Passivity, Disappointment and Democracy in Homeowner Associations' in S E Barton and J Silverman (eds), *Common Interest Communities: Private Government and the Public Interest* (Berkeley: Institute of Governmental Studies, University of California)

Blandy, S (2010) 'Legal Frameworks for Multi-owned Housing in England and Wales: Owners' experiences' in S Blandy, A Dupuis and J Dixon (eds), *Multi-owned Housing: Law, Power and Practice* (Farnham: Ashgate)

Blandy, S (2013) 'Collective Property: Owning and Sharing Residential Space' in N Hopkins (ed.), *Modern Studies in Property Law* vol. 7 (Oxford: Hart Publishing)

Blandy, S and B Goodchild (1999) 'From Tenure to Rights: Conceptualising the Changing Focus of Housing Law in England' 16(1) *Housing Theory and Society* 31–42

Blandy, S and D Lister (2005) 'Gated Communities: (Ne)gating Community Development' 20(2) *Housing Studies* 287–301

Boardman, B (2007) *Home Truths: A Low-carbon Strategy to Reduce UK Housing Emissions by 80% by 2050* (Oxford: Co-operative Bank and Friends of the Earth) www.foe.co.uk/resource/reports/home_truths.pdf

Bromley, R D F, A R Tallon and A J Roberts (2007) 'New Populations in the British City Centre: Evidence of Social Change from the Census and Household Surveys' 38(1) *Geoforum* 138–54

Bright, S and N Hopkins (2011) 'Home, Meaning and Identity: Learning from the English Model of Shared Ownership' 28(4) *Housing Theory and Society* 377–97

Butt, P (1993) 'Plain Language and Conveyancing' (July/August) *Conveyancer and Property Lawyer* 256–69

Callon, M (1986) 'Some Elements in a Sociology of Translation: Domestication of the Scallops and Fishermen of St Brieuc Bay' in J Law (ed.), *Power, Action, Belief* (London: Routledge)

Carr, H (2011) 'The Right to Buy, the Leaseholder and the Impoverishment of Ownership' 38(4) *Journal of Law and Society* 519–41

Clarke, A and P Kohler (2005) *Property Law: Commentary and Materials* (Cambridge: Cambridge University Press)

Clarke, D (2006) 'Long Residential Leases: Future Directions' in S Bright (ed.), *Landlord and Tenant Law: Past, Present and Future* (Oxford: Hart Publishing)

Cloatre, E (2008) 'Trips and Pharmaceutical Patents in Djibouti: An ANT Analysis of Socio-legal Objects' 17(2) *Social and Legal Studies* 263–81

Cowan D and Carr H (2008) 'Actor-Network Theory, Implementation and the Private Landlord' 35(2) *Journal of Law and Society* 149–66

Cowan, D, K Morgan and M McDermont (2009) 'Nominations: An Actor-Network Approach' 24(3) *Housing Studies* 281–300

Davey, M (2006) 'Long Residential Leases: Past and Present' in S Bright (ed.), *Landlord and Tenant Law: Past, Present and Future* (Oxford: Hart Publishing)

Department for Energy and Climate Change (2014) *2013 UK Greenhouse Gas Emissions, Provisional Figures and 2012 UK Greenhouse Gas Emissions, Final Figures by Fuel Type and End-User* www.gov.uk/government/uploads/system/uploads/attachment_data/file/295968/20140327_2013_UK_Greenhouse_Gas_Emissions_Provisional_Figures.pdf

Farias, I (2010) 'Introduction: Decentring the Object of Urban Studies' in I Farias and T Bender (eds), *Urban Assemblages: How Actor-Network Theory Changes Urban Studies* (Abingdon: Routledge), pp. 1–24

Faulkner, A, B Lange and C Lawless (2012) 'Introduction: Material Worlds: Intersections of law, Science, Technology and Society' 39(1) *Journal of Law and Society* 1–19

Fox, L (2007) *Conceptualising Home: Theories, Laws and Policies* (Oxford: Hart Publishing)

Gabriel, M and K Jacobs (2008) 'The Post-social Turn: Challenges for Housing Research' 23(6) *Housing Studies* 527–40

Grove, G A and J F Garner (eds) (1963) *An Introduction to the Principles of Land Law* (London: Sweet & Maxwell) (4th edn)

Guggenheim, M (2010a) 'The Law of Foreign Buildings: Flat Roof and Minarets' 19(4) *Social and Legal Studies* 441–60

Guggenheim, M (2010b) 'Mutable Immobiles: Building Conversion as a Problem of Quasi-technologies' in I Farias and T Bender (eds), *Urban Assemblages: How Actor-Network Theory Changes Urban Studies* (Abingdon: Routledge), pp. 161–78

Gurney, C (1990) *The Meaning of Home in the Decade of Owner Occupation: Towards and Experiential Perspective* (Bristol: School of Advanced Urban Studies, University of Bristol)

Harris, D C (2011) 'Condominium and the City: The Rise of Property in Vancouver' 36(3) *Social and Legal Inquiry* 694–726

Hyatt, W S (1998) 'Common Interest Communities: Evolution and Revolution' 31(Winter) *John Marshall Law Review* 303–95

Latour, B (1987) *Science in Action: How to Follow Scientists and Engineers through Society* (Cambridge, MA: Harvard University Press)

Latour, B (1991) 'Technology is Society Made Durable' in J Law (ed.), *A Sociology of Monsters: Essays on Power, Technology and Domination* (London: Routledge), pp. 103–31

Latour, B (2005) *Reassembling the Social: An Introduction to Actor-network Theory* (Oxford: Oxford University Press)

Latour, B (2010) *The Making of Law: An Ethnography of the Conseil d'Etat'* (M Brilman and A Pottage trans.) (Cambridge: Polity Press)

Lovell, H (2005) 'Supply and Demand for Low Energy Housing in the UK: Insights from a Science and Technology Studies Approach' 20(5) *Housing Studies* 815–29

Luhmann, N (2000) *Organisation und Entsheidung* (Opladen: Westdeutscher Verlag)

Moore, S F (1973) 'Law and Social Change: The Semi-autonomous Social Field as an Appropriate Subject of Study' 7 *Law and Social Change* 719

Rooke, C, E Cloatre and R Dingwall (2012) 'The Regulation of Nicotine in the United Kingdom: How Nicotine Gum Came to Be a Medicine, But Not a Drug' 39(1) *Journal of Law and Society* 39–57

Riles, A (2005) 'A New Agenda for the Cultural Study of Law: Taking on the Technicalities' 53 *Buffalo Law Review* 973–1033

Riles, A (2011) *Collateral Knowledge* (Chicago: University of Chicago Press)

Saunders, P (1990) *A Nation of Home Owners* (London: Unwin Hyman)

Smith, P (2009) 'Apartment Ownership – The Irish Reform Package' 73(1) *Conveyancer and Property Lawyer* 21–38

Valverde, M (2005) 'Authorising the Production of Urban Moral Order: Appellate Courts and their Knowledge Games' 39(2) *Law and Society Review* 419–56

8

Bringing the Technical into the Socio-legal: The Metaphors of Law and Legal Scholarship of a Twenty-First Century European Union

Paul James Cardwell and Tamara Hervey*

Introduction

The narrative form – particularly as an origin story and (folk) history – remains a potent constitutive mechanism for creating and sustaining communities, including legal communities. There is a way to tell the story of EU law or the roles of law in EU integration that begins from a faith in law in the 1950s, turns away from law (to governance) in the 1990s, and, after 2008, either returns to law, or even hyper-legalism, or, in the alternative, eschews law as a means to solve Europe's problems. This story may even be the 'received wisdom' as to EU law's foundations and development. It is at least a recognized dominant narrative. It is a narrative of both EU law and the study of EU law.

Put into the terms of this book, the dominant narrative therefore proceeds along the lines of a focus on 'the legal'; a focus on 'the socio'; followed by a return to a focus on the legal (either as a return to faith in the legal, or as a rejection of the legal (Sharon Cowan, this volume)). EU law was initially seen, and studied, as technical legal doctrine; there followed

*   We are grateful to the participants at the workshops on The Methods of European Integration, Central University Budapest, June 2012; the panel on Methods of Integration at the University Association for Contemporary European Studies Annual Conference, Passau, September 2012; and the workshops Exploring the Legal in Socio-Legal Studies, London School of Economics, September 2012; Theorising Integration and Governance after the Lisbon Treaty and During Crisis, Sheffield, July 2013; The New Intergovernmentalism, Budapest, November 2013, at which versions of this chapter were delivered, especially Dave Cowan, Uwe Puetter, Dermot Hodson and Simon Bulmer. We are also grateful to the editors and anonymous reviewer and to Pablo Castillo Ortiz, Niamh Nic Shuibhne and Nina Boeger for their useful comments and suggestions, although we were not able to incorporate all of those in this version of the chapter.

a turn to socio-legal scholarship of EU law, where law was understood through socio-legal approaches; and more recently there is either a return to legal doctrine, or a rejection altogether of law as an important factor in EU studies or the future of the EU. Of course, to cast the story in those terms implies a disconnection between the dyad 'legal'–'socio' – a relationship which scholars of the sociology of law have puzzled at for generations. Rather than engaging directly with that question, for the purposes of this chapter, we will accept the distinction as a useful device. We want to suggest a different way of telling the story of EU law and EU legal studies, particularly the story of its turn to (and away from) the socio-legal. We suggest that attention to 'legal technicality' (the legal of socio-legal, as the title of this book has it) has much to offer towards such a retelling. What if we seek to uncover the legal in the socio-legal, and vice versa? How might attention to legal technicality *as a socially understood phenomenon* enrich EU socio-legal scholarship? How does the story go then?

As well as demonstrating the method of 'telling' and 'retelling', we also investigate and interrogate *narration* as a socio-legal method(ology). In recognizing the provisionality of narrative, what do we reveal about the limitations and the promise of the legal or the socio-legal, for instance, in the 'project' of European Union? And what does such a retelling offer in terms of future research agendas for (EU) law?

Before we begin, a brief note on the object of study. We are interested in both EU law and EU legal studies. While we appreciate that these are distinct, we justify bringing them together here by reference to the ways in which (EU) lawyers and (EU) legal scholars are members of interlocking and overlapping communities (see also Sanders and Griffiths, this volume). One need think only of the permeability of the boundaries between the EU's Court of Justice (CJEU) and the legal academy (many of the CJEU's judges and référendaires (legal clerks) held academic positions before or after serving at the CJEU) to illustrate these connections.

Bringing the technical into the socio-legal: the power of metaphor

Drawing on much older debates about 'law and society' or 'law in society', contemporary scholars such as Riles (2005; 2011) and, following her lead, Cowan, Hunter and Pawson (2012) have rediscovered legal doctrine or technicality as an important asset in the study of law, in particular where attention is being paid to legal culture(s). Legal technicality resonates with Ewick and Silbey's (1998) notion of law or legality as a game, a 'terrain for tactical encounters' or a social resource to be deployed for strategic goals. Lawyers (in practice and in the academy) can be culturally understood as 'legal technicians', 'engineers' (Howarth, 2013), 'plumbers'

(Twining, 1967), or 'instrumentalists', who 'view law in primarily pragmatic instrumental terms, as a tool to be judged by its successes or failures in achieving stated ends' (Riles 2005, pp. 973–4). Intuitively, especially for those of us for whom the contrast between 'law in the books' and 'law in context' has formed an important part of our own professional stories (see Philippopoulos-Mihalopoulos, this volume), the technicalities of law, or legal doctrines, have little to do with law or legality understood as socially constructed. But new understandings of the relationships between law and society help us to see that legal technicality represents the very things that socio-legal scholars are interested in: the places where the politics (or economics, or ethics and so on) are actually played out 'along with the hopes, ambitions, fantasies and day-dreams of armies of legal engineers' (Riles, 2005, p. 975). For instance, the sites of 'exotic new forms of private governance' turn out to contain 'quotidian humdrum legal knowledge practices' (Riles, 2011, p. 15). A deep focus on legal technicality can also play a 'critical' role, in helping to uncover the ways in which law sustains certain assumptions that support structures of power as 'background rules of the game', essentially by hiding them from scrutiny.

A key narrative mechanism through which lawyers as legal technicians operate is that of the metaphor. Showing how law operates through metaphors, which become literalized, reified and extraordinarily resilient, is therefore an important task for socio-legal scholarship. As Cowan et al. (2012) have shown in the context of housing law, we think that exposing the metaphorical, expressed through legal technicality, offers great promise in the context of EU law. (For an example of work considering the metaphorical in EU legal scholarship that focuses on an analysis of legal textbooks, see Hervey, 2013). Uncovering metaphors allows us not so much to understand the technical legal rules, arguments and approaches of EU law in their own terms, 'but in appreciating the truths which they translate and which others translate through them' (Cowan et al., 2012, p. 277). By 'truths', we do not mean objectively verifiable facts, but cultural understandings; stories and myths; even dreams, hopes or fears. We are responding to and building on the discussion begun by Paul Craig (2013), discussing the *Pringle* ruling[1] on the European Stability Mechanism, of the 'implicit metaphors' of EU law: 'contractual', 'governance and integration', and 'governance and survival'. Craig understands these metaphors in instrumental terms and, to a significant extent, we would agree. But in what follows, we also show that the metaphors of EU law play a role that can be understood sociologically, of creating a community of which, by which and for which the 'origin story' of EU law is told.

---

1 Case C-370/12 *Pringle* ECLI:EU:C:2012:756.

We do so through a primary focus on the canonical metaphor of EU law: the idea that it is a 'single legal order', distinct from, and superior to, both international law and the legal systems of its member states. While we might quibble as to whether this is a metaphor, and some may claim that it is literally true, the very possibility of such a discussion is enough for us to be interested in considering the idea of EU law as a single legal order metaphorically. We also consider the instrumental metaphor of EU law as a tool to create peace and prosperity, which supports the canonical single legal order metaphor. And we consider the metaphorical support for the main counter-narrative to the single legal order story: the idea of EU law as a space or place. To summarize, we think these metaphors support Europeanization (a highly contentious process) in several interlocking ways. By implying that the CJEU holds a uniquely authoritative position within a single hierarchical legal order (cf. Přibáň, this volume), the metaphor paints reality through a beguiling narrative, framing the world in a way presented as unquestionable. This framing provides an apparently 'safe' space for resolving difficult and deeply contested political, economic or ethical questions. It works to support the claim that legal or judicial processes are a valid (or even the optimal) way to settle such contestations. It reifies and unifies what might otherwise be understood as much more contingent and multifaceted settlements.

Further, the metaphor operates to persuade that the settlement developed by the CJEU's jurisprudence (either a line of decisions, or a single case) – as opposed to that of other courts – is an optimal settlement. It thus masks and neutralizes matters that are deeply contested. Where we would go further than Craig is by also seeking to understand the metaphor of a single EU legal order through a sociological lens. As the scholarship noted above has shown, legal metaphors also do their work through the networks of legal actors who subscribe to and perpetuate them. An idea of a single EU legal order works to create and sustain a sense of a unitary community, or set of relationships, that is relatively fixed through time, and that self-defines through certain shared (legal) values. Therefore, the single legal order metaphor also masks the temporal contingency of EU law and the community of its lawyers (for an elaboration of the ways in which the community of EU lawyers – if it even exists as objective reality – is fractured, incomplete and contingent through time; see Cohen and Vauchez, 2011).

The metaphors of EU law I: a tool to create all that is good

According to the received wisdom, for at least the earliest generation of EU lawyers and legal scholars, the legal is instrumental. (EU) law was a means to an end – an end with a powerful, even urgent, normative basis, that of avoiding war in (western) Europe. Peace and prosperity were to be promoted by a process of 'integration', that is, an increasing enmeshment of the economies of (western) European nation states. The metaphor that EU law is a tool to achieve integration, order, peace, (economic) development and prosperity, both within the EU itself, and for a wider geographical area (through, primarily, the enlargement of the EU, but also through EU external relations law) endures. One can find many of its proponents among contemporary EU lawyers and legal scholars. For these instrumentalists, EU law fails or succeeds depending on the extent to which policy areas are Europeanized through law and (nationally determined) political or economic desires are subjugated to (EU level) legal rules. Technical legal argument is an important tool in the toolbox and can (and, implicitly, according to such scholars, should) be deployed to further these goals. We would argue that this notion – the *inherent* capacity of (EU) law to promote such self-evident benefits, both within and outside the EU's geographical territory – deserves to be investigated further.

The idea of EU law as a tool to create peace and prosperity was constructed in the imagination of EU legal scholars as essentially a court-driven phenomenon, built on the explication of generally applicable legal principles from often extremely open legal texts, through the standard modes of technical legal reasoning. Such formalistic deduction of consequences from abstract rules could be inspired by the 'civil law' method, that is, based on a positivistic determination of legal texts, followed deductively through syllogism. Increasingly, after the UK and Ireland joined the EU in the 1970s, the CJEU's reasoning was inspired by the 'common law' method (Arnull, 1999), that is, determined through a form of *stare decisis* (though the CJEU is technically not bound by its own previous rulings) and applied by analogy. A tight community of lawyers and legal scholars (especially before the 1970s accessions) consciously (Cohen, 2007; Vauchez, 2008; Stone Sweet, 2010; Cohen and Vauchez, 2011) drew on legal principles recognizable in national legal contexts. The *erga omnes* effect of EU law implied by the technical doctrinal method meant that apparently uncontroversial decisions, in abstruse areas, could have enormous consequences in practice across a range of other contexts. For instance, the CJEU decision to the effect that EU law is 'supreme', that is, must be applied in priority over conflicting national rules,[2] which was of the utmost significance to the future development of all EU law, was decided in a case involving electricity privatization where the damages due (for failure to pay an electricity bill) were the princely sum of 1925 Italian lira (Steiner, 1988, p. 32), the equivalent

---

2 Case 6/64 *Costa v ENEL* ECLI:EU:C:1964:66.

of £2.43/€3 in today's currency. The same point can be made about the doctrine of indirect effect, whereby all national law must be interpreted by national courts in conformity with EU law, as decided in a case relating to the reimbursement of travel expenses for a job interview (approximately 3 DEM/€6.50).[3]

A closer attention to metaphor as a social or cultural resource of the EU lawyer as pro-integration instrumentalist reveals that the low practical salience of the contexts in which such fundamental doctrines of EU law were established through technical legal argument is not irrelevant. Even in this phase of EU (legal) studies, a counter-narrative (provided largely by political scientists studying the CJEU) explains the legal as clothing or hiding the politics of integration (particularly as carried out by the CJEU) in the formal routines and practices of the law. EU law had a technical quality, but it was almost a parody of the technical that may have shielded or masked the integration process from some kinds of political pressure (Stein, 1981; Burley and Mattli, 1993). If the binary opposition of law and integration to anarchy and disintegration of European societies characterized the foundational phase of what is now the EU, fundamental challenges to that notion have arisen during the years that followed. For some legal scholars, the masking of politics by legal technicalities was far from benign. The debates between Coppell and O'Neill (1992) and Weiler and Lockhart (1995), on the effects on human rights protection in Europe of the CJEU's developing doctrine on EU human rights law, are a well-known example.

In the received wisdom, beginning from the 1980s, the changing features of the EU are reflected in the widening horizon of legal scholarship, which is interested in different research agendas and adopted alternative methods to the court-focused technical legal scholarship of the foundational phase. This evolution is encapsulated in Shaw and More's (1995) idea of 'new legal dynamics of European Union'. The turn to socio-legal approaches to studying EU law is accompanied by an interest in critical legal studies of EU law. Early (English language) socio-legal studies in EU law (Snyder, 1987, 1990) concentrated on uncovering the hidden power relationships in EU (administrative) law (for instance, of neocolonialism) and the institutional and ideological contexts within which substantive EU law was developed and applied. Explicitly postmodern approaches to EU law (Ward, 1996), and other critical approaches, such as those incorporating an explicitly critical feminist frame of analysis (Fenwick and Hervey, 1995; McGlynn, 2006), were developed.

But these studies by and large eschewed deep exploration of the legal doctrine applicable in the relevant policy areas, and how legal technicality,

---

3   Case 14/83 *Von Colson* ECLI:EU:C:1984:153.

expressed through the metaphorical, supports power relationships. Might there be aspects of EU technical legal reasoning, in areas as wide-ranging as social policy, fisheries, environment, energy, defence and so on, where this metaphor is so embedded in the law that we cannot see ways in which EU law disintegrates, disorders, destroys, for instance, through the power of the market? Where does EU law's 'naming' exclude the meanings or narratives of other (non-legal) professionals or the disempowered (Ohana, Carr, Hunter, this volume)? For whom is the 'origin story' of EU law being told, and who is excluded from the plot? Building on existing socio- and critical legal approaches to EU legal scholarship, we suggest that this possibility is worth further investigation.

Furthermore, in the latest phase of EU legal scholarship, the metaphor of EU law as a tool for peace, prosperity and development continues to resonate strongly. As Craig (2013) has shown, the response of the CJEU[4] to the tangled web of instruments that make up the EU's response to global financial and Eurozone crises can be understood through several possible 'implicit legal metaphors', including that of 'governance and survival' (2013, p. 268). The cost here to 'rule of law' protections, such as transparency, accountability and reviewability for consistency with human rights, is masked by the belief in the metaphor of EU law as a tool for all that is good.

The metaphors of EU law II: a single legal system

According to the 'standard foundation story', the process of European integration, though based in administrative cooperation (for instance, in agricultural policy, trade policy, or on coal and steel production), was to be underpinned by a body of (international) law. The instruments setting up what is now the EU are international treaties – legal instruments which express agreements between sovereign states. Technically, such an understanding of the contractual nature of the EU's treaties implies that EU law does not exist beyond that which is willed by the governments of its states. The implication of the metaphor of contract is that states are bound by EU law, but they can revise their obligations at will, and the 'rule of (EU) law' means no more than that.

But the EU's founding treaties also set up supranational institutions that escaped the control of the governments that set them up. The CJEU, in partnership with national courts, began with increasing confidence to build a body of legal principles that not only sought to ensure that the member states would not escape their (agreed) obligations in EU law (relying on the metaphor of contract), but that also expressed principles

---

4 In *Pringle*.

going beyond those explicitly agreed by the governments of the sovereign member states (relying on different metaphors altogether). The idea of EU law as its own, self-perpetuating, legal system, similar to that of a state, was born in the CJEU's imagination and accepted and perpetuated through legal scholarship. In so doing, the CJEU also sought to enrol private litigants (mainly firms which traded across EU borders) in the process of enforcement of EU law. Magisterial studies of the role of law in European integration (Cappelletti et al., 1986; Weiler, 1991) explained these processes, implicitly casting the CJEU as a technical genius in harnessing the ability of international agreements, expressed in very general terms, to condition and constrain state governments through its exercise of standard legal reasoning, recognized across Europe. In the predominant view of legal scholars of that generation, (EU) law was implicitly constructed as part of a binary opposition to the anarchy of war, or to the whim of political preferences of national governments (as expressed through contract). (EU) law represented order and certainty for private actors, and thence economic development.

This account of EU law has little to do with socio-legal studies, at least as traditionally understood. The law is the law of the text. The methods of its study are technical or doctrinal. What matters, and what is interesting ('where the action is'), are the decisions of courts – in particular the CJEU, but also national courts. National, higher level courts are cast either as 'progressives' or 'laggards'. The former are those that accept the authority of EU law in similar doctrinal/technical terms to those adopted by the CJEU (e.g. courts in the Netherlands or Belgium). The latter are those that fail to do so (e.g. Italian or German constitutional courts) (Schermers and Waelbroeck, 1992). Movement from the latter to the former camp is greeted enthusiastically by the academy, as evidencing compliance with the rule of law (Craig, 1991).

According to these legally defined principles, emerging from case law, rather than from the literal text of formal Treaty arrangements, EU law thus becomes understood as both implicitly embodying a distinct legal order and also occupying a superior position in a hierarchy with other (national) legal orders. At least arguably, they represent the most important, embedded and enduring metaphor about the EU: the idea that it is an entity that, like a state, has a single and unitary legal system,[5] and that its relationships with its component states are like those in a federal legal system. Recognizing these claims about EU law as metaphorical offers at least five benefits to EU legal scholarship.

---

5 Of course, a few states, e.g. the UK, have more than one legal system.

Illuminating 'puzzles' of doctrinal scholarship

First, seeing the claim that EU law is a single, hierarchically superior legal system as metaphorical assists enormously in illuminating what otherwise present as 'puzzles' of doctrinal scholarship. Certainly for the CJEU itself, and also for many legal scholars, the EU's self-declared 'new legal order'[6] provided the springboard for an entire body of scholarship that in practice interprets EU law as if it were the law of a state. The single legal order metaphor became reified in EU law and legal scholarship, in just the same way that Riles describes the metaphor of law as a tool becoming embedded in conflicts scholarship. The CJEU's reasoning in a very wide range of areas, including supremacy of EU law,[7] judicial protection,[8] relationships between the CJEU and national courts[9] and other international organizations,[10] relies on this metaphor. Understanding that the EU's single legal order is a culturally created metaphor, expressive of truths in the sense of hopes and dreams (for Europhiles), or fears (for Eurosceptics), rather than of objective reality, helps us to understand some of the apparently irresolvable puzzles of EU doctrinal legal scholarship, such as what the proper legal relationship is between the CJEU and the European Court of Human Rights (ECHR) in Strasbourg.

The metaphor of the EU's legal order as a unitary entity was crucial to the development of ideas of the constitutional basis of EU law, as opposed to notions of EU law as a variant of ordinary international law. The concerns with 'democratic deficit' and consequent turn in the 2000s to 'constitutionalism' in its general form was reflected in literature explicitly situating EU legal scholarship within a constitutional frame (Weiler, 1999; Weiler and Wind, 2003; Cremona and de Witte, 2008; Curtin, 2009). The law in context (or 'living constitutionalism' (Curtin, 2009)) approach to the administrative law aspects of EU constitutional law also gained prominence (contrast Schwarze, 2006, with Harlow, 2002, or Curtin, 2009). Taking this constitutionalist frame further, a significant body of EU legal literature draws on normative political theory (a selection includes MacCormick, 1999; Walker, 2005; Eleftheriadis, 2007; Somek, 2008; De Búrca and Weiler, 2011).

But the single legal order narrative, upon which the doctrines of EU law, and the methodological assumptions about its study, are based, became more and more difficult to sustain empirically, as socio-legal studies of EU law showed that a 'multi-speed' Europe emerged from at least the early

---

6 Case 26/62 *Van Gend en Loos* ECLI:EU:C:1963:1.

7 E.g. *Costa v ENEL*; Case C-213/89 *Factortame* [1990] ECLI:EU:C:1990:257.

8 E.g. Cases C-6 & 9/90 *Francovich* ECLI:EU:C:1995:372.

9 E.g. Case C-224/01 *Köbler* [2003] ECLI:EU:C:2003:513.

10 E.g. Case C-84/95 *Bosphorus Airways* ECLI:EU:C:1996:312; Cases C-402 & 415/05-P *Kadi* ECLI:EU:C:2008:461.

1990s. If there is an EU constitution, it is based on a constitutionalism that renders (representational) politics at best decentred and at worst arid and marginalized (Přibáň, this volume). Variable constellations of member states over areas of EU law such as opt-outs from stage three of economic and monetary union, the 'Schengen *acquis*', border controls on people, permanent structured cooperation in defence, and even core areas such as social policy, have proliferated since before the Maastricht Treaty of 1992 first set out the idea of 'differentiated integration' in Treaty form. The extent of these examples of variable geometry has gone beyond the stage where they could realistically be counted as exceptions to the general rule, and this has led some scholars to call for formalization of a 'two-speed' Europe (Piris, 2012).

Additionally, there is increasing dissatisfaction with older accounts of the ways in which EU law interacts with other legal systems, such as the law of the United Nations, the law of the Council of Europe/ECHR, and national law. This unease with the hierarchy implicit in the earlier approaches has resulted in an interest in legal pluralism, and heterarchical models, in EU legal studies (for instance, MacCormick, 1999; Walker, 2002; Krisch, 2008; Walker, 2008; Lock, 2009; Walker et al., 2011), much of which overlaps with the constitutionalism literature. Understanding that dissatisfactions with analysing EU law or understanding that Europeanization as based on a single legal system can be explained by the metaphorical nature of that contention reveals that the tools and methods of legal research that are deployed to understand such a system as if it existed in objective reality are inadequate to the task. The single legal order is like Teubner's 'constitutional illusion', driven by fantasies (Přibáň, this volume) of differentiated social or political actors.

Indicating new methods for studying EU law

Second, therefore, seeing the metaphorical nature of the claim of EU law as a single legal system opens up new ways of understanding and studying EU law that are both socio-legal and technical legal. We suggest that studies of EU substantive law would gain much by paying closer attention to the ways in which the metaphor of a single legal system supports and sustains, almost invisibly, the phenomena in which they are interested. Legal scholarship often leaves such conceptual questions implicit (Van Gestel et al., 2012), and EU legal scholarship is no different. In our view, analyses of EU law that rely (implicitly) on assumptions of systemic unity (with, for instance, implications of hierarchy)[11] and internal consistency, as well

---

11 For instance, early analysis of data on UK courts applying EU commercial/consumer law suggests that notions of hierarchy and systemic unity are woefully inadequate to account for judicial reasoning, suggesting that the methods of comparative law will be more appropriate in such contexts, see Harrison and Hervey, forthcoming.

as (relative) fixity through time – all underlying assumptions of technical legal analysis – would be significantly enhanced by illuminating the limitations of such an analytical frame. If EU law is not a unitary entity, but consists of 'common law', 'Scandinavian', 'civil law' versions and so on, then studies of particular substantive areas would be significantly enhanced by drawing on comparative law concepts that recognize the culturally contingent nature of law and legal systems (Cotterrell, 2006). EU law becomes 'domesticated' within each legal system: it is a 'hybrid' that is transformed by each national legal order (Walker, 2005) and needs to be studied as such. The technical doctrines of domestic and EU law, studied in their respective cultural and social contexts, have the potential to reveal much about how EU law supports or disrupts the positions of different actors. Equally, there is scope for work considering how metaphors of unity, and implied hierarchy, work to sustain legal relationships, for instance, in contracts operating across borders.

Understanding EU law as neutralizing contested questions

Third, the claim of EU law as a single legal system supports a key totalizing mechanism of EU law – the idea of 'read across' ('continuity', Ohana, this volume) in the sense of application of a legal principle developed in one particular context in other, unexpected contexts. Within a single legal system, a technical legal approach is to expect consistency of legal principles, and, indeed, such a concept in practice can tell us what the law *is*. Read-across can take place even if the application of legal principles in novel areas is not politically popular among (some) national governments, if the CJEU is involved, and national courts play along. This has happened in a very broad range of areas of EU law. In *Pupino*,[12] the principle of direct effect was read across from 'ordinary' EU law to (then) 'third pillar' law; in *Mangold*[13] and *Küçükdeveci*[14] direct effect, hitherto understood as a characteristic of some explicit written legal texts, was applied to fundamental rights as 'general principles' of EU law. The concept of market access was read across from the case law on goods to that on services and establishment (Barnard, 2001; Barnard and Scott, 2002; Spaventa, 2007). The principle of direct effect and the concept of market access (concepts from EU trade law) were used to challenge collective agreements in the context of an enlarged EU, with member states at very different stages of economic development, and hence wage levels (the context of employment relations) (*Viking* and others).[15] The broad concepts of 'restriction', and 'undertaking'

---

12 Case C-105/03 *Criminal Proceedings against Maria Pupino* ECLI:EU:C:2005:386.
13 Case C-144/04 *Mangold* ECLI:EU:C:2005:709.
14 Case C-555/07 *Küçükdeveci* ECLI:EU:C:2010:21.
15 E.g. Case 438/05 *Viking Line* ECLI:EU:C:2007:772.

were read across from regulation of services or anti-competitive behaviour in the private sector to activities (healthcare, pensions, education) seen as part of national welfare systems.[16] The concept of (social) citizenship as a 'fundamental status'[17] was read across from cases involving nationals of one of the member states (insiders) into cases concerning 'third country' nationals (outsiders).[18] Read-across has also been used in the context of judicial support for the European Stability Mechanism, from case law concerning development aid.[19] The technical legal concepts upon which read-across relies, including the implicit comparability of different situations (e.g. private healthcare and state-funded healthcare; development aid to the Global South and fiscal and economic stability for the EU), reasoning by analogy, and so on, operate to neutralize deeply contested questions in the EU, such as, for instance, whether internal market law should apply to disrupt historically embedded labour relations or whether human rights clauses should be part of EU external trade agreements.

The effect of the metaphor of single legal order here is to depoliticize. This is both in the sense of the double abstraction (the offering of an abstract set of legal rules, and the abstracting of ourselves from those rules, Cowan and Wincott, this volume), and in an instrumental sense. (EU) law is co-opted by the politically and economically powerful, to pursue particular agendas. But, as Přibáň (this volume) remarks, power cannot be removed by technology – including legal technologies such as single legal order – as in the case of decaffeinated coffee beans. Power remains. The method adopted in this chapter reveals legal technologies to be expressions of contingent power structures (see Cloatre, Carr, Sanders and Griffiths, Sharon Cowan, David Cowan, and Hunter, this volume). This observation also reveals one of the limitations of the method of narration – it can uncover, but it does not (seek to) change, or overtly and directly oppose or disrupt.

Enhancing 'law in context' and 'governance' studies of EU law

Fourth, the narrative of a single legal order was challenged by the turn in EU (socio-)legal scholarship away from court-focused studies towards, for instance, detailed assessments of EU legislation and its applications in

---

16 E.g. Case C-158/96 *Kohll* ECLI:EU:C:1998:171; Case C-372/04 *Watts* ECLI:EU:C:2006:325; Case C-67/96 *Albany* ECLI:EU:C:1999:430; Case C-180/98 *Pavlov* ECLI:EU:C:2000:428; Case T-289/03 *BUPA Ireland* ECLI:EU:T:2008:29; Case C-437/09 *AG2R Prévoyance* ECLI:EU:C:2011:112; Case C-73/08 *Bressol* ECLI:EU:C:2010:181.

17 E.g. Case C-184/99 *Grzelczyk* ECLI:EU:C:2001:458; Case C-224/98 *D'Hoop* ECLI:EU:C:2002:432; Case C-413/99 *Baumbast* ECLI:EU:C:2002:493; Case C-224/02 *Pusa* ECLI:EU:C:2004:273; see also Case C-85/96 *Martínez Sala* ECLI:EU:C:1998:217.

18 E.g. Case C-34/09 *Zambrano* ECLI:EU:C:2011:124; Case C-200/02 *Zhu and Chen* [2004] ECLI:EU:C:2004:639.

19 Cases C-181 & 248/91 *Bangladesh Aid* [1993] ECLI:EU:C:1993:271.

practice. Beginning in the mid-1980s, the increasing density of legislation, coupled with a diversifying range of policy areas dominated by the EU, brought sectoral studies in its various contexts. According to the 'standard narrative', an increasing interest in the *effects* of EU law on the ground ('law in action') came throughout the mid to late 1990s and into the 2000s. Such studies are often influenced by regulation literature (Ayres and Braithwaite, 1995; Morgan and Yeung, 2007; Baldwin and Black, 2008), rather than by court-focused notions of the law and legality. Law in action or law in context studies of EU law emerged in a wide range of areas of internal EU policy. Some of the most 'doctrinal' fields of EU legal scholarship, such as competition law, received a law in context treatment (Monti, 2007). Law in context studies of EU external policy came a little later (Cremona, 2008).

'EU law in context' scholarship emanating from the legal academy is accompanied by some interest from scholars of other disciplines (particularly political science) in the legal aspects of EU policy domains and in cross-disciplinary collaborations between EU law and economics (see, for instance, Ardy et al., 2006); EU law and political science and international relations theories (Wincott, 1995; Armstrong and Bulmer, 1998, De Búrca, 2005); and law and ethics or the values of the EU, in a range of contexts including human rights (Weiler, 1992; O'Keeffe, 1994; Kostakopoulou, 2001); criminal justice (Peers, 2000; 2006; 2011); public office (Harlow, 2002); bio-medicine (Farrell, 2006; McHale, 2009); and international development (Alston, 1999; Khaliq, 2008; Williams, 2010). From the 1980s, there is also interest in the implications of sociological work, such as systems theory, for EU law (Teubner, 1988). More recent new interdisciplinary collaborations, also drawing on sociology, include studies of the EU using science and technology studies (STS) as a lens for understanding the power relationships embedded in EU legislation and regulation (Flear et al., 2013; Flear and Pickersgill, 2013).

A related point, which emerges from the significant enlargements the EU has experienced since the 2000s, concerns the suitability of both traditional legal instruments in EU integration and our ways of studying them. In an EU of 28 members, the ability of the institutions to maintain the level of legislative output of earlier years, to adopt entirely new legislation or embark on comprehensive legislative reform is likely to be increasingly constrained (Piris, 2012). Less legislative innovation suggests that there will be fewer of the most identifiable *legal* aspects of Europeanization on which EU (socio-)legal scholars can comment. Further, the EU's increasing use of soft instruments of governance, rather than the 'Community method', enforced by the CJEU, and in particular by private individuals who enjoy legally enforceable rights in EU law, is another example of the decentring of legal technicality in EU studies, according to the standard narrative. The move from Community method to governance was seminally charted by Scott and Trubek (2002), and an interest in 'governance' among (legal) scholars has spawned a cottage industry of literature throughout the 2000s and 2010s, some of which explicitly draws comparisons with US experiences (De Búrca and Scott, 2006; Sabel and Zeitlin, 2010; Dawson, 2011). The 'European private law' project shares some of the features of this move to governance (Lando and Beale, 2000; von Bar et al., 2009; Brownsword et al., 2011), especially that it is focused around a 'soft' or voluntary legal instrument, the 'Common Frame of Reference'. However, it also relies on a heavy element of self-regulation. In the context of moves away from the Community method, the expectation is that 'hard law', legal obligations or entitlements are not the drivers that lead change. Rather, voluntary policy isomorphism – following target-setting, benchmarking, information comparison, 'name and shame', and peer learning – or choice of soft instruments in a 'regulatory competition' between optional norms, or both, are what is important to track in order to understand processes of Europeanization. Courts and individual legal rights are absent from the story (but see Hervey, 2010). Consequently, there would appear to be no room – in either the law in context approach to EU law, or in its 'governance' version – for technical doctrinal legal analysis.

But again, we would suggest that these kinds of socio-legal studies could be usefully supplemented by attention to the technical. Although the underlying implication of this scholarship is that court decisions, or even legislation, are of less importance, but that what matters is the realities of regulatory practice on the ground (particularly in the member states), we would argue that those very realities are supported by legal technicalities. Indeed, much of the literature outlined above implicitly supports such a suggestion, and there is scope for uncovering more of the ways in which the legal supports governance structures (an agenda explicitly pursued by scholars who are interested in law/governance hybrids). Bringing a socially or culturally understood reference to the technical notion of EU law as a single legal system brings together the legal doctrinal and 'law and' interdisciplinary scholarship. The claim is that 'where the action is' is neither the technicalities of the law, nor the law within its (political/economic/ethical) contexts *alone*, but the ways in which the technicalities support, enable, hinder or impede particular political, economic or ethical agendas.

Refuting the 'beyond the legal' narrative

In the 2010s, the idea of the EU as a *legal* order at all has been placed in question. There is one way to tell the story which says that a faith in (EU) law as the solution to political problems has almost entirely disappeared in the context of the Eurozone crisis. The populations of member states such as Portugal, Spain and Greece remain fundamentally unconvinced of the legitimacy of EU (and International Monetary Fund) rule-making and enforcement. The European Stability Mechanism is, legally speaking, outside of the framework of EU law (Peers, 2013). Even where technically binding law is in existence, if the rules are not enforced, or where law is eschewed in favour of political solutions, this is a parody of law, or a kind of hyper-legalism where law is nothing more than being 'seen to be doing something' even where there is no expectation that more law will 'fix the problem'. Another example where the legal (as opposed to the political) appears redundant is the question of EU membership of a future Scottish state (Edward, 2012).

The idea that solutions to Europe's problems cannot be found in the legal is in stark contrast to the faith in law of the EU's foundational phase. The sense of lack of faith in law as an agent for change is accompanied by a lack of hope in the continued 'heroism' (Hunt, 2007) of the CJEU, so crucial to the foundational stories. In the post-Lisbon settlement, a CJEU lacking in sufficient gravitas and authority (at least compared to national constitutional courts (Chalmers, 2012)), with inappropriate judicial architecture (Nic Shuibhne, 2009) can no longer be expected to develop the imaginative and 'activist' jurisprudence of its supposed heyday. Fewer really new legal principles emerging from the CJEU's case law, less legislation, more governance, 'soft law' and self-regulation, all mark out a narrative of a turn from law in the EU of the 2010s.

We are not supporting the position that written legally binding and enforceable texts (be that the treaties or EU legislation) are all that really matters. Legal accounts that are restricted to technical analysis of enforceable legal texts are unable to explain even partly some of the most dynamic or controversial areas of Europeanization. These include areas of internal activity such as economic and monetary union, criminal justice, commercial law, regulation of research, combating climate change, as well as areas of external activity, such as defence, trade conditionality, neighbourhood relations, enlargement or energy.

But, equally, an account of Europeanization processes in such areas that totally ignores the legal dimension is also impoverished. For sure, in many areas, the legal position does not explain relationships between the governments of the 28 member states, or between EU institutions and national governments. The obvious example is the Eurozone crisis, where the central Treaty agreed to solve the problem is not part of EU law and where legal rules appear to be easily flouted in view of political necessities or expediencies (depending upon one's view). The implication is that legal scholarship has little to contribute. We refute the claim that there are *any* dimensions of Europeanization where law has *no role whatsoever* to play, and consequently where technical legal scholarship cannot contribute to the debate. Typically, this notion of 'extra-legal' or 'intergovernmental' areas of EU activity refers to policy areas which have arisen beyond either the formal competences of the EU, or the legislative powers of the institutions. In our view, in the post-Lisbon EU, all dimensions of the European integration process involve law (or at the very least, law-like qualities) and an understanding of the politics/economics/sociology/and so on *only* is thus insufficient as an analytical frame, because it misses the ways in which law still supports European agendas.

A good example is provided by EU foreign policy. This was, historically, a 'purely' intergovernmental dimension, having begun as European Political Cooperation in the 1970s without a formalized framework for cooperation. Eventually, the existing processes gained Treaty recognition (in the Single European Act), and became the Common Foreign and Security Policy (CFSP) in the Treaty on European Union. Legal scholars initially pondered as to whether the instruments of CFSP could be termed as 'law' (Denza, 2002; Eeckhout, 2004). But since the *Kadi* case,[20] CFSP can no longer credibly be thought of as an area that is immune from either legal processes or legal analysis. The measure challenged in *Kadi* was, after all, in its origins a CFSP measure. Even the moves in the Treaty of Lisbon to 'isolate' or 'ring-fence' CFSP from other parts of the Treaty do not diminish the potential for legal analysis (Cardwell, 2013). On the contrary, the new Treaty provisions increase the role for a contribution from legal scholarship, since the general legal principles of coherence and so on (that are supported by the metaphor of the EU as having a single legal system) still apply.

The 'constitutionalization' of CFSP in Lisbon is characterized by Thym (2009) as 'legal intergovermentalism' (see also Bickerton et al., 2014). Such a novel theoretical or methodological framework would have been understood as oxymoronic at earlier stages of EU studies. But the 'intergovernmental' label is insufficient in itself to indicate that a policy area is (or should be) reserved for the methodologies of politics or economics. Technical legal analyses have something to offer even where it appears that the contrary is the case.

We would also argue that understanding EU regulation or governance is enhanced by attention to the legal. Governance is both 'law-light', hence claims that the methods of legal scholarship cannot and should not engage with governance (implicit in, for instance, Hatzopolous, 2007), *and* 'law-like' (which justifies claims to the contrary, as implicit in all the legal scholarship on governance). Governance is claimed to work because of the 'shadow' or 'backstop' of the law (Sabel and Simon, 2003). It does so within

---

20 *Kadi.*

a legal framework – law mandates activities such as the gathering of data in a particular form; reporting of that data; and comparison (Armstrong 2010). It follows that, in our view, there is much to be gained by explorations of hybridity, between law and governance, in studies of the EU (e.g. Trubek and Trubek, 2007; Dawson, 2011). Scholars such as Armstrong (2010) have already brought together discussion of governance with that of legal technicality, showing the enduring power of technical legal discourse, even in the context of what appear to be 'exotic' new governance practices.

Equally, we see examples of Europeanization processes that are very much *about* hard law without necessarily being done *through* hard law. We have already mentioned the European private law project, which works through soft instruments, but seeks to influence contractual arrangements between firms (and firms and consumers) operating across European boundaries. Another example is cooperation between the judiciaries and other (quasi-)judicial bodies across the EU, which is on the rise. Understanding of the workings of judicial processes, procedures and principles, in their technical doctrinal sense, brings an enriched account of what is occurring, or assists in considering what limitations or safeguards need to be in place in such an important dimension of Europeanization, with implications for the rights and duties of a range of individuals in both civil and criminal law settings.

In short, one cannot understand contemporary Europeanization without some reference to law. This claim points towards the promise of embedding studies of the 'technical legal' into both interdisciplinary and empirically grounded 'law and policy' studies of Europeanization processes. The most significant metaphor of EU law – that it is a single legal system, with a hierarchical relationship to the legal systems of its member states – supports processes of Europeanization in surprising areas of EU law, and in surprising ways. Uncovering those places and processes, and the power relationships that they might embed, is an important task for EU legal scholarship.

The metaphors of EU law III: a space or place

Dissatisfaction with the metaphor of EU law as at the apex of a hierarchical legal system has engendered important moves in the EU legal academy towards a different metaphoric language, involving terms indicating geographic or physical spaces for circulation and interaction, such as legal 'space' or 'architecture' (Krisch, 2008; Piris, 2012). There is obviously scope here for interdisciplinary approaches to EU law, which, for instance, draw on methods used in the study of architecture or geography (see David Cowan, this volume). The idea of EU law as a space for (legal) circulation implies 'a new kind of law than can no more be conceived of as being a legal order, as it is pluralist (rather than exclusive), contradictory (rather than consistent), unfinished (rather than complete)' (Itzcovich, 2012, p. 374). The language of constitutional pluralism has already emerged in EU legal scholarship since at least the early 1990s, at least in analyses of institutional, if not of substantive, EU law. Obviously, such scholarship will continue to make important contributions. But, going further, merely replacing one metaphor with another will not in itself achieve the insights that bringing the technical into the socio-legal might offer.

Metaphors of space or place for circulation of legal ideas depart from the assumption that EU law is somehow 'special' law,[21] and that, in particular, the CJEU is somehow a 'special' court. Here, a change in the practice of the CJEU, as compared to the foundational (Weiler, 1991) period, suggests that, at this stage of 'self-constitutionalization', the CJEU's *own* self-understanding is increasingly like an 'ordinary' constitutional court than hitherto assumed. This has implications for the roles of technical EU legal scholarship.

For instance, where different systems are in non-hierarchical relationships with one another, the role of technical legal reasoning takes on greater significance (Itzcovich, 2012). In the absence of authority, in the sense of a *de iure* claim based on hierarchy, dialogic relations between systems take place through the recounting of legal reasoning, particularly in the context of judicial activity, but also through scholarship. Over time, the shared notion of what counts as 'good' and 'less good' legal reasoning (based on internal coherence of the law, the construction of fact patterns as similar to or distinguishable from previous cases, and so on) becomes a sort of proxy for authority. Thus, if one of the roles of law is to provide a practical solution to the political problem of pursuing European integration without federal statehood, that process relies on shared European respect for the rule of law and the consequent respect of administrative and executive authorities for the judiciary. In this context, where scholarship assesses the relative merits of legal reasoning from different 'levels', 'units' or actors in a pluralist legal order, it also contributes to that dialogue. Examples may be found in the work of scholars who grapple with the relationships between the ECHR and the CJEU (for example, Krisch, 2008); and the CJEU and national constitutional courts, particularly with respect to human rights (see e.g. Sabel and Gerstenberg, 2010). The implication is that the standard methods and tools of comparative constitutional legal scholarship are equally applicable to EU law.

---

21 We wish we had a pound or a euro for every time we have read the phrase *sui generis* of the EU's legal order during our total of 30-plus years studying the EU!

There is important work to be done by EU legal scholars to scrutinize not only the quality of legal reasoning, using the classical and technical approaches of doctrinal law, but also the ways in which the technical reasoning supports the very metaphors on which it is based. They themselves are not expressions of objective reality, but of fears, hopes or dreams for Europe's future(s), and/or of relations of power, hierarchy and subordination. Much as Sharon Cowan's (in this volume) feminists believe in the possibilities of law to realize and, indeed, even conceptualize equality, Europhile EU lawyers continue to believe in legal techniques as ways to realize, and conceptualize, European Union. The method of uncovering the metaphors on which the narrations of EU law are based reveals inherent promise, but also limitations of such conceptualizations and reminds us of the necessity to maintain suspicion of law and to embrace other mechanisms of conflict resolution or social change. (EU) law can be an effective instrument for an agenda of social progression, but, as Carr (in this volume) so powerfully reminds us, technical law can also fail to do or deliver the very things we expect from it. Telling the story of (EU) law creates (a) community/ies, but also excludes from that community.

Conclusion

There is a sense in which this chapter is profoundly unsatisfactory. The chapter seeks to uncover some of the ways in which exploring the metaphors of EU law allows a retelling of the standard narrative of EU law and EU legal scholarship. It shows some of the ways in which the metaphors of EU law are pervasive and enduring; how they have a 'magic' of almost invisibility; and how they work through doctrinal legal analysis, to frame the world in ways which are presented as unquestionable. Doing so helps us to understand what appear to be irresolvable technical legal problems; to make sense of interactions between law and politics, economics, ethics and so on; and to uncover hidden patterns of empowerment and disempowerment. In so doing, we have made (more) visible some of that which is rendered less visible (or invisible) by the dominant narratives. And we have shown how this approach to socio-legal studies can be deployed in ways that give equal weight to the 'standard preoccupations' of (EU) legal scholarship and the 'standard preoccupations' of socio-legal, political science, or sociological (EU) scholarship, or at least that focused on the roles of law in Europeanization processes. But, in so doing, the chapter (like the book in which it appears) embraces the very dichotomy it rejects: that of the social and the legal. As Ohana (in this volume) puts it, we are 'complicit in the very phenomenon we seek to uncover', the process of naming as legal.

This leads us to reflect on the nature of the method which we have deployed here. Such 'metatheorizing', if you will, is our approach to the puzzle that Philippopoulos-Mihalopoulos (in this volume) articulates as 'how to deal with immanence without being locked up in it'.

So, we note that the narrative form itself almost forces the storyteller into using dyadic chronologies such as that deployed in this chapter. The form obscures that which does not fit within the dominant modes of understanding at different historical phases *as the story is told* (not as expressions of objective reality). We have shown how, particularly in the contemporary EU, there might be a temptation for EU (socio-)legal scholars to concentrate on matters other than the legal. As the dominant narrative would have it, law, in particular court-made law, seems to have moved from a central, instrumental role, to a peripheral, perhaps even obfuscating or window-dressing role, such as, for instance, where new legal instruments are agreed in an effort to be 'seen to be doing something' even where there is no meaningful expectation of compliance. Technical legal arguments about the proper meaning of legal texts, such as, for instance, the new Treaty governing financial stability mechanisms, are therefore pointless, except as exercises in abstract legal doctrine. Law means no more than text on a page, without concrete effects in social life, be that the life of the EU's institutions, those of the member states, or the lives of Europe's populations. On the contrary, we have argued that, even where law appears to be on the sidelines, even in modes and sites of EU legal scholarship that appear to be either the most socio-legal, or in places where legal scholarship seems redundant, a focus on legal technicality, as understood through the social or cultural lenses offered by recent scholarship, has much to offer. There is no such thing as mere 'abstract legal doctrine'.

One final thought. As well as being a powerful constitutive mechanism, the story is also a powerful didactic form. A story of the foundation and development of EU law, EU lawyers and EU legal studies is thus also a story from which lessons can be drawn. What might we take to be the 'moral of our tale'? Perhaps, quite simply, it is that 'good' (socio-) legal scholarship of the EU will also pay attention to the technicalities of law and legal doctrine. And (of course!) that is the kind of scholarship with which we ourselves – and we guess the contributors to this book – associate. One of the broader contributions of this chapter, therefore, is to illustrate that the stories we tell about our own disciplines *themselves* embody metaphoric language that serves a particular purpose. And, as good, self-reflexive critical scholarship tells us, that purpose could include perpetuating relations of power, both within the law and within the academy.

Cases

Albany Case C-67/96 ECLI:EU:C:1999:430
Bangladesh Aid C-181 & 248/91 [1993] ECLI:EU:C:1993:271
Baumbast Case C-413/99 ECLI:EU:C:2002:493
Bosphorus Airways Case C-84/95 ECLI:EU:C:1996:312
Bressol Case C-73/08 ECLI:EU:C:2010:181
Costa v ENEL Case 6/64 ECLI:EU:C:1964:66
Criminal Proceedings against Maria Pupino Case C-105/03 ECLI:EU:C:2005:386
D'Hoop Case C-224/98 ECLI:EU:C:2002:432
Factortame Case C-213/89 [1990] ECLI:EU:C:1990:257
Francovich Cases C-6 & 9/90 ECLI:EU:C:1995:372
Grzelczyk Case C-184/99 ECLI:EU:C:2001:458
Ireland Case T-289/03 BUPA ECLI:EU:T:2008:29
Kadi Cases C-402 & 415/05-P ECLI:EU:C:2008:461
Köbler Case C-224/01 [2003] ECLI:EU:C:2003:513
Kohll Case C-158/96 ECLI:EU:C:1998:171
Kücükdeveci Case C-555/07 ECLI:EU:C:2010:21
Mangold Case C-144/04 ECLI:EU:C:2005:709
Martínez Sala Case C-85/96 ECLI:EU:C:1998:217
Pavlov Case C-180/98 ECLI:EU:C:2000:428
Prévoyance Case C-437/09 AG2R ECLI:EU:C:2011:112
Pringle Case C-370/12 ECLI:EU:C:2012:756
Pusa Case C-224/02 ECLI:EU:C:2004:273
Van Gend en Loos Case 26/62 ECLI:EU:C:1963:1
Viking Line Case 438/05 ECLI:EU:C:2007:772
Von Colson Case 14/83 ECLI:EU:C:1984:153
Watts Case C-372/04 ECLI:EU:C:2006:325
Zambrano Case C-34/09 ECLI:EU:C:2011:12
Zhu and Chen Case C-200/02 [2004] ECLI:EU:C:2004:639

References

Alston, P (1999) *The EU and Human Rights* (Oxford: Oxford University Press)
Ardy, B, I Begg, D Hodson, I Maher and D G Mayes (2006) *Adjusting to EMU* (Basingstoke: Palgrave Macmillan)
Armstrong, K A (2010) *Governing Social Inclusion: The Law and Politics of EU Coordination* (Oxford: Oxford University Press)
Armstrong, K A and S Bulmer (1998) *The Governance of the Single European Market* (Basingstoke: Palgrave Macmillan)
Arnull, A (1999) *The European Union and its Court of Justice* (Oxford: Oxford University Press)
Ayres, I and J Braithwaite (1995) *Responsive Regulation: Transcending the Deregulation Debate* (Oxford: Oxford University Press)
Baldwin, R and J Black (2008) 'Really Responsive Regulation' 71 *Modern Law Review* 59–94

Barnard, C (2001) 'Fitting the Remaining Pieces into the Goods and Persons Jigsaw' 26 *European Law Review* 35–59

Barnard, C and J Scott (2002). *The Law of the Single European Market: Unpacking the Premises* (Oxford: Hart Publishing)

Bickerton, C, D Hodson and U Puetter (eds) (2015) *The New Intergovernmentalism: States and Supranational Actors in the Post-Maastricht Era.* (Oxford: Oxford University Press)

Brownsword, R, H Micklitz, L Niglia and S Weatherill (eds) (2011) *The Foundations of European Private Law* (Oxford: Hart Publishing)

Burley, A-M and W Mattli (1993) 'Europe before the Court: A Political Theory of Legal Integration' 47 *International Organization* 41–76

Cappelletti, M, M Seccombe and J H H Weiler (eds) (1986) *Integration through Law: Europe and the American Federal Experience* (Berlin: de Gruyter)

Cardwell, P J (2013) 'On Ring-fencing the Common Foreign and Security Policy in the Legal Order of the European Union' 64 *Northern Ireland Legal Quarterly* 443–63

Chalmers, D (2012) 'The European Court of Justice Is Now Little More Than a Rubber Stamp for the EU' http://blogs.lse.ac.uk/europpblog

Cohen, A (2007) 'Constitutionalism without Constitution: Transnational Elites between Political Mobilization and Legal Expertise in the Making of a Constitution for Europe' 32 *Law and Social Inquiry* 109–35

Cohen, A and A Vauchez (2011) 'The Social Construction of Law: The European Court of Justice and its Legal Revolution Revisited' 7 *Annual Review of Law and Society* 417–31

Coppell, J and A O'Neill (1992) 'The European Court of Justice: Taking Rights Seriously?' 29 *Common Market Law Review* 669–92

Cotterrell, R (2006) *Law, Culture and Society: Legal Ideas in the Mirror of Social Theory* (Farnham: Ashgate)

Cowan, D, C Hunter and H Pawson (2012) 'Jurisdiction and Scale: Rent Arrears, Social Housing and Human Rights' 39 *Journal of Law and Society* 269–95

Craig, P (1991) 'United Kingdom Sovereignty after *Factortame*' 11 *Yearbook of European Law* 221

Craig, P (2013) '*Pringle* and Use of EU Institutions outside the EU Legal Framework: Foundations, Procedure and Substance' 9 *European Constitutional Law Review* 263–84

Cremona, M (ed.) (2008) *Developments in EU External Relations Law* (Oxford: Oxford University Press)

Cremona, M and B De Witte (eds) (2008) *EU Foreign Relations Law – Constitutional Fundamentals* (Oxford: Hart Publishing)

Curtin, D (2009) *Executive Power of the European Union* (Oxford: Oxford University Press)

Dawson, M (2011) 'Three Waves of New Governance in the European Union' 36 *European Law Review* 208–26

De Búrca, G (2005) 'Rethinking Law in Neofunctionalist Theory' 12 *Journal of European Public Policy* 310–26

De Búrca, G and J Scott (eds) (2006) *Law and New Governance in the European Union and the United States* (Oxford: Hart Publishing)

De Búrca, G and J H H Weiler (2001) *The European Court of Justice* (Oxford: Oxford University Press)

De Búrca, G and J H H Weiler (2011) *The Worlds of European Constitutionalism* (Cambridge: Cambridge University Press)

Denza, E (2002) *The Intergovernmental Pillars of the European Union* (Oxford: Oxford University Press)

Eeckhout, P (2004) *EU External Relations Law* (Oxford: Oxford University Press)

Edward, D (2012) *Scotland and the European Union* Scottish Constitutional Futures Forum Blog, www.scottishconstitutionalfutures.org/OpinionandAnalysis/ViewBlogPost/tabid/1767/articleType/ArticleView/articleId/852/David-Edward-Scotland-and-the-European-Union.aspx

Eleftheriadis, P (2007) 'The Idea of a European Constitution' 27 *Oxford Journal of Legal Studies* 1–21

Ewick, P and S S Silbey (1998) *The Common Place of Law: Stories from Everyday Life* (Chicago: University of Chicago Press)

Farrell, A M(2006) 'Governing the Body: Examining EU Regulatory Developments in Relation to Substances of Human Origin' 27 *Journal of Social Welfare and Family Law* 427–37

Fenwick, H and T K Hervey (1995) 'Sex Equality in the Single Market: New Directions for the European Court of Justice' 32 *Common Market Law Review* 443–70

Flear, M L, A M Farrell, T K Hervey and T Murphy (2013) *European Law and New Health Technologies* (Oxford: Oxford University Press)

Flear, M L and M D Pickersgill (2013) 'Regulatory or Regulating Publics? The European Union's Regulation of Emerging Health Technologies and Citizen Participation' 21 *Medical Law Review* 39–70

Harlow, C (2002) *Accountability in the European Union* (Oxford: Oxford University Press)

Harrison, J and T K Hervey (forthcoming) 'Judicial Method of UK Courts in EU Law Cases: A Case Study in Commercial Law'

Hatzopolous, V (2007) 'Why the OMC Is Bad for You: A Letter to the EU' 3 *European Law Journal* 309–42

Hervey, T K (2010) '"Adjudicating in the Shadow of the Informal Settlement"?: The Court of Justice of the European Union, "New Governance" and Social Welfare' 63 *Current Legal Problems* 92–152

Hervey, T K (2013) 'Realism, Empiricism and Doctrine in EU Legal Studies: Views from a Common Law Perspective' in R Nielsen and U Neergaard (eds), *European Legal Method: Towards a New European Legal Realism* (Copenhagen: DJØF) 125–60

Howarth, D (2013) *Law as Engineering: Thinking about What Lawyers Do* (Cheltenham: Edward Elgar)

Hunt, J (2007) 'The End of Judicial Constitutionalisation?' 3 *Croatian Yearbook of European Law and Policy* 135–55

Itzcovich, G (2012) 'Legal Order, Legal Pluralism, Fundamental Principles: European and its Law in Three Concepts' 18 *European Law Journal* 358–84

Khaliq, U (2008) *Ethical Dimensions of the Foreign Policy of the European Union: A Legal Appraisal* (Cambridge: Cambridge University Press)

Kostakopoulou, D (2001) *Citizenship, Identity and Immigration in the European Union: Between Past and Future* (Manchester: Manchester University Press)

Krisch, N (2008) 'The Open Architecture of European Human Rights Law' 17 *Modern Law Review* 183–216

Lando, O and H Beale (2000) *Principles of European Contract Law Parts I and II* (The Hague: Kluwer)

Lock, T (2009) 'The ECJ and the ECtHR: The Future Relationship between the Two European Courts' 8 *Law and Practice of International Courts and Tribunals* 375–98

MacCormick, N (1999) *Questioning Sovereignty: Law, State, and Nation in the European Commonwealth* (Oxford: Oxford University Press)

McGlynn, C (2006) *Families and the European Union: Law, Politics and Pluralism* (Cambridge: Cambridge University Press)

McHale, J (2009) 'Nanomedicine and the EU: Some Legal Ethical and Regulatory Challenges' 16(1) *Maastricht Journal of European and Comparative Law* 65–89

Monti, G (2007) *EC Competition Law* (Cambridge: Cambridge University Press)

Morgan, B and K Yeung (2007) *An Introduction to Law and Regulation* (Cambridge: Cambridge University Press)

Nic Shuibhne, N (2009) 'A Court with a Court? Is It time to Rebuild the Court of Justice?' 34 *European Law Review* 173–4

O'Keeffe, D (1994) 'Union Citizenship' in D O'Keeffe and P Twomey, *Legal Issues of the Maastricht Treaty* (Chichester: Wiley Chancery), pp. 87–107

Peers, S (2000, 2006, 2011) *EU Justice and Home Affairs Law* (Oxford: Longman) (1st edn), (Oxford: Oxford University Press) (2nd and 3rd edns)

Peers, S (2013) 'The Stability Treaty: Permanent Austerity or Gesture Politics?' 9 *European Constitutional Law Review* 404–41

Piris, J-C (2012) *The Future of Europe: Towards a Two-Speed EU?* (Cambridge: Cambridge University Press)

Riles, A (2005)'A New Agenda for the Cultural Study of Law: Taking on the Technicalities' 53 *Buffalo Law Review* 973–1033

Riles, A (2011) *Collateral Knowledge: Legal Reasoning in the Global Financial Markets* (Chicago: University of Chicago Press).

Sabel, C F and O Gerstenberg (2010) 'Constitutionalising an Overlapping Consensus: The ECJ and the Emergence of a Coordinate Constitutional Order' 16 *European Law Journal* 511–50

Sabel, C F and W H Simon (2003) 'Destabilization Rights: How Public Law Litigation Succeeds' 117 *Harvard Law Review* 1016

Sabel, C F and J Zeitlin (eds) (2010) *Experimentalist Governance in the European Union: Towards a New Architecture* (Oxford: Oxford University Press)

Schermers, H G and D F Waelbroeck (1992) *Judicial Protection in the European Communities* (The Hague: Kluwer)

Schwarze, J (2006) *European Administrative Law* (London: Sweet & Maxwell)

Scott, J and D Trubek (2002) 'Mind the Gap: Law and New Approaches to Governance in the European Union' 8 *European Law Journal* 1–18

Shaw, J and G More (1995) *The New Legal Dynamics of European Union* (Oxford: Clarendon Press)

Snyder, F (1987) 'New Directions in European Community Law' 14 *Journal of Law and Society* 167–82

Snyder, F (1990) *New Directions in European Community Law* (London: Weidenfeld & Nicolson)

Somek, A (2008) *Individualism* (Oxford: Oxford University Press)

Spaventa, E (2007) *Free Movement of Persons in the EU: Barriers to Movement in Their Constitutional Context* (The Hague: Kluwer)

Stein, E (1981) 'Lawyers, Judges, and the Making of a Transnational Constitution' 75 *American Journal of International Law* 1–27

Steiner, J (1988) *EEC Law* (Oxford: Oxford University Press)

Stone Sweet, A (2010) 'The European Court of Justice and the Judicialization of EU Governance' 5(2) *Living Reviews in European Governance* http://digitalcommons .law.yale.edu/cgi/viewcontent.cgi?article=1069&context=fss_papers

Teubner, G (1988) *Autopoietic Law: A New Approach to Law and Society* (Berlin: De Gruyter)

Thym, D (2009) 'Foreign Affairs' in A von Bogdandy and J Bast, *Principles of European Constitutional Law* (Oxford: Hart Publishing), pp. 309–43

Trubek, D and L Trubek (2007) 'New Governance and Legal Regulation: Complementarity, Rivalry or Transformation' 13 *Columbia Journal of European Law* 539–64

Twining, W (1967) 'Pericles and the Plumber' 83 *Law Quarterly Review* 396–426

Van Gestel, R, H Micklitz and M Poiares Maduro (2012) *Methodology in the New Legal World*, EUI Working Papers in Law 2012/13 http://cadmus.eui.eu/bitstream/ handle/1814/22016/LAW_2012_13_VanGestelMicklitzMaduro.pdf?sequence=1

Vauchez, A (2008) 'The Force of a Weak Field: Law and Lawyers in the Government of Europe' 2 *International Political Sociology* 28–144

von Bar, C, E Clive and H Hans Schulte-Nölke (2009) *Principles, Definitions and Model Rules of European Private Law: Draft Common Frame of Reference* (Munich: Sellier)

Walker, N (2002) 'The Idea of Constitutional Pluralism' 64 *Modern Law Review* 317–59

Walker, N (2005) 'Legal Theory and the European Union: A 25th Anniversary Essay' 25 *Oxford Journal of Legal Studies* 581–601

Walker, N (2008) 'Beyond Boundary Disputes and Basic Grids: Mapping the Global Disorder of Normative Orders' 6 *International Journal of Constitutional Law* 373–96

Walker, N, J Shaw and S Tierney (2011) *Europe's Constitutional Mosaic* (Oxford: Hart Publishing)

Ward, I (1996) *A Critical Introduction to European Law* (London: Butterworths)

Weiler, J H H (1991) 'The Transformation of Europe' 100 *Yale Law Journal* 2403–83

Weiler, J H H (1992) 'Thou Shalt not Oppress a Stranger: On the Judicial Protection of the Human Rights of Non-EC Nationals – A Critique' 3 *European Journal of International Law* 65–91

Weiler, J H H (1999) *The Constitution of Europe* (Cambridge: Cambridge University Press)

Weiler, J H H and N J S Lockhart (1995) '"Taking Rights Seriously" Seriously: The European Court and its Fundamental Rights Jurisprudence – Part I' 32 *Common Market Law Review* 51–94

Weiler, J H H and M Wind (2003) *European Constitutionalism Beyond the State* (Cambridge: Cambridge University Press)

Williams, A (2010) *The Ethos of Europe: Values, Law and Justice in the EU* (Cambridge: Cambridge University Press)

Wincott, D (1995) 'Institutional Interaction and European Integration: Towards an Everyday Critique of Liberal Intergovernmentalism' 33 *Journal of Common Market Studies* 597–609

9
Territory and Human Rights: Mandatory Possession Proceedings

David Cowan

[F]or territory to 'work' effectively *the basic principles* of territoriality cannot be seriously questioned. When they are ... then the contingencies of territory are more clearly revealed and the claims that these territorializations are necessary or natural features of our life-worlds are more easily discounted. Territorial configurations are not simply cultural artifacts. They are political achievements. (Delaney, 2005, pp. 11–12, original emphasis)

Getting to convergence is actually arduous work. It is partly enabled by a mix of conditions ranging from unequal power among states to the fact of emergent global publics among the powerless pushing for more social justice across nation states. These developments entail a move toward centrifugal, and away from centripetal dynamics that have marked the development of nation states. (Sassen, 2008, p. 309)

Introduction

For legal geographers, such as Delaney (2005), that law and space are mutually constitutive has become both a given and a rallying call (Blomley, 1994). Whether one is researching the mundane (pedestrianism or shopping malls) or the global (respectively, Blomley, 2010; Layard, 2010; Sassen, 2008), the productive capacity of this splicing has become apparent (Philippopoulos-Mihalopoulos, 2014). In this chapter, following Sassen (2008), I open out one particular aspect of space – territory – for consideration of its productive capacity as a way of reading, or thinking about, law.

My contention in this chapter is rather mundane, despite the intense political frisson which discussion of human rights seems to engage in the

UK: it is about how we might read law as an interdisciplinary exercise. We can, of course, read it as doctrine, but doctrine so often masquerades as something else. Although mundane, this chapter also has ambition in its own right. The ambition is to be 'simultaneously inside and outside law, simultaneously technical and theoretical, legal and socio-legal' (Valverde, 2009, p. 153; Cotterrell, 2008).

I do so in a particular context – mandatory possession claims – in which (for want of a better expression) there is a clash of values between Anglo-American liberal property rights and the interpretation given to Article 8 (of the European Convention for the Protection of Human Rights and Fundamental Freedoms 1950 (ECHR)) by the European Court of Human Rights (ECtHR). I argue that territory and its relative, territoriality, enable us to develop an appreciation – if not quite, an understanding – of a recent historical period in which there has been a jurisdictional collision between the House of Lords/ Supreme Court and the ECtHR about the substance of mandatory possession procedure in relation to land (as to which, see Cowan et al., 2012). Put simply, the basis of certain claims to possession which used to be mandatory can now be challenged either on conventional public law grounds and/or that they are disproportionate to the occupier's right to respect for their home (*Manchester CC v Pinnock* [2010] UKSC 45; [2011] 2 AC 104 (*Pinnock*); *Hounslow LBC v Powell* [2011] UKSC 8; [2011] 2 AC 186 (*Powell*)).

That context pits an idea of territory against those property rights; or rather, an understanding of an ontology of home, with constraints on interference, as envisioned by the ECtHR, on the one hand; with asocial property rights, with their emphasis on exclusion and a treatment of the individual as an abstract equal, on the other hand. Whether the property owner is public or private (or somewhere between), a strong version of liberal property theory focuses property rights principally on the owner's right to exclude; as Blackstone (1809, p. 2) has it, their 'sole and despotic dominion'.

Of course, such a perspective is regularly discussed and disputed in the literature, but the right of exclusion is generally said to be an important incident of property rights, which requires coercive enforcement (Alexander and Penalver, 2012, ch. 7). As Ellickson (2008, p. 15) puts it: 'This liberal entitlement [to exclude], which of course is subject to limitations, makes the owners of dwelling units the gatekeepers who control the identities of occupants and additional owners.' Mandatory possession proceedings are the epitome of such a property right. They operate irrespective of the identity of the landlord, the purpose for holding the property (e.g. as an investment) and eviction (e.g. to obtain a higher rent) because of the focus on abstract individuals and equality. Justice is blind but, in its blindness, it neatly ignores a social rationality.

What comes to be at stake, we see, is how we map territory and, just as with reading cases, it is a conflict between insularity and openness. As Ward LJ put it, perhaps most elegiacally:

> The idea that an Englishman's home is his castle is firmly embedded in English folklore and it finds its counterpart in the common law of the realm which provides a remedy to enable the owner of the castle to secure the eviction of trespassers from it. But what if the invaders occupy for long enough to establish their home within the keep? Whose castle is it now? Whose home must the law now protect? (*Malik v Fassenfelt and Others* [2013] EWCA Civ 798, [1])

This collision between jurisdictional territory and individualistic territory in the form of liberal property rights has given rise to some quite wild claims, for example, about 'trumping the will of Parliament', but, as I argue, this can be seen as historical moment in time when, as Sassen (2008, p. 8) argues, our capabilities are beginning to jump track, intermediating between old and new orders; or, to put it another way, folding or splicing jurisdictions (Blomley, 2004). It has been a moment in time (quite a lengthy moment really, spanning seven years) when what is up for grabs is what is often left silent, the identity of 'territory'.

In the first section, I develop an understanding of territory which weaves together geography and law/geography scholarship. In the second section, the case study itself is laid out. Much of this work has already been done elsewhere (Loveland, 2011; Latham, 2011; Cowan and Hunter, 2012a, 2012b), so the discussion can be brief. Rather than focus on the law as it has developed, the discussion considers the key role played by one of the actors, Lord Scott, in the developing jurisprudence. I do so because he had been a chancery barrister so his legal education was imbricated with the values of liberal property rights; and because he appeared as a House of Lords judge in all the relevant cases until the Supreme Court stepped into line with the ECtHR.

In the third section, I draw attention to the way the courts have reached a pragmatic compromise – what has emerged from the jurisprudence is a narrow crack in the strongest version of liberal property rights, as the courts have managed to repel the borders. It involves territorializing the territory, so to speak, through the creation of boundaries; but these boundaries are constantly being shuffled, as territory is being remade. If it is the case that different jurisdictions move at different velocities, then the velocity of jurisprudence in the English jurisdiction has rapidly developed while it might be said that the ECtHR is now following in the slipstream. As Sassen (2008, p. 389) puts it, 'in this assembling they bring together what are often different spatio-temporal orders, that is, different velocities and different scopes'. It has produced an 'eventful engagement' and a frontier zone into which the English courts are now regularly delving.

Territory and territoriality

Until the 1980s, geographers tended to think of territory in two-dimensional, cartographic terms. Jurisdiction and territory were often regarded as being consonant with each other. Both are often still regarded as fixed in time and space, a given. However, the more recent insight is that they are neither fixed nor given, but constantly being made and remade; they are produced. Indeed, it has been said that the assumption of fixity 'obscure[s] the interaction between processes operating at different scales'; in short, it is a territorial trap which presumes its object of study (Agnew, 1994; Akinwumi, 2013). In turn, the idea of territory being fixed offers an assumption of sovereignty which has been destabilized.

This destabilization is what Sassen describes as processes of de-nationalization through the remaking of territory. Sassen's particular targets are globalizations, which destabilize the scalar assemblage of the sovereign as the exclusive grantor of rights. However, the process of de-nationalization, of rewriting sovereignty, is one in which a range of new capabilities are also in the process of being shifted towards objectives outside their original development, paradoxically re-enforcing sovereignty at the very moment it is being questioned (Foucault, 2007, p. 106; Sassen, 2008, p. 6). These new capabilities create tipping points between old and new; but also jumping track between old and new. As Sassen puts it:

> The critical issue is the intermediation that capabilities produce between the old and the new orders: as they jump tracks they are in part constitutive and at the same time can veil the switch by wearing some of the same old clothes. (2008, p. 8)

Territory does not fit into nested hierarchies, but is messy (Elden, 2010; Painter, 2010; Allen, 2011). As Painter puts it:

> [T]erritory is necessarily porous, historical, mutable, uneven and perishable. It is a laborious work in progress, prone to failure and permeated by tension and contradiction. Territory is never complete, but always becoming. It is also a promise the state cannot fulfil. (2010, p. 1094)

The porousness of territory in this context requires its redrawing of the boundaries so as to account for 'geographically expansive legal action' (Akinwumi, 2013), criss-crossing UK and European courts.

Sassen (2008, p. 388) argues that new jurisdictional geographies have emerged in this process. There is a splicing in the production of territory and jurisdiction. Although we might dispute her chronology, Sassen argues that the new territories being produced by the global have resulted in a transnational geography of law. She makes a key point (2008, p. 390) about the different velocities of different jurisdictions in that 'they bring together what are often different spatio-temporal orders'. The research agenda she sets in part is a search for specificity in the 'embeddedness of the global'; and 'we might find that some instances of the national have a greater capacity for resistance to denationalization or, alternatively, for accommodation than others'. The case study discussed below suggests that resistance and accommodation are not necessarily alternatives, but intertwined.

To an extent, we can say that much of the above was already part of socio-legal scholarship. De Sousa Santos' path-breaking work (1987) on law as a map of misreading had already alerted us to the significance of the interaction of law and maps. His development of 'interlaw' and 'interlegality' to describe the ways in which different scales of law (local, national, global) come together at the same point, defining in and out different issues, lies behind much of the law/geography literature (Ford, 1999; Valverde, 2009; Cowan et al., 2012; Johns, 2013). As he puts it (at p. 290), 'each scale of legality has a specific regulation threshold which determines what belongs to the realm of the law and what does not'. In this sense, perhaps reading between the lines, what these different scales of law do is produce not just different versions of legality, but also different identities.

In this chapter's case study, territory and territoriality are produced in different locations through the weaving together of small scale and medium scale legality (European Convention and national law respectively). They are produced in Strasbourg, the Supreme Court, the County Court; indeed, in every case where a landlord claims mandatory possession and the tenant seeks to argue an Article 8 defence, there are assertions of territory and territoriality is in question. Furthermore, if territory can be reduced to a single person's identities, the process of de-nationalization inheres in the productiveness and re-construction of legal statuses – in other words, perhaps we should no longer think of 'trespassers' or 'unlawful occupiers' but as rights-bearers, because identities are themselves mobile. First, we must proceed to outline the distortions in our map of legality.

Towards convergence

> the reason why we represent justice as blind, and holding scales in her hands, is precisely because she hesitates, and proceeds feeling her way forward … For her to speak justly, she must have hesitated. (Latour, 2010, pp. 151–2)

The Human Rights Act 1998 (the 1998 Act) appears to have ushered in a new discursive juridical relation through which the Supreme Court and the ECtHR interact; these are moments of tension and contradiction, of networks in the making (as we are witnessing at the time of writing with the UK's Conservative party proposal to make the ECtHR judgments advisory only). The root question lies in the extent to which each is sufficiently porous to accede to the territorial rule of the other (on which different views have been expressed extra-judicially: Scott, 2009; Hale, 2012).

Convergence in this case study of mandatory possession cases has, indeed, been arduous work – involving five House of Lords/Supreme Court decisions, numerous decisions of (let alone applications to) the ECtHR – and it remains both a work-in-progress as well as perhaps the most contentious property law issue, as well as engendering fractious public law debate (compare Thompson, 2011, and Goymour, 2011; and Irvine, 2012, and Sales, 2012). It is, from one point of view, an invasion at two levels of territorial metaphor – a fundamental challenge to property rights from outside (Darian-Smith, 1995); and, from another point of view, a set of practices of everyday life, or, at least, the everyday life of that mundane institution, the County Court (Cowan et al., 2012).

My argument is that the 1998 Act has reinforced territory and territorial integrity; it constructs political subjectivity in its defence of territorial autonomy (Ford, 1999, p. 899); indeed, the Act is primarily about resisting the processes of de-nationalization. As Ford (1999) puts it, legal discourse 'to some extent *creates* these dialogically opposed modes of human selfhood, such that an attack on a given jurisdictional arrangement can become an attack on the very subjectivity of the individuals who are invested in the arrangements'.

Mandatory possession proceedings and Article 8: a brief orientation

In essence, the question facing English courts during the period from 2004 to 2011 was how to weave the requirements of Article 8 ECHR (as directly implemented in Schedule 1, Human Rights Act 1998) – with its right to respect for an amorphous, psycho-social concept of 'home' – within a liberal property law doctrine which prioritizes the integrity of, and formal rights in, property. The issue was raised across a series of different types of mandatory possession proceedings – where the court *must* grant an order for possession if certain conditions have been fulfilled – spanning different legislative and common law regimes (see Cowan, 2011, p. 380).

One way of conceiving this seven-year period of hesitation is through a triptych of theses from property rights – to public law – to public law/ ECHR. Each employs different versions of territory – whether of property, the state, or the home – and the jurisdictional splice. What comes across clearly from the cases is judicial protectionism. That is, the courts were seeking to protect the County Court, both implicitly and explicitly, thus allowing the property thesis to trump this home right.

At the outset, the House of Lords, by a majority, emphasized property rights as trumping Article 8. So in *Qazi v Harrow LBC* [2003] UKHL 43; [2004] 1 AC 98, Mr Qazi's challenge to Harrow LBC's mandatory claim for possession was unsuccessful. Lord Scott's opinion is perhaps emblematic of the discursive appeal to property right:

> If Mr Qazi has no contractual or proprietary right under the ordinary law to resist the council's claim for possession, and it is accepted he has not, the acceptance by the court of a defence based on article 8 would give him a possessory right over [the property] that he would not otherwise have. It would deprive the council of its right under the ordinary law to immediate possession. It would constitute an amendment of the domestic social housing legislation. It would give article 8 an effect it was never intended to have and which it has never been given by the Strasbourg tribunals responsible for implementing the Convention. ([151]; an opinion from which he subsequently resiled in *Kay v Lambeth LBC* [2006] 2 AC 465, at [150])

In retrospect, one might see Lord Steyn's dissenting judgment (at [27]) as both prescient and discursively in tune with the premise of this article, for he emphasized the way that the 1998 Act had changed the jurisdictional 'landscape' of property rights.

The public law period was ushered in by two House of Lords judgments concerning trespassers in/on property owned by local authorities: *Kay v Lambeth LBC* [2006] 2 AC 465 and *Birmingham CC v Doherty* [2009] 1 AC 367. In these cases, by narrow majorities, two gateways were expounded that could be used by occupiers to challenge public authority decision-making, but only if they were 'seriously arguable' (a significantly higher threshold than normal). Gateway (a) was a straight incompatibility challenge, but the prospects of success of such a challenge were clearly slim because of the margin of appreciation accorded social legislation and the 'search for balance' between individual and community rights inherent in the ECHR (Lord Bingham, *Kay*, [32]). As Baroness Hale put it in *Kay* (at [182]):

> [T]he court is entitled to make two assumptions. The first is that the domestic law has struck the right balance between the competing interests involved: those of a person occupying premises as his home and those of the landowner seeking to regain

possession of those premises in accordance with the law. The second is that the landowner, if a public authority, has acted compatibly with the Convention rights of the individual occupier in deciding to enforce its proprietary rights.

Gateway (b) entitled the occupier to challenge the public authority's claim to possession through 'conventional' public law grounds. This was, in effect, a restatement of the law (*Wandsworth LBC v Winder* [1985] AC 461). In *Doherty*, at [55], Lord Hope qualified the notion of 'conventional' public law grounds by adding, somewhat elliptically, 'that in this situation it would be unduly formalistic to confine the review strictly to traditional Wednesbury grounds. The considerations that can be brought into account in this case are wider.'

But by the time these cases had been heard, the ECtHR jurisprudence had been moving at a different velocity. The general principle in a succession of cases beginning with *Connors v UK* (2002) 35 EHRR 28 was that the Article 8 rights conveyed a procedural and substantive point. As expressed in *McCann v UK* (2008) 47 EHRR 40, at [50]:

> The loss of one's home is a most extreme form of interference with the right to respect for the home. Any person at risk of an interference of this magnitude should in principle be able to have the proportionality of the measure determined by an independent tribunal in the light of the relevant principles under Art. 8 of the Convention, notwithstanding that, under domestic law, his right of occupation has come to an end.

The House of Lords swept this line of authority under the carpet in *Kay* and *Doherty*. But it subsequently became crystal clear that the issue was not going away for Mr Kay's application to the ECtHR was successful. The court simply repeated the *McCann* assertion and said (again elliptically) that the House of Lords had probably not gone far enough: *Kay v UK* [2011] HLR 2. These cases before the ECtHR to which the UK was a party were supplemented with others which demonstrated a 'coherent and consistent' jurisprudence.

In *Manchester CC v Pinnock* and *Hounslow LBC v Powell*, the Supreme Court performed the folding of ECtHR jurisprudence and English law. It recognized that an occupier, faced with a proper mandatory possession claim, could properly defend that claim by pleading that the eviction, and any notice to quit, was disproportionate to their right to respect for their home. Little guidance was provided beyond imposing a threshold again that the defence must be 'seriously arguable', and the height of that threshold was emphasized particularly in *Powell* (Lord Hope, [33]). The court was, perhaps, more forthcoming on the landlords' rights – for this was a pyrrhic victory – making clear that their housing management rights and responsibilities, their unencumbered property right and housing management duties are taken as read (and do not need to be pleaded) and of 'real weight' (*Pinnock*, at [52]–[54]). As Lord Neuberger MR has framed the test subsequently: 'it will only be in "very highly exceptional cases that it will be appropriate for the court to consider a proportionality argument", although "exceptionality is an outcome and not a guide"' (*Corby BC v Scott* [2012] EWCA Civ 276, at [18]). The final point is that the County Court should decide the case summarily (*Pinnock*, at [62]).

While *Pinnock* and *Powell* ushered in the third element of the triptych for all mandatory possession proceedings, so effectively undermining gateway (a), the public law defence (gateway (b)) remains open to occupiers as well. Thus, there is a jurisdictional weave in many such defences although it remains important that an eviction may be proportionate but defeated on public law grounds (although the same may not be true the other way around).

Lord Scott

Lord Scott's approach, from *Qazi* to *Doherty*, has been identified above as emblematic of the liberal property rights approach, of the property lawyer's territorial approach to rights. Faced with Article 8 claims, Lord Scott began with the assertion that such claims could not deprive the owner of their right to immediate possession (*Qazi*), proceeding to admit of the limited exception based on public law grounds. His retirement pre-dated *Pinnock*. What is interesting for the purposes of this chapter is his version of truth about the ECtHR jurisprudence with which he was confronted in *Doherty*. After oral argument in *Doherty*, the ECtHR gave judgment in *McCann v UK*, which reaffirmed the proposition that mandatory possession proceedings offended against the procedural requirements inherent in the right to respect for the home in Article 8. The House of Lords took written submissions on *McCann*.

Lord Scott asserted (at [69]), first, that the gateway (b) route of challenge could only be mounted against a public authority, and not against a private owner. In a lengthy addendum, he provided what can only be described as a vigorous critique of the *McCann* decision, arguing in summary that it 'appear[ed] to be based on an imperfect understanding of domestic law or procedure' (at [88]). He regarded Mr McCann's Article 8 defence as unarguable in light of the facts of the case, in particular Mr McCann's abuse of his wife (he 'had shown a truly lamentable want of respect'), which was the principal cause of her giving up the tenancy, the scarcity of housing available to local authorities, and their allocation obligations. That the authority had procured Mrs McCann's notice, as suggested by the ECtHR, was 'at variance with the facts' ([86]–[87]).

Lord Scott's appreciation of the summary possession hearing as being one in which Article 8 defences would be considered was at variance with the reality of such hearings, let alone the law at the time of *McCann* (Cowan et al., 2012). His description of the type of proportionality review undertaken by a County Court judge to determine whether the defence was 'capable of being sustained by serious argument' was similarly at variance with those hearings (and possibly still is). But it was an attempt to shore up the territorial integrity of the jurisdiction against the incursion of the ECtHR's development of Article 8 jurisprudence; or limit the effect of the latter on the former. Perhaps it can be regarded as a question of different jurisprudential velocities or trajectories – certainly this can be said in retrospect – but, at heart, the knee-jerk response of Lord Scott was consistently to reassert the sovereignty of the owner as regards exclusion and choice, while limiting restrictions on those rights.

There is a further point which one can draw out of Lord Scott's denunciation of the ECtHR approach, which concerns the territorial integrity of the county court. In the face of this welter of law from the senior courts and the ECtHR, it is the location of this jurisdiction in the County Court which was being protected. It was judicial protectionism, or preservation; as Cowan et al. (2012, p. 280) put it: 'Protecting the process must be managed against the contrary proposition of allowing occupiers to give full vent to their challenges as a result of the procedural and legal checks at this stage.' One sees this time and time again throughout the cases, not just in the opinions of Lord Scott and not just in the gateways cases (e.g. *Kay*, at [31], Lord Bingham; *Powell* at [35], Lord Hope). Lord Hope is perhaps most eloquent in his affirmation of the everyday life of County Court possession hearings because of the ECtHR's proposition that it would only be in 'exceptional' cases that a proportionality defence would be successful. The problem with this was the ambit of exceptionality:

> Every solicitor who is asked to advise an occupier will have to consider whether it is arguable that the decision to seek his eviction was not proportionate. If he decides to raise this argument the court will have to examine the issue. The whole point of the reasoning of the majority was to reduce the risks to the operation of the domestic system by laying down objective standards on which the courts can rely. I do not think that the decision in *McCann* has answered this problem. Until the Strasbourg court has developed principles on which we can rely for general application the only safe course is to take the decision in each case as it arises. (at [20])

Others have taken this point further, but, in the context of de-nationalization, and the reassertion of sovereignty, this jurisdiction-based territorial integrity of the County Court is not particularly hard to rationalize.

Confining the jurisdiction

> [S]ince scale creates the phenomenon, the different forms of law
> create different legal objects upon eventually the same social
> objects. They use different criteria to determine the meaningful
> details and the relevant features of the activity to be regulated.
> They establish different networks of facts. In sum, they create
> different legal realities. (de Souza Santos, 1987, p. 287)

In this section, I take forward the argument about the demands of liberal
property theory, arguing that the pragmatic acceptance by the Supreme
Court of the proportionality jurisdiction is strictly confined by the territorial demands of that theory. That is the first point taken in this section.
This is as much a question of procedure as one of substance, but at heart
is also about the weaving of conventional public law and proportionality
jurisdictions (as opposed to grounds).

The second point considers how far the logic of this new jurisdiction
should go, picking up on the current burning doctrinal questions about its
reach into the private sector; the porosity of proportionality and human
rights thought. At the heart of this discussion is the question of velocity,
for it may well be that the development of the jurisprudence in English law
will lead to a rather different set of outcomes which, perhaps paradoxically,
lead to a reinvention of the territory of government – as Sassen has it, in
de-nationalizing, new territories and territorialities are produced. Indeed,
I would go further and argue that these legal texts constitute a new construction of the social from the margins (a point to which I return in the
conclusion).

The compelling logic of property law

What we find, after the legion of senior court decisions, is the narrowness
of the new jurisdiction – as Cowan and Hunter (2012b, p. 18) have put it,
'if the proportionality jurisdiction offers anything, it is a "white elephant"'.
They are referring to the exceptionality of the jurisdiction; its assertion that
it will only be the exceptional case which will surmount the seriously arguable threshold. And the odds are sharply stacked against the occupier seeking to surmount that threshold. Indeed, there has only been one successful
reported decision in which the jurisdiction was invoked (*Southend-on-Sea
Borough Council v Armour* [2014] EWCA Civ 231).

There are two reasons why this is so, the former providing the justification. It can only be the exceptional case because of the particular power
of liberal property theory's discourse. Its narrative is compelling because
the vindication of property rights has such a hold over us. Nevertheless,
there is an acceptance of the fallacy in the binary separation operated by
liberal property theory's division between the private right of exclusion,

protected by law, as opposed to the fulfilment of public values, which are othered by this discursive narrative and certainly not the appropriate domain of private law (classically, see Demestz, 1967; also Weinrib, 2012, pp. 43–54). This binary can be overemphasized, but occupies a significant tension in liberal property theory (for discussion, see Rose, 1986; Layard, 2010; Bottomley and Moore, 2007; Alexander and Penalver, 2012). It is this tension, which is being balanced in this new jurisdiction, for public values are evident in the proportionality balance. Thus, it is possible that the balance will weigh in favour of the 'vulnerable' tenant where the social landlord has not offered suitable alternative accommodation, the public value being the societal duty towards the vulnerable (*Pinnock*, [64]). However, as Etherton LJ explained (*Thurrock BC v West* [2012] EWCA Civ 1435, [31]), even where the defence is made out, this public element causes problems in identifying the status of the occupier:

> [I]t is difficult to imagine circumstances in which the defence could operate to give the defendant an unlimited and unconditional right to remain: comp. Pinnock at [52]. That might be the effect of a simple refusal of possession without any qualification. It is particularly difficult to imagine how that could possibly be appropriate in a case where the defendant has never been a tenant or licensee of the local authority. Otherwise, the effect of the Article 8 defence would be that the Court would have assumed the local authority's function of allocating its housing stock, preferring the right of the defendant to remain, without any tenancy or contract, over all the other people entitled to rely on the local authority's statutory housing duties and without the benefit of any knowledge of who those people are and their circumstances and of other relevant matters which would properly guide the local authority in housing management decisions.

Although exceptionality is not the criterion, only an exceptional case can overcome the apparent power of property rights (which are taken as read such that they do not need even to be pleaded). As the Supreme Court put it in *Pinnock* ([52]):

> Where a person has no right in domestic law to remain in occupation of his home, the proportionality of making an order for possession at the suit of the local authority will be supported not merely by the fact that it would serve to vindicate the authority's ownership rights. It will also, at least normally, be supported by the fact that it would enable the authority to comply with its duties in relation to the distribution and management

of its housing stock, including, for example, the fair allocation of its housing, the redevelopment of the site, the refurbishing of substandard accommodation, the need to move people who are in accommodation that now exceeds their needs, and the need to move vulnerable people into sheltered or warden-assisted housing. Furthermore, in many cases (such as this appeal) other cogent reasons, such as the need to remove a source of nuisance to neighbours, may support the proportionality of dispossessing the occupiers.

So, having accepted the new jurisdiction, the Supreme Court was placating fears about its potential ambit – it was not an attack on property rights to exclude and choose (which are 'of real weight when it comes to proportionality': *Pinnock*, at [54]), because 'in virtually every case' possession would be ordered if the occupier has no contractual or statutory right to remain. The extra-national logic of proportionality was tamed by the territoriality of territory. *Pinnock* can be seen as a watershed moment or, rather more mundanely, as a pragmatic compromise which involves only limited movement (beyond reducing the transnational geography of national jurisprudence). It has been a partial unbundling of the 'territory of the national' – indeed, as Sassen argues (2008, p. 6; in line with much socio-legal theory), such unbundlings are overlain with the past leaving an 'in-betweenness' in which old and new capabilities combine and 'some capabilities can be shifted toward objectives other than the original ones for which they developed'.

There is also an empirical point about procedure. Socio-legal scholars are only beginning to appreciate the significance of court procedure as a structuring device (in particular, Mulcahy, 2005; 2012). The Civil Procedure Rules require an occupier to show that they have a 'substantial defence' to a possession claim (rule 55.8). To pursue an Article 8 defence, by contrast, the occupier must show that they have a 'seriously arguable' case. This phrase was first used in the context of gateway (b) (*Kay*, [110]), but ironically sets the threshold higher than that for permission to bring an application for judicial review. In *Powell* (at [92]), Lord Phillips perhaps set the test even higher in arguing that it would only be in 'very highly exceptional cases' that the occupier would be able to cross that threshold.

Further, it is also clear that the occupier must demonstrate that they cross that threshold at an early stage in the proceedings, prior to disclosure of documents, policies, files etc. Although court practice differs, the senior courts have emphasized the summary nature of the proceedings to avoid the risk of prolonged and expensive proceedings; while, at the same time, refusing to give guidance on the procedure to be adopted (e.g. *Powell*, at [47] (Lord Hope) and [101] (Lord Phillips)). In *Corby*, Lord Neuberger MR:

emphasise[d] the desirability of a judge considering at an early
stage (normally on the basis of the tenant's pleaded case on
the issue) whether the tenant has an arguable case on Article 8
proportionality, before the issue is ordered to be heard. (at [39])

The problem for those representing occupiers is that, by this stage, the
file is unlikely to have 'ripened' sufficiently to know whether the defence
meets the threshold. They operate to a large extent in the dark. *Holmes v
Westminster CC* [2011] EWHC 2857 offers a particularly stark example of
this in that the pleaded defence was struck out summarily; when a potentially seriously arguable defence did emerge (either on proportionality or
gateway (b) as well as other grounds), it was effectively too late as these
matters were only raised on appeal but could not have been developed at
the summary hearing.

Questioning the jurisdictional limit

While the courts have emphasized the limits of this new jurisdiction, the
question is whether it can be kept in check.[1] The outstanding question is
the reach of the jurisdiction beyond local authorities to other providers of
'social housing', and beyond that to the private sector (landlords, mortgage
lenders, receivers and other private entitles – see, for example, Nield and
Hopkins, 2013). Here again, then, we face denationalization, the different
legal matrices depending on jurisdictional perspective. The possibilities
have been left open (*Pinnock*, at [4] and [50]).

I will unpack the doctrinal argument briefly here because it goes to the
questions addressed in this chapter. The point being discussed – the hori-
zontality of the 1998 Act – has been the subject of many learned papers
(e.g. Hunt, 2001; Hickman, 2010), and so the argument here is restricted to
the specific context. The actors here are not just judges, but the rules, regulations and other orderings, as well as their interpretation by the experts,
which are made to speak as '*the* law'. It is their association and the translation of the latter by the former which produces, in this limited context, the
social (and which then moves on).

On the one side, then, the argument for restricting the proportionality
doctrine to public bodies appears to be based in part on s. 6 of the 1998 Act,
which restricts the Act's ambit to core public authorities and those hybrid

---

1 Although see *R(JL) v SSD* [2013] EWCA Civ 449, where the Court of Appeal allowed
   only a limited right to use the jurisdiction at this stage where either the occupier was
   prevented from raising the defence at the possession hearing or there has been a fundamental change in the occupier's circumstances after that hearing: 'That is because,
   under English procedure, it is those proceedings, and in particular the hearing of them,
   which are designed finally to determine (subject only to any appeal) the lawfulness
   or otherwise of the owner's claim for possession': [39], Briggs LJ (emphasis added).

public authorities ('any person certain of whose functions are functions of a public nature') provided that the nature of the act is not private. That was the approach adopted by the Court of Appeal in *R (Weaver) v London & Quadrant HT* [2010] 1 WLR 363. Further, and perhaps most eloquently among those in this camp, Thompson (2011, p. 438) argues that such an extension of Article 8 would undermine various fundamental principles of property law concerning third-party rights (overreaching, purchasers from mortgagees) as well as their rights to possessions. For him (at p. 440), 'the basis of judicial intervention is, in essence, an extension of judicial review'; he thus elides gateway (b) and Article 8 (in similar vein to Lord Scott in *Doherty*).

By contrast, the argument for expanding the jurisdiction lies in the procedural nature of the requirements of Article 8, in accordance with the jurisprudence of the ECtHR. Mandatory possession proceedings must have some outlet to enable the proportionality of an eviction to be considered, given the significance accorded to the right to respect for the home irrespective of the nature of the claimant. The substantive arguments are secondary, although they do follow on from the opening up of that jurisdiction. The court itself is a public authority and must, therefore, accord that procedural protection to occupiers. The further one goes into the 'private', the less substantive protection one is likely to obtain (and that is particularly the case with trespassers).

It is not the purpose of this chapter to mediate between these two arguments; rather, I seek to identify their root concerns to see how they speak to the themes of this chapter. As Sassen (2008, p. 13) argues, the process of denationalization 'reconstitutes the construction of the public and the private, and of the boundaries between these domains'. In this new mentality, the public–private binary makes no sense (even if it ever did), so that the process of de-nationalization 'makes possible kinds of engagements for which there are no clear rules. The resolution of these encounters can become the occasion for playing out conflicts that cannot easily be engaged in other spaces' (at p. 389).

If liberal property theory depends on the abstract individual and equality for its strength, what has happened has been a rather different make-up of public–private. For the reconstituted public – which includes some charities and most housing associations (which are funded through a mix of public and private funds) – the rights of exclusion are slightly tempered and limited; they are less individual, less liberal and decontextualized. In a word, their role has been made up to be more 'social'. For the purely private, if there is such a thing, we have 'an important principle, namely the principle that parties who have exercised their contractual freedom to agree terms should not be allowed to invoke Convention rights to relieve themselves of the terms of the bargain' (*McDonald v McDonald* [2014] EWCA Civ

1049, [37], Arden LJ). Further, precisely because we are dealing with a private landlord, even if proportionality was relevant:

> the balance is almost always going to be struck in the landlord's favour because the landlord is enforcing his property right to return of the property. Moreover, he may well have suffered loss (most obviously, arrears of rent) which he may not be able to recover if the tenant has few means and continues in possession. The position of the landlord may be even stronger if there are third parties who are directly concerned in the protection of the landlord's rights and who are liable to be prejudiced by the refusal to make a possession order, such as mortgagees of the property or other creditors of the landlord. The position of those third parties is no less relevant to the balancing exercise than the position of homeless persons who are interested in the enforcement by social landlords of their rights to recovery of their housing stock from tenants to whom they no longer owe any housing duty. ([50], Arden LJ)

The point, though, is that the ECtHR jurisprudence has been inverted; it reaches into the fabric of court processes and, in turn, the activities and mentalities of what was once seen as private. The 1998 Act facilitated this jump from the national to supranational and back again; indeed, it was inherent in the title of the White Paper, *Rights Brought Home* (Home Office, 1987). There is a two-way effect at least in this context, and the velocities of those ways differ. In those shifting networks, what is apparent also is that power itself is flattened – if the nature of power lies in the ability to make things happen, it is independent of size (Foucault, 1982, p. 221; Callon and Latour, 1981). The newly constituted trespasser/rights-bearer has been weaved together with proportionality into a new vocabulary of property, which is productive of both territory and jurisdiction. Further, the 'triumph' of the lengthy campaign described in this chapter has been woven into the processes of government – the justification for a new mandatory ground of possession for antisocial behaviour across all forms of housing tenure (a substantial rewriting of security of tenure laws in its own right) has been that occupiers will have the proportionality defence (Department for Communities and Local Government, 2012, para. 2.6).

Conclusions

The argument in this chapter has been that we socio-legalists have a considerable amount to offer the ways in which law can be read. Our interdisciplinary starting points enable us to unpack the ideologies of legal instrumentalism and managerialism; to see law from different perspectives takes it away from its technicality; and, in the context of this case study, how law and lawyers protect their ideological terrain.

Indeed, one message of this chapter concerns the significance and problematization of territory through the case study. What has been at risk in the case study is nothing less than the most significant principle of the common law of property – exclusivity – and what we have found is that this principle has had to give way to an awkward, pragmatic, narrow and limited compromise. In so doing, different conceptions of territory were contested and remain contested, for this is law in action as boundaries are remade continually; it is the stuff of the everyday, the mundane, the territory of the County Court five-minute possession hearing. Territory is constructed, and constantly reconstructed; it is a set of processes in the making; and that making happens in a crowded, contested space, from whatever point one looks at it. Territory, perhaps counter-intuitively, is about processes, proximity and distance; it is about movement, velocity (velocities), and mobilization of people and rules – indeed their weaving together.

In the case study, the jurisdiction itself is still in action, although the ECtHR is now largely absent, for the velocity is now with the English courts. In this case study, there is now no apparent need for a voltage transformer when one moves between jurisdictional scales (to adopt de Souza Santos' metaphor), but that is not to say that the translations are uncontested; these contestations were at the heart of the Conservative offer in the 2015 election (see Conservative Party, 2015). As Sassen suggests, convergence is hard work. Perhaps the reason for that is the totalizing discourse of law, the way law formats the social (Latour, 2010, pp. 260–3) and has to respond to challenges from outside, translating those challenges into its own jurisprudence.

Thus, in law, the identity of the trespasser is now as a rights-bearer, at least in the case where they are defending a claim against a public body. The shifting sands and arguments about the imposition of this obligation on private landlords reflects something of an understanding about what has come to be known as 'social housing'. That label, which, as Cowan and McDermont (2006, p. xi) argue, is both constructed and contingent, carries particular meaning in this context. If these housing providers are 'social', that conveys a sense of obligation. What is being knocked out in this case study is the shape of that social obligation; and it is incredibly narrow. Private landlords, on the other hand, have no such social obligation. They are othered in this narrative because of the discourse of the private, of the exclusivity of rights, the governing power of the individual contract, the power of exclusivity. In short, private landlords owe nobody anything. They are beyond the social, whether or not their rent-seeking behaviour is funded by the state through social security benefits or they hold the property simply as an income-earning or capital-enhancing security. What has been emphasized is that the free market works – and, of course, the free-market ideology is entirely attuned to the asocial liberal property thesis.

In these epoch-defining controversies, the land itself, of course, remains immobile. However, in Latourian terms, land is made mobile by the different contours of the law as it has developed over time. If the rights of humans are to bite, the land must be the trespasser/rights-bearer's *home*, which implies some form of ontological relationship with the land. That is already well-covered terrain itself when we think about human actors (e.g. Fox, 2006), but what is potentially more interesting is how the land itself comes to speak – for example, the trespassers in *Malik* were able to demonstrate how the landowner had neglected and abused the land, whereas they were exercising good stewardship. However, as we saw in the previous paragraph, ontological relationships between, say, trespassers and the land, are moved out of sight by liberal property theory.

Thus, we return to the mundane readings of law. Lord Scott and Lord Irvine's positions can just as easily be read as political disagreement with the ECtHR and, indeed, their brethren. A focus on territory, as opposed to say exceptionality or proportionality, enables these positions to be exposed. What comes to be at stake is how we map territory and, just as with reading cases, it is a conflict between insularity and openness. We have moved to a point where we are able to note that the heterogeneity of the 'public' in housing (at least) speaks to a broader construction of the social, rather than a binary public–private which are, as Rose (1993, p. 286) puts it, 'the ghosts of liberal political philosophy' – ghosts which are very real in the political rationality of property.

Cases

Birmingham CC v Doherty [2009] 1 AC 367
Connors v UK (2002) 35 EHRR 28
Corby BC v Scott [2012] EWCA Civ 276
Holmes v Westminster CC [2011] EWHC 2857
Hounslow LBC v Powell [2011] UKSC 8; [2011] 2 AC 186
Kay v Lambeth LBC [2006] 2 AC 465
Kay v UK [2011] HLR 2
Malik v Fassenfelt and Others [2013] EWCA Civ 798
Manchester CC v Pinnock [2010] UKSC 45; [2011] 2 AC 104
McCann v UK (2008) 47 EHRR 40
McDonald v McDonald [2014] EWCA Civ 1049
Qazi v Harrow LBC [2003] UKHL 43, [2004] 1 AC 98
R (Weaver) v London & Quadrant HT [2010] 1 WLR 363
R(JL) v SSD [2013] EWCA Civ 449

Southend-on-Sea Borough Council v Armour [2014] EWCA Civ 231
Thurrock BC v West [2012] EWCA Civ 1435
Wandsworth LBC v Winder [1985] AC 461

References

Agnew, J (1994) 'The Territorial Trap: The Geographical Assumptions of International Relations Theory' 1(1) *Review of International Political Economy* 53

Akinwumi, A (2013) 'Powers of Reach: Legal Mobilization in a Post-apartheid Redress Campaign' 22(1) *Social and Legal Studies* 25.

Alexander, G and E Penalver (2012) *An Introduction to Property Theory* (Cambridge: Cambridge University Press)

Allen, J (2011), 'Topological Twists: Power's Shifting Geographies' 1(2) *Dialogues in Human Geography* 283

Blackstone's *Commentaries on the Laws of England* 1809 (15th edn)

Blomley, N (1994) *Law, Space, and the Geographies of Power* (New York: Guilford Press)

Blomley, N (2004), 'From "What" to "So What"? Law and Geography in Retrospect' in J Holder and C Harrison (eds), *Law and Geography* (Oxford: Oxford University Press)

Blomley, N (2010) *Rights of Passage* (London: Glasshouse)

Bottomley, A and N Moore (2007) 'From Walls to Membranes: Fortress Polis and the Governance of Urban Public Space in 21st Century Britain' 18(2) *Law and Critique* 171

Callon, M and B Latour (1981) 'Unscrewing the Big Leviathan: How Actors Macro-structure Reality and How Sociologists Help Them to Do So' in K Knorr and A Cicourel (eds), *Advances in Social Theory and Methodology: Toward an Integration of Micro- and Macro-Sociologies* (London: Routledge)

Conservative Party (2015) *The Conservative Party Manifesto 2015* London: Conservative Party. https://s3-eu-west-1.amazonaws.com/manifesto2015/ConservativeManifesto2015.pdf

Cotterrell, R (1998) 'Why Must Legal Ideas Be Interpreted Sociologically' 25(2) *Journal of Law and Society* 171

Cowan, D (2011) *Housing Law and Policy* (Cambridge: Cambridge University Press)

Cowan, D, L Fox O'Mahony and N Cobb (2012) *Great Debates on Property Law* (Basingstoke: Palgrave)

Cowan, D and C Hunter (2012a) '"Yeah But, No But" – *Pinnock* and *Powell* in the Supreme Court' 78(1) *Modern Law* Review 78

Cowan, D and C Hunter (2012b) '"Yeah But, No But" or Just "No"? Life after *Pinnock* and *Powell*' 15(1) *Journal of Housing Law* 58

Cowan, D, C Hunter and H Pawson (2012) 'Jurisdiction and Scale: Rent Arrears, Social Housing and Human Rights' 39(2) *Journal of Law and Society* 269

Cowan, D and M McDermont (2006) *Regulating Social Housing: Governing Decline* (London: Routledge)

Darian-Smith, E (1995) 'Rabies Rides the Fast Train: Transnational Interactions in Post-colonial Times' 6(1) *Law and Critique* 75

de Souza Santos, B (1987) 'Law: A Map of Misreading. Toward a Postmodern Conception of Law' 14(2) *Journal of Law and Society* 279

Delaney, D (2005) *Territory: A Short Introduction* (Oxford: Blackwell)

Demestz, H (1967) 'Towards a Theory of Property Rights' 57(2) *American Economic Review* 347

Department for Communities and Local Government (2012) *A New Mandatory Power of Possession for Anti-Social Behaviour: A Consultation* (London: DCLG)

Elden, S (2010) 'Land, Terrain, Territory' 34(6) *Progress in Human Geography* 799

Ellickson, R (2008) *The Household: Informal Order around the Hearth* (Princeton: Princeton University Press)

Ford, R (1999) 'Law's Territory (A History of Jurisdiction)' 97(4) *Michigan Law Review* 843

Foucault, M (1982) 'Afterword: The Subject and Power' in H Dreyfuss and P Rabinow (eds), *Michel Foucault: Beyond Structuralism and Hermeneutics* (Chicago: University of Chicago Press)

Foucault, M (2007) *Security, Territory, Population* (G Burchell trans.) (Basingstoke: Palgrave)

Fox, L (2006) *Conceptualising Home* (Oxford: Hart Publishing)

Goymour, A (2011) 'Property and Housing' in D Hoffman (ed.), *The Impact of the Human Rights Act on Private Law in England and Wales* (Cambridge: Cambridge University Press)

Hale, Baroness (2012) '*Argentoratum Locutum*: Is Strasbourg or the Supreme Court Supreme?' 12(1) *Human Rights Law Review* 65

Hickman, T (2010) *Public Law after the Human Rights Act* (Oxford: Hart Publishing)

Home Office (1987) *Rights Brought Home* White Paper CM 3782 (London: The Stationery Office)

Hunt, M (2001) 'The "Horizontal Effect" of the Human Rights Act: Moving beyond the Public–Private Distinction' in J Jowell and J Cooper (eds), *Understanding Human Rights Principles* (Oxford: Hart Publishing)

Irvine, Lord (2012) 'A British Interpretation of Convention Rights' *Public Law* 237

Johns, F (2013) *Non-Legality in International Law: Unruly Law* (Cambridge: Cambridge University Press)

Latham, A (2011) 'Talking without Speaking, Hearing without Listening? Evictions, the Law Lords and the European Court of Human Rights' *Public Law* 730

Latour, B (2010) *The Making of Law: An Ethnography of the Conseil d'Etat* (Cambridge: Polity Press)

Layard, A (2010) 'Shopping in the Public Realm: A Law of Place' 37(4) *Journal of Law and Society* 412

Loveland, I (2011) 'The Shifting Sands of Article 8 Jurisprudence in English Housing Law' (2011) *European Human Rights Law Review* 151

Massey, D (2004) 'Geographies of Responsibility' 86(1) *Geografiska Annaler* 5

Mulcahy, L (2005) 'Feminist Fever? Cultures of Adversarialism in the Aftermath of the Woolf Reforms' in J Holder and C O'Cinneide (eds), *Current Legal Problems*, (Oxford: Oxford University Press)

Mulcahy, L (2012) 'The Collective Interest in Private Dispute' 33(1) *Oxford Journal of Legal Studies* 59

Nield, S and N Hopkins (2013) 'Human Rights and Mortgage Repossession: Beyond Property Law Using Article 8' 33(3) *Legal Studies* 431–54

Painter, J (2010) 'Rethinking Territory' 42(9) *Antipode* 1090

Philippopoulos-Mihalopoulos, A (2014) *Spatial Justice* (London: Routledge)

Rose, C (1986) 'The Comedy of the Commons: Custom, Commerce, and Inherently Public Property' 53(4) *University of Chicago Law Review* 711

Rose, N (1993) 'Government, Authority and Expertise in Advanced Liberalism' 22(2) *Economy and Society* 283

Sales, P (2012) 'Strasbourg Jurisprudence and the Human Rights Act: A Response to Lord Irvine' *Public Law* 253

Sassen, S (2008) *Territory, Authority, Rights: From Medieval to Global Assemblages* (Princeton: Princeton University Press)

Scott, Lord (2009) 'Property Rights and the European Convention on Human Rights', paper delivered to the Property Bar Association, London

Thompson, M (2011) 'Possession Actions and Human Rights' *Conveyancer and Property Lawyer* 421

Valverde, M (2009) 'Jurisdiction and Scale: Legal "Technicalities" as Resources for Theory' 18(2) *Social and Legal Studies* 139

Weinrib, E (2012) 'Poverty and Property in Kant's System of Rights' in G Alexander and H Dagan, *Properties of Property* (New York: Wolters Kluwer)

10

Legal Technology in an Age of Austerity: Documentation, 'Functional' Incontinence and the Problem of Dignity

Helen Carr[1]

Introduction

> It's very shameful, writing about diapers, it's completely with-
> out dignity.[2] (Barron, 2013)

Critical characteristics of the contemporary 'crisis' in the provision of care for vulnerable adults within England are its inadequacy, its unfairness, its complexity and as Barron (2013) so eloquently points out, its failure to treat people with dignity (Age UK, 2012). The failure to care is made manifest in high-profile scandals, such as the collapse of private care providers; but also, perhaps more worryingly, in routine neglect – for instance, the lack of attention to basic human rights such as liberty and family life, or proper support for bodily functions such as feeding and continence (see, for example, Local Government Ombudsman and Parliamentary and Health Services Ombudsman, 2009; House of Lords Select Committee, 2014). The problems of care are intensified by the politics of austerity that followed the financial crash of 2008, although, as this chapter makes clear, austerity has long been associated with state provision of care for vulnerable adults.

The chapter focuses on the important, but arguably undertheorized, legal dimensions of the 'crisis' of adult social care, asking two questions of

---

1 The author is very grateful for the opportunity provided by the Socio-Legal Studies Association-funded one-day conference to explore the case and for the comments of Dave Cowan and the independent reviewers of the chapter which have significantly improved the argument presented. The usual caveats of course apply.

2 Karl Ove Knausgaard in a 2013 interview with Jesse Barron.

the law. First, it considers whether, and in what ways, the technical legal devices deployed to resolve disputes about provision between the state and the citizen are implicated in the apparent insolubility of the problems of adult social care. Second, it asks whether it is still possible to reason within law about concerns of dignity, civility and social health (Carr and Hunter, 2012; Dorsett and McVeigh, 2012, p. 89). It raises these questions in the context of a technical think through of a decision of the Supreme Court: *R (on the Application of McDonald) v Royal Borough of Kensington and Chelsea* UKSC 33. This case concerns functional incontinence, absorbent sheeting and a claim to dignity in the context of a cost-cutting austerity. The judicial reasoning in this case provides essential material for my argument; it is determinedly technical – having been described as 'a triumph of black letter law' (Clements, 2011, p. 675) – and provocative. Not only did the media and voluntary sector voice their disappointment with the court's support of the authority's decision to replace the night-time carer with absorbent sheeting, something quite extraordinary happened within the decision itself – the majority expressed, in strong terms, their indignation at the dissenting reasoning of Baroness Hale (George, 2011; Carr, 2012).

The chapter is structured as follows: it starts by considering the 'turn to the technical' within critical social and legal theory, and, in particular, the theoretical 'unpacking' of the technical tool of jurisdiction; it then sketches a story of legal provision for adult social care through the lens of jurisdiction, noting jurisdictional contradictions, complexities and shifts in the legal architecture of the British post-war welfare state. The next section of the chapter considers the *McDonald* case, focusing on judicial treatment of the documentation prepared by the social workers, which became the technical linchpin of the case. The chapter concludes by reflecting upon the potential of technical thinking as a means of revitalizing conscience as a critical component in the jurisdiction of adult social care.

Legal technicalities as critical tools

Nelken alerted social welfare scholars to the significance of the technicalities of law. In his characterization of the Rent Act 1965 as a 'technocratic response to one prominent example of the "rediscovery of poverty" in the 1960s ... with the overall intention of taking "the rent out of politics"' (Nelken, 1983, pp. 34–5) he made the important observation that the legal technicalization of social welfare is used as a tool for its depoliticization. This, together with Mitchell Dean's argument that we should reveal and repoliticize the technical as part of resistance to neoliberal rationalities (Dean, 2007), has always been persuasive and important for me (see Carr and Hunter, 2008) as social welfare law is a critical component in the system through which contemporary transformations of the state are played out in the realities of poor people's lives.

The current focus on legal technicalities seems a quite different intellectual project emerging from a concern that the 'how' of legal practice is rarely considered by critical scholarship (Valverde, 2009). Our new agenda involves revealing, embracing and mining law's technical characteristics. As Riles argues:

> Humanists should care about technical legal devices because the kind of politics that they purport to analyze is encapsulated there, along with the hopes, ambitions, fantasies and daydreams of armies of legal engineers. (Riles, 2005, p. 975)

The politics of which Riles speaks is distinct from the political task that is the more frequent focus of critical legal scholarship, which explains the ways in which law represents the 'embodiment of norms, the outcome of political compromise, and the repository of social meaning' (Riles, 2005, p. 973). Rather than relating law to external political forces, or even not doing 'law' at all, Riles wants us to think about the politics that is internal to law, the politics of the legal rules used to resolve legal problems. Using the analogy of the leaking faucet, she suggests that critical legal scholars might typically critique:

> The distributive consequences of plumbing, or the gendered division of labor it has produced, or ... might explore the persons and practices that produced the leaky faucet: he or she might describe the meetings of the leaky faucet fixers' association in all its exotic and ironic detail and show how the fantasies of repair and disrepair mirror wider forces at work in parallel fields of greater interest to humanists ... (Riles, 2005, pp. 979–80)

For Riles, this is problematic. As Zumbansen puts it, 'the critical legal scholar risks losing law as form by decrying it as camouflage for different emanations of power' (Zumbansen, 2008, p. 807). What Riles points out is that, by ignoring the technical aspects of legal thought, critical legal thinking becomes complicit in its own marginalization. Instead, she argues that the legal dimensions, the 'technical aesthetics of law' (Riles, 2005, p. 976), should be at the heart of the critical legal project. Agency is crucial here. The point of focusing on legal techniques is:

> To bring the technical into view not as an effect or a byproduct, a tool of more important agents and forces, but as the protagonist of its own account. (Riles, 2005, p. 985)

Here Riles, drawing on her science and technology studies roots, seeks to persuade socio-legal scholars to think about law's materiality and to reflect upon what Bennett subsequently described as its 'vitality'. 'Vitality' means:

The capacity of things ... not only to impede or lock the will and designs of humans but also to act as quasi agent or forces with trajectories, propensities or tendencies of their own. (Bennett, 2010, p. viii)

Although it is perhaps difficult for lawyers to grasp that legal artefacts, rather than lawyering, may have agency, Riles' piece has both stimulated and coincided with a new interest in technicalities within critical socio-legal scholarship. The technical practices of jurisdiction have been particularly productive. Questions of jurisdiction are central to the practices of law yet, as Pisca points out, have been undertheorized (Pisca, forthcoming).

Two distinct, although overlapping, strands of jurisdictional thinking can be identified (Pisca, forthcoming). Valverde demonstrates that theorizing about scale, for instance, is further enriched by relating it to the machinery of jurisdiction. She points out that:

Jurisdiction ... distinguishes more than territories and authorities, more than the where and the who of governance. Jurisdiction also differentiates and organizes the 'what' of governance – and, most importantly because of its relative invisibility, the 'how' of governance. (Valverde, 2009, p. 144)

The invisibility means, for instance, that:

The effects of consigning a particular problem to a local rather than a national jurisdictional are rarely analyzed even in appeal cases in which levels of government fight with one another. (2009, p. 153)

What Valverde alerts us to is that jurisdiction is as much a tool of governance as a way of doing law.

The second strand emerges from the work of Dorsett and McVeigh. For them jurisdiction is foundational:

We will have lived in a world of jurisdiction. We are brought into life and set in motion according to the authority of law, our conduct is shaped according to civil order, and our conscience created and turned to political faith in law and community. (2012, p. 1)

In their work, jurisdiction becomes very rich; it is, and more than, the most technical and prosaic ordering of legal authority, the means of pronouncing existing law and inaugurating law, the visible forms that law takes, a distinct way of representing authority and a practice or craft that actively produces something. As Barr explains:

Technologies of jurisdiction create and arrange the institutional practices of law as well as creating and conducting lawful

relations. This is technology in its classical sense of craft; a practical knowledge or wisdom, which places the technology of
jurisdiction as a craft, practice, activity and prudence of law that
requires a practical knowledge of law. (Barr, 2013, p. 62)

Importantly for this chapter, which examines the competing legal tensions in the provision of adult social care, Dorsett and McVeigh identify a
need for a jurisdictional space of conscience. For them, its formulation 'has
become the most pressing concern of social life' (2012, p. 45). Their work,
prompted by the uneasy acknowledgement of indigenous jurisdictions by
non-indigenous jurisdictions within Australia, focuses on rival forms of
authority and rival positions. They are intrigued by the progressive possibilities of judicial encounters.

These approaches share an interest in legal techniques identifying,
for instance, the work done by practices of categorization, mapping
and precedent. For neither, however, is an analysis of technicalities sufficient. Valverde suggests a dual methodology, arguing that, in addition to analysing the work done by the machinery of jurisdiction 'one
would have to ask extra-legal questions, such as: how did the party that
decided to launch, say, a constitutional challenge against a city by-law,
imagine the space of their dispute?' (see Cowan and Carr, 2008). For
Dorsett and McVeigh, the concern is not governmental but jurisprudential, mining technicalities is a crucial precursor to any consideration of
questions of how we live with law and how our lives with law may be
made more just.

Drawing on both of these approaches, this chapter now turns to the par-
ticularities of jurisdictional thinking in the *McDonald* case. My concern is
with the judgment of the dispute between McDonald and the state – how
do the judges validate the technical decision-making of the local authority
and what does this tell us about our lives with law? First, however, I consider the vulnerable adult as a jurisdictional project suggesting that some of
the current complexity emerges from the different strands of jurisdictional
thinking at work.

The rise and fall of the vulnerable adult as a jurisdictional project

The National Assistance Act 1948 (the Act) was one of a suite of statutes
including the Education Act 1944, the National Health Service Act 1946
and the Children Act 1948 which provided the legal foundations of the
British post-war welfare state. These created, in its modern form, the vulnerable adult as a jurisdictional subject. As a subject, the vulnerable adult
was 'an exception to the (natural) legal person' (Dorsett and McVeigh,

2012, p. 87) because of their need for state assistance. Section 21(1) of the Act imposed a duty on local authorities to provide:

> residential accommodation for persons who by reason of age, infirmity or any other circumstances are in need of care and attention which is not otherwise available to them.

There was a simultaneous crafting of the jurisdiction of the national welfare state, an assemblage of measures that enabled the vulnerable adult to live well according to the interests of the state and the public interest (Dorsett and McVeigh, 2012, p. 85). This was achieved symbolically through the formal termination of the jurisdiction of the poor laws in s. 1 of the Act, and more substantively through distinguishing the jurisdiction from the previous, now discredited, workhouse system. There was an emphasis on the welfare of the service users and the importance of appropriately differentiating provision by recognizing different categories of need.

The legislative emphasis was on creating bureaucratic, rather than legal, relationships between the national state and local government and local government and the recipient of provision. Schemes of provision designed by local authorities had to be approved by the Minister of Health, who was able to order local provision if a local authority defaulted on its responsibilities. The statute set out systems for the registration, inspection and regulation of residential provision. Complex reimbursement provisions applied when a local authority provided welfare services for someone ordinarily resident in another local authority. The state-centric nature of the jurisdiction reflected the wide public trust in state institutions that followed the Second World War (Baldock, 2003).

Perhaps the particular blend of paternalism, expertise and public interest that characterized the jurisdiction is exemplified by s. 47 of the Act (only recently repealed by the Care Act 2014). This section authorized state intervention when someone refused welfare. The section enabled a local authority to apply to the magistrates' court for an order to remove someone from their home when they 'are suffering from grave chronic disease or, being aged, infirm or physically incapacitated, are living in insanitary conditions, and are unable to devote to themselves, and are not receiving from other persons, proper care and attention' (s. 47(1)). What was required was certification from the local medical officer of health that it was in the interests of that person that they were removed, or that it was necessary for preventing injury to the health of, or serious nuisance to, other people.

Within the jurisdiction created by the Act, the vulnerable adult is a welfare subject, rather than a rights-bearing citizen, and issues of legal authority arise between the welfare expert and the courts, rather than the individual whose rights are at stake. As Baldock puts it, what the Act established was:

> 'social administration' rather than social politics and it gener-
> ated a particular formation of social care provision, limited by
> the Treasury's definition of what could be afforded and man-
> aged in such a way that no categorical citizenship rights to care
> were established. (Baldock, 2003, p. 113)

A significant jurisdictional shift, triggered by a political crisis about the
costs of welfare, occurred with the implementation of the National Health
Service and Community Care Act 1990. This enabled the marketization of
the welfare state by splitting the planning and purchase of welfare services
from their provision and transforming the role of the local authority. The
authority was to plan services in response to need, and then procure those
services from a 'mixed economy of care'. The jurisdictional inspiration was
contract, the driving force neoliberalism, with its overriding concern to protect the individual, 'at all costs from the collective power of a coercive state
that is always on the verge of becoming totalitarian' (Campbell and Sitze,
2012, p. 13); with the market, of course, being the best means to that end.

The vulnerable adult, while remaining exceptional, was also to be
reformed; the Community Care (Direct Payments) Act 1996 empowered
local authorities to make direct payments to people assessed as in need of
services to make their own arrangements to meet their needs. 'Personaliza-
tion', the ability for service users to have choice and control over service
provision, was a transformational tool, the new key to living well, providing
individual independence, well-being and dignity (Department of Health,
2008). Here, appeals to conscience were resolved through re-imagining the
service user as a consumer.

The relationship between conscience and civil jurisdiction is important; the civil jurisdiction relating to vulnerable adults was, I would argue,
underpinned by a prior and inaugurating jurisdiction of conscience which
re-emerges in projects of reform. There is no doubt that in the interwar
years the workhouse system and the poor laws provoked national shame,
and the welfare state was a response. Its subsequent destabilization and
marketization was not solely as a consequence of a rhetoric of unafford-
ability; there was a gradual recognition of its potential to oppress resulting
in decarceration of individuals from institutions to the community during
the 1980s and 1990s (for details, see e.g. Ungerson, 2000); and there was an
acknowledgement of the justice of the claims of disability rights activism,
as well as a belief that autonomy potentially provided a better, as well as a
cheaper, means for guaranteeing individual dignity (Oliver, 1995).

Two statutes in particular – the Chronically Sick and Disabled Persons
Act 1970 (CSDPA) and the Disabled Persons (Services, Consultation and
Representation) Act 1986 (DP(SCR)A) – demonstrated the existence of

an alternative, conscience-based jurisdiction in connection with societal responses to the needs of disabled people. Section 2 of the CSDPA imposes a duty on local authorities to provide a range of community-based services for vulnerable adults which can be individually enforced. The DP(SCR)A places an express obligation on local authorities to assess the needs of people for services, thus increasing vulnerable adults' leverage upon the state and providing tools for legal arguments. The CSDPA started as a private member's bill sponsored by Alf Morris only five years after he became a Labour MP. He was the sixth child of a family of nine, born in one of the worst of Manchester's slums, whose father had been seriously disabled during the First World War. His speech introducing the bill concluded with a powerful appeal:

> Mr. Speaker, if we could bequeath one precious gift to posterity, I would choose a society in which there is genuine compassion for the very sick and the disabled; where understanding is unostentatious and sincere; where needs come before means; where, if years cannot be added to the lives of the chronically sick, at least life can be added to their years; where the mobility of disabled people is restricted only by the bounds of technical progress and discovery; where the handicapped have the fundamental right to participate in industry and society according to ability; where socially preventable distress is unknown; and where no man has cause to be ill at ease because of disability. (HC Deb. 5 December 1969, vol. 792, col. 1863)

The DP(SCR)A, another statute initiated by a private member's bill, drew its inspiration from Alf Morris's legislation but also from obligations articulated on the international stage. Tom Clarke MP explained, as he introduced the Bill at its second reading:

> Over 10 years ago, the United Nations General Assembly adopted a declaration on the rights of disabled people and called for national and international action to ensure that it would be used as a common base and frame of reference for the protection of those rights. The declaration said: 'Disabled persons have the inherent right to respect for their human dignity. Disabled persons, whatever the origin, nature and seriousness of their handicaps and disabilities have the same fundamental rights as their fellow citizens of the same age which implies, first and foremost the right to enjoy a decent life as normal and full as possible.' I believe that the Bill represents a small step in that direction. Given imagination and positive support, I believe

that it represents a major beacon which, in time, the rest of the world may wish to copy. (HC Deb. 17 January 1986, vol. 89, col. 1353)

Conscience worked as an inspiration for these statutes that expanded and added dignity to adult social care but it did not displace the bureaucratic character of the pre-existing civil jurisdiction. Instead, the bureaucracy itself expanded, in order to manage and make governable the potentially disruptive consequences of conscience. It developed documentary tools for the assessment of need and the rationing of resources.

The complexity of the resulting jurisdictional amalgam is demonstrated by the judicial responses to the claims made in the case of *R v Gloucestershire CC ex parte Barry* [1997] AC 584. The case concerned the decision of Gloucestershire County Council to reduce the care services provided to Mr Barry, an 82-year-old living alone with limited mobility and limited sight, because its budget from central government to fund adult social care had been cut by £2.5 million. The majority of the House of Lords, in over-ruling a majority decision of the Court of Appeal, were clear that needs were relative and therefore intimately connected with resources. Gloucestershire County Council was thus entitled to reduce provision for Mr Barry provided that such reduction followed a reassessment of his needs. The decision, shaped by the traditional limitations of judicial review, ratified the dominance of civil jurisdiction by prioritizing the interests of the state and relying on procedural requirements to protect Mr Barry's individual rights. Simultaneously, it intensified the legal role of the social worker by making the task of assessment of need central to legally robust decision-making about the allocation of resources. In contrast, the dissenting judges acknowledged the alternative argument pleaded by Mr Barry's counsel that the evaluation and resourcing of need should be founded upon the values of a civilized society. The opinion of Lord Lloyd in the House of Lords was particularly powerful:

> Who then is to decide what it is that the disabled person needs, and by what yardstick does he make his decision? I do not find the answer difficult. In the simplest case it is the individual social worker who decides. In more complicated cases there may have to be what is called a comprehensive assessment. But in every case, simple or complex, the need of the individual will be assessed against the standards of civilized society as we know them in the United Kingdom, or, in the more homely phraseology of the law, by the standards of the man on the Clapham omnibus. ([598])

For Lord Lloyd, the role of the social worker is not solely to administer scarce welfare resources, it is the office through which our collective conscience becomes activated when judging claims upon the state. So, although Mr Barry lost his case, the dissent and the lack of judicial unanimity about the outcome remind us of the jurisdiction of conscience and its progressive potential – something of particular importance in the problematic present of provision for vulnerable adults.

The Department of Health introduced further assessment requirements in response to the complexities of the decision. As a result, not only did documentation become even more pivotal in managing claims upon the state, its focus was increasingly resource management rather than needs assessment. The decision was reached prior to the implementation of the Human Rights Act 1998 which can be understood as providing a new jurisdictional space for claims of conscience, a legal means, in Dorsett and McVeigh's terms, of 'putting the state in its place' (2012, p. 51). As such, it gave hope to non-governmental organizations and other lobbyists on behalf of the vulnerable. They saw the *McDonald* case as particularly important as it provided an opportunity for mobilizing the notion of 'dignity'. However, in the encounter between civil jurisdiction and conscience the expectations of activists were disappointed. Age UK, which intervened in the case, described the judicial decision as 'shameful'. Its views were reported in the *Guardian*,

> While Age UK is acutely aware of the current difficult economic climate, the right balance must be struck between the rights of the individual and the interests of the community, and Age UK continues to find it difficult to understand how it can be rational or reasonable to expect an older continent person to use incontinence pads rather than to assist them to access a toilet. (the *Guardian*, 2011)

In the same article, John Wadham, legal officer for the Equalities and Human Rights Commission, commented:

> Ms McDonald is not incontinent. However, this judgment means she will be treated as such. Local authorities will now have greater discretion in deciding how to meet a person's home care needs and will find it easier to justify withdrawing care. This means that older people's human rights to privacy, autonomy and dignity will often be put at serious risk. (the *Guardian*, 2011).

The mismatch between activists who expected the judges to use dignity substantively to redress injustice and the decision of the Supreme Court justices is provocative. Its significance is heightened by the response to Baroness Hale's dissent, which, in its concluding paragraph, echoed Lord Lloyd:

> In the United Kingdom we do not oblige people who can con-
> trol their bodily functions to behave as if they cannot do so,
> unless they themselves find this the more convenient course.
> We are, I still believe, a civilized society. I would have allowed
> this appeal. ([79]).

The majority found the need to repudiate Hale's claim upon the collective conscience within their speeches. This suggests that such claims now fall way beyond the norms of legal discourse and that, despite the potency of the Human Rights Act 1998, it is now not possible to reason about dignity and civility within the law. My explanation for this is twofold. First, the jurisdictional project is no longer the vulnerable adult, but rather the documentation of that person's needs and jurisdictional responsibility is devolved from the judiciary to the social worker; second, the documentation acquires a life and vitality of its own which the judges seem willing to preserve. As long as it manages the questions asked of it, then the judges will not intervene.

Documentation and *R (on the Application of McDonald) v Royal Borough of Kensington and Chelsea 2011*

The legal problem

Elaine McDonald, who was 67 years old at the time of the proceedings, suffered a stroke in 1999 that left her with disabilities including severely limited mobility. She fell severely at night in April 2006, breaking her hips, and was hospitalized as a consequence for four months. Subsequently, and relatively rapidly, she suffered two more falls leading to further hospitalization. In addition (and at the heart of the legal dispute), Ms McDonald, although not incontinent, suffers from a small and neurogenic bladder causing her to urinate two or three times during the night. Kensington and Chelsea funded a night-time carer who helped Ms McDonald access a commode. This ensured her safety and prevented falls. The dispute between the parties arose because Ms McDonald wanted to continue to use a commode for night-time urination, whereas Kensington and Chelsea wanted her to use incontinence pads or special absorbent sheeting making the night-time carer redundant and reducing the cost of the care package by more than £20,000. For Kensington and Chelsea, this provided an appropriate solution. The borough argued that incontinence pads have the potential to improve the quality of life of vulnerable adults who have difficulty accessing toilets by protecting them from harm and allowing a degree of privacy and independence. Ms McDonald objected strenuously to Kensington and

Chelsea's proposed course of action. She was appalled at the thought of being treated as incontinent when she was not, and at having to use incontinence pads. For her, this was an intolerable affront to her dignity.

As *Barry* made clear, Kensington and Chelsea are legally obliged to meet Ms McDonald's assessed needs irrespective of cost and the impact the cost may have on its resources, although it can have regard to resources in deciding how to meet needs. What this means is that, if Ms McDonald's assessed need is a need for 'assistance at night to use the commode' (how it was initially expressed in a needs assessment begun in July 2008 and completed in October 2008), Kensington and Chelsea would be required to provide her with assistance to use her commode at night, which would require a night-time carer, regardless of the expense. If the assessed need is understood more generally in terms of safe urination at night, which is what Kensington and Chelsea successfully argued before the High Court, then the borough would be entitled to have regard to its resources in deciding how to meet that need. So, it would be entitled, subject to human rights considerations and disability discrimination laws, to decide that a reasonable and adequate solution to Ms McDonald's needs is provided by absorbent sheeting.

The Court of Appeal decided that Kensington and Chelsea was entitled to reduce its provision to Ms McDonald because the need the borough was meeting was the need for safe urination at night. Ms McDonald appealed to the Supreme Court. The majority (Lords Walker, Brown, Dyson and Kerr) affirmed the decision of the Court of Appeal. Baroness Hale dissented.

Reading the case informed by Riles' leaking faucet analogy, it is interesting how narrowly the majority of the judges understood the problem before them, despite the political and social crises enveloping adult social care. No new system of decision-making about needs was required to cope, for instance, with the European Convention demands of dignity, or to respond to the complex and unsatisfactory consequences of the majority decision in *Barry* which left service users without legal protections against inadequate resourcing of adult social care. For the majority, the case was about the documentation which recorded Kensington and Chelsea's decisions about Ms McDonald's needs: *it* was the faucet and the judicial role was first to identify whether or not there was any leakage, and if so, to see if it was remediable.

The documentation

Socio-legal scholarship has alerted us to the significance of documents. They are 'paradigmatic artefacts of modern knowledge practices' (Riles, 2006, p. 2) 'ubiquitous features of late modern life ... the emblem of modern bureaucracy' (Riles, 2006. p. 6). As we have seen, they are particularly potent in social welfare law where they play a crucial part in resource allocation. Indeed, within the decision, Lord Dyson reflects upon the particular nature of the documentation in adult social care:

> In construing assessments and care plan reviews, it should not be overlooked that these are documents that are usually drafted by social workers. They are not drafted by lawyers, nor should they be. They should be construed in a practical way against the factual background in which they are written and with the aim of seeking to discover the substance of their true meaning. ([53])

The reference to the 'true' meaning of the document is tantalizing. It was, of course, always unlikely that Lord Dyson would begin to unravel the network of the material and non-material, the human and the non-human that make up assessments and care plan reviews. What Lord Dyson meant is much more mundane. For him, the role of the court is to reveal rather than obscure the meaning ascribed to the document by Kensington and Chelsea. This is a benevolent task, which requires a kind of double translation – first of the document, and second of the judge who must put himself in the position of the administrator of resources.

Nonetheless, we should reflect a little further on the multilayered complexity of these documents. On one level, they are incredibly intimate records of the needs of individuals who, in order to get resources to meet those needs, must disclose their lack of autonomy and their inadequacies (Engel, 1993). The documents have an interesting temporality – they are constructed over extended periods, during which time the vulnerabilities of the people they concern may intensify or diminish. They must also anticipate the future. Central government funding may be reduced, costs of provision may rise and demand across the borough may escalate. As Lord Dyson notes, they are drafted by social care professionals who have bureaucratic responsibilities to ensure that statutory duties are met within the limited resources available, which they must reconcile with their professional responsibilities to the vulnerable adults who are their clients. The documents thus simultaneously construct the bureaucrat, the bureaucracy, the social care professional and the applicant for services. The form and content of the documents are determined by statutory guidance (at the time of the hearing, Fair Access to Care Services, 2003), so they are legal documents, which become judicial artefacts once decisions are challenged. But they are shaped by more than legal technology; the range of technical devices available to provide for the service user's needs, the hoists, the adaptations or, as in this particular case, the availability of absorbent sheeting and incontinence pads, has a direct impact on the responses proposed to difficulties faced by service users (as does our often limited technical understanding of the physical and mental problems facing the service user).

The problem with the documentation in this case was the shifting identification of Ms McDonald's needs from 'assistance to use the commode at night' to 'night-time toileting needs'. The shift justifies the reduction in provision but no specific reassessment of Ms McDonald's needs has taken place. Yet, despite the fact that the documentation is the crucial component of legal decision-making in adult social care and provides the only protection for the rights of the service user, the majority did not regard the omission as problematic. They were prepared either to imply the required reassessment or to decide that judicial discretion could remedy any defect. For them the faucet was not leaking. This pragmatic approach to the documentation is compounded by the role the documentation plays in determining dignity.

Dignity

Only Lord Brown addresses the Article 8 claim directly, rejecting Ms McDonald's argument that to require her to use absorbent sheeting when she was not in fact incontinent was a breach of her right to a private life, to human dignity and autonomy. For him, the process of consulting with Ms McDonald recorded in the documentation demonstrates Kensington and Chelsea's respect for her private life:

> The respondents went to great lengths both to consult the appellant and Mr McLeish about the appellant's needs and the possible ways of meeting them and to try to reach agreement with her upon them. In doing so they sought to respect as far as possible her personal feelings and desires, at the same time taking account of her safety, her independence and their own responsibilities towards all their other clients. They respected the appellant's human dignity and autonomy, allowing her to choose the details of her care package within their overall assessment of her needs: for example, the particular hours of care attendance, whether to receive direct payments in order to employ her own care assistant, and the possibility of other options like extra care sheltered housing. ([19])

The documentation is the means through which dignity is demonstrated. Dignity is elided with consultation and its purpose is procedural. Because dignity is documented, the necessary transparency and information transfer is revealed. Baroness Hale in her dissent points out the limited connection between consultation and substantive justice:

> But the fact that they have been trying so hard for so long to persuade her to accept their point of view does not mean that it is a rational view or one which she is bound to accept. ([76])

However, making consultation procedural closes down, indeed makes unhearable, the counter argument. Clements puts it well:

> In effect, that 'dignity' becomes something defined by a process and perforce 'indignity' in terms of a flawed process – and not as an issue of substance. Conceptions of dignity, such judges would claim, are (like all legal principles) matters for the head and not the heart, and certainly not to be identified by reference to non-rational emotional benchmarks such as revulsion or the mores of a civilized society. (Clements, 2011, p. 676)

The documentation achieves something else of contemporary importance. It enables the reconciliation of the conflict that is at the heart of the neo-liberalized and constricted welfare state which simultaneously repositions the service user as a consumer whose preferences should be met and tells the service user, in a revitalized and more punitive form of welfare's long-standing paternalism, how he or she should behave. In this particular case, in a rather remarkable twist, safety (provided by confining Ms McDonald to her bed) and privacy and independence (provided by absorbent sheeting) trumps Ms McDonald's claim to dignity via help to use the commode. This is perhaps best illustrated by Lord Brown's final dismissal of any Article 8 argument, as he describes the decision as:

> a proportionate response to the appellant's needs because it affords her the maximum protection from injury, greater privacy and independence, and results in a substantial costs saving. [19]

The extraordinary elasticity of the documentation, and its crucial role in facilitating neoliberal welfarism, reminds us of the consequences of inscription, the ways in which people represent themselves and others within written artefacts. The imprecision of dignity cannot survive as a legal claim when pitted against such substantive and documented outcomes.

Functional incontinence

There is a third technical move within the documentation, made by the social workers in the case and unchallenged by the judges. What happens is that Ms McDonald's condition is re-labelled as functional incontinence. Functional incontinence describes the urinary incontinence that occurs when a person is aware of the need to urinate, but is unable to get to a bathroom for physical or mental reasons. Like all medical labels it has significant power, and it is arguably that move which prevents Ms McDonald making an effective claim for dignity because it removes her body, and indeed all of our bodies, from the dispute. For we are all functionally incontinent and the management of the consequences of this is one of our constant although invisible concerns. Urination and its management is an overlooked technology which is simultaneously intimate, mundane, complex and fragile. When bodily technology fails, as it commonly does, there are physiological consequences, embarrassment, depression and frequently withdrawal from social life.

Sanitary facilities are, of course, crucial to our management of our continence and our dignity, although as the quotation at the start of this chapter suggests, it is shameful to talk about them (Barron, 2003). As Braverman points out:

> In our sanitary, well-plumbed lives, the toilet – an engineering marvel – removes waste out of sight and out of mind. Indeed, the wash-room, and the water closet ('WC') in particular, is an ingenious invention on the immediate physical level. At the same time, the WC does not only flush water; it also flushes the human fear of its own organic nature and, consequently, of mortality. (Braverman, 2009, p. 50)

She notes that when the toilet is one that is public in any sort of way, then it becomes hyper-regulated. This is a consequence of:

> the physical, symbolic, and imaginary sanitary status of the wash-room ... the mixed public/private status of commercial washrooms, which makes them more prone to various provisions and to extensive modes of surveillance and discipline ... (and) the dense physiological faculties performed in the limited physical space of the public wash-room. A thick regulatory web is thus applied so as to make the public washroom accessible to the 'normal' user. (Braverman, 2009, p. 70)

This makes clear that toilets are crucial to our understanding of what is 'normal' in our social functioning. When we are forced to behave in a way which is inconsistent with the discipline that has been imposed upon our bodies from a very early age, then our dignity is placed in jeopardy. This is illustrated by Hollins' account of the management of continence on the first American space flight on 5 May 1961. Although schoolchildren had written to NASA to ask them what the astronaut would do when he needed the toilet, for NASA it was not a relevant issue. The expectation was that the astronaut would urinate just before they closed his pressure suit and then hold it until he was on the rescue ship. Unfortunately, there was a four-hour delay on the launch pad and he needed to urinate. The only answer that could be given to his question about how he was to do this was to 'do it in the suit' regardless of the damage caused to the electronic devices within the suit (see Hollins, 2013). The story fascinates because of the juxtaposition of the achievements of space technology and the failure of the scientists to provide for the mundane, and the consequent human physical discomfort and embarrassment amidst the success of the flight.

In *McDonald* the unquestioning acceptance of the label – functional incontinence – prevents judicial examination of a crucial issue: the consequences for Ms McDonald's dignity of the replacement of the technology of the toilet with the technology of absorbent sheeting. The first technology enables her to be normal, the second allows us to keep her safe. It seems that it is our dignity rather than hers, which is preserved. This judicial failure is facilitated by a particular legal technology, reasoning by analogy. Lord Brown uses *Bernard v Enfield* [2002] EWHC 2282 (Admin); [2003] HRLR 111, a case relied upon by Ms McDonald, to bring home the hopelessness of her claim:

> But really what is striking about *Bernard* is the contrast between that case and this. The claimants there were husband and wife. They had six children. The wife was severely disabled and confined to a wheelchair. In breach of their duty under section 21(1)(a) of NAA 1948 , the respondent council failed for some 20 months to provide the family with accommodation suited to her disability. The consequences were appalling. The wife was doubly incontinent and, because there was no wheelchair access to the lavatory, was forced to defecate and urinate on the living-room floor. And she was unable to play any part in looking after her six children. Small wonder that Sullivan J, at para 31, described the article 8 case as 'not finely balanced' and awarded £10,000 damages. ([17])

So the extreme case is deployed to defeat the instant case but simultaneously overlooks the importance of the mundane. Baroness Hale attempts to disrupt this logic through her own analogy. She suggests that:

> Logically, the decision of the majority in this case would entitle a local authority to withdraw this help even though the client needed to defecate during the night and thus might be left lying in her faeces until the carers came in the morning. ([77])

This analogy is, however, of quite a different order from Lord Brown's. Rather than using settled legal cases to solve a legal problem, what Hale does is to use an analogy to demonstrate the insufficiency of the legal solution reached by the majority. It is an analogy which does not solve, but rather exacerbates, the problem that the judges are faced with. It brings the body back in, but in a way that appals Lord Walker in the affront it represents to the dignity of the court:

> I totally disagree with, and I deplore, Lady Hale's suggestion that the decision of the majority would logically entitle a local authority to withdraw help from a client so that she might be left lying in her faeces day and night, relieved only by periodic changes of absorbent pads or sheets. ([32])

I too have difficulty with the way in which Baroness Hale deploys Ms McDonald's body in her reasoning, for she exacerbates McDonald's victimhood and, indeed, the disgust we feel for the vulnerable body to make her point. We should take care in how we utilize the body in our arguments for, as Twigg makes clear, the intensity of our gaze can work to dehumanize rather than humanize (Twigg, 2000; 2002). Despite this, it is insufficient to articulate, 'the greatest sympathy for the appellant's misfortunes and a real understanding of her deep antipathy towards the notion of using incontinence pads' (Lord Brown, [19]). More is required of the judges in acknowledgement of the particular although mundane incursion into human dignity, the peeling away of years of discipline that is required when someone is told to wet her bed.

Conclusion

Ms McDonald's claim upon the state was unconventional and inspirational. Rather than constructing herself as a victim in the way that the bureaucratic system which underpins welfare provision for vulnerable adults requires, she asserted a right to be treated with dignity. The failure of the British courts to respond to her claim was particularly dispiriting to anyone concerned with the contemporary problematization of adult social care.[3] The concern of this chapter has been to explore the extent to which technical legal thinking explains the failure of that claim. My argument is that the particular evolution of jurisdictional thinking about vulnerable adults and the role of the state is deeply implicated in the outcome of the case. What my review of the emergence of the law demonstrates is that, while claims of conscience have been of significance in the development of the jurisdiction, they are constantly changing – so, for instance, welfare mutates into rights, subjects into citizens and freedom from want into independence. Meanwhile, governmental concerns about the affordability

---

3 The European Convention on Human Rights subsequently recognized that Ms McDonald's Article 8 right to dignity had been breached, albeit only for the limited period when the reduction in provision was not justified by a specific reassessment of her needs.

of welfare are increasingly neoliberal, resisting new claims and requiring austerity. Judicial thinking struggles with the complexity of reconciling these two modes of jurisdictional thinking and responds by making the documentation rather than the vulnerable adult its major concern. Yet the shift is problematic; it devolves jurisdictional thinking to social workers who are more and more managers of scarce resources and transparent procedures, and less and less advocates for service users. If judges simply oversee processes putting right technical failures, they erode possibilities of reasoning about concerns of dignity and conscience and increase the vitality of the bureaucratic documentation at the expense of the service user. They delegate to non-lawyers the responsibility of ensuring that a life lived with law is a life of dignity.

Yet, perhaps there are some possibilities in judicial technical thinking – deconstructing technicalities such as functional incontinence and interrogating their relationship with law and dignity may well be productive. However, that would require judicial recognition of the problems of reasoning by analogy, so beloved by lawyers, because such reasoning requires extreme humiliation and victimization before the law will intervene. When it comes to responding to the needs of vulnerable adults, it seems to me that Braverman's observation is most apt:

> From minute dressing codes, such as zippers, to the potty training of toddlers, recognizing the importance of washroom design in governing our everyday conduct is not unlike realizing the importance of salt to King Lear – namely that small things govern our everyday lives and make all the difference in the world. (2009, p. 46)

Cases

Bernard v Enfield [2002] EWHC 2282 (Admin); [2003] HRLR 111
Holmes-Moorhouse v LB of Richmond upon Thames [2009] UKHL 7 [2009] 1 WLR 413
R v Gloucestershire CC ex parte Barry [1997] AC 584
R (on the Application of McDonald) v Royal Borough of Kensington and Chelsea [2011] UKSC 33; [2011] 4 All ER 881

References

Age UK (2012) Care in Crisis www.ageuk.org.uk/documents/en-gb/campaigns/care_in_crisis_report_2012_pro.pdf?dtrk=true
Baldock, John (2003) 'Social Care in the United Kingdom: A Pattern of Discretionary Social Administration' in Anneli Anttonen, John Baldock, Jorma Sipila (eds), *The Young, The Old and the State Social Care Systems in Five Industrial Nations* (Cheltenham and Northampton: Edward Elgar)

Barr, Olivia (2013) 'Walking with Empire' 38 *Australian Feminist Law Journal* 59–72

Barron, Jesse (2003) 'Completely without Dignity: An Interview with Karl Ove Knausgaard' *Paris Review* 26 December 2013 www.theparisreview.org/blog/2013/12/26/completely-without-dignity-an-interview-with-karl-ove-knausgaard

Bennet, Jane (2010) *Vibrant Matter: A Political Ecology of Things* (Durham and London: Duke University Press)

Braverman, Iris (2009) 'Loo Law: The Public Washroom as a Hyper-Regulated Place' *Buffalo Legal Studies Research Paper* No 2009-03

Campbell, Timothy and Adam Sitze (2012) 'Introduction' 8(1) *Law Culture and the Humanities* 6–16

Carr, Helen (2012) 'Rational Men and Difficult Women – R *(on the Application of McDonald) v Royal Borough of Kensington and Chelsea* [2011] UKSC 33' 34(2) *Journal of Social Welfare and Family Law* 219–30

Carr, Helen and Caroline Hunter (2008) 'Managing Vulnerability: Homelessness Law and the Interplay of the Social, the Political and the Technical' 30(4) *Journal of Social Welfare and Family Law* 293–307

Carr, Helen and Caroline Hunter (2012) 'Are Judicial Approaches to Adult Social Care at a Dead-End?' 21(1) *Social and Legal Studies* 73–92

Clements, Luke (2011) 'Disability, Dignity and the Cri de Coeur' 6 *European Human Rights Law Review* 675–85

Cowan, David and Helen Carr (2008) 'Actor-Network Theory, Implementation, and the Private Landlord' 35(1) *Journal of Law and Society* 149–66

Cowan, David, Caroline Hunter and Hal Pawson (2012) 'Jurisdiction and Scale: Rent Arrears, Social Housing, and Human Rights' 39 (2) *Journal of Law and Society* 269–95

Dean, Mitchell (2007) *Governing Societies: Political Perspectives on Domestic and International Rule* (Maidenhead: Open University Press)

Department of Health (2008) *Transforming Adult Social Care* LAC (DH)(2008) (London: Department of Health)

Dorsett, Shaunnagh and Sean McVeigh (2012) *Jurisdiction* (Oxford: Routledge)

Engel, David M (1993) 'Origin Myths: Narratives of Authority, Resistance, Disability, and Law' 27 *Law and Society Review* 785

George, Robert (2011) 'In Defence of Dissent: R *(McDonald) v Royal Borough of Kensington and Chelsea*' 41 *Family Law* 1097–103

Guardian (2011) 'Carer Battle Over as Ex-ballerina Loses Supreme Court Fight' 6 July 2011 www.guardian.co.uk/society/2011/jul/06/care-battle-ballerina-supreme-court

Hollins, Hunter (2013) 'Forgotten Hardware – How to Do It in A Space Suit' 37 *Advances in Physiology Education* 123–28

House of Lords Select Committee (2014) *Mental Capacity Act 2005: Post Legislative Scrutiny* (London: The Stationery Office)

Local Government Ombudsman and Parliamentary and Health Service Ombudsman (2009) *Six Lives: The Provision of Local Services to People with Mental Disabilities* Second Report Session 2008–2009 HC 203-1 (London: The Stationery Office)

Nelken, David (1983) *The Limits of the Legal Process: A Study of Landlords, Law and Crime* (London: Academic Press)

Oliver, Michael (1995) *Understanding Disability* (Basingstoke: Macmillan)

Pisca, Nick (forthcoming) 'Understanding Jurisdictional Thinking'

Riles, Annelise (2005) 'A New Agenda for the Cultural Study of Law: Taking on the Technicalities' 53 *Buffalo Law Review* 973–1033 http://ssrn.com/abstract=558605

Riles, Annelise (2006) 'Introduction: In Response' in A Riles (ed.), *Documents: Artefacts of Modern Knowledge* (Michigan University of Michigan Press)

Riles, Annelise (2011) *Collateral Knowledge: Legal Reasoning in the Global Financial Markets* (Chicago: University of Chicago Press)

Twigg, Julia (2000) 'Social Policy and the Body' in G Lewis, S Gewirtz and J Clarke (eds), *Rethinking Social Policy* (London: Sage)

Twigg, Julia (2002) 'The Body in Social Policy: Mapping a Territory' 31(3) *Journal of Social Policy* 421–39

Ungerson, Clare (2000) 'Thinking about the Long Term Production and Consumption of Care in Britain – Does Gender Still Matter?' 29(4) *Journal of Social Policy* 623–43

Valverde Mariana (2009) 'Jurisdiction and Scale: Legal "Technicalities" as Resources for Theory' 18 *Social and Legal Studies* 139–58

Zumbansen, Peer (2008) 'Law after the Welfare State: Formalism, Functionalism, and the Ironic Turn of Reflexive Law' 56 *American Journal of Comparative Law* 769

11
Following the Law or Using the Law? Decision-Making in Medical Manslaughter

Andrew Sanders and Danielle Griffiths

Introduction

Over the course of a lifetime most of us will put our lives in the hands of one or more healthcare professionals. Many of us will do this several times, sometimes knowingly and sometimes not. Much medical and surgical treatment is intrinsically dangerous, but so would be the failure to treat many people who are ill or injured. And so, inevitably, many people die in the course of medical and surgical treatment. Sometimes this is simply because some people cannot be saved, and much treatment is inherently risky. But sometimes it is because of negligence. Many people also suffer hugely without dying and are left permanently damaged or traumatized by the experience, but what should be done in these cases is not for this chapter but a different one (Griffiths and Sanders, 2013).

So how should we think about appropriate legal responses to deaths arising from negligent treatment or negligent failure to treat? There is, of course, the law of tort, but with cuts to legal aid, invoking this increasingly depends on having the money to hire a lawyer or such a strong case that it will be taken on a 'no-win no-fee' basis. And there are complaint and discipline procedures. But many people lack confidence in such processes, often with good reason (Dixon-Woods et al., 2011). So both courses of action are problematic in very large numbers of cases.

Then there is the criminal law. The Health and Safety Executive (HSE) has criminal powers to prosecute healthcare trusts and individual healthcare professionals. However, currently the HSE does not, in general, investigate matters related to quality of care or clinical judgement, leaving it to other bodies due to lack of resources (Kazarian et al., 2011). The police and

Crown Prosecution Service (CPS) conduct criminal investigations into the majority of cases that involve a potential negligently caused death.[1]

Most serious crimes in England and Wales have two main elements: the act or omission itself; and the doing of that act or omission deliberately or recklessly. The second element, the mental element, is very often determined 'subjectively'. That is: did the defendant know or intend that the consequence would be the one for which he or she is being prosecuted?

Manslaughter is an exception. There are many types of homicide, of which murder is the most serious, and there are many types of manslaughter (see Ashworth and Horder, 2013). 'Gross negligence' is the mental element of one type of manslaughter. This will be discussed in more detail later. But the basic principle is that one cannot be convicted for killing people by 'mere' negligence. It has to be gross. There are many examples: *R v Wacker* (2003) QB 1203, where illegal immigrants were crowded into a lorry and died from suffocation; *R v Kite and OLL Ltd* (1996) 2 Cr App R (S) 295, where a small outward bound company failed to heed safety warnings and several young people drowned as a result. And then there are medical cases, two of which helped shape the modern law of 'gross negligence manslaughter' (GNM). In *R v Adomako* (1995) 1 AC 171, an anaesthetist did not realize his patient had stopped breathing; and in *R v Misra* (2005) 1 Cr App R 21, two doctors failed to diagnose and treat an infection.

Technically, 'medical manslaughter' (MM), as cases like *Adomako* and *Misra* are known in prosecution circles, is no different to other GNM. But it can be argued that MM cases are morally dissimilar to cases like *Wacker* and *Kite and OLL*. Moreover, the defendants in *Adomako* and *Misra* are arguably less morally blameworthy than those in many health and safety cases where there is no manslaughter conviction, such as in *Director of Public Prosecutions (DPP) ex parte Jones* (2000) IRLR 373, where a young worker was struck by a crane after the company had several warnings about dangerous working conditions. So, should healthcare professions be treated more generously than employers and landlords, on the basis that the former caused death in the course of socially vital, risky and life-saving work? Or should they be treated less generously than other people because the potential for causing death and injury is so much greater and they have (or should have) more awareness of the danger their negligence can cause? Or perhaps law-makers and law-enforcers should pay no attention to the context at all and simply apply the legal principles in a formalistic way?

---

1   The CPS is usually involved in criminal cases only at the end of investigations. However, in MM cases prosecutors from the Special Crime and Counter Terrorism Division have a broader role in investigations, often guiding the police and offering advice at the earliest stages of investigations.

This chapter will not debate how healthcare professionals should be treated. Instead, an essential prior issue will be examined: how health care professionals are *actually* treated. In both the civil and criminal law there appears to be an underlying deference on the part of juries and the judiciary which often works to the benefit of healthcare professionals (Miola, 2011). In this chapter we look at another agency where such deference could be displayed: the CPS. We shall discuss the way prosecutors use the law to justify a particular stance towards the prosecution of MM. In cases of MM this leads to some not proceeding as far as they perhaps should. This can be seen as deference and a departure from the 'law in the books' in so far as the CPS seems to be reluctant to prosecute doctors without an element of 'badness', more often assuming them to be of 'good character' on the basis of belonging to the medical profession.

It is not that the law in the books and the 'law in action' are different, nor that they are the same. What we will demonstrate is that the desire to see a particular type of law in action leads prosecutors to shape the law in the books. As McBarnet (1981) argued over 30 years ago, it is often necessary to understand the technicalities of the law in order to understand what legal professionals do, even though (contrary to the stance of legal positivism) those technicalities do not determine what legal professionals do. More recently, Riles (2005) has extended this argument: she shows that, in the context of conflicts of laws, doctrinal thought (and doctrinal thinkers) are worthy of attention in themselves. This chapter extends this approach yet further, viewing agencies of law enforcement as doctrinal thinkers too.

Background: too many prosecutions for medical manslaughter?

In 2006 Ferner and McDowell looked at trends in the prosecution of doctors. Based on media reports and the low conviction rate in MM cases, they concluded that prosecutions had risen in the last 20 to 30 years. They asserted that the CPS charges too many cases. The CPS does so because it is 'an emotionally satisfying way to exact retribution' rather than from a concern to protect patients (Ferner and McDowell, 2006, p. 314).

This is rejected by the CPS. Prosecutors argue that their decisions are based on the law and on the interpretations of/elaborations on the law set out in documents such as the *Code for Crown Prosecutors* and not because of emotion or political pressure (O'Doherty, 2006). Although there is discretion to not prosecute on 'public interest' grounds, even if the evidence is strong, this discretion is eschewed in most homicide cases. This is because 'seriousness' is the most important factor taken into account when considering whether to prosecute (Sanders et al., 2010, ch. 7). Homicide is almost always 'serious'.

However, we shall see that the gross negligence test is too vague to act as a legal straitjacket. Indeed, 'The CPS has told us that prosecutors find it difficult to judge when to bring a prosecution ...' (Law Commission, 1996, para. 3.9). So, prosecutors who wish to exercise discretion not to prosecute when the evidence is 'thin', for example, will often be able to do so on the basis that drawing the evidential sufficiency line in such cases is a matter of judgement on which opinions can legitimately differ. So the mere existence of apparently strict legal rules does not negate the claims of Ferner and McDowell.

Oliver Quick's (2011) previous work confirms this. Accepting Ferner and McDowell's evidence on an increase in prosecutions, he found that prosecutors' and experts' evaluations of gross negligence were very broad and subjective. Quick argues that this lack of consensus about gross negligence is leading to particular harshness for doctors who are exposed to such an uncertain crime through working in their high-risk profession. For Quick (2010), the best solution would lie in replacing 'gross negligence' manslaughter with 'manslaughter by subjective recklessness'.

If Ferner and McDowell are correct, such use of the criminal law against healthcare professionals marks a relatively recent shift in attitudes. It has long been accepted that the civil courts used to hold deferential views towards the medical profession. This was seen most starkly in the *Bolam* test (*Bolam v Friern Hospital Management Committee* (1957) 1 WLR 582; Miola, 2011) used in civil law and which effectively allowed doctors to set their own legal standards. Emilie Cloatre (this volume) shows how shifting definitions of what counts as acceptable in pharmaceutical treatment has numerous social and legal implications. Under the *Bolam* test, allowing doctors to define what counts as acceptable in medicine meant social and legal disadvantage for many patients. The advent of *Bolitho v City and Hackney Health Authority (1997)* 4 All ER 771 marked a turning point away from such deference. An increase in prosecutions of doctors would indicate that the criminal courts are also more willing to subject the medical profession to increased legal scrutiny.

Numerous scandals have exposed the medical profession as being often fallible and sometimes even incompetent and dangerous. From the recent reports of terrible neglect at Mid Staffordshire NHS Trust (2013) to the stories which populate the media of doctors making fatal mistakes, there have been numerous high-profile examples of doctors being discredited and more open to legal redress through the criminal law. Robert Wheeler (2002) notes that aggrieved patients have found that their rights cannot be adequately exercised and accountability cannot be laid firmly at the door of the transgressor through the traditional routes of the civil courts or professional regulators. Yet, as Wheeler points out, prosecution for manslaughter changes all of this and brings punishment and accountability straight to the door. Police and coroners are much more aware of medical accidents and more likely to investigate when a complaint is made than they were even just ten years ago (Griffiths and Sanders, 2013). 'Just' being investigated, let alone prosecuted, by the state for a serious crime is quite different from local, civil or professional disciplinary proceedings that doctors may be more used to. A criminal investigation carries strong connotations of moral opprobrium. In these ways, the old culture of deference to doctors has certainly shifted.

The picture is, however, complex. Even if there has been a rise in prosecutions, Miola (2011) shows how in the criminal sphere generally, and in MM cases in particular, doctors are still treated relatively favourably. Conviction rates are low and, until recently, non-custodial sentences have been the norm even where there haves been appalling levels of disregard for patients (*R v Misra and Srivistava* [2004] EWCA 2375). In many cases, and regardless of the verdict, the courts have commented on the 'good' character of the defendant doctors. Miola gives the example of two junior doctors involved in the case of *R v Prentice* (1994) QB 302 (which we discuss in more depth later) where vincristine was fatally injected into the spine of a patient. Despite being found guilty, the trial judge pointed out that they were not 'bad men [but] good men who ... were guilty of a momentary recklessness' (*R v Misra and Srivistava*).

For Miola, in criminal cases, the courts have often assumed that doctors are of good character, by virtue of them belonging to the medical profession. Their crimes are treated as momentary lapses in the otherwise exemplary characters of the doctors concerned. Whatever the action which has led to the prosecution, such presumption of good character does not fit well with the name of the crime charged. Manslaughter is not easily associated with the medical profession. Arguments to change criminal charges for medical error to more context-specific offences, which do not include slaughter in the name, such as 'medical neglect endangering life', as we have argued elsewhere (Griffiths and Sanders, 2013), may change such reticence to find doctors guilty. As Natalie Ohana argues (in this volume), 'legal naming is an act of knowledge-production by which a social phenomenon is granted a name accepted by legal discourse' (p. 82). The social phenomenon of the 'good doctor' does not fit with the name of the crime they can be charged with, most often despite their actions.

Much work on deference in the criminal courts and the medical profession has looked at judges' and juries' reluctance to convict and condemn. Relatively little work had been done to explore the decision-making of agencies responsible for prosecution decisions. Have agencies such as the police and CPS become less deferential, less likely to be biased by the presumptions of good character, and more likely to subject a doctor to prosecution?

Consequently, as part of a large Arts and Humanities Research Council project headed by Margot Brazier and a team from the University of Manchester School of Law, we sought to find out on what basis the CPS decides to prosecute doctors (or not); what issues arise in decision-making; and whether or not Ferner and McDowell and Quick were correct. With the cooperation of the CPS, we looked at a selection of the cases it considered over a five-year period and conducted semi-structured interviews with the prosecutors involved in those cases.[2] There were 75 cases in total, of which only four were prosecuted. This is, by any standards, a low figure (Devlin, 2010). It appears, on the face of it, that – rather than too many cases being prosecuted – there could be too few cases prosecuted. To assess whether or not this is so, we will examine prosecution decision-making. First, though, let us see what we know of the law of GNM.

The law of gross negligence manslaughter

Twenty years ago, in *R v Adomako* (1995) 1 AC 171, it was clearly established in the leading judgment by Lord Mackay that four elements need to be proved for GNM.

The existence of a duty of care to the deceased

Lord Mackay envisaged that this would be determined by the law of tort. In reality, a wider view of 'duty' has been taken (tortious duty probably did not exist in *Wacker*, for example, as the victims voluntarily participated in the illegality). But establishing the existence of a duty is rarely, if ever, problematic in MM cases.

Breach of the duty of care

In most MM cases it is also evident whether a duty was breached (unlike in many other GNM situations, such as where drugs are supplied to a friend) (Wilson, 2008). It should not matter, in principle, whether the duty was breached by an act (e.g. a particular medical treatment or operation) or omission (e.g. failure to treat a post-operative infection, as in *Misra*).

Cause of death of the victim

Causation in GNM and MM cases is determined in the same way as it is determined in all other crimes. Thus, for the legal requirement of causation

---

2   Due to the way in which the CPS stored its files we were not able to get all the cases they dealt with during that period. While the sample was not representative and could not give a reliable indication of the rates of prosecutions over the period, the analysis of decision-making within the case files was our major concern in order to discern how prosecutors were applying the law.

to be satisfied, the act (or omission) need not be the only cause of death if it significantly contributes to the death. Its effect must not be *de minimis* (*R v Cato* (1976) 1 All ER 260), but it need not be the main cause if its contribution is more than negligible (*R v L* (2010) EWCA Crim 1249).

Gross negligence

As stated earlier, mere negligence will not suffice. But how 'gross' need the negligence be? According to Lord Mackay, whether a breach of duty

> should be characterised as gross negligence and therefore as a crime ... will depend on the seriousness of the breach of duty committed by the defendant in all the circumstances in which the defendant was placed ... The essence of the matter which is supremely a jury question is whether, having respect to the risk of death involved, the conduct of the defendant was so bad in all the circumstances as to amount in their judgment to a criminal act or omission. (*R v Adomako* (1995) 1 AC 171, 187)

This is as close to a definition of gross negligence as we have. In practice, it seems that the offence of GNM involves circularity; juries being told in effect to convict of a crime if they think a crime has been committed (Law Commission, 1996, para. 3.9; Brazier and Allen, 2007, p. 21). Circularity was a frequent criticism of the *Bateman* test of gross negligence (*R v Bateman* (1925) Cr App R 8)[3] on which the test in *Adomako* is based. A type of homicide that has been criticized so frequently and so consistently yet which was affirmed – largely unchanged – 70 years after first being formulated seems curiously indispensable.

The test for GNM is supposed to be objective (if we leave aside the subjective nature of a circular test!). Disregard and recklessness are not required for conviction. Cases involving a momentary (but major) error with no evidence of subjective fault, such as miscalculating the dose of diamorphine, have therefore resulted in conviction (*CA & R v Becker* (2000) WL 877688). Thus, caring doctors who do their best for patients but who make a terrible mistake have found themselves cast into the criminal process. This is unusual, but not unique. A doctor who misdiagnosed (as depression) a serious side effect of diabetes – which, because it was untreated, killed the patient – was convicted of MM and imprisoned.[4] Other recent MM convictions, also where doctors were imprisoned, are more typical. In one, in 2013, where the doctor ordered tests that revealed a serious condition but delayed the required operation, the

---

3   See criticism by, for example, Williams (1983); successive editions of Smith and Hogan.
4   www.bbc.co.uk/news/uk-england-south-yorkshire-21434488

CPS commented that: 'This doctor's actions were not mistakes or errors of judgement' but a series of failures to act.[5] In *R v Garg* [2012] EWCA 2520 the doctor made numerous clinical errors that were ultimately fatal.

Prosecution decision-making and healthcare deaths

We categorized the 75 CPS cases we examined according to the *Adomako* tests (b, c and d set out above), although this is rather schematic as some cases inevitably encountered difficulties relating to two or three of the tests.

Prosecution – all tests met

In 5 per cent (four) of cases the CPS prosecuted. There were two convictions, one acquittal, and one case never got to trial as the defendant fled the UK and could not be extradited. In three of these cases there was strong evidence that the doctors had been warned by colleagues and/or the patient not to proceed with the particular procedures that caused death. In the other, had basic protocols been observed, the patient would probably not have died.

We return to these cases later. At this point it is important to note that these data cast considerable doubt on Ferner and McDowell's claims of increased prosecutions and shows that there has been no lowering of the de facto prosecution threshold.

No breach of the duty of care

In 25 (33 per cent) of the cases, the CPS decided or advised that there was no breach of duty of care in relation to the individuals being investigated (these include five 'advice' cases where no decision was made by the CPS).

(i)   In around half of these cases it was clear that there would be difficulty identifying a breach from the beginning. For example, a 9-week old baby bled to death after a routine circumcision. The post-mortem was inconclusive as to why the bleed occurred and there was no evidence that the operation was performed negligently. Despite the early finding that causation could not be proved, a full one-and-a-half year police investigation was initiated, after which it was concluded that there were no grounds to argue that the GP who performed the operation had breached his duty of care.

(ii)   In one-third of the cases where no breach of duty was established, there was clear evidence of individual error. Three cases involved individual faults that contributed to a death yet no one individual could be identified as the cause of the particular error/incident. For

---

5   www.bbc.co.uk/news/uk-england-london-24825665

example, one case involved a toddler who died after a naso-gastric tube was inserted into his lung and feed was introduced. Three nurses were involved in his care but not one admitted making the mistake. One of them was almost certainly to blame but it was impossible to identify which one.

(iii) The rest of the cases involved errors or adverse incidents that could be directly related to systemic faults. For example, a man was refused treatment on arrival at an accident and emergency department: the hospital staff had deemed that he posed a threat to staff because they believed he was using drugs and had shown slight aggression. He was taken to a police station where he suffered a cardiac arrest and died. The police investigation concluded that he did not have capacity on arrival at the hospital (he was suffering from 'excited delirium' in relation to his drug use) and should have been sedated and treated on the basis of his severe symptoms. Three individuals were investigated but the hospital trust's policies on 'violent and aggressive behaviour' had never been communicated to the individuals or tested, so no individual breaches of duty were found.

Failure to establish causation

In 33 cases (44 per cent) the CPS decided that causation would probably not be proved were prosecutions to take place (and, as we have seen, some 'breach of duty' cases also had causation difficulties). Causation is particularly problematic in MM cases because, by definition, they involve situations where the victims are already ill or injured and so are at greater risk of death than 'normal' people. Even when someone has a non-life-threatening condition, the administration of an anaesthetic or drug to which they have an undisclosed allergy or their exposure to hospital 'superbugs' can lead to unexpected death without any negligence at all, let alone gross negligence. Vulnerable patients, particularly the elderly and the terminally ill, are (by definition) more vulnerable. Not only are they more susceptible to 'things that go wrong' (such as exposure to superbugs), but they usually present to hospital with a series of existing ailments. In one case the pathologist concluded 'establishing causation in the case of an eighty-five year old woman with a history of heart disease is near impossible even if gross negligence was present'. This was despite the fact that the woman had died following extreme failures in the level of nursing care. We identified different types of case where causation was difficult to prove.

(i) Only four of these cases could be said to involve no evidence of a substantial fault or error. For example, a baby born at 25 weeks died due to natural causes. A doctor treating the baby had made a minor error which was found to be unrelated to the cause of death yet the police still pursued a lengthy investigation after the family had raised concerns. In a similar case a baby died of meningitis that was quite advanced when he arrived in hospital.

(ii)   In some cases there was clear error. For example, a surgeon proceeded with a non-essential operation despite knowing that the patient was at serious pre-operative risk and then failed to adequately treat her when she suffered a cardiac arrest during the surgery; a nurse failed to treat an elderly woman who had suffered a non-life-threatening injury to her left foot and who progressively deteriorated due to the lack of care, despite the nurse being warned of the deterioration. Existing medical conditions meant that proving causation would have been very difficult.

Failure to reach the 'gross' threshold

Thirteen cases (17 per cent) fell into this category.

(i)   In about three-quarters of the cases there was clear evidence of gross negligence on our interpretation. In all of these cases, the CPS took into account circumstances that could be characterized as 'mitigating', which were said to have affected the healthcare professional's behaviour, e.g. pressure, stress, end of long shift. For example, in one case a doctor accidentally inserted a chest drain into the patient's heart causing a catastrophic and fatal haemorrhage, and in another a nurse mixed up two bags and accidentally and fatally administered a pain relief infusion intended for epidural use into a patient's arm. Both healthcare professionals were said to have worked very long shifts without adequate breaks due to understaffing and had previously displayed exemplary character and work. Another example included a nurse who incorrectly placed a naso-gastric tube into a patient's lung, yet this failure was found to be a result of poor practice that had developed on the ward and was condoned by clinicians and more senior management. This was an example of a management-produced incompetence, while in other cases incompetence was attributed to poor training: for example, a doctor whose failings demonstrated a 'clear need for assessment and further training within the field of paediatrics'.

(ii)   One-quarter of the cases included evidence of subjective recklessness, but there were 'circumstances' (that could be characterized as 'mitigating') or other reasons why they were judged not to meet the gross negligence threshold. For example, a surgeon perforated a major organ during an operation to take a biopsy and the patient subsequently died. Nurses attending the operation stated that they expressed worries to the surgeon about the procedure. Subsequent investigations showed that the particularly difficult nature of the operation meant that the perforation that caused death was understandable. The surgeon knowingly took a risk that may or may not have been justified, but it was not a grossly negligent decision 'in the circumstances'. Other cases involved failures in care by a number of persons yet none of which individually reached the threshold for gross negligence. To quote a common theme within many of these files, despite a case being caused by minor and reckless failures by a number of individuals, these failures could not be summed in order to reach the threshold required.

How the CPS interprets the gross negligence manslaughter tests

It is hard to escape the conclusion that in many of the cases that were not prosecuted the public interest test was applied under the guise of the evidential test; and/or that in cases such as these the two tests merge. The tests could merge because juries would be expected to have the same feelings of sympathy towards the healthcare professionals in question that the prosecutors expressed (e.g. 'tragic mistake by a dedicated professional'). Acquittals would therefore have been likely in many of these cases even if all the elements of *Adomako* were satisfied.[6] For example, a police doctor was recently prosecuted for MM after a man held in custody died. The man was a heavy drinker, was schizophrenic and epileptic, and banged his head and became unconscious during his arrest; the doctor examined him for less than a minute in his cell, did not try to rouse him and did not take a medical history. Despite such obvious failures in care, the jury found him not guilty. This is arguably related to the reluctance of juries to convict (Dyer, 2012). But prosecutors are supposed to ask what a 'reasonable jury' would be likely to decide, not what a jury that was unreasonably swayed by sympathy and potential deference to the medical profession would decide. So there has to be something more going on.

That something more appears to be subjective recklessness and moral culpability. This is surprising since the gross negligence test is an explicitly *objective* test. But, in assessing the grossness of the breach, prosecutors highlighted subjective recklessness in all the (admittedly few) prosecuted cases. And the language used in some of the files denoted that the healthcare professional involved displayed an element of additional 'bad' character. Take these examples.

---

6   'Jury equity' is a recognized feature of jury decision-making, i.e. some acquittals are made in the face of evidence of guilt because of sympathy for the defendants and/ or dislike of the criminal law under which they were prosecuted. For discussion, see Sanders et al. (2010, ch. 10).

- A prosecutor described how one doctor displayed great arrogance and little remorse: 'we knew he wasn't going to go down well with the jury, he was cold and so unapologetic about the incident'.
- 'You know the young doctor who had been clearly exhausted but trying his best ... juries are going to have sympathy, we even have sympathy for them.'
- 'There is an element of second guessing what a reasonable jury would do, would they say what this individual did amounts to homicide and evidence shows that juries are reluctant to say that this is a homicide. It would be true to say a prosecution is far more likely to be successful when there is a degree of recklessness on the part of the individual, we know this.'

Many prosecutors told us that 'badness' is often crucial in securing a guilty verdict. To quote one lawyer, 'you need something more than a serious error of judgement; you need something "dirty" something the jury can latch on to'. Another prosecutor put it more explicitly: 'yes I suppose the one off pure mistake is probably going to be dropped, those kinds of cases where there is little culpability, it is in no-one's interests to prosecute those'. Another explained: 'Some judges don't understand gross negligence and have a negative reaction to it and sometimes that influences the jury, the judge just doesn't want the doctor in their court. We know this.' Or, as a prosecutor put it to Quick (2010): 'In reality I can't see how we would bring a prosecution without an element of subjective recklessness.' This is borne out in many reported cases: for example, the two doctors who, over a period of two days, ignored warnings and failed to act on evidence that their patient was critically ill and so were subjectively reckless (*R v Misra* (2005) 1 Cr App R 21).

Further, we have seen that in 17 per cent of the non-prosecuted cases all the *Adomako* tests, including gross negligence, appeared to be satisfied. But either there was little evidence of subjective recklessness, or – if there was evidence – there were significant mitigating factors. In many of the cases, incompetence rather than deliberate wrongdoing was identified. Examples include a GP who, over a period of two months, failed to diagnose an infection in a young child. Despite the child's dramatically worsening symptoms, the GP failed to chase urine tests or make an urgent referral. The prosecutor concluded that this was a 'tragic mistake by a dedicated professional'. She commented to us that 'you could see that this was not a bad doctor and it is so hard to judge illness in children sometimes, I did feel so sorry for her, sometimes the punishment of knowing what you've done is enough.' Two nurses had caused the death of a diabetic patient due to incorrect treatment for hyperglycaemia. The errors were put down to a lack of experience and failure to check the original prescription rather than a 'wicked and abysmal act'. Another prosecutor commented to us:

> in the bad cases you have a mistake that has been done by someone trying to do the job the best they can, often in

difficult circumstances. We're all human and make mistakes and some of the things we see are not the usual clear homicide committed by the bad person, it's the good person who has accidentally done something bad.

Cases outside the time-frame of our sample show similar patterns. A classic example is the case of two patients who died as a result of being given a cancer drug that was 500 per cent too concentrated. This happened because: (a) the prescribing doctor did not specify the brand of the drug, a crucial error since different brands came in different concentrations; and (b) the nurses administering the drug did not heed the warning on the drug containers to check that the dosage was appropriate. On the face of it, this was gross negligence on all their parts because the drug was known to be highly toxic in large quantities and so they would or should have known that there was a risk of death if a mistake of this kind was made. The police investigated and consulted the CPS over an MM prosecution, but the CPS declined to prosecute, despite this clearly being no momentary slip (*Birmingham Post Late*, 13 July 2010).

Other cases in our sample involved momentary errors on the part of otherwise competent practitioners. For example, a doctor had accidently given a fatal overdose of a drug to a patient but the CPS review note in the file concluded that the doctor had clearly 'made a mistake which he has now recognized but the breach of duty was a serious error of judgement rather than a gross and therefore criminal act'. The note makes reference to this being 'a tragic mistake by a dedicated professional', how remorseful he was, how his motivation had clearly been to act in the best interests of his patient, and how the family were very sympathetic towards the doctor and were aware that he had done his best to care for their relative. The prosecutor in this case noted that 'we couldn't take this to court, it was a tragic case but the doctor had clearly suffered enough, it was just an awful mistake'. In another case a doctor had wrongly prescribed a drug which led to the death of her patient. The review note concluded that 'this appears to be a tragic error of misjudgement by the professional involved', not a criminal breach of duty. Her previous good conduct, and the fact that she had previously on that day issued the right dosages of the same drug, went in her favour. The nurse in the naso-gastric tube case (above) was described as a hard-working and dedicated professional who had never displayed any previous bad character, and the paediatric doctor (above) ('a dedicated professional') had made a 'tragic mistake'.[7] The

---

7   As noted, some cases of non-reckless momentary error are sometimes successfully prosecuted (e.g. *Becker* (2000)). So we know that 'badness' and subjective recklessness are not necessary ingredients. The point being made here is that there were no such cases in our sample. Thus, unless some cases were missed, there were none over a five-year period, which indicates a change in practice in recent years.

prosecutor stated in interview that 'it was clear she was acting with the best of intentions, it was a terrible mistake but that wasn't enough to prosecute'.

Sometimes prosecutors would recognize the family's sympathy towards the doctor. Particularly in cases where the patient has been terminally ill and a doctor has had a good relationship with the family, prosecutors regarded the views of the family as important: 'the family had no desire to see him in prison, quite the opposite, they realize that something went wrong but they were more grateful for the things he did right for their relative'.

This all sounds like excellent material for speeches in mitigation or to justify decisions to not prosecute on 'public interest' grounds (the views of victims and their families are explicitly recognized in relation to the public interest, but not as evidential factors). But what has it to do with the law of GNM? To answer this we need to return to *Adomako*.

'Badness' – a fifth element?

Dr Sullman and Dr Prentice were junior doctors who had their case heard in the House of Lords at the same time as *Adomako*. They made the error of injecting vincristine into the spine of their patient, having been put in the position of administering such treatment untrained and unsupervised. The error was fatal, and the 16-year-old patient died some days later in agony. The judge at their trial expressly told them that they were not 'bad men' but they were nonetheless convicted (*R v Prentice; R v Sullman* (1994) QB 302). However, their convictions were quashed by the Court of Appeal. Now it has been suggested in *Rowley v DPP* (2003) EWHC Admin 693 that:

> It is clear from what Lord Mackay said [in *Adomako*] that there is a fifth ingredient: criminality ... or 'badness'. Using the word 'badness', the jury must be sure that the defendant's conduct was so bad in all the circumstances to amount 'to a criminal act or omission'.

This is the source of the CPS determination to prosecute only the morally culpable professional. However, Mackay did not conclude in *Adomako* that the *defendant* must be 'bad' – i.e. subjectively culpable – in order to satisfy this test. While a defendant's recklessness may be one of the 'circumstances' that forms part of the evidence that negligence was gross, subjective recklessness is not a requirement. Thus, as far as 'the law' is concerned (in the strict black-letter sense), it is hard to see how this really is an additional test. Indeed, neither the Law Commission (1996, para. 2.10) nor most of the standard textbooks that we scrutinized for this purpose mention *Rowley* which is, after all, a rather obscure challenge to a decision not to prosecute for MM. And in no other substantial discussions of GNM have we seen mention of a 'fifth test'.[8]

Only one case could be found – in the ten years since *Rowley* was decided – that mentioned it. Referring to *Rowley*, it was stated in *Misra*, the leading MM case since *Adomako*, that 'the defendant's state of mind ... will often be a critical factor in the decision'. But the judgment made clear that subjective recklessness is not required. The judgment went on:

> The jury concluded that the conduct of each appellant in the course of performing his professional obligations to his patient was 'truly exceptionally bad', and showed a high degree of indifference to an obvious and serious risk to the patient's life. Accordingly, along with the other ingredients of the offence, gross negligence too, was proved.

There are three points to note here: first, it is the conduct, not the defendant or his/her mental state, that must be 'truly exceptionally bad'; second, this badness seems to be relevant to the Court of Appeal in respect of proof of gross negligence and 'the other ingredients of the offence' not as a fifth test; third, no fifth test was mentioned in the judgment. And to take a more recent case at random, in *R v Evans* (2009) 2 Cr App R 10 only the four *Adomako* tests were put to the jury, and this approach was endorsed by the Court of Appeal; no fifth test was mentioned (also see *R v Connolly* (2007) 2 Cr App R (S) 82, where *Misra* and the *Adomako* tests were discussed and applied but no fifth test was mentioned).

Why rely on *Rowley*?

Prosecutors in the Special Crime and Counter Terrorism Division strongly suggested to us that badness in a general sense – that we found difficult to understand as other than subjective recklessness – is needed. We questioned them about this self-imposed need to find moral culpability as a prerequisite for prosecuting. They said that they were required to do this because it is the fifth test in *Rowley* – not a case of which we had previously heard and, as explained above, not a case that any legal commentators regard as important, nor one that establishes a fifth test. The prosecutors knew about *Rowley* because it was in the DPP's *Legal Guidance* to crown prosecutors on homicide (CPS, 2014). Prosecutors also rely heavily on the obligation to consider 'all the circumstances' highlighted in the judgments

---

8   We could find only two mainstream writers – Quick and Herring – referring to *Rowley*. Quick (2007) draws attention to the endorsement in that case and in *Misra* of the use of evidence of subjective recklessness by Lord Mackay in *Adomako*. But he does not identify any 'fifth test'. Herring (2010) comments that the court 'approved of the use of 'badness', the 'badness' of the defendant's actions' (p. 278). There are a few other scattered comments.

in *Rowley* and in *Misra*. But this is a meaningless obligation. Presumably prosecutors, judges and juries are not being asked to consider irrelevant circumstances. But, logically, no one should need to be told to consider all *relevant* circumstances, for to fail to do so would by definition be failing to make a full consideration. The result of the fifth test and of being asked to do something that need not be stated is that prosecutors strain to find something over and above objective gross negligence. What, in another context, might seem to be evidence of recklessness can be regarded as 'bad' and a relevant 'circumstance', justifying the view that there is sufficient evidence of gross negligence for prosecution; while what, in another context, might seem to be a mitigating factor comes to be seen as a 'circumstance' that makes the action less 'bad' and thus justifying the view that there is insufficient evidence of gross negligence to justify prosecution.

But to say, as prosecutors do, that they have to follow *Rowley* is not true. *Rowley* is only in the DPP's *Legal Guidance* because the DPP decided it should be. Neither legal logic nor precedent requires this. Following *Rowley* is a deliberate choice that enables the CPS to follow its instinct, rather than the black letter of the law as it is understood by the overwhelming number of commentators and reported court judgments.

Underlying this instinct is the presumption of the good character of doctors which lies at the heart of traditional deferential attitudes towards the medical profession. Such attitudes seem to live on not only in judges and juries who are often reluctant to convict, but also prosecutors. This reluctance to see a doctor in court unless there is a profound element of 'badness' that clearly distinguishes them from the rest of the 'dedicated' profession, and justifying this through the use of a fifth test that does not need to be used, shows that doctors are benefiting from a layer of protection that other professionals or individuals do not seem to have. This argument is not contradicted by the more recent cases, outside our sample, discussed above. These cases displayed negligence that is truly 'gross' by any standards. And in *Garg* (also discussed earlier) the doctor tried to falsify the records that proved his errors – as good an example of badness as the CPS could wish for. It is hard to believe that the doctors concerned were not reckless ('bad' in the sense of displaying indifference to suffering that is hard to believe of doctors), but proving that would have been another matter.

Oliver Quick argued that 'prosecutors work within climate of increased suspicion of professionals which is likely to impact on the "frames" they adopt in exercising their discretion' (2006, p. 429). We would agree with Quick, but, from our research, any public distrust and increase in complaints does not seem to have overcome the protection that doctors have traditionally benefitted from in the criminal sphere as regards prosecutions (although it is likely that they have come under greater pressure from inquests and police investigations). Instead, ingrained within prosecutors' 'frames' are traditional forms of deference disguised through the adoption of a legal test that is not required.

Conclusion

The vagueness of the gross negligence and badness tests (such as they are) leads to substantial reliance on the judgement and opinion – or as some prosecutors told Quick (2006), 'gut instinct' – of the prosecutor and the specialists (usually doctors) instructed to be expert witnesses (Quick, 2011). Thus, prosecutors who wish to prosecute only where they find subjective recklessness are able to do follow their preference. The result is discretion based on public interest considerations (particularly blameworthiness) but hidden under the guise of a determination that the negligence was insufficiently gross.

This gives some support to Quick's view that GNM is 'unclear, unprincipled, and often unfair' (2010, p. 186). However, it does not support his recommendation that it should be abolished and that we should rely instead on (subjective) reckless manslaughter. For we have seen that many cases involving subjective recklessness are not prosecuted anyway. The subjectivist mind of the legal academic would be put at ease by implementing his proposal, but the reality of the law would remain unclear, unprincipled, and often unfair. For although Quick rightly criticizes 'the powerful prejudicial force of adverse assessments of character' under the law as it currently operates (2010, p. 194), this would remain true if the law were changed in the way he advocates – for a determination of whether someone was subjectively reckless is informed by precisely those considerations. This is apparent from our discussion of many of the cases in our sample.[9] Nor would Quick's proposal lead to many fewer prosecutions. Instead of a lowering of the prosecution threshold over the last 20 years, and too many prosecutions, our research shows that there are fewer prosecutions than one would expect from the conventional understanding of GNM.

If our goal is more certainty, the best solution would be to retain the gross negligence test, and no longer rely on the fifth element in *Rowley*. Although gross negligence would still embody elements of circularity and uncertainty, it would do so less than now. Whether the consequent increase in prosecutions for MM would be desirable from a policy point of

---

9   For a different type of example, and an extended discussion of the problems involved in 'proving' subjective recklessness – showing, in particular that it does not eliminate unprincipled, unpredictable and unfair decisions – see Sanders (2015).

view is another matter. Also as Sharon Cowan (this volume) argues, while they can sometimes permit certain kinds of agency, legal techniques can leave intact underlying problematic foundations. While an increase in prosecutions may increase the agency of victims and victims' families, it is questionable how far they will decrease future medical errors and improve healthcare systems. As far as this chapter is concerned, the important point is that prosecutors are being disingenuous when they claim 'simply' to follow the law. But nor does this research support the extreme realist view that the law in action is entirely removed from the law in the books. In this case study, the prosecutors decide what law in the books they wish to adhere to and construct it accordingly. They follow the laws that they choose to follow.

The broader message is that we – that is, those of us committed to a critical and/or socio-legal project – ignore legal technicalities at our peril. This should not be surprising. Riles, for example, discusses the work of the legal realist Walter Cook. Cook's analysis of the technical doctrinal aspects of conflicts of laws made 'explicit the tacit knowledge practices of lawyers and judges' (2005, p. 1030). Riles therefore argues that no legal writers should ignore legal technicalities because 'any approach to the law that ignores what is the very core of legal thought cannot escape its own marginalisation' (2005, p. 975). This is evident if we consider the work of the CPS in deciding MM cases. To simply dismiss them as deferring to doctors by prosecuting too rarely, or condemn their punitiveness for supposedly prosecuting too frequently, is naive. The CPS does operate within some kind of legal boundaries. The exact placing of those boundaries is currently a matter for the CPS itself, but that task could be appropriated by Parliament, the courts or policy-makers. But in each case the attempt would be unsuccessful without taking on the CPS in the terms by which it is legitimated and by which it legitimates itself: criminal law doctrine.

This type of confrontation is rarely made. The failure to 'take law seriously' perhaps explains, as Riles suggests, why critical legal studies and socio-legalism remain so marginal in the UK, as in the USA. Despite protests to the contrary, the socio-legal project has hardly penetrated most 'social' legal subjects (such as environmental, labour and welfare law) let alone 'core' legal education and scholarship (Sanders, 2015). But to get sucked back into doctrinalism alone would be a mistake. As Valverde (2009) puts it, 'analyses need to be simultaneously inside and outside law, simultaneously technical and theoretical, legal and socio-legal' (2009, p. 153).

Cases

Bolam v Friern Hospital Management Committee (1957) 1 WLR 582
Bolitho v City and Hackney Health Authority (1997) 4 All ER 771
CA & R v Becker (2000) WL 877688
DPP ex parte Jones (2000) IRLR 373
R v Adomako (1995) 1 AC 171
R v Bateman (1925) Cr App R 8
R v Cato (1976) 1 All ER 260
R v Connolly (2007) 2 Cr App R (S) 82
R v Evans (2009) 2 Cr App R 10.
R v Garg [2012] EWCA 2520
R v Kite and OLL Ltd (1996) 2 Cr App R (S) 295
R v L (2010) EWCA Crim 1249
R v Misra and Srivistava [2004] EWCA 2375; (2005) 1 Cr App R 21
R v Prentice; R v Sullman (1994) QB 302
R v Wacker (2003) QB 1203
Rowley v DPP (2003) EWHC Admin 693

References

Ashworth, A and J Horder (2013) *Principles of Criminal Law* (Oxford: Oxford University Press)
Birmingham Post Late, 13 July 2010
Brazier, M and N Allen (2007) 'Criminalising Medical Malpractice' in C Erin and S Ost (eds), *The Criminal Justice System and Health Care* (Oxford: Oxford University Press), p. 21
Crown Prosecution Service (2014) *Homicide: Murder and Manslaughter* www.cps.gov.uk/legal/h_to_k/homicide_murder_and_manslaughter
Devlin, M (2010) 'Medical Manslaughter' 26 *Medical Defence Union Journal* 7–8
Dixon-Woods, M, K Yeung and C Bosk (2011) 'Why Is UK Medicine No Longer a Self-regulating Profession? The Role of Scandals Involving "Bad Apple" Doctors' 73(10) *Social Science and Medicine* 1452–9
Dyer, C (2012) 'Police Doctor Is Cleared of Manslaughter But Criticised as "Negligent"' 344 *British Medical Journal* 739
Ferner, R and S McDowell (2006) 'Doctors Charged with Manslaughter' 99(6) *Journal of the Royal Society of Medicine* 309
Griffiths, D and A Sanders (2013) 'The Road to the Dock: Prosecution Decision-making in Medical Manslaughter Cases' in D Griffiths and A Sanders (eds), *Bioethics, Medicine and the Criminal Law Volume 2: Medicine, Crime and Society* (Cambridge: Cambridge University Press), p. 117
Herring, J (2010) *Criminal Law Cases and Materials* (Oxford: Oxford University Press) (5th edn)
Kazarian, M, D Griffiths and M Brazier (2011) 'Criminal Responsibility for Medical Malpractice in France' 27(4) *Journal of Professional Negligence* 188–99.

Law Commission (1996) *Legislating the Criminal Code: Involuntary Manslaughter* (London: The Stationery Office) http://lawcommission.justice.gov.uk/docs/lc237_Legislating_the_Criminal_Code_Involuntary_Manslaughter.pdf

McBarnet, D (1981) *Conviction* (London: Macmillan)

Mid Staffordshire NHS Foundation Trust (2013) *Report of the Mid Staffordshire NHS Foundation Trust Public Inquiry* (London: The Stationery Office) www.midstaffspublicinquiry.com/report

Miola, J (2011) 'The Impact of the Loss of Deference towards the Medical Profession' in A Alghrani, B Bennett and S Ost (eds), *The Criminal Law and Bioethical Conflict: Walking the Tightrope* (Cambridge: Cambridge University Press)

O'Doherty, S (2006) 'Doctors and Manslaughter – Response from the Crown Prosecution Service' 99(11) *Journal of the Royal Society of Medicine* 544

Quick, O (2006) 'Prosecuting "Gross" Medical Negligence' 33 *Journal of Law and Society* 429–40

Quick, O (2007) 'Medical Manslaughter: The Rise (and Replacement) of a Contested Crime?' in C Erin and S Ost (eds), *The Criminal Justice System and Health Care* (Oxford: Oxford University Press)

Quick, O (2010) 'Medicine, Mistakes and Manslaughter: A Criminal Combination?' 69(1) *Cambridge Law Journal* 186–203

Quick, O (2011) 'Expert Evidence and Medical Manslaughter: Vagueness in Action' 38(4) *Journal of Law and Society* 496–518

Riles, A (2005) 'A New Agenda for the Cultural Study of Law: Taking on the Technicalities' 53 *Buffalo Law Review* 973–1033

Sanders, A (2015) 'Poor Thinking, Poor Outcome?: The Future of the Law Degree after the Legal Education and Training Review and the Case for Socio-Legalism' in H Sommerlad et al. (eds), *The Futures of Legal Education and the Legal Profession* (Oxford: Hart Publishing)

Sanders, A, R Young and M Burton (2010) *Criminal Justice* (Oxford: Oxford University Press)

Smith, J and B Hogan (successive edns) *Criminal Law* (Oxford: Oxford University Press)

Valverde, M (2009) 'Jurisdiction and Scale: Legal "Technicalities" as Resources for Theory' 18(2) *Social and Legal Studies* 139–57

Wheeler, R (2002) 'Medical Manslaughter: Why This Shift from Tort to Crime?' 152 *New Law Journal* 593–4.

Williams, G (1983) *Textbook of Criminal Law* (London: Stevens)

Wilson, W (2008) 'Dealing with Drug-induced Homicide' in C Clarkson and S Cunningham (eds), *Criminal Liability for Non-Aggressive Death* (Aldershot: Ashgate)

12
Conclusions: A Socio-Legal Metatheory
Andreas Philippopoulos-Mihalopoulos

The tension of this book

There is a tension in this book. Just as with any tension, this is both problematic and creative. Just as with any tension, it makes things much more exciting. The tension is this: on the one hand, the book attempts to engage with the 'technical aesthetics of law' towards which Annelise Riles (2005, p. 976) has convincingly urged legal academics. On the other hand, the book resists doing this fully, avoiding thus the risk of locking itself up in the ivory tower of law's lingo. This would be an all too familiar space, unfrequented by non-legal scholars due to its prohibitive technicality and its self-enforced closure. The tension is palpable, not least because this book is, as our editors write in their introduction, the groundwork for nothing less than a *socio-legal metatheory*.

The book goes straight to the core of what socio-legal research is and, in so doing, addresses the following issues: how to observe the technicalities of the law while remaining untechnical, horizontal, open? How to play with the law without indulging the play of the law? How to take the law seriously without being subsumed by it? All the chapters in the book perilously balance between these two aspects and most of them manage a convincing tightrope excursus. But perhaps the most adventurous funambulists are the editors of the volume. Their metatheoretical ambition is how they would like the tension to be bridged: a metatheory firmly rooted in this most forgotten and least sexy epithet of our interdisciplinary, radical, critical, emplaced, embodied, impactful research: the *legal*. The challenging irony of this must be savoured in its fullest. A personal anecdote: when I accepted the invitation to give the concluding plenary for the very successful conference that operated as a springboard for this volume, I did so, believing that the object of exploration was not the legal but *law's place*. False pretences (but of benign intent), administrative noise, late-stage additions and subtractions, tongue slips, email ghost: whatever the cause of this might have been, it is a clear indication (to me at least) that when these socio-legal scholars began organizing the conference, they still considered the legal a rather unattractive object unable in itself to warrant an interesting conference. Something needed to be added to make it a bit more relatable, to soften the blow of the ruler as it were. I also know I would not have accepted had I known that the object was, quite simply, the *legal*. Why would I be interested in this cantankerous old beast that brought to (my) mind wigs and dust and uncomfortable seating, irrelevance and bad infinite historicity, slow tempi and even slower interdisciplinary connections? Little did I know that attending the conference and reading this book would change my understanding of the legal – but I wonder whether this happened in the intended way.

Let me return to the quest for metatheory, which is the challenge I set myself, in full awareness of the paradox (a *grounded* metatheory!). Following the editorial decree and relying on the chapters of the book, in this concluding/summing-up/critically appraising/furthering/solidifying chapter, I attempt to bring together the cornerstones of what I would consider a metatheory for socio-legal research. Since my objective is to focus on this book, I avoid injecting other references except for the absolutely necessary, using the preceding chapters as my reference corpus. I am mainly interested in building on their impressive richness, and draw some generalizing but not abstracting conclusions on the potential of a socio-legal metatheory. The questions underlining this short text, therefore, are: what is the main challenge and responsibility of a socio-legal metatheory and of a socio-legal researcher in particular? What are the emerging tensions of socio-legal research in relation to interdisciplinarity, critical legal theory and doctrinal law? What are the underlying unifying conditions behind a socio-legal metatheory? And, finally, what are the emerging socio-legal positions as witnessed in the chapters of this volume?

For the editors, the current absence of a socio-legal metatheory can be attributed to the way socio-legal research theory and method have developed. This is probably a strategic and possibly polemical omission: socio-legal research prides itself on its groundedness, social contextualization and transformative potential. This, combined with a widespread scepticism towards theory, makes it hard or even undesirable for socio-legal research to think of a metatheory, namely *to observe itself as theory*. For this reason, any socio-legal metatheory, namely a theory that reflects on the way socio-legal method understands the world and itself, must perforce be 'accessible and appealing to (mainstream) scholars of legal technicalities' as the editors admonish. In other words, the nascent socio-legal metatheory should be *rooted in the law and its technicalities* in order to guarantee accessibility; and at the same time, *exceeding the law and its observation*, in order to observe itself observing the world. This is indeed the difference between a theory and a metatheory: the former answers to the question *what*; the latter answers to the question *how*, namely how is it that we socio-legal researchers observe what we observe? Metatheoretical observation necessitates both a distance from the subject matter and an immersion in it.

This is what I would call an *immanent placing* of the metatheory. This formation is not my figment. Rather, it is dictated by the one most overwhelmingly pivotal preoccupation of the book: how to deal with immanence (in this case, legal technical immanence) while not being locked up in it. Indeed, immanence puts in an appearance in every single chapter of this book. To define it briefly and crudely, immanence is absolute interiority, where the outside does not play a role in the way things are determined inside. Immanence can be distinguished from transcendence because immanence does not rely on an external source of validity, justification, origin or destination. Immanence is the preferred locus of current discourses that deal with materiality, networks and assemblages, things and objects, post-human agencies and new ontologies.

But these are already vertiginous terminological leaps for the more traditional legal academic. We risk losing sight of the groundedness of it all, despite the fact (and this is the paradox) that all the above refer to nothing other than legal documents, statutes, court decisions, objects, bodies and other matter that become part of any legal case, as Emilie Cloatre's chapter discusses. So, although all chapters are characterized by an intense immanent predisposition, this immanence never assumes its name. There is not a single mention of it. This is true immanence: we do what we do. We engage with the thing in hand without the need to define it. At the same time, this is a clever immanence: it manages to dissimulate itself as business-as-usual. It is folded inside, discounting external explanations, yet without imparting the narrow or asphyxiating affect of a world without outside, or a Leibnizian monad with no windows. The present immanence affords glimpses of a transcendence (beyond law, beyond matter, beyond society) without, however, dwelling on them. Rather, the immanence that emerges in this volume is both *infinite* and *all-inclusive*. The infinity is best revealed when some chapters delve into the technicalities of the law. To take an example: Helen Carr's exquisite disquisition on the intimacy of documents opens up a vast immanence of schizophrenic opposition: unfolding official documents that, origami-like, reveal bodily surfaces, leakages, extended technologies of the body, and personal suffering. Their immanence is *infinite* because it is based on always superimposing documents, one written on top of the other, yet all retaining their individual nuances when thrown into different contexts. Helen Carr's documents are not palimpsestic. Their geology is constantly splayed open, their layers fully fleshed out in their fragility. Their immanence is *all-inclusive* because it contains the public and the private, the differentially temporal, the law that remains inscribed within the law (and its technicalities) *and* the law that eschews that and tries to form itself out of the rarefied air of human dignity, only pathetically able to be circumscribed within the law.

The socio-legal metatheory is at the stage of looking at itself in the mirror and trying to understand how it does what it does, namely what its own technicalities are. I hope it will be read affirmatively when I write that this book wishes for nothing less than having its cake and eating it. On the one hand, the book works at a distance from its object of observation, thus looking at what the socio-legal gaze looks at and how. On the other, it defeats this distance by claiming groundedness: it whispers in the ears of the legal system, it understands and at points sympathizes (however critically) with its bedfellow, this rather compulsive obsessive nerd who calculates legal technicalities; it even plays along the old game of offering ways in which the law can change/the law can change society. The perseverance of offering suggestions for improvement in the concluding remarks, or even earlier in some chapters, is a luminous albeit perhaps a little unexamined (hence the need for metatheory) indication that the promise of law's transformative effect is still taken seriously. In sum, this book replicates the old understanding of a theory that informs practice by offering a distance that bridges. This is the grand irony of our research. Behind this, however, there lies one of the most enticing illusions of the legal system: that academic research still has the ear of the law.

Why is this an illusion? Not because it does not happen (we have solid, 'impactful' research cases that demonstrate how the law has listened) but because it does not happen in the smooth, directly causal way that the bridging between law and legal academic research promises. It is not only this book or the editorially suggested metatheory that are enclosed in their own infinite and all-inclusive immanence. The law is too. The law is the great dweller of this immanent bubble which we all try to pierce a little in order to have access to it. And how do we do this? By evoking *legality* instead of the law, as the editors suggest; or by spreading the law to include social customs even on a global scale which, however, remains community or locality-based as Jiri Přibáň following Ehrlich suggests in his work on *living law*; or by resisting the law bottom-up as Sharon Cowan urges us, thus bravely leaving behind, in a dustcloud of realization of immanence, the famous Butlerian 'double-gesture' of using and undermining the law at the same time. As Sharon Cowan amply reveals, the law is reformed, but this causality is never straightforward. Everything needs to pass through law's immanence which by definition is this: that the law is a fissure, a crack that allows ideological draughts to circulate and move the law this way and that (however glowingly right-on and just it might have been imagined in its emergence). Nothing predetermined, no facile causalities here. Nor, however, a level playing field where everything becomes determined anew at every situation. The law has constructed its immanence sentence by sentence, body by body, movement by movement, slowly but surely revolving around itself like a self-absorbed DNA-helix, never deviating except through and by its own allocation of deviation. Caroline Hunter puts it excellently: 'what we see here is a legal aesthetic generating a particular legal form, which becomes a hardened technology, to be used in a variety of circumstances with no thought for its content' (p. 146). So we may carry on calling this legality or living law or legal technicalities, as long as we are aware that these are tiny piercings on the great immanence of the law.

Where is the legal?

Since I am still evidently espoused to the idea of the *place* of the legal, I can only apologize for this section's title and ask for your indulgence. Indeed, I intend to begin by positing that 'the place of the legal' is the same as 'the legal'. I therefore propose to answer this question in the only way possible: spatially. Seeking for the place of the legal is an exploration of boundaries, as David Cowan reminds us in his contribution to this volume while tightrope-walking between a territory that is both spatial and discursive, both open and closed. Boundaries, however, are nothing but a way of circumscribing identity. Boundaries are the substance of the self and its differentiation from other (even an immanent other). This means that '*where* is the law' is not dissimilar to '*what* is the law'.

While I am not sufficiently delusional to believe that I could give an answer to the question of what the law is here, I draw from Chris Tomlins' chapter in this volume to revive the by now standard sociological and, from a certain perspective, positivist question of law's autonomy, and connect it to a question that characterizes this book: what makes the law law? (Read: where are law's boundaries? Does immanence have an external boundary? Are these boundaries porous? And so on.) More tightrope balancing here. Chris Tomlins has a philosophically complex answer to this: it is not just the historical conditions that determine what makes the law law, but rather the resilience of another juxtaposition that emanates from the heart of the law: 'This essay does not dissent from the base proposition that explanation of the legal is materially enhanced by summoning perspectives that do not themselves originate within the legal. Nevertheless, it targets the assumption ... that "the social" is the essential explanatory other of "the legal"' (p. 35). In a remarkably contained way, Tomlins establishes the contextual immanence of the law – only to shake it up at the next turn of phrase where he draws out the *soterial*:

> If social connotes the profane, the world of the creature, the
> world of fallen humanity, where law reigns and justice is an
> afterthought, soterial connotes the sacral, beyond law, where
> justice is eternal ... The soterial stands at about as stark a polar
> opposite to the social as it is possible to imagine. (pp. 36–37)

The soterial is a messianic salvation, except that, in the way employed and
elaborated here, it becomes a pole within the immanence of the legal. Here
is our tension again: doing archaeology between the legal and the soterial, while the social becomes an ancillary parameter of the legal. And here
is the immanence: although juxtaposed to the legal, the soterial is to be
found within the law. This is not a transcendental salvation. For Tomlins,
the waiting is over. The messiah has come and gone, and what is left is
a vast immanence that manages to accommodate both the legal and the
soterial. The metaphysics Tomlins is looking for are not transcendental but
deeply immanent. They are steeped in history and time, with an eschatology embodied in black and white spirits. This law is divine but is breathed
in the bodies who in their turn make the law. The law is what the law
makes it to be, via its bodies of emergence.

What is the soterial for the purposes of this tension? It is, quite simply,
justice. Justice is the immanent other of the law, only understood from
within the legal technicalities. Yet, at the same time, it is only the *fissures*,
gaps, or ruptures of such technicalities that in their turn reveal the possibility of the horizon of justice. These are the ruptures through which Tomlins
peers in order to discover 'other orderings, other *taxes*, of the phenomena
with which as scholars we concern ourselves' (p. 54). The otherness of the
legal is justice – still legal justice, still deeply immanent, *but also the polar
opposite of the technicalities*. Inside, looking in, Tomlins understands immanence as fractured, folded and twisted because he finds himself 'peering
through this particular fracture in the continuum of normalcy' (p. 54). This
peering through yields a glimpse of a different justice but justice nevertheless. A different history but history nevertheless. We are buoyant, gaz-
ing from the heights of our metatheory to what makes the law law. The
answers are always surprising.

Jiří Přibáň's take is closer to a sociological understanding of the law but
the answers are no less surprising. Přibáň's funambulism takes him on a
re-examination of legal pluralism that sits uncomfortably in the suprasys-
tem of global constitutionalism's normative claims. Inspiringly drawing
from Eugen Ehrlich's research on living law, where the law has expanded to
include social customs and other social norms, Přibáň comments on phenomena of spontaneous juridification and functional differentiation, both
of which are relevant in the assembling of a socio-legal metatheory. The
first one refers to what I would name legal assemblages, more on which

below. The latter, however, drawn directly from the autopoietic theory of social systems, is a useful addition to the question of where the legal is. Niklas Luhmann has dealt with functional differentiation, drawing on Weber before him but also enriching it with a strong emphasis on autopoietic closure. To put it simply, each social system (such as law, politics, economy and so on) is determined by its function in terms of society, in its turn acknowledged by the social expectations of the specific system. Thus, the social expectations of the law are that the law will carry on considering lawful (or unlawful) what has been considered lawful (or unlawful) previously, unless of course the conditions change. If I steal a loaf of bread today, I know that my act is unlawful. If I carry on walking on the pavement, I assume that my act is lawful just as it has always been lawful to walk on the pavement. Law's particular function is to bind social expectations over time.

This does not say much about the law; only what the law does. Is this enough? Is this the idea of technicalities, namely to go deeper into what the law does in order to see *how* the law does, thus inverting the levels of observation and placing the second-order deeper in the system rather than at a distance from it? The answer is a qualified 'yes', but only when functionalism in its flipside is taken into consideration. I have previously (2010) described systemic function, not as the positive aspect of a system going about its job, but as the negative aspect of a system existing because of social necessity. Function creates a space in which several equally plausible solutions to a problem may be tried out. Luhmann has put it similarly: 'Orientation by function alone is not sufficient. This follows from the simple fact that the reference to a function is always an invitation to look for functionally equivalent alternatives, that is, to cross systems boundaries' (Luhmann, 2004, p. 93). So the desire to cross is there. But so is closure, which for systems theory is draconian. Each system is normatively closed to other systems. Its immanence is absolute, its boundaries are watertight. Even so, upon closure rests openness: while normatively closed, a system is cognitively open. This means that it learns from other systems by way of observation. But how does it observe other systems if it is normatively closed? This is the most counter-intuitive and, for this reason, the most valuable idea that has come from systems theory: every observation is self-observation. *The law learns from other systems, from 'the social', only by looking deeper into itself.* Legal technicalities are fleshed out, small blurry mirrors reflecting a whole world translated into the law's own language. Natalie Ohana in this volume puts it accurately: 'this is essentially a process of translation: processing a social phenomenon in order to render it legal in its form and nature, an integral part of the legal discourse' (p. 92).

The value of the above formulation for a socio-legal metatheory should not be underestimated. Immanence, in the form of normative closure for the law, requires a re-examination of the facile causal links between the legal and the social. To talk about control or even unmediated influence is misplaced. Causality must be worked out internally, from within the law, by observing how the law observes. *The socio-legal researcher has this unique responsibility: to delve deeper into the law in order to see how the law really connects with the social.* The answer will be surprising and most likely resoundingly negative: the connection is a matter of epistemological positioning (yes, the law does change as a result) but its ontology is much more complex than that, and nearly always requires a translation into legal language. However, the socio-legal responsibility is not exhausted here. If we were to leave it at this, we would only be resuscitating the cantankerous beast that both socio-legal and critical theorists have successfully put to sleep (at least in some circles). *The responsibility is to carry on walking the tightrope, keeping technicality on the one hand and the horizon on the other. The other of the law is justice, and this risks being forgotten when delving in the technicalities without at the same time, paradoxically, retaining a distance from them.* And, to come full circle, justice can only emerge from within the legal. The immanence is absolute, the closure complete. Our only playing field is the law as it opens its immanence to include the world. The law cannot be thought of independently of its spatiality. I have called this *the lawscape*, namely the epistemological and ontological confluence between law and space. The lawscape is all there is, continuous, fractal, post-human, immanent. The lawscape is legal technicalities *and* openings of justice, legal continua and just ruptures. There is nowhere else to go but deeper into the lawscape.

Legal matter

Deeper in the law, there is only skin. All technicality is surface, all folding is conduit, all immanence is rupture. Skin separates as much as it bridges. Never connection, never direct affect, but always atmospherically spread, the law slides parallel to the world, forever shut in its immanence. So although never connecting directly and causally, the law co-emerges with other bodies and constructs the world as we know it. The law is everywhere, as has become apparent in the previous section. One of the problems, therefore, addressed in this volume is how to escape the law. Sharon Cowan, for example, muses on the declining faith we have in the law while we observe that the law is everywhere. The easy answer is: well, we cannot escape the law because there is nothing outside the law. This is especially the case if one accepts that the lawscape contains both lawful and unlawful movements of the various bodies that co-constitute the lawscape.

The difficulty comes after such an answer: how do we handle a law that is everywhere in terms of both epistemological delineation (where do we stop when we research the law) and ontological survival (is there nowhere to hide, to breathe free from the law)?

The latter is tackled by the lawscape itself: the basic characteristic of the lawscape is that it dissimulates the law and makes it invisible. From absorbent sheeting (Carr) to solar panels (Hunter) and counterfeit medicines (Cloatre), the law only appears when it appears. Until then, it is 'just' matter, things, stuff. No law, right? Well, not quite. This book *in toto* shatters one of the grand illusions of the law: that the law is abstract, universal and immaterial; that it applies equally and regardless of who, what, when or where; that it hovers above matter; and when it does gather in a material form, it is in the courtroom or the Conseil d'Etat or perhaps the arbitration room. And it is usually documents, files, books. Sometimes symbols, sometimes clothing, but basically texts. Yet, this book shows beyond any doubt how the law is not only everywhere but also everything and everyone, every body, animate or inanimate, of matter or of discourse, of different temporality and geography. One of the greatest and most refreshing achievements of this book is that it shows from a solidly socio-legal angle that the law is through and through material. Law's abstraction is subsumed in the folds of the everyday materiality of human and nonhuman bodies that move around, with and against each other. Emilie Cloatre's perspicacious description of how counterfeit drugs can be captured by various kinds of legal definitions is interestingly contrasted to the otherwise different reception of these drugs in practice. The material discourse comes to its full fruition in Caroline Hunter and Helen Carr's chapters, where it is amply demonstrated how the legal and the social are found in a relation of mutual form-giving.

Once this is established and empirically demonstrated, as so many chapters here do, the return to the discursive is no longer the same. Metaphors in the EU context are not simply the law as it is but the law as it wants to appear, as Paul James Cardwell and Tamara Hervey show in their chapter. Likewise, Andrew Sanders and Danielle Griffiths demonstrate the permeability of these two categories in the context of medical manslaughter, although putting it in terms of the received distinction of law in books and law in action. *The material and the discursive share the same surface.* Each one folds in its own immanence, and in this interiorized, indirect and affective way, it affects the way the other is formed. I shall allow Natalie Ohana to address the immanent technicality of the discursive in this extensive quote from her chapter:

> the act of classification constructs the meaning of a named
> element by defining the limits within which it can be understood

> and thereby separating it from other possible meanings. Classification thus prevents a new, challenging and different meanings from entering the discourse that do not correlate with that defined space. First acts of classification divide the element off and set the paths through which it can be further understood. Additional classification acts continue through the directions set by those first acts and by that strengthen and solidify them. The more classification acts that pile on top of that initial definition and are guided by it, the harder it becomes for new and different possibilities of meaning to uproot the existing realms of understanding in order to be heard and accepted. (p. 87)

This astute description of the mechanics of classificatory violence, itself a grand technicality of the legal, resonates with the previously quoted description by Caroline Hunter of the passage from discourse to hardened technology by means of superimposition.

To the above, I would like to add two brief considerations. The fact that the material and the discursive share the same surface means, first, that matter is not outside the law but immanent to it. In my work I have consistently found that the legal discourse is through and through material, despite legal pretences to the opposite. It is our responsibility to emphasize the relevance of the material, and socio-legal research seems the natural and most efficient field for this kind of thinking. What is more, it is our responsibility not to be taken in by the grand legal illusion: that through the neutrality of technicalities, the law remains objective. Technicalities are material, as Riles repeatedly states, and materiality is not neutrality but immersion. Naturally, the law often dissimulates this in order to retain both its much-prized façade of neutrality, and its social function as the system that binds social expectations. The extent to which the socio-legal researcher demolishes this or works with it is a matter of tension.

The second consideration I would like to add is also a consequence of the immanence between the material and the discursive, and it refers to the way a legal assemblage emerges. Assemblage is a term introduced by Deleuze and Guattari (1988) and connotes the way in which various bodies (human and nonhuman, animate and inanimate, material and immaterial) come together and form a composition that assumes agentic abilities. The original French term *agencement* offers a better understanding of what the authors intended. I have argued elsewhere (2014) that legal agency emerges through assemblages that form, at a given time, a material legal presence. These emerge within the legal system, whether in its material or discursive form, and their legality is emphatically not ascribed by law. Legality is an emergence. This is what Jane Bennett (2010) in her book *Vibrant Matter* means when she refers to the vibrant self-organizing nature of both organic and inorganic matter. Although Bennett is not taking into consideration the legal, the pervading discursive and material presence of the law obliges, not just legal scholars, but all of us who surf the interdisciplinary wave as a matter of ethical refusal to be shut in one discipline, to focus on the law in its relation to the world. This is the ethical basis of the demand for a socio-legal metatheory, so amply demonstrated in this book.

Five socio-legal positions

Allow me by way of conclusion to synthesize this concluding comment of a chapter, and suggest five positions that constitute the groundwork for a metatheory of socio-legal research.

Position one

The responsibility of the socio-legal researcher is to retain the tension between the exploration of legal technicalities and the thinking of the law as a contextualized whole with its particular social function and horizon.

Position two

The tension between technicalities and horizon cannot be resolved through binary opposition but through immanence, namely an interiority specific to the legal and without recourse to external origins, grounds for justification, or final purposes. This does not exclude the social and the interdisciplinary from socio-legal research. Rather, it places them in the heart of the legal, making the legal an all-inclusive immanence, emerging alongside other all-inclusive spheres of immanence, such as the political, the economic, the religious, the scientific and so on.

Position three

The other of the law is neither the social nor the material but justice. Justice is immanent to the legal, and for this reason it has to be sought from within legal technicalities. However, legal technicalities are also the playing field of a law that pretends to be neutral, objective, universal, equal for all, abstract, immaterial and so on. The way legal technicalities are used, yields unequally distributed social outcomes. Material ontologies are *not* flat but *tilted* according to distributions of power. Yet, they remain the only way in which legal justice may materialize from within the legal system. For this reason, justice emerges *through* and at the same time *despite* the law. Justice can only be revealed from within the legal technicalities but by focusing on their gaps and ruptures. The socio-legal responsibility is to keep an eye on both the legal wall and the awnings of justice.

Position four

An immanent socio-legal research requires a reconfiguration of causality. In the epoch of the Anthropocene and the era of the post-human, rationalized causalities in the form of control or direct influence are more than ever comfortable epistemological constructs that retain the ossified, hardened technology of a law that does not deviate from its prescribed path. Socio-legal causality is a complex, internalized observation of how the law observes. The socio-legal researcher has the responsibility to delve deeper into the law in order to see how the law actually contains with and is contained by the social.

Position five

The legal is at the same time both material and discursive. The two share the same immanent surface. There is not an exclusive direction of influence: the material affects the discursive to the same degree as the discursive affects the material. Legal agency is a composition of material and discursive bodies that emerge from within the legal in a self-organizing manner. Legal agency is not ascribed by the law in the form of top-down distribution, but is acquired from within the law in the form of embodied confluence with or resistance to the law. This accentuates the socio-legal tension between the legal technicalities and the horizon (of justice) but also offers new critical positions on how to accommodate this tension.

References

Bennet, Jane (2010) *Vibrant Matter: A Political Ecology of Things* (Durham: Duke University Press)

Deleuze, Gilles and Felix Guattari (1988) *A Thousand Plateaus: Capitalism and Schizophrenia* (B Massumi trans.) (London: Continuum)

Luhmann, Niklas (2004) *Law as a Social System* (K Ziegert trans.), F Kastner, R Nobles, D Schiff and R Ziegert (eds) (Oxford: Oxford University Press)

Philippopoulos-Mihalopoulos, Andreas (2010) *Niklas Luhmann: Law, Justice, Society* (London: Routledge)

Philippopoulos-Mihalopoulos, Andreas (2014) 'Critical Autopoiesis and the Materiality of Law' 27: 2 *International Journal of Semiotics of Law* 165–77

Riles, Annelise (2005) 'A New Agenda for the Cultural Study of Law: Taking on the Technicalities' 53 *Buffalo Law Review* 973–1033

Afterword: A Method More Than a Subject

Annelise Riles

This fascinating collection addresses the topic of legal technicalities from a remarkable variety of theoretical and methodological perspectives. Some authors view a focus on legal technicalities as an extension of a long-standing socio-legal studies concern with the relationship between the social and the legal, a way to 'draw on diverse ways of understanding ... the legal' (Cowan and Wincott, this volume, p. 2) while other authors embrace the concept of technicalities precisely as a place of respite from the explanatory power of the social (Tomlins). Some view technicalities as an important concern for legal reform projects; others view technicalities in precisely the opposite sense, as a site for legal critique projects. The editors propose that we make sense of the 'meanings' of legal technicalities – that we bring technicalities into the sphere of things that can be studied from a humanistic or culturalist point of view. The chapters respond to this call in a variety of registers. There are feminist, legal pluralist and Foucauldian chapters, as well as chapters inspired by science and technology studies.

Not surprisingly, the authors of these chapters have differing reactions to my own work on legal technicalities. Some find my work helpful. Others sound a note of caution. Sharon Cowan, for example, reads me as overly optimistic about legal doctrine and as exemplifying feminists' enduring obsession with law despite the many disappointments of law reform projects. Most intriguing of all, Chris Tomlins takes my project as a source of inspiration or licence to engage in a project of his own that, on the surface, has nothing much to do with either my work or legal technicalities. His work and mine meet here, not on the ground of the subject matter, but in the way his moves evoke mine, but are also entirely his own, from the standpoint of his particular disciplinary concerns and techniques as a legal historian.

In this short response, I wish only to clarify what I mean by legal technicalities and to explain why and how this focus emerged for me in the context of my own scholarly trajectory. I do this to emphasize two points.

First, legal technicalities are not so much a subject of study (and even less a normative position, something to be for or against) so much as they are for me a way of looking, acting and responding, a method. Second, that method is surely idiosyncratic to the specific challenges and opportunities I have faced, as a scholar at the confluence of specific disciplines writing at a specific moment in the debate. Since these are unlikely to be anyone else's immediate concerns, I am delighted to learn that the work can be taken in other directions, in the service of so many other kinds of normative, critical, scholarly and law reform projects.

What are legal technicalities?

It may be helpful for me to begin by summarizing what I have meant by the technical quality of law when I have used the term. First, the technical for me is what defines and differentiates legal thought from other kinds of knowledge. In *Collateral Knowledge*, I set out a number of elements (Riles, 2011, pp. 64–70). First, the technical is a package of different phenomena of different orders. It includes categories of experts (see Sanders and Griffiths, this volume), certain ideologies about the power of law and place of law in society and markets, but also certain forms of reasoning – especially a problem-solving paradigm, that is, an interest in law as a means to an end. It also includes certain artefacts such as contracts or statutes. Despite the propensity of some legal scholars to associate legal technicalities with private law, there is nothing inherently public or private about technicalities. Technicality can be a technique of legal knowledge within the state as much as within the market. When I use the term 'technical', I mean a routinized, compartmentalized form of knowledge that is designed to travel – from one social or political or cultural space to the next. What makes law global is the technical, in other words, the fact that a lawyer in Dubai or in London will approach a legal document from a largely similar set of routinized pathways of thought.

All this is to say that legal technicalities are both ideas and things in the world. And, as speech act theorists have noticed, it is a feature of the technicality of law that these ideas take 'real' form. The legal fiction that a corporation is a person transforms a corporation into a person as an operation of law, for example. In this understanding, obviously legal thought can be more or less technical. Indeed, legal thought often mixes with other forms of expertise (such as social-scientific expertise) and hence becomes less technical. This point is noted in several chapters in this volume, including especially Cloatre's study of counterfeit medicines in which legal technicality merges other forms of knowledge (science, rumour, etc.) to produce artefacts such as 'counterfeit' which are 'neither legal nor non-legal'.

More generally, however, what I mean by legal technicality is those aspects of legal practice that cannot be reduced to norms, trust and other sociological concepts. In other words, what I find so challenging about legal technicalities is that they resist theorization precisely by posturing as unimportant, non-theoretical, 'meaningless' stuff (Riles, 2005). Technicalities are 'thin', conceptually speaking. There just isn't that much to be unpacked about them; it is all there on the surface. They are remarkably Teflon-like in the way they survive critique. Whatever a critic might say about legal technicalities is, on the one hand, already very obvious to all the users of these technicalities, and, on the other, not at all damaging to their continued use. Some of the chapters in this book are frustrated by this dimension of technicalities where they seek to engage them in the modality of critique.

I also understand legal technicality as a profoundly aesthetic practice – a practice of fidelity to proper form. This is important for me because I have repeatedly argued that the legitimacy of law inheres in its aesthetic dimensions and practices (Riles, 2001). This legitimacy, in turn, becomes 'a script for a particular kind of collaboration' (Riles, 2011, p. 59). The editors provide a beautiful example of the collaborative possibilities of legal technicalities in their analysis of the balance of convenience test. This test, they write, is a 'vehicular idea'. It 'moves things on; it brings in critique and shifts in meaning' precisely because of its 'shallowness' and the way it becomes 'second nature for lawyers' (p. 26).

Why the focus on legal technicalities?

My own engagement with the technical quality of law is very much the product of the particular moment and disciplinary configurations in which I have found myself, and the intellectual and institutional challenges those have posed. As a law student and graduate student in anthropology, I began from a point of deep dissatisfaction with socio-legal studies. All of the efforts to combine, or relate law and society, to show how each was engendered by the other, seemed parasitic on some outmoded assumptions about what these two things to be related – law and society – really were (Riles, 1994). Like Tomlins in this volume, I also began from a point of view of profound scepticism about 'the social' or 'the cultural' as explanatory categories for law or anything else, and so, when as a doctoral student a year after finishing law school, I encountered the work emerging in science and technology studies challenging the concept of the social as an explanatory device for science and technology (Latour, 1996), I immediately saw potential opportunities for an understanding of law.

My experience as a law student at Harvard Law School after the demise of critical legal studies (CLS) had also left me searching for something beyond what was on offer within that movement (and the critical traditions it borrowed from, from Marxism to literary criticism to feminist theory and post-colonial studies) – something motivating several chapter in this volume (Sanders and Griffiths, Cardwell and Hervey). But it also left me curious: the critiques of law produced by CLS were so obviously correct as a matter of logic or empirical observation. How could such critiques then 'fail' institutionally or intellectually? How was it that the law just kept on trucking? Might there be something in the nature of law as knowledge that is impervious to critique?

I went back to graduate school after law school to work with the feminist anthropologist Marilyn Strathern, to whom I owe my own understanding of the word 'techniques' – a word she used to describe gender (Strathern, 1988). From Strathern, and from other anthropologists of the Pacific, I gained an appreciation of debates in the anthropology of exchange and, in particular, of the work of form, or aesthetics, in calling forth many of the phenomena taken as given in socio-legal and critical legal studies debates, such as society, politics, gender, the self and so on. My first article emerging from my doctoral work sought to engage seriously with the role of form in United Nations (UN) proceedings, as a kind of methodological respite (for both UN officials and myself as a scholar) from politics (Riles, 1998).

The almost self-consciously autistic attitude of many British social anthropologists towards those dominant traditions of critical theory – their insistence that they didn't really read outside their discipline, for example – seemed like a refreshing respite, in a monastic sort of way. What also appealed to me about anthropology was the large element of intellectual risk involved in the methodology. One was expected to go where the material took you, to put the question of what was interesting or important in the hands of one's interlocutors. My first book, for example, puts side by side subjects that have no relationship whatsoever from a prior theoretical vantage point (land use among part-Europeans in Fiji and women's activism at the UN) because these 'fit' together for the people with whom I was conducting the investigation. The question of what these things have to do with one another becomes a later problem of analysis, or what I call 'unwinding' (Riles, 2008). This idea that one should risk common scholarly sense to place the intellectual reins in the hands of one's subjects later motivated my effort to take legal technicalities seriously.

By a fortuitous set of events I found myself hired almost immediately into a law school where the kinds of traditions of doctrinal work that socio-legal studies scholars had laboured hard to deconstruct were alive and well. I was expected to be a mainstream law professor and I found most of what that entailed to be boring, difficult and politically distasteful. It took me a while, but after some time I began to wonder whether this strange subject position could be a new kind of fieldwork project. Rather than fight legal formalism (or, for that matter, legal instrumentalism), could I seek to understand it on its own terms? In particular, I was drawn to what a focus on form, as in my prior research, could not fully explain. Legal technicalities had powerful aesthetic dimensions – yet, if one were to confront an expert in these tools and suggest that they could be explained in terms of aesthetics, one would get scoffed at. These practitioners themselves disavowed any greater 'meaning' to the tools than the tool-like quality of the thing. They insisted on the thin-ness of the thing, the boringness of the thing, telling me to go find culture and meaning elsewhere. It was a direct experience in the limits of humanistic analysis, an actual pushback from the subject of study itself (Riles, 2005). And yet lest this lead us to exoticize legal knowledge – to treat it as fundamentally other to humanistic or critical analysis – I discovered that the fountain of much of the exchange theory in anthropology that had so inspired me, Hans Vaihinger (2009), was also the fountain of contemporary debates about that core legal technique, the legal fiction, and the inspiration for much twentieth-century pragmatist jurisprudence (Riles, n.d.).

In the closing lines of their chapter, Cardwell and Hervey call for greater reflexivity about our place in all that we are describing as legal technicalities. Cardwell and Hervey turn their lens on how, at various moments, the socio-legal displaces the legal, or is in turn displaced, in the construction of European Union legitimacy, in order to emphasize how socio-legal accounts bolster the law and perpetuate their own power relations. They give us a picture of socio-legal accounts of doctrinal law as collaborator, in all the positive and negative senses of that term. I certainly would embrace the same description of my own explorations of the technical. Anthropologists by definition work collaboratively – their empirical findings and theoretical interventions are always somewhat serendipitous artefacts of the particular professional situation in which they have found themselves, and they are always at a risk of going native. My own story is also meant to emphasize how particular this trajectory has been. My own need for, and hope for, legal technicalities can't be expected to be anyone else's.

Collaboration in the technical

My point then is that this work with legal technicalities can't be applied to anyone else's subject. In that respect, it is like legal technicalities themselves: it is not a theory. So what can one do with it, or with legal technicalities for that matter? Legal technicalities exist to be appropriated: anyone trained in the techniques can use them, can redeploy them, for any purpose. Here inheres their power. If legal technicalities cannot be described, cannot be critiqued, cannot be humanistically situated, they certainly can be used or appropriated. Here we find another deep connection to the anthropology of the gift, in which, as the anthropologist Hirokazu Miyazaki writes, the hope of the gift can't be described but only 'replicated on another terrain' (Miyazaki, 2004).

The feminist science studies scholar Donna Haraway compares such appropriations to the childhood game of cat's cradle in which one person makes a shape out of string, then stretches out their hands and passes it on to someone else, who then destroys the prior shape but turns it into something further (Haraway, 1994). Haraway has in mind the particular knowledge practices that define feminist scholarly engagement, but her description captures the way in which feminist anthropologists have long imagined their relationship to their work, to one another, and to their research subjects. Can we have an equally playful, disruptive and collaborative relationship to legal technicalities (Riles, 2006, 2013, 2014)? My current work, an experimental virtual community of scholars, legal practitioners and policy-makers known as Meridian 180, seeks to emulate and appropriate certain aspects of legal technicalities on another political and experiential terrain, rather than describing them. In this project, we make the collaborative work explicit and, building on the understanding that the technical is both a set of ideas and institutions in the world, we explore how collaborative knowledge work can take forms other than the written text – how it might be an institution, or a movement, for example. This is a long way from the critical interventions of CLS as a political and intellectual movement against the technicality of law. Here, acknowledging the problems of complicity inherent in the nature of the endeavour, and the possibility of unintended consequences, we treat the technical as a medium for a cat's cradle.

In this spirit, I am moved and inspired by Chris Tomlins' own appropriation of my work in his own entirely different direction. Tomlins reads the Turner Rebellion as an account of another kind of technicalities – the technicalities of theology – played out in a space of legal contestation, and also in a wider cultural condition in which legal technicalities and theological technicalities are mutually referencing, mutually interpolated and mutually meaningful. The piece has a clear theoretical agenda – against social contextualization and against historicism as habitually practised. But what intrigues me is the allegorical shape of the argument, the way it finds in its subject new possibilities of form, from the double entendre to the analogy. The case of the Turner rebellion is, of course, calculated to skewer the conventional legal historian, who as Tomlins tells us, is drawn again and again to this event as one of the few actual examples of a semi-successful violent slave uprising in the USA. For Tomlins, however, these mainstream socio-legal scholars can applaud a slave rebellion but only if they can domesticate it once again as a vindication of the 'right' kind of (social) consciousness. He then presents them with a troubling mirror image of themselves – Gray, the professional historian who 'takes 24 hours of confusion and methodically *organizes* it. Here temporality is linear and causality is secular' (p. 39). The ensuing 'problematic text' points directly to what is wrong with mainstream historiography: it literally divides experience in two, banishing the theological, and hence telling only half the story since the very category of social context is, in Tomlins' view, only half of a longstanding Euro-American binary of sacred and profane modalities of thought.

Tomlins then follows this allegorical critique with a proposal that 'instead we start with belief. And instead of trying to construct belief as a consequence of context, let us allow belief its own primal force' (p. 40). Belief is, of course, the ultimate anti-empirical. The fact that belief can never be confirmed has led anthropologists of religion, for example, to abandon it entirely and focus instead on such things as ritual practice and ritual language. What would a focus on belief actually look like?

Here, Tomlins introduces Jonathan Edwards – a towering figure in American intellectual history who nevertheless remains largely unknown in the secular social science renderings of American historical identity. And when Tomlins reads Edwards seriously, what we find is that a focus on belief takes the form of ... history. Indeed, Edwards' theology is profoundly historical. It is an account of the unfolding of messianic time told through biblical events (themselves read as historical events) combined with events from more recent history. So what differentiates this history from the kind of historiography Tomlins would critique? For one thing, he tells us, it is imbued with an aesthetics of typology: the object of historical analysis is to reveal a series of types and antitypes. Tomlins enacts this methodology in the essay itself: Edwards' representations of Christ are placed side by side with Turner's self-description, as two examples of a type, while Gray and Edwards figure as historiographic anti-types. As the account progresses, Tomlins gently demonstrates that we social scientists have nothing to fear about belief – it is not beyond our intellectual grasp. On the contrary, it is far more familiar, and also far more generative, that our intellectual divisions of experience would allow us to imagine.

So, in place of text and context as organizing metaphors for socio-legal studies, Tomlins offers us type and anti-type. As in the delicious double entendre of the 'act of God', itself the ultimate legal technicality, the type can be both legal and non-legal, both sacred and profane at once. But what inspires me here is that it is above all both subject and method: 'discovered' in a reading of Jonathan Edwards, it is reappropriated on Tomlins' own intellectual terrain. It is this method – the fearless discovery of an Other technique, the analogical exploration of its workings and ultimately its redeployment on one's own intellectual terrain that I would claim as the promise of legal 'technique' – as a method, more than a subject.

References

Haraway, Donna Jeanne (1994) 'A Game of Cat's Cradle: Science Studies, Feminist Theory, Cultural Studies' 2(1) *Configurations* 59–71

Latour, Bruno (1996) *Aramis, or, the Love of Technology* (Cambridge, MA: Harvard University Press)

Miyazaki, Hirokazu (2004) *The Method of Hope: Anthropology, Philosophy, and Fijian Knowledge* (Stanford: Stanford University Press)

Riles, A (1994) 'Representing In-Between: Law, Anthropology, and the Rhetoric of Interdisciplinary' (3) *University of Illinois Law Review* 597–650

Riles, A (1998) 'Infinity within the Brackets' 25(3) *American Ethnologist* 378–98

Riles, A (2001) *The Network Inside Out* (Ann Arbor: University of Michigan Press)

Riles, A (2005) 'A New Agenda for the Cultural Study of Law: Taking on the Technicalities' 53 *Buffalo Law Review* 973–1033

Riles, A (2006) 'Introduction: In Response' in A Riles (ed.), *Documents: Artifacts of Modern Knowledge* (Ann Arbor: University of Michigan Press)

Riles, A (2008) 'Anthropology, Human Rights, and Legal Knowledge: Culture in the Iron Cage' 108 *American Anthropologist* 52–65

Riles, A (2011) *Collateral Knowledge: Legal Reasoning in the Global Financial Markets* (Chicago: University of Chicago Press)

Riles, A (2013) 'Market Collaboration: Finance, Culture, and Ethnography after Neoliberalism' 115(4) *American Anthropologist* 555–69

Riles, A (2014) 'From Comparison to Collaboration: Experiments with a New Scholarly and Political Form' 77 *Law and Contemporary Problems* 14–35

Riles, A (n.d.) *Is the Law Hopeful? In Hope in Law and the Economy* (Philadelphia: University of Pennsylvania Press)

Strathern, M (1988) *The Gender of the Gift: Problems with Women and Problems with Society in Melanesia* (Berkeley: University of California Press)

Vaihinger, Hans (2009) *The Philosophy of 'As If': A System of the Theoretical, Practical and Religious Fictions of Mankind* (Eastford: Martino Fine Books)

Index